OXFORD MONOGRAPHS ON
SOCIAL ANTHROPOLOGY

General Editors

MAURICE FREEDMAN   B. E. B. FAGG

A. C. MAYER   E. ARDENER

Ujo léwun, kajaq tené,
Dorong dopéq, oté né.
Kara oné pana weq,
Ular naga, ara bora,
Ahin tutuq kara dora.
Pan ebéng, balé boraq.

Udjolévung, the mountain of Kédang

KÉDANG

A STUDY OF
THE COLLECTIVE THOUGHT
OF AN EASTERN
INDONESIAN PEOPLE

BY

R. H. BARNES

WITH A FOREWORD
BY
RODNEY NEEDHAM

CLARENDON PRESS : OXFORD

1974

Oxford University Press, Ely House, London W.1

GLASGOW   NEW YORK   TORONTO   MELBOURNE   WELLINGTON
CAPE TOWN   IBADAN   NAIROBI   DAR ES SALAAM   LUSAKA   ADDIS ABABA
DELHI   BOMBAY   CALCUTTA   MADRAS   KARACHI   LAHORE   DACCA
KUALA LUMPUR   SINGAPORE   HONG KONG   TOKYO

ISBN 0 19 823185 7

© OXFORD UNIVERSITY PRESS 1974

PRINTED IN GREAT BRITAIN BY
BUTLER AND TANNER LTD
FROME AND LONDON

FOREWORD

RODNEY NEEDHAM

DR. BARNES HAS kindly paid me the very considerable compliment of asking me to write a foreword to his first book. I am much abashed to do so, for this entails publishing some assessment of it; yet the fact of the matter is that he has splendidly accomplished what I myself greatly wish I had done, and his monograph therefore needs no endorsement of mine to commend it. *Kédang* is a very fine ethnographical achievement; analytically it is impressive, constantly intriguing, and on occasion quite brilliant. It strikes me indeed as one of the most masterly studies to have emerged from Oxford social anthropology as it was under the aegis of the late Sir Edward Evans-Pritchard.

The success of Dr. Barnes's undertaking derives in large part from the premiss that his ethnographic task is to extract principles of order, so that his exposition is governed throughout by a pursuit of principles. It is this profound and constant preoccupation which permits him not only to dispense with a conventional arrangement of topics but also to adopt a methodically discursive style of argument. At first, this may seem unduly digressive, but there is never any dropping of the thread of relevance: the interconnexions are made by the connotations of Kédang verbal concepts and by the concinnity of Kédang modes of representation; that is, the exposition does indeed follow, as Dr. Barnes intends, 'the lines of greatest fluency' in tracing the distinctive contours of Kédang collective thought. In these regards a discursive account is even particularly appropriate to an inquiry which is primarily directed to thought rather than to social action, and which concomitantly therefore is a study of language and the various contexts of use in which it conveys significance.

In paying recognition to the models that he has followed, Dr. Barnes gives special credit to Edmund Leach's outstanding paper 'The Language of Kachin Kinship'. This well merited citation is very pleasing, to me at any rate, but there is another parallel, not adduced by Dr. Barnes, which I find just as noteworthy and methodologically even more instructive. This is to be found in

Gregory Bateson's *Naven* (first edition, 1935). A main resemblance consists in Bateson's concern to elicit the motifs of Iatmul ideology: complementary and symmetrical dualism, monism, seriation, and alternation. There is also a resemblance of intellection in the analytical imagination so strikingly shown both by Bateson and by Dr. Barnes (as, for that matter, by Professor Leach as well): an agility of thought and an unconstrained preparedness to make whatever connexions of structure, form, image, or metaphor seem apt to an understanding of the case. These qualities are not common in anthropological writings (I suppose they could not be common in any), and their presence in this monograph lends it a fine distinction. There is, too, a directness of expression which for me associates *Kédang* with the style of argument characteristic of the late A. M. Hocart; this is an additional virtue in Dr. Barnes's work and makes a further link with a scholarly tradition.

Underlying such theoretical considerations, however, there are the properties intrinsic to the object of study itself. Despite all the anthropological contention about whether structure is an aspect of social reality or a relational abstraction made up by the observer, it is hard to deny that Kédang society possesses an order of a 'total' kind. At the level of categories and social action this is displayed and secured by the absolute nature of a prescriptive system, and here Dr. Barnes has made an invaluable contribution. Asymmetric prescriptive alliance has in recent years been made the focus of a great deal of clamour in anthropological debate, with some critics of the notion going so far as to assert that societies of this type do not and even cannot exist. This extreme and rather doctrinaire view has not been well argued by its proponents, and it was in any case controverted in advance by published ethnographic accounts—especially from Indonesia—attesting the actual existence of a number of societies of the kind. But for those critics who most obdurately rejected the type there was, it appeared, a grave difficulty about these accounts: some of the most crucial, including those from eastern Indonesia, were in Dutch and thus inaccessible to scholarly attention. It will doubtless be found a grateful convenience, therefore, that Dr. Barnes has now supplied in plain English a description of asymmetric prescriptive alliance in yet another society of Indonesia. The Kédang relationship terminology is clearly ordered by an asymmetric prescription, and an asymmetric contraction of alliances corresponds with this categorical directive. Kédang social classification has cyclic consequences, moreover, and these are well known to the people themselves.

Subsidiary to these main concerns there are many particulars which further augment the value of Dr. Barnes's monograph: for instance, the many points at which his comparative allusions extend our grasp of the general features of east Indonesian forms of civilization, or such more technical matters as the singular constitution of Kédang social classification (which lacks terms for the second descending genealogical level) and the new demonstration of the contingent connexions between categories and institutions. But the sustained interest of the entire account is to be found centrally in what Dr. Barnes so skilfully elicits from the multifarious details of Kédang collective representations and customs, namely the implicit principles of Kédang collective thought: in so far as there is motion it is oriented to the right, and in so far as being has structure this is segmentary and consists of inter-nodes and points of transition. By reference to these principles Dr. Barnes subtly demonstrates that there is a general concordance throughout all phases of Kédang conceptual order: the order is dualistic, composed of pairs of ranked and complementary opposites; and complementary opposition is 'the germ of a number of systems of oriented relations which show the features of segmentation, irreversibility, and self-closure'. Ultimately, he concludes, the most irreducible conceptual distinction at work is that by which the form or structure of being is contrasted to the spiritual essence that moves through it.

In thus discerning what may properly be regarded as Kédang metaphysics, Dr. Barnes has ingeniously executed what is at once a superb addition to Indonesian ethnography, a genuinely structural analysis of social thought and action, and a singular contribution to a comparative understanding of certain primary modes of human consciousness and experience.

Merton College, Oxford
April 1974

ACKNOWLEDGEMENTS

THE fieldwork upon which this book is based was undertaken with the aid of a Graduate Fellowship from the National Science Foundation (of the United States) and a grant from The Committee for Graduate Studies, University of Oxford and was conducted under the auspices of the Lembaga Ilmu Pengetahuan Indonesia, to whom I express my gratitude.

Although I do not agree in principle with the purposes of the Catholic mission, I must remark that the Indonesian and European members of the *Societas Verbini Dei* were always gracious and helpful to us and provided a crucial service in forwarding our mail and currency. I thank especially Msgr. A. H. Thijssen, formerly Bishop of Larantuka and now Bishop of Bali, and Father A. J. F. de Rechter.

I am especially thankful to the people of Léuwajang for their kindness in taking us in and for their ceaseless help while we were there. Though it is perhaps not proper to single anyone out, I wish to mention in particular M. Suda Apelabi, Kepala Desa Gaja Baru Leuwajang, and Peu Langun Wajan in whose house we lived.

I also wish to express my deep appreciation to Dr. Rodney Needham for six years of supervision during my studies at the University of Oxford and in Kédang and for his preface to this work. My wife has been constantly involved in all levels of this project, and this has been to a great extent a joint study. Her most recent contribution has been to prepare the figures and maps and Tables 8–13.

An important change has been made in Chapter XIII, in response to helpful discussions with several persons including, in particular, Professor A. Teeuw and Dr. J. C. Anceaux of Leiden, whose generosity in providing their time and attention I gratefully acknowledge.

At various stages in the research for this project, unpublished colonial reports in several Dutch archives have been made available for my inspection. I am very thankful for this valuable service and wish to express my indebtedness in particular to the sources of the two reports cited here, Professor J. van Baal and the Tropen Museum, Amsterdam for Seegeler and the Algemeen Rijksarchief, The Hague for Munro.

CONTENTS

LIST OF PLATES

LIST OF MAPS

LIST OF FIGURES

LIST OF TABLES

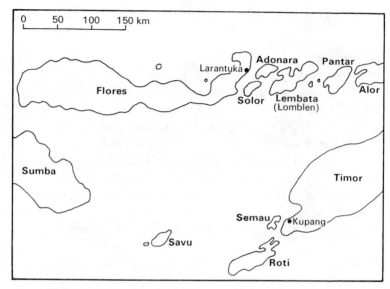

MAP 1*a*. Lembata in relation to neighbouring islands.

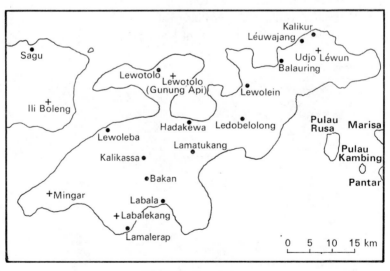

MAP 1*b*. Lembata.

INTRODUCTION

KÉDANG is a district located at the extreme east of the small eastern Indonesian island Lembata (see Map 1). Until the present its people have very nearly escaped all attention in the published literature, and this book presents an almost completely original contribution to the ethnographic record. At another level, it attempts a form of reporting in which the diversity of ethnographic detail is conceived of as forming a whole. The major task is to extract the principles of order; and to this end the facts must be set out in a way which most facilitates the pursuit of principles. The success of this undertaking is made the more likely by the fact that Kédang possesses a social order of the kind which best exemplifies Mauss's conception of '*total* social phenomena'. Whatever chapter divisions may be imposed on the facts in order to facilitate the exposition are likely to be arbitrary and external because they do not correspond to inherent divisions within the culture of Kédang. Here it seems possible to demonstrate the closest correspondence among the principles governing the, apparently, most diverse realms of thought and action, whether it be in ceremonials, the construction of buildings, conceptions of space or time, techniques and attitudes connected with birth, ageing and death, or even social relations. Necessarily, this study is concerned primarily with collective representations. Space does not permit an elaborate description of subsistence activities, tools, and other features of purely or primarily economic or material concern; and Kédang is an area in which there is the least to be gained from such treatment.

Throughout, a search has been made for the conceptual unities and distinctions which are those of the people of Kédang themselves; and the exposition has attempted to follow the lines of greatest fluency. This means that it has tried to begin where the culture of Kédang begins and to unfold as that culture most naturally unfolds. It should not cause surprise, then, that what elsewhere is often put at the last is here found at the beginning, and what is traditionally put at the beginning must sometimes wait here until the end of the exposition.

I. THE TERRAIN

The island of Lembata has been described by Beckering as resembling a flying bird of which Kédang forms the head and the peninsula of the Lewotolo volcano in the north and the district of Labala in the south form the wings. A central spine of ancient volcanic mountains and hills runs directly up the island from the mountain Mingar at the western end to the mountain of Kédang at the east. On either side of this spine are found the three active volcanoes of the island, each forming a peninsula of its own. To the north is the spectacular, constantly smoking Lewotolo or Gunung (Ili) Api—Lembata's Etna, as Wouter Schouten called it in the seventeenth century. On the south coast is the island's highest mountain, the still slightly active Labalekang, which at 1,644 metres towers over the whaling village Lamalerap. On the same coast is the volcano Ili Werung on the Labala Peninsula, which last erupted in 1963.

Geologically, the island is very similar to its neighbours. It consists primarily of volcanic soil, interrupted in some places— particularly in the north—by high-lying beds of ancient coral. High savannah plains are found in the mountainous central region, which are still largely unpopulated. There are a few streams which run all the year round, but the largest of these, Wai Komo, does not permit navigation by even the smallest boats.

Until this century, the island's population lived almost exclusively on the slopes of the highest mountains. Decades of effort by the colonial and later the Indonesian governments have broken this pattern to the extent that the major part of the villages in many districts have moved down towards the base of the mountains near Dutch-built roads, and many areas formerly untouched have been opened for farming. In Kédang, in particular, the plains west of the mountain are now widely exploited, whereas until a few decades ago most people were afraid even to travel in this area. To this day, few people live there permanently and even they return to their village at the end of the agricultural season. In the west, in the region of Kalikasa, new villages have been opened in formerly uninhabited regions under the encouragement of the government.

Lembata is one of a series of small islands called the Solor

Archipelago, situated east of Flores and north of Timor.[1] It lies on trade routes connecting eastern and western Indonesia and the island of Timor with Makasar; and it has certainly always had contact with Indonesian traders. Furthermore, there have been European garrisons and missionaries on Solor and at Larantuka, East Flores intermittently since 1555, but Lembata remained almost completely unknown to Europeans until the end of the last century.

Like its neighbouring islands, it has been known under several names: Lomblen, Lomblem, Lombatta, Quella, Kawella, Kawoela. The last three names derive from the name of the district Kawela at the western tip of the island. In this century, Lomblen has come to be accepted as standard, and it is this form which will be found on most modern maps. Lombatta seems to be the oldest recorded name and is to be found in Wouter Schouten's account of his East Indian voyage. In the middle fifties, when the island's administrative status was raised to that of an autonomous district (*Daerah Autonom*), the name of the island was changed to what was considered its original form with certain spelling alterations to bring it into line with modern Indonesian orthographic conventions. It is now officially called Lembata, a fact which unfortunately seems to be at variance with international convention.

Where the names Lomblen or Lembata (if they are really the same) originate is not at all clear. Van Lynden (1851: 318) suggests that they are bastardizations of village names: *Lawo leing, Leoew batan*, or *Lob'mata*. I have encountered similar ideas on the island. One also hears that the name comes from the mountain Lompo Batang in the Celebes, or the two islands, Lapang and Batang, in the strait between Lembata and Pantar, which is supposed to be the site of the land where the ancestors of many Lamaholot clans once lived before it sank into the sea. The most popular theory in Kédang (particularly among government officials) is that the name originated from the mythical hero of Kédang, Pulau Lama Léqang. One even encounters versions of this theory which have Pulau Lama Léqang himself coming down to the beach to meet the first Dutchman. Since the first word of his name (*pulau*) means 'island' in Malay, this allows the Dutchman

---

[1] Lembata lies between 123° 12′ 36″ and ± 123° 54′ 11″ east, longitude, and between 8° 10′ 18″ and 8° 31′ 14″ south, latitude, and is about 1,180 square kilometres in size (Beckering 1911: 184).

to ask the name of the island, and Pulau Lama Léqang to think he is being asked his own name. The Dutchman, not knowing the language, then goes away to perpetrate the colossal mistake of naming an island after an individual—and mispronouncing the name at that.

If there is any connection at all between the names Lomblen and Pulau Lama Léqang, it is probably the reverse. The latter is constructed on the model of the ceremonial names for villages, in which two elements are joined by the word *lama*, which in Lamaholot seems to mean 'place' or 'region'. The ceremonial name for the village Léuwajang for instance is Wajang Lama Hoténg, Ruba Lama Léwaq or Wajang Lama Hoténg, Nuba Lama Léwaq, Ruba Lama Lai, Léwa Lama Doa. This name contains an admixture of Lamaholot and words of the Kédang language of such unusual form that I could not get an exact translation for each word. To translate it accurately is actually beyond my capacities, but I will offer this attempt: the village where (spirit?) is called, and offerings are made at altars; deer (spirit?) come high, sail far.

Léqang is the sort of mindless commotion a chicken makes when it is searching for a place to nest; so Pulau Lama Léqang might well be translated, 'the island where chickens nest'. The story of this figure is given in Appendix I.

2. REMARKS ON THE HISTORY OF LEMBATA AND KÉDANG

When the Dutch began serious administration of the island, after 1910, they adopted the more or less traditionally existing districts: in the north Lewo Tolo and Kédang, in the west Kawela—all three of which were placed under the Radja of Adonara—in the centre the *kakang*-ship Lewoleba, in the south the *kakang*-ship Lamalerap and the radjadom Labala—all eventually put under the Radja of Larantuka. The historical background of these districts was obscure then and remains so to this day.

East Flores and the three islands to the east, Solor, Adonara, and Lembata, are inhabited by a population which, everywhere except in Kédang, speaks the Solor or Lamaholot language. There are many dialectal and cultural differences within this area, especially on Lembata, which is the least homogeneous of the islands; but everywhere there is essentially the same language and same culture. This language is even found in scattered enclaves on the coast of Pantar and Alor. There was no comparable political unity in this area; this was only established by the Dutch after decades of gradual elimination of local political powers and the drawing together of an administrative district which is now the *Kabupaten Flores Timur* or the East Flores Regency (East Flores, Adonara, Solor, and Lembata). What the Dutch began to work with was a disparate collection of local powers and independent regions of quite unequal importance. With some of these small radjadoms, they had treaties dating from as far back as the seventeenth century. Others came decisively under their influence only after Portugal sold its holdings in the islands to Holland in 1859. Neither power seems ever to have made any serious effort to establish ties with Lembata. Solor, Larantuka, and Adonara were the centre of their interest.

There exists among the Lamaholot communities a division of considerable ethnographic interest into groups called Padji and Demong. The division is found on each of the islands, and the two groups are traditional enemies, formerly in a state of perpetual if sporadic warfare. The Demong of East Flores consider themselves the militarily stronger late-comers who drove the original population, Padji, out of the good lands in the centre of the islands into the rougher and less productive extremities. In most areas this seems to fit well with the distribution of the two groups but not everywhere, certainly not in eastern Adonara where the Padji are strong. All of the areas are either Demong or Padji, but there was no over-all system of alliances, nor was there any over-all political structure based on the division before the Dutch stepped in. As it happened, the two most powerful radjas in the area, the Radja of Larantuka and the Radja of Adonara, were Demong and Padji respectively. Furthermore, there was an ancient league called in Malay 'the five coasts' (*lima pantai*) among the five Muslim and Padji radjas of Adonara, Trong and Lamahala on Adonara and Lawajong (Lohajong) and Lamakera on Solor. The Radja of Larantuka controlled the whole of eastern Flores with the exception of seven villages at the tip of the Tandjung Kopondei (Tandjung Bunga or Flores Cape) in the possession of the Radja of Adonara. He also claimed holdings in central Adonara and eastern Solor. The Radja of Adonara had control of Lewotolo on Lembata and claimed Kawela and Kédang.

The Dutch saw in the real and putative holdings of the two

radjas of Larantuka and Adonara the embryo of a convenient administrative division. By 1931 all the land had been consolidated under Larantuka and Adonara, which were the only radjas still holding office (Dijk 1925: 34).

Lembata, excepting only Lewotolo, was least tightly bound by these traditional ties, and they were here at best mostly nominal. The Kapitan of Kédang claimed then, and it is still claimed in Kédang, that his district was independent of the Radja of Adonara, and this claim is verified by Munro, a lieutenant of the Dutch infantry, in an official report in 1915 (pp. 1–2). Munro says that Kédang was originally a radjadom, but M. A. Sarabiti, the last Kapitan, told me that his family bore only the Kédangese designation *Rian-Baraq*, an honorific composed of the words 'great' and 'heavy'. Van Lynden lists Kédang in 1851 as standing under the Radja of Adonara, but he no doubt relied on the Radja of Adonara for this information for he remarks that '*Lomblem* is still very little known'.

The remembered history of Kédang was gathered by Guru J. Bumi Liliweri of the village Léunoda, who kindly allowed me to copy from his record. Though it is not possible to date the various wars which occurred in Kédang before the Dutch take-over, one receives the very strong impression that the ruling family of Kalikur managed to consolidate its control of Kédang only after the Dutch forced their subjection to the Radja of Adonara. In the nineteenth century there were attempts to take over Kédang by both the Radja of Lamahala and the Radja of Adonara, as well as a series of expeditions by the head of Kalikur, twice with the aid of soldiers from Timor, to subject the villages of the interior.

Lamahala is an ancient kingdom on the south coast of Adonara which appears in treaties with the Dutch as early as 1613. Unlike the other Muslim radjadoms, it lacks a hinterland and seems always to have depended on trading. Wichman describes the village as having the best craftsmen. They are goldsmiths and silversmiths, carpenters, woodcarvers, and blacksmiths (Vatter 1932: 158), and they still provide the other islands with spear-points, bushknives, and jewellery. Kluppel describes them as seditious and homicidal, and speculates that they derive from pirates—though his dating of their settling on Adonara at around 1770 overlooks the long history of their diplomatic relations with the Dutch. They seem to have revolted from Dutch control in

1868 and driven the Dutch post-holder to seek refuge in neighbouring Trong, which they then attacked the next year. The
Radja was deposed in 1872 because of his 'turbulent and bellicose
disposition and double dealings with the Government' and the
village then placed under the Radja of Lamakera (Kluppel 1873:
380). Again in 1888 they were involved in a war with Adonara,
which ended when the Dutch brought in the two gunboats *Prins
Hendrik* and *Benkoelen* to bombard the village, finally razing
the village and burning all its boats (Wichman 1891: 264–6).
Vatter (1932: 158) describes it in the late twenties as a centre of
the anti-Dutch movement and Bolshevistic propaganda.

Lamahala's interest in Kédang seems to have developed during
this period of belligerence in the middle of the nineteenth century,
though a more exact dating is not possible. What this interest
was founded on is not difficult to determine. Kédang was regarded as one of the richest areas on the island, especially in such
goods as coconuts, candlenut, assam, and citrus fruit. Rice and
maize seem to have been abundant enough to play a large part in
external trade, and Kédang provided also a steady supply of slaves.
Settlers from Lamahala founded the village Dolulolong (Dulolong)
on the northern coast (see Map 2), and from there attempted to
wrest the villages of the interior from the control of Kalikur. This
led to at least two wars in which many villages allied themselves
with Lamahala, but in both cases Kalikur managed to break the
overt revolt without being entirely able to suppress the resistance.
As late as 1913, representatives from Dolulolong were sent to the
district commissioner in Larantuka with the claim that they stood
under neither Kalikur nor Adonara but under Lamahala (Munro
1915: 1).

Towards the end of the last century, the Radja of Adonara,
Arikian Kamba, who claimed ancient supremacy in this area, led
a force in person to conquer Kédang. This army landed at
Dolulolong, but was met and defeated by soldiers under the
leadership of the head of Kalikur near the village Léuhoéq. Some
time later, the head of Kalikur went to the village Tanah Merah
(Tanah Mean) on the west coast of Adonara just opposite Larantuka to attend the funeral of the father-in-law of a member of his
own clan. He was there captured by order of the Radja of Adonara
and turned over to District Commissioner Misroop at Larantuka.
They kept him there for about a month, until the two gunboats

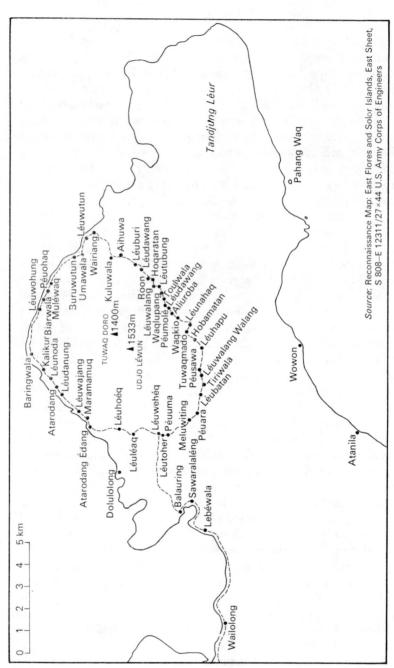

Source: Reconnaissance Map: East Flores and Solor Islands, East Sheet, S 808–E 12311/27×44 U.S. Army Corps of Engineers

MAP 2. Kédang.

Prins Hendrik and *Benkoelen* arrived. These boats then carried a party consisting of the Commissioner of Kupang, the district commissioner, the district officer, the Radja of Adonara and the captured head of Kalikur back to Kédang, where they cruised back and forth in front of the village Kalikur. The Dutch officials then presented the head of Kalikur with an ultimatum demanding that he recognize the supremacy of the Radja of Adonara on pain of watching the bombardment of his own village. Under this pressure he formally submitted Kédang to rule by the Radja of Adonara. The Dutch stationed soldiers in Kalikur, whose head they then officially appointed *kapitan* of Kédang, the local delegate of the Radja.

The Dutch demanded a payment of Rp 1,000 in silver for the cost of the expedition. This they received from the Radja of Adonara, who in turn received an equal sum from the ruling clan of Kalikur, Léu Tuang. In addition he demanded as a fine a large tusk and a large gong from each of the villages of Kédang. He also ordered that every three months for a year each village of the interior must bring its entire crop of copra, candlenut or assam to the coast to be picked up by his boats and taken back to Adonara.

The villages which had fought so long to escape control by Kalikur and whose resistance had never been completely suppressed, found themselves suddenly subjected to three governments and burdened with the costs of conquest as well. Ironically, they were surrendered by a man who had no clear claim to do so, in order to save a village whose destruction they would probably have welcomed. Though the action was taken in the name of the Radja of Adonara, the real force was provided by the Dutch military, without which neither the Radja nor the newly appointed Kapitan of Kédang could have carried through their political control.

Another consequence of this defeat was that Kédang came to be reckoned as Padji because they stood under the Radja who controlled all the Padji territories. One of my aims in going to this area was to study the Padji/Demong division from the point of view of a Padji population. Most of the information available comes from Demong (Arndt 1938). I learned absolutely nothing of the question in Kédang, where the people claim to have had no relation to either group prior to the Dutch conquest. It is likely that they were regarded as Padji before this time, but it is also quite certain that the Padji/Demong conflict has nothing to do with the indigenous culture of Kédang and is purely a Lamaholot institution.

At some time, probably in about 1904, the Dutch collected all the firearms on the island. These were brought in by traders from Makasar and Buton and traded for, in particular, slaves. Beckering (1911: 196) says that of the 1,400 rifles gathered on the island, 1,100 came from Tanah Padji, that is, the parts of the island under the Radja of Adonara. Today there seems to be no such weapon in private hands in Kédang.

In 1915, the Dutch established an elementary school at Kalikur. The second school was opened in 1925 by the Catholic mission in Aliuroba; they opened more schools in 1927 at Léudawan, 1928 at Meluwiting and Buruwutung, in 1929 at Léuwajang. Islam was introduced to Kédang early in the last century through the ruling family of Kalikur and the settlers from Lamahala at Dolulolong. It was largely confined to these two villages until around 1931, when Muslims from Kalikur began to proselytize in the interior. Catholicism was introduced in the island first through the village Lamalerap. Already in the last century, missionaries stationed in Larantuka made periodic visits there. They first began to work in Kédang during the early part of the decade of the twenties. According to the census of 1970, forty-five per cent of the population is Muslim, twenty-eight per cent Catholic, and twenty-seven per cent retain the traditional religion. In addition some of the Chinese traders in Balaurin are now Protestant.

Chinese merchants first came to Kédang in 1910 where they settled in Kalikur. Most now live in Balaurin which was recently made the centre of the government of the Ketjamatan Omesuri. Munro mentioned three markets in Kédang in 1915 (p. 8) at Pasar Wairiang, Kalikur, and Dolulolong. Balaurin was then a favourite market for smugglers because it lay far enough away from the mountain to escape the supervision of the *kapitan*; but according to Munro, the Dutch shut it down and moved it to Dolulolong. It could not have remained shut for long.

Kalikur was in ancient times already a port for traders. When the ship *Victoria* of Magellan's expedition sailed past the island in January 1522, the helmsman, Francisco Albo, recorded the name Alicura in the ship's log. Le Roux (1929: 14) identifies this with Kalikur. He is certainly correct: the version given by Albo curiously combines the form of the name known outside Kédang with the form it has in the indigenous language. Within Kédang, it is known as Aliur. The loss of the two *k*'s is a regular shift found when comparing Lamaholot with Kédangese. The indigenous name of Kédang is actually Édang. It is easy to understand why the Lamaholot form should have received precedence, since traders from Lamaholot provided important ties to the outside for this relatively isolated area. It is curious that the first circumnavigation of the world should have given us this proof of Kalikur's importance as a port even then as well as evidence of the antiquity of this shift in the Kédang language. The name of Kalikur could only have been known to the two Tidorese pilots of the *Victoria* if it figured as an important centre of trade.

It was originally founded by people from the village Aliuroba, which lies on the south side of the mountain, and the ruling clan (Léu Tuang) are of Kédang descent. But there had been strong mixture with foreigners, particularly with traders from Celebes, Adonara, and Alor. Le Roux says there has been mixture with people from Ternate as well. I do not know how to assess this claim, which seems in any case speculative. He refers to the fact that the Sultan of Ternate claimed the islands in this area until 1683 when he signed a treaty with the United East India Company (*Vereenigde Oostindische Compagnie* or the *V.O.C.*) renouncing his claims. That ties with the Moluccas may once have been more than nominal is quite possible, but this phase is part of Kédang's prehistory. The ancestors of the clan Honi Ero of Kalikur are said to have come from Seran, as are also those of the Radja of Adonara. The clan Marisa of Kalikur is said to descend from Madjapahit Javanese.

That Kalikur had by itself partly succeeded in establishing its suzerainty over the rest of Kédang is due to its control of trade with the interior. Most of the list of items van Lynden (p. 324) found in the Solor trade in the 1850s is representative for Kédang as well. From Makasarese, Buganese or Endehnese merchants came cloth (the cheap, machine-woven cotton sarongs or *lipaq*, which still serve as everyday wear), silk thread (yellow, red, and white) used as decoration in locally woven cloth, elephant tusks, ivory bracelets, gongs, beads, field knives and swords, rifles, medicinal herbs, arak (distilled palm wine), and jenever (gin). The return was maize, rice, copra, candlenut, assam, and slaves.

The contact with strangers gave Kalikur an advantageous sophistication and knowledge of the outer world; their position as intermediaries for the trade with the mountain population gave them power and wealth. They took advantage of this position to establish an arrogant and extortionate supremacy over the rest of Kédang. Even in recent decades they allowed themselves to confiscate the goods of people going to market, and there were numerous instances of beatings and terrorizing by villagers of Kalikur so long as they remained in power. Until the change of government in 1965, the villages Léuwohung, Biarwala, Péuoha, and Mulé Waq were considered actual possessions of Kalikur, a situation resulting from a war in which the determined resistance of Léuwohung was finally broken by a force from Léuwajang under the leadership of the locally famous Boli Talé. As reward for the assistance rendered to Kalikur, Boli Talé's delegate, Leraq Nara, was sent to Timor, where he was awarded the title Fettor (a term of Portuguese origin frequent on Timor, where it means a sort of district head or lieutenant to a radja). The title seems to have had no enduring consequences, but Léuwajang retained fairly favourable relations with Kalikur, though they, too, were exploited from time to time.

The relation to the outside provided Kalikur its first opportunity to attempt serious conquest. No more than the incident just described can these events be dated, but they certainly belong to the second half of the nineteenth century. Through traders from Alor, Kalikur heard of the famous warriors of Timor called *meo* (reputedly Amfoan). The word *meo* occurs in several Timorese languages where it designates a war leader (Vroklage 1952: 1: 646; Schulte Nordholt 1971: 338–45). Kalikur brought a party of *meo* or Timorese warriors to Kédang to help in suppressing the villages of the interior. These troops then burned all the villages of Kédang except Léutubung, which defended itself ingeniously by bending back a stand of bamboo which stood at the entrance to the village. This they tied in such a way that when the rope was cut the bamboo swept the path before it, and the first group of *meo* which entered the village were swiftly decapitated. This seems to have been their only defeat, and after twice coming to Kédang in support of Kalikur, their name became greatly feared.

Today, when someone is startled or frightened, he may still utter the conventional cry, '*Béjéng! Méo!*' ('Run! *Meo!*').

3. THE MOUNTAIN OF KÉDANG

The district of Kédang is dominated by its mountain which is so imposing that any attempt to account for the culture of Kédang must begin with this landmark. It consists of two peaks; modern maps give the heights of these as 1,400 and 1,533 metres respectively, figures which make it the second highest on the island. It appears variously on maps and in publications under the name Ili (mountain) Kédang and Udjoléwung (on Dutch maps Oedjole-woeng). Both names are correct. Opinion differs in Kédang as to which is the more traditional, but I find no good reason to suppose, as some Kédangese claim, that one or the other has been simply invented and imposed by the Dutch colonial government. I was once told by a man from the village Baringwala that the original name was Ili Kura or 'Cassava Mountain', but I have encountered no other support for this, and the word *kura* is not even recognized in the village in which I lived. The meaning of Udjoléwung will be discussed later.

The smaller peak of the mountain is labelled on some maps Toewadoro (i.e. *tu(w)aq doro*). I encountered no one who recognized this name, but inquiries revealed no substitute for it. It is quite likely that some regions of Kédang consistently employ the name. However, in the region where I lived, absolutely no interest was shown in this peak. It is virtually treeless and not very striking.

When viewed from the north or northeast, the mountain gives the impression of having split and the eastern half then slowly tumbling or sinking into the sea. Viewed from the east, the mountain presents its least attractive aspect. Here it appears as a rather jumbled collection of hills and ravines; and, as the eastern side characteristically suffers from insufficient rain, it is considerably more barren than are the northern and western sides. The summit displays a feature not found on other nearby mountains: there is a quite distinct change in vegetation from that at lower levels. As one climbs, one leaves behind the familiar palms, banyans, candlenut trees, tamarinds, etc. and in the last few hundred metres enters an area of very large trees of various types (unfortunately unknown to me) all called *lu* in the local language. These trees, which are now being pushed back by the opening of new fields, may once have extended farther down the sides of the mountain. Until recently they were somewhat protected by a traditional prohibition on opening fields near the summit. When one leaves the lower skirts of the mountain and climbs to the top, one gets the very strong impression of having entered a quite different world. In contrast with the vast, sulphurous and constantly smoking open crater of Lewotolo (which is easily viewed from Kédang), the crown of the mountain here displays a quiet sylvan atmosphere, a sort of eternal restfulness belying any possibility of historically recent activity. This atmosphere fits quite well with the cultural place of the top of the mountain and underlines the absence among the population of any memory of eruption.

Brouwer (1940: 23), referring to an unpublished paper by M. A. Hartmann, incorrectly reports that no distinct crater forms can be recognized on the mountain. The cone, however, is quite easily seen on cloudless days from the north and west (U.S. Navy H.O. 1962: 259), and, as will later be shown, the crater itself is of considerable importance in the culture.

Vatter (1932: 15) says that Kédang was still active in the middle of the last century, and Brouwer (1917a: 429; 1917b: 998) makes a similar report. This mistake is traceable to Verbeek (1908: 365–6), who, in referring to nineteenth-century reports on activity of the 'Lobétolé' volcano, remarks that in two sea-charts available to him this name is applied to Kédang and refers to van Lynden (1851: 319) who speaks of 'the almost constantly smoking volcano *Lobetolle* (the northeast hook of the island)'. He notes that the name Lobétolé is incorrectly applied to Kédang and that it actually refers to the Lewotolo volcano to the west; but for some reason he maintains the misconception (which Hartmann 1935: 824, at least, regards as 'very unlikely') that these reports were actually referring to Kédang and not to Lewotolo. There are in fact a number of notices of unusual activity of Pulau Komba and Lewotolo in the years 1849 and 1852 (Anon. 1850a; 1850b; 1851; 1852). In one of these (1850b: 154) smoke is reported from Lobetolle, and the volcano is assigned the correct co-ordinates for Kédang; but these are surely taken from a faulty sea-chart. None of these reports mention two active volcanoes on the north coast, and it is hardly likely that Lewotolo was quiet in this period. Wouter Schouten (1676: 80) already describes the 'wonder high burning mountain' of the island Lembata, which shows that in the seventeenth century, as now, only one volcano gave a striking display to ships sailing past the island.

At no point on the mountain are sulphurous fumes given forth, but there are hot springs along the beach.

4. THE NAME

The name Kédang, or in the local form Édang, means the bamboo jew's harp. Why it has this name is open only to speculation. The jew's harp plays no significant part in their present culture, and only a very few people know how to make it. I found no myths or stories which mention it, and the people themselves seem to have no theory to explain the name. That the name rests on a pun is quite possible. The word can be analysed into two parts, *é* and *dang*. *É* (in some regions *ké*) is the form of the first person plural pronoun which excludes the person addressed; *dang* is the verb used for playing a percussive instrument. This allows one to imagine that the people of the region characterized themselves to strangers as 'the people who play percussive instruments'. But this is only one possibility of the word; the undivided form is possibly related to Indonesian *gendang* (drum).

Kédang stands out in comparison to many regions of Lamaholot in the number of gongs it owns and especially in the fact that they are used as bridewealth. They have a marked fondness for percussive instruments, of which the jew's harp is only one version.[2] There is a line from a song in Kédang which demonstrates the possible range of reference of this word: *édang tatong, lia namang*. *Tatong* is the bamboo zither. *Lia* may be the morning star and God; and I was told that in this case it means the words of the song (cf. Lamaholot *liang*, 'to sing', 'song'; Leemker 1893). *Namang* means to circle dance. This line could mean simply 'jew's harp, bamboo zither; song, dance'; but another possible reading of the line would be 'we play the bamboo zither, God dances'. Since God cannot circle dance by Himself, the phrase

---

[2] The jew's harp, which appears on the Barabudur reliefs, is even used on Bali in orchestras which imitate the great *gong gede* orchestras (Goris and Dronkers n.d.: 184). It is perhaps of use to compare the name of Kédang and their use of percussive instruments to the similar role of drum and gong orchestras (*gondang*) among the Toba Batak before their forcible suppression by the colonial government at the instigation of the missionaries, where a lineage may be called *sagondang*, 'belonging to one *gondang*' (Vergouwen 1964: 34).

may imply His participation in the very dance of those who are singing the song. Needham has drawn attention to the role of percussion in ceremonies of transition (1967a), and circle dances are particularly associated with ceremonies of this type in Kédang. So too is the use of percussive instruments. They are also part of a cycle of exchange which is fundamental to the social order and which is occasioned by the most important gift one group of people may give another: life itself, the possibility of continued existence. If the people of Kédang call themselves players of percussive instruments, they mean quite a bit more by this than we might at first think, as it is an expression of their sense of religious order.

5. SUBSISTENCE

Most Kédangese are agriculturalists. Maize is the staple. Rice—cultivated on dry fields—Job's tears, millet, *sorghum vulgare*, cassava, and other tuberous plants are less significant. Other crops include bananas, beans, peanuts, pumpkins, cucumbers, melons and other gourds, eggplant, sugarcane, red peppers, pineapples, tobacco, coconuts, *pinang* (areca), and *sirih* (betel). Also exploited is an important list of crops which are not planted or usually cared for: tomatoes, ginger, curcuma, cotton, a large variety of citrus fruit, candlenut trees, the lontar palm, *motong* (*Moringa oleifera* Lam.), spinach, papaya, paria (*Memordica charantia* Lam.), cassambai, mangoes. Wood for building purposes may be taken from the many varieties of trees growing wild. The areng palm provides a good quality of cord. The coconut palm, and to a just slightly less extent the lontar, is a wonder plant, the parts of which are employed for an uncountable variety of purposes. Bamboo groves are individually owned.

Farming is done on dry fields on the terraced slopes of the mountain or, in other areas, of hills and ravines. The rotation of fields is irregular, depending on the situation of the fields and the quality of the soil. On the sides of the mountain, fields are often planted year after year until they no longer return the seed. All ground within the village is planted every year without let. Irrigation is not possible in most areas because of the shortage of water, and there is little chance of providing fertilizer. The fields are burned off each year, and all work is done with the aid of a field knife and a digging stick with a small iron blade, the only locally available implement suitable to the rocky soil. There is no communally organized work on the fields, though friends who have fields in the same area usually help each other. Work which requires a number of people, such as threshing rice or carrying the crops from the fields, may be arranged by forming a group which does the same job for all of its members in succession, or the owners may invite people to help, and repay them by providing a small feast. There are no village-owned fields. A field is owned by the first person to open it, and his claim is permanent; it does not lapse even after the field is long abandoned. A person can open a field anywhere where there is no field, or he may ask permission to reopen an abandoned one. Now that the population is large, many people have their fields many kilometres away from their village.

The main domestic animals are chickens, pigs, and goats. Sheep are rare. Van Lynden (p. 321) said in 1851 that there were no horses on the island; in 1911 there were only about sixty (Beckering 1911: 193). There are now quite a few, mostly in the possession of people living on the coast. Game animals include principally deer and pigs. There are no longer deer on the mountain itself, but they are numerous in the area to the west. Wild pigs can still be hunted near the top of the mountain; they seem to be the same species as the domesticated pigs. There are no monkeys on either Lembata or Solor, although they occur on Flores and Adonara. It is a curiosity of the Kédang language that there is nevertheless a term for monkey, *luka-leki*. The island was once known for its numerous wild buffalo. These are now much less numerous. The Kapitan of Kédang, at one time the richest man on the island, owned a herd of 300 buffalo, but these were rounded up and slaughtered in the thirties. The village Lamalerap at the other end of the island hunts whales, and edible birds' nests are gathered in the district Kawela. Rienzi (1836–7: 1: 205) describes the island of Solor as producing nothing but bamboo and birds' nests, but the latter are found only on Lembata. Neither island has the kangaroos he says are to be found here.

6. CLOTHING

Schouten described the islanders of Adonara in the seventeenth century as wearing nothing but loincloths, but the people of the island Solor were said to desire cloth more than money. *Lipaq*, the thin cotton sarongs, which actually should be worn only by men but which are standard wear for both sexes in this part of Indonesia, are mentioned as trade items in the middle of the last century. The original clothing for men in Kédang were the loin-cloth (*tariq*) and the *sedé*, a circular piece of clothing made from gebang leaf, which had a draw-string around the waist and covered the loins, reaching a little above the knees. A cap which used to be worn was made from the burlap-like covering at the base of the branches of the lontar palm. Women would have worn the loin-cloth as well, but it is possible that sarongs were made in the islands for local trade before clothing was available through foreign merchants.

The term for the woman's sarong in Kédang is *wéla*, a word which also refers to the mountain. Traditionally it is forbidden to weave or make clothing in Kédang. Vatter found that a clan in the Lobetobi region of East Flores which originally came from Kédang retained this prohibition. He says that he was told on Lembata that the coastal population had bribed the witch-doctors into imposing this prohibition in order to ensure their own monopoly (1932: 150–1). He does not say who told him this, and the story seems in some ways unlikely. Whatever truth it may have, it cannot be the full explanation, for the prohibition is hardly so superficial. Even today when weaving is done by the mountain population, the proscription applies in full force within the boundaries of the old village. It may be that making clothing is regarded as an alien process and possibly also as polluting to the village. The Japanese first introduced it on a large scale to Kédang. They brought in a superior type of cotton, and then trained the population in the methods of cloth making used in Lamaholot. Nowadays, many women make sarongs for everyday use; but they cannot produce the expensive and highly decorative pieces made in Lewotolo (Gunung Api) or Lamalerap.

It was traditional for the hair to be worn long and tied on the top of the head for a man or at the back for a woman. The opposi-tion represented by these two ways of wearing the hair is between up and down and corresponds to the symbolic position of male and female in other cases. When I was in Kédang, there was only one old man who still wore his hair this way. Vroklage (1952: 1: 164) says that on Timor the Dutch forced the men to cut their hair short 'for reasons of health'. He did not say why it did not occur to them to shave the heads of the women as well. I do not know if these measures were ever introduced into Kédang, but the businessman's haircut became an Indonesian fashion in the early years of this century, and it has now completely taken over in Kédang.

7. POPULATION SIZE AND ADMINISTRATIVE STATUS

Beckering (p. 186) gives the population of Lembata in 1911 as 31,000 to 32,000. According to the census of 1930, there were 47,000 people on the island; according to the 1970 census there are now 82,000. In 1930 there were 16,318 people in Kédang (*Volkstelling 1930* 1936: 5: 137); in 1970, 25,440. In the last several decades there has been a large influx of settlers from Lamaholot areas, in particular from Lewotolo. Very nearly half the village Léuléaq is now Lamaholot speaking. Wailolong, Lebé, Sawaralaléng, and Balaurin are inhabited predominantly by people of foreign descent. There are a number of families of the Badjo Laut at Balaurin, Kalikur, and Wairiang.

At the time of the coup in 1965, the Indonesian government was already beginning to ease the Kapitan from power. During that coup he found himself on Java and did not deem it wise to return to Kédang until 1970. After his departure, Kédang was split into two administrative units, each under an acting Tjamat or sub-district head. In June 1970 new men were put into these offices which were then raised to full status. The two *ketjamatan* were named after the ancestral couple of Kédang, Bujaq Suri (the male), and Omé Suri (the female). In 1968 the villages were rearranged to form, where possible, new administrative units of no fewer than 1,000 members. Frequently two or more old villages were combined to form one of these 'new form villages' (*desa gaja baru*).

8. LANGUAGE

The people of Kédang speak a so far unrecorded language. Their term for it is *tutuq-nanang wéla*, or 'the language of the mountain'. Whereas *tutuq* means 'to talk', *nanang* otherwise means 'to weave' (baskets); so the phrase suggests the interweaving force of conversation. It stands in opposition to *iwang-kariq*, which is their term for the Lamaholot-speaking Lewotolo region and means language they cannot understand, thus any strange language.

Disregarding slight variations of pronunciation and vocabulary, the language is homogeneous throughout Kédang. Since an increasing number of the population are becoming literate, they now can apply the model of Bahasa Indonesia for writing their own language.

Prof. Karl van Trier of Madiun prepared (in the late forties) some word lists in Kédang (which, together with some other word-lists prepared by missionaries and in the possession of the mission in Kédang, were kindly lent me by Father Geerts) and introduced the convention of using a *q* for the glottal stop. This is now often employed in Kédang, and I have decided to use it in this book rather than the apostrophe. The glottal stop is so frequent that it seems to deserve a character of its own, and the *q* is not otherwise required. I do not indicate the initial glottal stop. As in Bahasa Indonesia, their *w* ranges between our *v* and our *w*. I have retained the familiar Indonesian *w* for this sound. The Indonesian silent *e* is unknown in the language of Kédang; instead they have two *e*'s pronounced like the French *è* and *é*. I use the unaccented *e* for the first and the *é* for the latter. The initial and internal *w* is dropped more frequently in Léuwajang than elsewhere. The *dj* (pronounced as English j) usually gives way here to the *j* (pronounced as English *y*). I have kept to the forms most commonly used in Léuwajang, which are the ones I know best, but a dictionary of the language of Kédang might well choose a different village for its model.[3]

There are many words of very similar form, and related meaning, which are distinguished in pronunciation only by an initial relaxing or tightening of the throat. In some cases this can be seen to be a superficial feature used to distinguish two senses of the same word. An example of this is *iné-amé*, which can mean, depending on whether the throat[4] is relaxed or not, either the members of the wife-giving line or one's own mother and father, or the equivalent level of one's clan. Here there is no question of the etymological connection. In other cases, this feature seems to distinguish homonyms of different origin: I suspect that *apé*, which is probably derived from Indonesian *kapas*, and means

---

[3] In the Kédang language, the possessive precedes and the adjective follows the noun (cf., Vatter 1932: 275–6).

[4] Dr. J. C. Anceaux of Leiden tells me that this may be what linguists working in the African field call a 'tongue-root retraction'.

'cotton', and *apé*, meaning 'what?', are in this category. In a number of cases, an argument is made in this dissertation that near homonyms of this sort demonstrate a common etymology and a common idea, such as in the two versions of *anaq*, meaning 'child' and 'complete'. The reader may react as he wishes, but he should be aware that there is a phonetic basis for such an argument.

I have used certain words from Bahasa Indonesia frequently in this dissertation because no easy English equivalent seems to exist. The reader should be alerted then to the following: (1) *balai*, a bamboo platform, ubiquitous in Indonesia, which serves in one as table, chair, bed, and storage platform: (2) *sirih-pinang*, a mild narcotic, constantly used, consisting of the nut of the areca palm (*pinang*) and the pepper of the betel plant (*sirih*), or sometimes (in Kédang less frequently than elsewhere) the leaf of this plant, and chewed together with lime; (3) *sarong*, a tube of cloth worn by women as a kind of dress; (4) *lipaq*, the equivalent for a man.

Munro (1915: 11) says that the language of Kédang is not a Lamaholot dialect, but is related to the language spoken on Pantar. This idea that there is a close linguistic connection between Kédang and Pantar-Alor seems to have been quite common, and is adopted by Salzner (1960). Vatter (1932: 276), on the other hand, says that it must be regarded as an independently developed form of Lamaholot and not an Alor-Pantar language. Comparison with the word-lists in Anonymous 1914: 94–102, which is the only published evidence we have on the languages of Alor and Pantar, shows a certain relation with the Coastal Alor language, but none at all with the others. The Coastal Alor language spoken in coastal regions of Alor and Pantar are dialects of Lamaholot, and it seems incorrect to class them with the other Alor and Pantar languages. My experience in Kédang is that there is a high percentage of the vocabulary which is shared with Lamaholot. I would not know how to estimate this, but I am sure it is not over fifty per cent. The elements of this common vocabulary belong to all historical levels of the language; the two are obviously connected in their origins, but there seems to have been a continual influx of Lamaholot words into Kédang, and this still goes on. What is remarkable is how many fundamental elements in the language have nothing to do with Lamaholot or, from what little we know, with Pantar or Alor languages either. It seems to me that the language of Kédang is best considered a language in its own right, and should not be listed as a dialect of any of its neighbours.

In addition to ordinary language, there is a repertory of phrases used in ceremonies, songs, and public oratory. These are not ordered into long texts of fixed form, as happens in some neighbouring societies. The texts of chants used during ceremonies approach this to some extent without ever achieving a determined order of lines or a stable content and fixed length. Oratory on festive occasions is always an extemporary selection from traditional lines. The performances I saw were rather lacklustre; and this form of oratory is not developed to the extent that one finds in Lamaholot. A good bit of this special language is known by everyone, but certain people are recognized to excel in it, especially priests (*molan-maran*). It is 'formal, formulaic, and parallelistic' (Fox 1971a: 215). Most words of the ordinary language come in dyadic sets. These sets are often composed of synonyms, such as *huna-wetaq* ('house'), but other principles are also employed, including antithesis. In ordinary conversation the full dyadic pairs are brought in only occasionally for stylistic colouration; but in the ceremonial language they are used to construct formal phrases which are often combined into two lines of parallel meaning. There is no clear border between ordinary language and the ceremonial language either in use or vocabulary. In the latter one encounters words and phrases which the Kédangese themselves consider abstruse and sometimes even untranslatable. There are also many borrowings from Lamaholot or use of Kédangese words in the ancient form common to both languages, and there are some borrowings from Malay and modern Bahasa Indonesia. But in the main, the vocabulary of the ceremonial language is largely familiar words of ordinary use.

Kédang is a very democratic society, without a genuine class of nobles, and there seems to be little competitive impulse to develop jealously guarded reputations as experts in these matters. There was no clear authority to turn to who could give me carefully constructed versions of chants for various occasions, so the best I could collect were rather short and repetitious 'representative' pieces. To some extent what I received deserves to be called representative for just these reasons; for the chants I heard during ceremonies were repetitious and not exceptionally long. My record comes primarily from Bala Béjéng, a priest, and Molan Bala who is a layman.

9. CONDITIONS OF WORK

This inquiry is by necessity a study of language. It is therefore a great disadvantage that there has not been any extensive work previously done on the language of Kédang. It is proper here then to explain why Kédang was chosen and to describe the conditions of work.

My intention in choosing a location for fieldwork was to find a place which was as little subject as possible to foreign influence and which had not been previously studied. These criteria do not have to govern every ethnographic study, but they are justifiable enough in themselves, and permit the anthropologist to confront himself with a situation that places his own categories in the clearest relief. Kédang was a community which came close to this ideal, and after conversation with missionaries of the *Societas Verbini Dei*, I chose to go there. It now appears to me that I might have chosen any number of other communities in the Flores region with equal justification, but Kédang was by no means a bad choice. It is unlikely that we would ever have known much about them had I not gone there, and their very interesting society forms an important link in the cultural make-up of the Solor Archipelago.

They are very easily distinguished as a society on its own, whether by the criteria of language, history, geography, or distribution of population. They have a society based on an ideology of asymmetric prescriptive alliance, and this provides one of the major interests of the study. I was able to record relationship terminologies of asymmetric prescriptive alliance in the Lamaholot language on each of the islands: Flores, Adonara, Solor, and Lembata. I also recorded terminologies of symmetric prescriptive alliance in the related Coastal Alor languages on Pantar and Alor. The study of Kédang not only provides a contribution to the topic of prescriptive alliance, but also prompts field research into the relation between symmetry and asymmetry in prescriptive alliance in closely related languages within a small geographic region and related historical setting. I intend to return to the area to conduct studies of Lamaholot culture and society.

I first went to Kédang in early October 1969. After reporting to the acting Tjamat of the Ketjamatan Omesuri and the chief of police in Balaurin, I walked with the personal escort of the police chief and the government messenger to the village Léuwajang. There I requested permission for my wife and myself to live in the village and to study the culture—and this was kindly granted. I chose Léuwajang because of its spring. Kédang is extremely short of water, and I intended to live in the old part of a village, usually situated in the mountain and far from springs or wells. Léuwajang is the only village in Kédang with a strong spring running all the year round, reasonably close to its old village.

The village head agreed to arrange for a house for us and then guided me on a walk round the mountain. I returned to Lewoleba, the main centre for the island's government and waited for two weeks while the house was being prepared. Then, on 17 October, my wife and I took a mission boat which dropped us off at Léuwajang.

Our house was situated in the hamlet Napoq Wala, which lies just below the old village (*léu tuan*) of Léuwajang; and it was identical with the houses of our neighbours except for its separate kitchen and an outdoor privy. We were given the house of one of the villagers, who moved next door into his son-in-law's house for the duration of our stay and became our very close friend and daily associate. On 23 October we were ceremonially received into the old village and, following dancing and feasting, moved into our new house. We lived in the old part of the village, rather than in the large hamlet at the beach with its schools, church, mosque, and village government, because my intention was to concentrate on the traditional culture. It is well to remember that this interest is carried over into the report, which does not present a study of culture change or attempt to give an account of what the Kédangese regard as the 'modern' elements in their life. This does not mean that we could not have studied Kédangese traditions in the new hamlet; quite the contrary. Nor does it mean that we did not have frequent contact with this part of the village. However, the religiously pre-eminent part of the village is *léu tuan*, the oldest hamlet, and many of the people who maintain traditional ways of life lived here or in the nearby hamlets. For my purpose, this was the best place to stay. Observation of ceremonies and of many features of daily life was considerably easier here.

Léuwajang has a population of 1,060, distributed among the hamlets Léu Tuan, Napoq Wala, Uru, Perung Baring, Édang, Riding, and the new beach settlement. The latter was first established when the Dutch ordered the mountain villages to move down to the coast where they could be more easily controlled. Several policies of the Indonesian government encourage settling in the new part of the village and the abandoning of the traditional religion. About a third of the village have their principal dwelling there. The oldest hamlet, *léu tuan*, lies at the highest part of the village. Napoq Wala is just below it, Uru to the east, Perung Baring farther east, Riding to the west and Édang, which at one

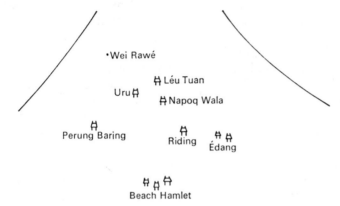

MAP 3. Schema of the hamlets of Léuwajang.

time in this century was the site of the village government, farther west. Of these older hamlets, Édang is the largest and lowest-lying, but even it is still relatively inaccessible from the road.

There are other former sites of small hamlets, the most recently abandoned being a place called Tanga Laléng. I do not include in this list any of the places where houses have been built at fields. During the length of a lifetime, the population of any of these hamlets will be relatively fluid. They are also not spaced so far apart nor are they so isolated that they have become divisions of major sociological significance nor are they associated with factions. Napoq Wala was supposedly formerly known as *léu tana* because it was once the site of fields for the inhabitants of *léu tuan*, and it and Uru are in a sense associated with *léu tuan* and share some of its aura as the old part of the village.

Before we went to Indonesia I had a few hours of training in Bahasa Indonesia at the University of Leiden, and in Oxford and I had studied the language on my own, but I could still not speak it. When I arrived in Kédang, my knowledge of the language was not much farther advanced. Since this was the only means of access to the language of Kédang, it was necessary to learn Indonesian. My study of both was carried on simultaneously in Kédang. It was important to learn Kédangese not only because it was a major part of the object of research, but also because many of the older men who were our daily companions could speak no Indonesian. By the time I left the field I was fluent in conversational Indonesian and in the language of Kédang, but this study can still only be considered an introduction to a language which could probably provide material for a lifetime's work for several linguists and philologists.

The stay in Kédang amounted to over nineteen months from October 1969 until June 1971. It was broken in July 1970, when we toured the Lamaholot area of Lembata and East Flores. We stayed a week in the villages of Lamalerap, Lembata, and Wailo-long, East Flores. This trip allowed me to make a preliminary reconnaissance of this people. In Lamalerap, I participated in a (successful) whale hunt. In Wailolong, I gathered information to complement Raymond Kennedy's unpublished notes on the alliance relationships among the lineages. We spent in all nearly twenty-three months in Indonesia.

Our life in the village was very similar to that of the villagers, with whom we were in constant contact. Though we depended on what was locally available for much of our food, our staple was rice, which we bought locally or got through the mission. We had to rely on medicines we brought with us to maintain our health. Our contact with Europeans during the months in Kédang was almost nil. The hamlet we lived in was so high, that for many days during the rainy season we were constantly in the clouds, which drifted through the house, covering everything with mildew. Our cameras, films, and tape-recorder did not stand up under these conditions, and most of our film record was destroyed; other parts of it disappeared in the post. Msgr. A. H. Thijssen, then Bishop of Larantuka, kindly loaned us his tape-recorder for the second year, and it was a great help to us.

10. SOURCES

I was not quite the first professional ethnographer to visit Kédang. That honour goes to Ernst Vatter who spent two days in Hobamatan during his tour of the archipelago in 1929. His three pages (1932: 212–14) present useful facts and bring to mind how much help it would be if the published record were larger. Some information is contained in the official reports of Beckering and Munro, the latter unpublished. In 1880 the naturalist Albert Colfs visited the village Kalikur. Intending to stay six weeks, he seems to have stayed hardly two and described his visit to the island as 'unproductive'. Of Kalikur he said the land had a miserable air, but that the interior was generally more fertile. He made a trip into the mountain to visit some villages, but said he had never seen such a path. In places one had to climb huge boulders, and he could cover only a half-league an hour. 'The terrain is rocky and produces nothing but lontar palms; the rest of the vegetation is miserable' (Colfs 1880: 86–7). His description of the trails is only too familiar.

Finally the dentist and naturalist, Lie Goan Liong (now A. Adi Sukadana), made some archaeological investigations on the island in 1961 near Lewoleba. He also visited Kédang and has published some articles on his observations, particularly pertaining to the filing and blackening of teeth. I have not been able to see these publications in Europe, and although I have attempted to contact him by letter and through mutual acquaintances, I have not yet had a direct response.

The models for this inquiry are many and I have cited several of them in the text. There is one paper which I have had no opportunity to cite but which I hope will be regarded in some ways as paradigmatic for the study. This is the paper 'The Language of Kachin Kinship' (Leach 1967). The language of Kédang differs from the Kachin language in the possibilities it offers the analyst, and in particular the relationship terms do not permit such wide-ranging pursuit of meaning; and, additionally, there was no room to pursue some forms of linguistic analysis which might have been possible. I think, however, that some of the considerations put forward here concerning other areas of the Kédang culture might be thought in the same spirit.

I

THE MOUNTAIN

THE mountain of Kédang is of considerable mythological
significance; and it is, I think, the logical starting-point for
the examination of the categories of Kédangese thought—
a process which one might compare with the botanical dissection
of a bud or flower, but which I prefer to compare to the experi-
mental tracing of the development of an embryo or the development of a seed into a full-grown plant. I choose these images,
especially the latter, because they are of the type which we will
find in the ethnographic record from Kédang.

I. THE ORIGIN OF MEN

There are many different origin myths told by different clans
and villages in Kédang. These characteristically recount the
emergence of the ancestors from a bamboo, a rock, a dog or goat,
or some similar object or animal; and a few clans report the history
of their travels to Kédang from some other place. These stories
cannot be collated to give a consistent 'history' of the origin of
the people of Kédang—though we may judge them to be structurally almost identical.

However, there is an ideology of common origin which the
majority of the population (excluding only those who are aware
that their ancestors came from outside) subscribe to, even though
this may not in each case fit their particular histories. It is thought
that the original ancestors lived at the top of the mountain; and
all original clans of Kédang are capable, at least theoretically, of
tracing their ancestry to the original pair, Bujaq Suri and Omé
Suri. These are brother and sister and descendants of the sun
and moon. Unfortunately, I could find no stories or myths connected with this pair, but they are known as the original incestuous
couple, Bujaq the brother, Omé the sister, the first humans and
the ancestors of humanity. In the genealogies in my records (see
Appendix II), they occur near the top of the series, where the
names have already become completely mythological and are
composed of combinations of names of the heavenly bodies.

Though there is little more that can be said of them, they do establish the connection between the origin of man and incest; and they show the mythological character of the latter (a point to which I will return in a later chapter).

There is another widely accepted tradition which may be described here. In Kédang it is believed that all of humanity descend from people who originally lived at the crown of the mountain and then left, one by one, to settle new lands. According to this tradition, there were once seven brothers who became the ancestors of humanity. I received various versions of this story. The names are never exactly the same, and there were not usually exactly seven mentioned on any one occasion; a total of the names given in the different accounts amounts to more than seven. It is nevertheless important that there are *supposed* to be seven, as this orders the ancestors within the opposition between odd and even numbers—a symbolic distinction which will receive repeated attention.

Here is one version: the seven brothers were named Gadja Léwun, Kajaq Léwun, Rai Léwun, Tana Léwun, Ejeq Léwun, Béha Léwun, and Udjo (or Ujo) Léwun.

These names are subject to translation in most cases, and their meanings throw light on their assignments. *Gadja* means 'elephant' and Gadja Léwun was the ancestor of the Chinese and other Asians. *Kajaq* means 'rich' and Kajaq Léwun became the ancestor of the Europeans. *Rai* means 'many' and Rai Léwun was said to be the ancestor of the Indonesians (those not living on Lembata or adjacent islands). *Tana* means 'earth' and for some reason Tana Léwun was said, in one case, to have become the ancestor of the people to the east (Irian, etc.). In another report, Tana Léwun was said to be the ancestor of a group of people who lived at the beach and, according to tradition, later became the ancestors of Bernusa on Pantar; and this seems to me more to the point. *Tana* sometimes refers to the fields, below the traditional village site, and thus this assignment accounts for the beach people (merchants of foreign origin) living below the village and standing in opposition to the people of the mountain. I cannot translate *ejeq* and *béha*. Ejeq and Béha Léwun were the ancestors of the animals, including the snakes, lizards, goats, pigs, and so on; and they establish a genealogical tie between men and animals. Another report mentioned Oka Léwun, who was the ancestor of the spirits; so man, the animals, and the spirits all have a common ancestry.

Léwun means 'village' and is the original form of the modern Kédangese word *léu* (cf. Lamaholot, *lewo*). It forms the second element in each name and allows us to assume, following Kédangese practice, that the father of these brothers was named Léwun. We could just as well go further and draw the conclusion that the father was the village itself, which would then have been a single village for the entirety of humanity. The word now stands, in the names of the brothers, for the entire population of each region associated with one of the brothers.

The personal ancestor of Kédang was Udjo Léwun, regarded as the youngest brother—the older brothers having all left and founded the populations of the rest of the world. This is in keeping with the Kédangese attitude that strangers are generally superior and deserving of respect. I have found little evidence, however, that this is associated in Kédang with cosmic symbolism, or that elder and younger represent a distinction between spiritual and temporal authority such as is common in other parts of eastern Indonesia (van Wouden 1968: 114–15).

Udjo Léwun does not appear in the mythological genealogies I collected, but the story is generally accepted nevertheless. The myths of origin may not be consistent with each other in detail, but we must realize that their validity for the people of Kédang lies in the fact that they attempt to account for similar problems.

It has already been noted that Udjo Léwun is one of the names of the mountain. In fact the full ritual name is *udjo léwun, kajaq tené*. *Udjo* is identical with the contemporary Kédangese word *ujung*, which means 'to tie' or 'fasten'; *kajaq* has the meaning in this case of 'many', 'a wealth of'. *Tené* means 'boat', but it may serve to symbolize the village; and in this case it represents the whole population. The implication of the entire phrase would be more easily translated into Bahasa Indonesia than English. What is intended can be explained in a circumlocution like the following: 'the community of Kédang—which may be compared to the occupants of a boat—is united by a single tie, although dispersed among many individual communities'. The Kédangese would readily apply a similar sentiment to the whole of humanity.

Having translated the first line of the song given on the fly-page at the beginning of the book, it is well to translate the rest of it.

Dorong dopéq, oté né.	Descend from the mountain and disperse.
Kara oné pana weq,	Do not be angry,
Ular naga, ara bora,	The dragon, the giant squid,
Ahin tutuq kara dora.	Do not follow opposed counsel.
Pan ebéng, balé boraq.	Go to see distant lands, but return to see us.

There is a short song which represents the unity of origin of humanity.

Oté koda, roda udéq;
Olé wadé puan sué.

Koda is the crown of the mountain, specifically the region of the first village of mankind *léu rian, léu éhoq*; but characteristically the old part, *léu tuan*, of each village has an offering stone called *koda* somewhere near the top of the village. *Koda* stands, therefore, for the connection which each village maintains with the original site of habitation and, consequently, with the descendants from that site in other villages. *Roda*—a word which has connotations very much like 'top' or 'head', as for instance when it is applied to the tassel of a corn plant—means in this case 'the mast of a boat'. *Puan* also means 'the mast of a boat'. These lines translated literally then mean, 'Up at *koda*, one mast; down [below] divides into two masts.' From the contexts in which I have heard this song, I propose the following interpretation: when mankind lived at the top of the mountain, they were one and did not divide until they descended, when they became two branches: the people of Kédang and strangers.

3. THE ORIGINAL VILLAGE: 'LÉU RIAN, LÉU EHOQ'

The common phrase for the dispersal from the mountain is *bua bikil* 'to give birth and shatter'. The villages of Kédang—by tradition, originally forty-four—are fairly evenly distributed around the slopes of the mountain. By ideology, if not in fact, they trace their origin to a common ancestor. By the same ideology, their ancestors originally lived in a village at the top of the mountain. This village is named *léu rian*, but because of the character of the ceremonial language it must be complemented by a dyadic pairing, and the full phrase is *léu rian, léu éhoq* ('the big village, the small village'). I made two trips to the top of the mountain to witness the site of this original village. Unfortunately, the photographs I made there disappeared in the post; so the reader will have to rely entirely on a written description.

léu rian ('the big village') is located in a flat plain a few hundred metres square, just below the very pinnacle of the mountain, which lies to the northwest and perhaps about ten metres above it. In the centre of this plain, oriented towards the pinnacle and on the side closest to it, is a small rectangular wall, made of piled, flat stones, and called *kota-bubuq*. It is about a metre square and stands about forty centimetres high. In the centre lies a round flat stone, such as are used for ceremonial offerings. Formerly, there stood inside this wall a post, said to have been shaped like a house post (*lili*). This still existed within memory of men in their fifties, who had observed it. It was reportedly destroyed by fires started in the vicinity to flush game. According to witnesses, it was cut to accommodate one of the wafer-shaped rat-guards which are used on the posts of a granary. Some people spoke of it as if it were a house post, but if it were within the stone wall it is more likely that it was an altar post. Altar posts of this type are not common in Kédang, but from its description it sounds very much like those found among the Belu of Timor (cf. Vroklage 1952: 3: pl. L). That it could nevertheless have represented a house post is not only possible but can be inferred from similar ceremonial houses (*huna lélang*) which often consist of a single post (cf. Vatter 1932: pl. 42, 2). This post is said to have stood on the side closest to the peak.

There are two slits in the sides of this stone construction, one in each of the two side walls. These slits represent doors, in this case called *balowé*. The *kota-bubuq* itself represents a house erected as an ancestral shrine for the inhabitants of the original village. One door is the exit for those people who founded the villages roughly on the east side of Kédang, the other for the villages on the other side. It is necessary to remark, however, that the orientation is not really east–west. The orientation is to the peak, and the whole lies in a way skewed to the direction of the passage of the sun.

Near the peak, above *léu rian*, is a grave. This looks much like a normal grave in Kédang and is made of piled stones. At either end a flat stone has been set upright (which is not common practice in Kédang). The grave is so oriented that it points towards the highest part of the peak. I tried to see if it pointed in the opposite direction to any particular landmark, especially Pulau Rusa, but there was no obvious orientation. Unfortunately I had no compass, and I had to estimate co-ordinates by eye, but the grave points down the island roughly in the direction of Labala. The orientation of this grave does not fit the pattern common in Kédang, which adds to its mystery. Like *kota-bubuq*, it is unquestionably of great antiquity. It is known always to have existed within memory of those now living, but no one is certain of its significance. The former Kapitan of Kédang, M. A. Sarabiti, assured me of its antiquity and that it is neither a Muslim grave nor the grave of one of his own family. I have myself often been

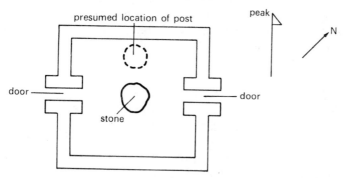

FIG. 1. *Kota-bubuq* at *léu rian*.

asked in Kédang if I knew whose it was. My guide on both occasions when I saw it, Kéwa Pajong, who is more familiar with the area than anyone I know, speculated that it was the grave either of Bujaq Suri or of Pulau Lama Léqang. The story of the latter is given in Appendix I. Although generally known in Kédang, the story seems to be particularly associated with the village Péusawa, and it is certainly possible that members of this village once constructed this monument. The grave could quite easily be seen as lying on a line between the highest point of the mountain and the village Péusawa. Of the two upright stones, the largest is on the end away from the peak. We might conclude that this is the head. Next to the grave at this end is a small stone circle, said to represent a well.

Nothing more can be said about this construction or its

significance, but considering the importance of this area and its monuments to the people of Kédang and their history, it is certainly worth taking the effort to give as accurate and detailed a description as possible of what is to be found there. The urgency of this is all the greater since in recent years school-teachers have begun taking their classes on outings to the top of the mountain, and the children have started defacing the area with stone constructions of their own. Some of these appeared after my first visit.

Below *léu rian* and to the west is the crater. It is not much larger than the plain of *léu rian*, a circular depression surrounded by walls of uneven height. The centre is marked by a small rounded hill. This crater is *léu éhoq* ('the small village'). There is no construction; and it may be remarked at this point that nowhere at the top of the mountain is there any signs of terracing or other indications of farming or genuine habitation.

There is, however, a small vent called *wélong* of great importance.

3. THE VENT WÉLONG

There are several vents of this kind on the mountain, all called *wélong*; and they are often associated with myths of origin or dispersal. The ancestors of mankind emerged from such a hole at the top of the mountain, which has since closed over; and we may presume that this too was a *wélong*. One of the uses of the word *wélong* is to mean 'whirlpool' (also known as *pilar*). The *wélong* at *léu éhoq* is said to run down through the mountain and to emerge in the sea at a place on the south coast near the village Atanila called *wowon*, where the dead souls go before departing to the land of the dead. Another example suggests, in fact, that vents of this sort characteristically emerge at places associated with the dead. At a place in the mountain near Léuwajang, called *uar néung*, there is such a hole, which is supposed to come out in the sea near the small point of land *rauq utuq*—which (as can be discerned from the name) is the mouth of a ravine where victims of certain unpropitious types of death were formerly set out to decompose.

Concerning the *wélong* at *léu éhoq*, a friend once compared it to the holes in the nose of a human. Just as humans must breathe so must the mountain. If a piece of wood is put into the *wélong* in the original village, it will emerge at *wowon*. Spray from breakers at *wowon* is said to emerge from this vent. This, however, occurs, according to witnesses, only at the beginning of the rainy season. I think there is a factual explanation, in so far as one is required, for this spray. When I was at *léu éhoq*, I naturally made an effort to locate this vent. My guide led me to the spot and we looked around without success until I stepped into it. Its mouth is a circular depression, which at that time was covered with a thick layer of loam, leaves, and branches. We cleared this away, and there was at the bottom a small vent large enough to put one's leg into. The mouth, according to my guide, used to be much larger, but boulders have fallen into it. This is quite possible as the ground is very soft. The vent itself, he said, was, however, never larger. This vent was surprisingly clean once the leaves and branches had been removed, and I suppose that an explanation for the vapour may be that rain water flowing into it becomes heated at some point and then turns to steam.

4. THE DISPERSAL FROM THE TOP OF THE MOUNTAIN

The connection of the top of the mountain with the sea and of the source of life with death which is found in *wélong* is of great interest. There is a story from the village Aliuroba, of which I have unfortunately only a partial account, which also demonstrates these features. The name of the village is to be analysed into Aliur, a culture hero, and Oba, the octopus. The ancestors of this village used to live near the top of the mountain. Near their village was a hole in which lived Oba. The village discovered to their alarm that their children were disappearing one by one. Through some course of events they discovered that they were being eaten by Oba. The villagers poured hot water into the hole to kill Oba, and his poison came bubbling back up, causing everyone to flee—leading to the foundation of the present villages. Very similar stories are told by other villages, among them Léuléaq. The key to these stories lies in the fact that a creature of the sea is found in the mountain or in the village, a confusion which leads to disaster and then to dispersal, thereby accounting for the present distribution of the human population.

The story told in Léuwajang to account for the dispersal from the top of the mountain occurs in two slightly different versions. According to this story, a village temple was being built at *léu rian*. They killed a pig for the feast associated with building this temple and divided it among those present, but because the villagers had become so numerous there was not enough. They then divided the teeth, bones, and skin among those who had no meat, but this still was not enough. This led to a fight, and subsequently everyone fled down the mountain to found the present villages. According to the second version, on the night of the feast, the villagers were circle-dancing. A dog was sleeping at the edge of the circle, and the dancers kept kicking it to get it to go out of the way. It finally woke up and joined the circle saying:

Ko au iku bojang,	I am the dog Iku Bojang,
Manuq laka waraq.	The bird Laka Waraq
Namang meté namang,	Let us circle-dance together.
Nédung meté nédung.	Let us dance [as individuals] together.[1]

The dancers were so frightened to hear a dog speak that they fled and eventually formed the present villages of Kédang.

5. DESCENT FROM THE MOUNTAIN

The descent from *léu rian, léu éhoq* is conceived of as having taken place in a series of stages, and each village has a list of former village sites which mark its descent down the mountain. These names are identifiable places. Those for Léuwajang are:

1. *tuén tubar, éjéq deler*—the head of the forest, the slope (dale) beneath.
2. *nara napoq, ruha alang*—a flat wide place, a grazing place for deer.
3. *dolu laléng, boté dolu, bai biri*—inside the stone terrace, where the soil is fertile.
4. *péu léu, loboq laléng*—a village with mango trees, situated in a space sheltered by surrounding hills.
5. *wajang hoténg, ruba léwaq*—this is the ritual name of Léuwajang and refers to the present site of the old part of the village (*léu tuan*).

The first of these, *tuén tubar*, is located in an area where the forest surrounding the crown of the mountain has recently been opened up for use as fields. Formerly, it was prohibited to have fields here because of its association with the ancestors. My guide, who, despite his firm adherence to traditional culture, had been one of the pioneers in opening this region, and has his fields

---

[1] *Nédung* or *hédung* are individual performances, though more than one person may dance at the same time.

adjacent to *tuén tubar*, led me to the site. It is heavily overgrown with bushes and thorny vines; so that we had to cut our way in. It consists of a circular pile of stones, similar to that in *léu rian*. As it is located on a steep slope, one side of this construction consists of a terrace wall of stones about two metres high. Although the area was too overgrown for me to see for myself, my guide said that there is no other terracing nearby, showing that the location has never actually been used for habitation. We dug around in the centre of the circle and found a few small flat stones of the sort used for offerings, indicating that it has been used for ceremonial purposes, but we found nothing else. There is no memory of there ever having been an altar post here.

I have never seen the sites 2 and 3. No. 4, which is just above the present village, has no monuments or signs of habitation, but the stand of bamboo which grows there is of ceremonial significance in connection with birth.

Although it pertains to another village, I would like to take this opportunity to describe the last authentic monument on the crown of the mountain. This is a location called *witing tun* ('roasting the goat') about half-way up between *tuén tubar* and *léu rian* and on the side near the village Meluwiting. It consists of two small graves. Although small, they would accommodate a large child and are oriented with the head towards the peak of the mountain and with the feet more or less in the direction of Meluwiting. The grave on the observer's left, if facing away from the mountain, has a headstone made of flat volcanic rock which looks as though it might have been slightly worked. These graves mark the site of the first village of the ancestors of Meluwiting. According to the version of the story told me by my guide, there was originally a woman named Ula Suri who lived by herself and had just one goat. This goat died, and, in order to dry it and keep it from rotting, she put it on a platform under which she built a fire. This is a procedure very similar to the way they dry copra, and the intention in this case was to embalm the goat by smoking it. However, it evidently became pregnant from the fire, and the woman after a few days heard a child crying inside the goat. Cutting it open she found two babies in the womb, called *witing dua* ('two goats'). One was male and the other female. The people of Meluwiting descend from this pair, and the village takes its name from the female goat (*witing meluq*).

6. THE SIGNIFICANCE OF THE MOUNTAIN

Attention has been given to the top of the mountain as the origin of mankind, and some mention has been made that in particular stories the same function has been assigned other locations. I hope the reader has acquired from this description a sense of the suitability of the mountain as an image for the various ideas associated with it by the Kédangese. Later arguments will turn upon the point that the mountain is, after all, only one of such images in Kédangese thought, and to attribute to it too great influence in determining the structure of that thought would be mistaken. I have also indicated the association between death and the origin of life, and between the mountain and the sea, which is to be uncovered by a detailed examination of the top of the mountain and of Kédangese ideas about it. A phrase from the ritual language shows the association of the sea and the mountain in the origin of life: *neda bua, hari belé*. On one occasion, I was told that *neda* means the mountain; on another I was told that it means more specifically the water which comes out from below the surface of the earth. It is also like a spirit (*sehar-metung*) which comes out from the earth. *Bua-belé* means 'to give birth'. *Hari* is the sea. The phrase then means as much as, 'the mountain brought forth, the sea gave birth'.

In the following are several stories and traditions which are concerned with maintaining a categorical distinction between the mountain and the sea or the mountain and the beach.

First is a simple example which concerns a distinction between two types of caterpillars or worms which cause damage to the crops. The first of these is honoured with the term *goa*, otherwise used to refer to large rock faces (cliffs) which harbour spirits (Ind., *gua, goa* means 'cave'). This is found only in the mountain and eats only the leaves of cassava. The second is found near the beach where it eats several kinds of crops and is simply called 'worm', (*ulé*). These two creatures supposedly never mix, each staying on its own side of a line which in Léuwajang runs, as it happens, just below the hamlet in which I lived.

A second case concerns the wood of the large trees, *lu*, found only around the crown of the mountain. I was once told that this wood may not be brought to the beach. It later transpired that this report was incomplete. It may be brought to the beach and used (as it is) in the construction of houses of the modern type in Kédang, which simply rest on the top of the ground; but it must not be used for a house with house posts, which are in a sense planted. Failure to observe this prohibition would cause a flash-flood.

A third case concerns the two monsters, of which mention has already been made, the *ular naga* and the *ara bora*. *Ular* occurs in many Indonesian languages, including Kédangese, with the meaning 'snake'. *Naga* is also widespread in Indonesia and also occurs in Sanskrit where it means 'snake' or 'dragon' (Vatter 1934: 119; Gonda 1952: *passim*). A tradition of a snake-like monster living in the mountain is common. The *ular naga* of Kédang is of this type. It lives near the top of the mountain. No one seems to have seen it, but it was described as being very big round, and was said to come out of its hole at the top of the mountain during the rainy season. A very large destructive flash-flood is said to be caused by the emergence of the *ular naga*.

Mention has been made of *oba*, the octopus. In the version of the myth concerning this creature which tells the origin of the village Léuléaq, it is the *ara bora*, rather than *oba*, that plays the destructive role. Both are virtually the same creature, either in the form of an octopus or in that of a giant squid. A tradition of a similar sea-monster is also well known from other parts of Indonesia. The names are not so invariable as that of the *ular naga*, however, and I do not know if an etymological connection is to be traced between *ara bora* and such terms as, for instance, the *anta boga* of Java and Bali.

In Kédang the *ara bora* is especially feared by boats at sea, and the ocean is named *ara bora loboq* which means 'the *ara bora* swallows'. It is clear that it is related to the sea spirit *hari botan* of Lamaholot, which is also described as a squid or octopus (*Polyp.* Arndt 1951: 28–30, 169–70). Though the term *hari botan* is not recognized in Kédang, all sea snakes are called *ular hari*. Furthermore, a large wind storm at sea is called *hari bura kéu*, that is, '*hari bura* rises'. As no one in Léuwajang knew any more about the *hari bura*, this phrase would have remained unintelligible to me had I not been told in the village Léuwutun that the *hari bura* is a huge wave. This wave was described as drawing back and leaving a large dry space and then rushing in to cover it. The *hari bura* is prevented from inundating the land by the *ular naga*, which descends to meet and clash with the *hari bura* at the beach. At Passar Wairiang there is supposed to be a stone (called *nuba-lapaq*) which marks the point where the *hari bura* and the *ular naga* meet. The water cannot cover this spot. From this it is clear that *hari bura* is another name for the *ara bora*.

It is also clear that a categorical distinction between the monsters of the mountain and those of the sea is considered essential to well-being and that certain disasters are readily explained by a descent of the *ular naga* or the rising of the *hari bura*, through which this distinction is confused.

Finally there is the story of 'Bota Ili and Wata Rian', which was given me by Guru A. Sio Amuntoda. This seems to be a story of the origin of civilization, in particular of fire, cooked food, clothing, and marriage. It undoubtedly deserves a more detailed analysis than can be given here, but a warning must be made in this connection. Arndt (1940: 61 ff., 155 ff., 160–1, 166) records several versions of this tale from Lamaholot; and some of the important equations which might be drawn from the one recorded here, such as that between the woman and the uncivilized state, and the man and civilization, are contradicted by them. Nevertheless, that culture is seen as coming from the shore is very appropriate, not only in Kédang but also in other parts of Indonesia. The names of the protagonists must be analysed at the beginning. Bota is a woman's name, and *ili* means 'mountain'. *Wata* means 'beach', and *rian*, which means 'great', is often employed in mythological names as a sort of implied honorific.

Bota Ili and Wata Rian

Bota Ili lived at the top of the mountain. Her body was covered with long hair, and she had extremely long fingernails and toenails. The hair on top of her head was a large tangled pile. She ate snakes, lizards, geckos, and iguanas. In order to light a fire to cook these animals, she would strike her arse on a rock. Before long the fire would begin to glow and she would cook the animals to eat them.

Wata Rian lived at the beach.

In the mornings he looked up at the top of the mountain and saw smoke from a fire. One morning he thought that the smoke in the mountain must mean that a human lived there.

Therefore, he decided, 'I must climb the mountain and see who is there.'

In preparation, he went fishing and got several fish; then he tapped a little palm wine. Then one morning, quite early, he set out to climb the mountain. He climbed and climbed until—precisely at noon—he finally arrived. There he saw a place where a human lived and a hearth. However, no one was there because Bota Ili had gone hunting and had not yet returned. He waited and waited, but she did not soon return. Therefore, taking his dog with him, he climbed a tree and sat waiting in the branches. He waited and waited, until finally he saw that Bota Ili had come back.

She was bent over carrying on her shoulder snakes, lizards, geckos, and iguanas. She tossed off her heavy load and rested a little. When she had finished resting, she struck her arse again and again on a rock to get fire; but the fire would not light; so she stopped and thought, 'Who can be here?' She looked to the left and looked to the right, above and below. She looked here and looked there. Suddenly she saw the shadow of a human being on the ground. Looking up she saw Wata Rian sitting in the branches of the tree. Then she got very angry.

'Hey, you there kept my fire from lighting,' she said. 'Come down so I can bite you to tatters.'

Wata Rian replied, 'Don't make trouble. If you do, I'll let my dog loose and he will bite you.'

Bota Ili then said, 'Just come down. I won't do anything, if you don't let your dog bite me. Climb down so we can cook the animals and eat.'

Wata Rian climbed down.

When he was down, Bota Ili tried to start the fire and the fire lit. They built the fire and cooked the animals along with the fish Wata Rian had brought. When the food was ready they sat down and ate. Wata Rian had brought a bamboo of palm wine so they could drink palm wine with their meal; however, he did not drink much himself, but poured a lot for Bota Ili.

Down, down, Bota Ili fell down drunk. She fell so fast asleep that she was no longer aware of her body. After a while, Wata Rian took a knife and shaved Bota Ili. He shaved her from head to foot. When he was through he saw that Bota Ili was a woman.

Afterwards they lived together and married.

Although it is not said so, it is almost certainly implied that in connection with being shaved and marrying Wata Rian, Bota Ili learned to wear clothing.

That this is somewhat more than an interesting story is shown in this account which I was given of a huge flash-flood which occurred in Léuwajang around 1932. The part of Léuwajang which is located at the beach is in a somewhat exposed position. The neighbouring village Léudanun, when it was situated at the beach, was once washed out to sea. Therefore, during a storm, if the alarm gongs indicating a flood are heard, everyone in the low-lying houses (which are built in what is actually the mouth of a ravine) flees to the houses built on the canyon walls on either side. This occurred in 1932, in a storm which was so huge that witnesses described great boulders being brought down and thrown into the sea, and one mentioned a large tree which came down in the flood still in a vertical position. The villagers fled to the higher parts and spent the night beating their gongs and eating and drinking. Before this flood several people had dreams predicting it. One man dreamed seven days before that Bota Ili would come down to the beach and wash her clothes. Another man dreamed two days before the storm that Bota Ili and Wata Rian would, in two days, exchange bridewealth. It was explained that the boulders and trees thrown into the sea by the flood were to be regarded as the bridewealth brought by Bota Ili. The huge waves thrown towards the land by the sea were the bridewealth brought by Wata Rian.

II
THE OLD VILLAGE, *LÉU TUAN*

A STUDY of the village must begin with the *léu tuan*, a term which is translated literally as 'the old village', although this rendering seems very flat to anyone familiar with the original idiom.

Almost all villages have a hamlet, designated as *léu tuan*, which is conceived of as the old site of the village. We have already seen that this is only the last in a series of supposed former village sites, but the *léu tuan* is the only one of these with which there is a connection in recent history and which has not therefore faded into the mythological, and it is probably the only one which was actually ever inhabited.

A few villages have no *léu tuan*. The best example of this is the ancient coastal village Kalikur. Kalikur was originally founded by settlers from Aliuroba, but it became a trading village without fields. It is situated at the water's edge and has always depended on its position as a port and intermediary between foreign traders and the mountain population. Several villages in the east are situated so near the shore that their *léu tuan* are just a short walk up a hill from the newer part of the village. A few other villages, such as Waqlupang—which is now entirely Muslim—have completely abandoned their *léu tuan*.

However, the *léu tuan* of most are still inhabited, and they are characteristically situated far inland at a considerable distance from the Dutch-built road, where, under orders from the Dutch and later Indonesian governments, the newer parts of the villages have been located. Among the highest must be those of Léutubung and Léudanun. How high the first is I have no way of knowing, but I would estimate that of Léudanun at about 600 to 700 metres above sea level. Léuwajang's *léu tuan* is about 500 metres and contrasts with that of neighbouring Atarodang Édang which nestles under an arm of Léuwajang and can hardly be more than 150 metres high.

I have studied the *léu tuan* of Léuwajang, just below which I lived, very closely; and, although what I have to record is broadly representative of the *léu tuan* of the other villages of Kédang, my description is drawn primarily from Léuwajang.

1. DESCRIPTION OF 'LÉU TUAN'

Léu tuan is directly associated in the minds of the Kédangese with the ancestors. It tends to attract very old people, though certainly not exclusively nor even predominantly. It is clear that several people living there do so through their attachment to the traditional culture and through their rejection of Catholicism and Islam; and during our stay several old people moved up to *léu tuan* to die. When we first arrived there were thirteen houses with about fifty inhabitants and ten granaries.

I tried to uncover evidence whether the clans of the village were traditionally assigned sections of the old village but came to the conclusion that, with one exception to be described later, this was never the case. It is true that at present the houses of the clans Buang Leraq and Hiang Leraq tend to be found near the top and those of Boli Leraq and Apé Tatu near the bottom, but this seems fortuitous. Most other clans are not now even represented. Before the Dutch began to make their rule felt strongly, *léu tuan* was much more heavily populated, and in fact one whole side of the site is now empty of residences.

Léu tuan is situated on top of a sort of hill which projects out away from the mountain. Despite this it rests on a very steep slope, and the houses stand on a series of narrow but very high terraces. The location was obviously chosen for defensibility and the remnants of a wall of cactus which used to encircle the village is still to be found above and below it.

In the following description of the ceremonial make-up of *léu tuan*, it must be remembered that it stands for—and at one time may very well have been identical with—the whole village. Its boundaries are the boundaries of the village, and what lies outside them is for ceremonial purposes outside the village.

To begin with, *léu tuan* (that of Léuwajang and of all other villages) is represented as consisting of the following—in all but the last case, unmarked—divisions: the head of the village (*léu tubar*); the feet of the village (*léu léin*); the left (*hikun*); the right (*wanan*), and the centre or navel (*léu puhé*). This orientation is not to our cardinal points, but is for all *léu tuan* related to the slope of the mountain. The head is the highest part and the feet the lowest.

This means that the head is towards the peak of the mountain, the feet towards the sea or, on the west and southwest side, then, towards the rest of the island.

In order to find *hikun* and *wanan*, the reader will have to learn to employ a technique which will be called upon several times in the course of this book. He must assume that his back is to the slope, in this case to the mountain. His right, then, corresponds to *wanan*, the right of the village, his left to *hikun*. Figure 2 demonstrates this orientation.

It might be thought that these divisions imply that the village is considered a sort of animate being. It must be remarked that there is no clear evidence for this, nor any indicating that the village is considered as a human being. Far from being an anthropomorphic

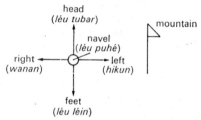

F IG. 2. Orientation of the old village, *léu tuan*.

conception, the image might just as well be that of an animal, or even more likely it may be that no analogy of the sort is intended and that the Kédangese simply regard the village as having the same divisions as many other kinds of (even inanimate) beings. My suggestion that the village was a human being never met with any clear conviction on the part of my friends, and the response it usually elicited, other than a laugh, was an account of the *mier ringa*, to which I will turn shortly. One does not, however, need to exclude the possibility that an anthropomorphic analogy may be part of the imagery of the village, but this cannot be taken as the primary or defining aspect of Kédangese imagery (cf. Endicott 1970: 31–2).

At any rate, the village is clearly facing away from the mountain. If we are to view *léu tuan* from the foot of the village, as the Kédangese certainly often do and as I have drawn Figure 2, then we will see that its orientation corresponds to that used in heraldry: its right appears as the heraldic right. In my opinion, what is of interpretative interest here is that the orientation corresponds to that of a person who is descending the mountain. For the moment I will only remark in this connection that this association certainly fits well with the tradition of descent from *léu rian, léu éhoq* recorded earlier.

Associated with the village are two snakes called *mier ringa*; both are of the kind called *ular pupun*, the spitting cobra. By tradition one is female, and is recognized by the fact that its tail is cut off short and that it has a hole in the side. The other is male and is complete. According to one old and authoritative man, the female snake lost its tail when someone (a human) cut it off. It seems to me that this tradition is to be directly interpreted, at the least, as a comment on the fact that a woman has a vagina but no penis. A story of a woman with a hole in her back is common in Indonesia, and one may refer to Kole Robak of Lamaholot (Arndt 1951: 172) and the *sundel bolong* of eastern Java (Geertz 1960: 18), figures which combine seductiveness with sexual threat. I received a slightly different version of this tradition which I consider symbolically confused, but which I nevertheless report for the record. In this version the sex of the snakes was not mentioned, but one was said to have the scar of a healed wound on its side and the other a short tail.

Explanation of the name is difficult. Inquiry yielded no translation of *ringa* and hardly any for *mier*. *Mier* seems to contain in its connotation the sense of protective spirit. It also occurs in the name *mier rian* which is applied to a war leader and in the name for the stand of (*aur*) bamboo located near the centre of the village, *aur mier*. The *mier ringa* represent the spirit of the village and are associated in particular with the centre, *léu puhé*. As such, they protect the inhabitants, but they are also frightening. They were once described to me as being 'too furious'. They protect the various groves and trees in *léu tuan*, which it is prohibited to cut; and if one does cut any of these trees, the *mier ringa* will come out and kill one's chickens. It is said that the *mier ringa* are snakes in the daytime, but that they may appear to those who have the eyes to see such things at night in the form of a human being. In this connection it may be useful to mention a tradition of the village Léuwehéq, who believe themselves descendants of a snake. When they have feasts (at night) it is thought that this snake will take the form of a human being and attend. He always comes, though they do not know who it is; and it seems that they always arrange to have their feasts so that he may.

The borders of the village are broken at two points where major paths enter. These points are regarded as doors and called *wéloq matan*, an expression which might be translated as 'strong door'. There are no doors, however, nor any other construction to mark these points. Just below the *wéloq matan* at the foot of the village is a stand of bamboo of a small type called *aur*. This stand is called *aur boher*, but some usages indicate that it too is regarded as *aur mier* and may therefore be a dwelling of the village spirit. Bamboo from this grove cannot be cut without an offering.

Near the door at the top of the village grows a banyan, known as *béu mier-ringa*, which used to figure in war ceremonies. Just above the old village wall at the top is another banyan known as *béu ula-lojo*, which will come into discussion later. At the top of the village is the site of *koda* already mentioned. At *léu puhé* in the centre of the village is a fairly large clear plain or yard (*alang*). This used to be the site of dancing at village festivals. Near this plain are the stand of bamboo known as *aur mier*, some trees of the type *ité*, known in this case as *ité marén* or *ité mier-marén* ('the prohibited *ité*') and a large banyan which seems to mark the site of the house of the now mythical former 'lord of the land' (*léu-auq wala*), Hoéq Rian.

At *léu puhé* is a flat stone known as *lapaq léu*, 'the village offering stone', and near it a small circle of stones on the ground with an upright stone slab in the centre. This is called *lado angin*, and it is here that one makes rain offerings. Also near *lapaq léu* are some ruined gongs lying on the ground, which were once given as reparation for some serious delict. Just to the right of *lado angin* is the site of the former village temple, *huna halé*. Below it is a circular, though fairly flat, heap of stones about two metres in diameter, which is the grave of the torso of Nibang Naran, killed by Hoéq Rian in a war between Léuwajang and some villages near the present Léudanun.

Although the trees planted in *léu tuan* may be cut down by their owners, those trees just mentioned which are situated at the centre of the village (*léu puhé*) are under an absolute prohibition. Furthermore, one must not defile *léu puhé* (with excrement, urine, or spittle), a prohibition which applies most strongly to *lapaq léu*. I was told that in the nearby village Maramamuq it is forbidden to plant maize inside *léu tuan*, though it is possible that there is no prohibition on planting rice (which, however, could probably not be planted for practical reasons). Such a prohibition certainly does not exist in Léuwajang, where even in *léu tuan* every year maize is planted in the space between the houses. However, absolutely nothing may be planted in the yard (*alang*) at *léu puhé*. I was told that kerosene may not be burned in *léu tuan*, but in fact it is regularly done. Another person, however, told me of this restriction that it applied only to ceremonies in the village temple, where only torches made from the candlenut (*miréq, Aleurites moluccana*) may be employed. In Léuwajang—though, according to the results of inquiries, perhaps not in other villages, such as Léudanun and Léuléaq—the lontar palm may not be allowed to grow within *léu tuan*, nor may its parts be used in the construction of any buildings. According to observation, this prohibition seems to be strictly followed. The prohibition on all work involved in making cloth which formerly applied on the mountain still obtains within *léu tuan*.

This is a heterogeneous list of prohibitions, and the grounds for some of them are still a puzzle for me. Let us observe for the moment that there is some sign that various of these prohibitions have been, through history, progressively weakened. Where they have weakened there seems to be a regular pattern of retreat. What once was prohibited on the mountain may not now be done within *léu tuan*. What once was proscribed within *léu tuan* may not now be done within *léu puhé* or within the temple. Impurities which may defile *léu puhé* are especially defiling for *lapaq léu*. This pattern, from the exterior to the centre, follows the path of increasing ceremonial importance.

It may also be observed that certain of the things prohibited are of foreign importation. Although maize is the staple in Kédang and has been for centuries, it is clearly in this category. So is kerosene, which only in this century has begun to supplant homemade candlenut or resin torches. I have discussed the prohibition on making clothing which seems also to belong to this category. That the lontar is so prohibited provides a particularly difficult problem.

The reason for the prohibition on the lontar palm could never be explained to me. It contrasts strongly with the practice in the villages around the Ili Mandiri in East Flores, where I was told that the village ritual house (*koke*) must be re-roofed each year with leaves from the lontar palm (cf. Vatter 1932: 92), a form of roofing which seems to be intentionally chosen for its lack of durability. In Léuwajang the lontar stands in opposition to the coconut palm. This latter may be planted in *léu tuan*, and in fact there are a few coconut palms growing there.

As a matter of fact, one of the principal differences between the two palms is that the coconut may be planted and cared for, while the lontar may not (Vatter 1932: 84 says the lontar is not planted in East Flores, and the same is true on Roti, Fox 1971b: 245). For the lontar, one may only let the nut fall to the ground and germinate by itself. In certain ceremonies one must use palm wine from the coconut palm rather than from the lontar. Although I have often been told this, I have never seen the rule observed, even in cases where the coconut palm wine was available. Although the principal palm tapped in the vicinity of Léuwajang is the lontar, in a large area of Kédang—from around Péusawa to Aliuroba—there are very few lontar palms and the coconut is tapped almost exclusively.[1] The restrictions on the lontar, particularly that it may not be planted, and its uneven distribution, suggest that in Kedang it may well have been introduced from outside.

There is one final prohibition to be mentioned. No one may be buried within *léu tuan*; and observation shows that with one exception all graves have been carefully placed outside its borders. It is said that it is forbidden to bury within *léu tuan* because after the first burial the land would never close, i.e. soon thereafter an unending series of deaths would begin, necessitating repeated digging of fresh graves. In contrast with this rule is the tradition—now of no practical effect—that if an enemy is killed in battle, his head or right hand, if his whole body cannot be obtained, should be brought back to be buried in *léu tuan*. It is said this is done to 'feed the village', *paro-baq léu-auq* or *paro mier-ringa*. *Léu-auq*, composed of the words for 'village' (*léu*) and 'earth' (*auq*), is the ceremonial phrase for the village; thus, the first phrase is literally 'to feed the village'. The second means 'to feed the *mier-ringa*', which makes explicit that it is the village spirit that is being fed. If the whole body is retrieved, it will be divided and the parts buried in the corresponding parts of the village: the head at *léu*

---

[1] Seemingly, only in Meluwiting do a few individuals know the tapping of the areng palm (*poléq, Arenga saccharifera*).

tubar, the legs at *léu léin*, the left arm at *hikun*, the right at *wanan*, and the torso at *léu puhé*, *alang-ajaq* ('the navel of the village, the centre of the yard').

2. THE WAR 'UNO PATANG, TÉBAN NOTING'

Mention has already been made that there is one grave in *léu tuan*, this being of the torso of Nibang Naran, killed by Hoéq Rian. Nibang Naran was the war leader of a group of four villages —now extinct—formerly situated near what is now Léudanun. Hoéq Rian was the *léu auq wala*, 'lord of the land', of Léuwajang. The war came about because Koko Bako and Leki Bako—who are the ancestors of the people of Béan or Bernusa on Pantar and who figure prominently in one of the origin myths of Léuwajang—had trouble with people from the four villages mentioned above. The two brothers then had a fish market at Rauq Utuq (where Léuwajang's market is now situated) and sold dried fish. A fight started because people from the four villages refused to pay. The two brothers then requested and got help from Léuwajang, which was drawn into the war called *nuq uno patang*, *téban noting* ('the war of the cooked fish called *uno*, the tied dried fish'). One of the events of the war was that the people of the four villages under the leadership of Nibang Naran invaded and burned the *léu tuan* of Léuwajang.

Everyone fled except Hoéq Rian who was old and blind and could not leave his house. As he was lord of the land, he lived in the village temple (which of course would not be done today). This was constructed on poles and could be reached only by climbing a ladder which had, according to prescription, seven rungs. Nibang Naran, with the intention of killing Hoéq Rian, mounted the steps. Although Hoéq Rian was blind, he waited with a spear, counting the steps as he heard Nibang Naran come up the ladder. When he had climbed six steps and was putting his foot on the seventh, Hoéq Rian speared him through the door, shouting at the same time, '*Petéq, Hoéq Rian sobé doq!*' ('Look out, Hoéq Rian is falling down!') As it was night, those below did not see that it was their own leader. Tricked in this fashion into thinking it was Hoéq Rian, they cut him to pieces. The next morning, when they saw who it was, they fled. The people of Léuwajang then buried him in the village in the manner described above for a fallen enemy.

As I have just described a war, perhaps I should explain here what little I know about war ceremonial. As I have said there is a banyan near the door to the village on the upper side called *béu mier-ringa*. It is here that they used to make offerings before going to war. So far as I know only a chicken was required, but this probably stood for a larger animal such as a goat or pig. If a bee, *méqo*, came and took one of the chicken feathers, it was a sign that the fight would be successful, that they would not be hurt. I asked what would happen if the bee did not come, and was assured that it would always come.

3. THE VILLAGE TEMPLE, 'HUNA HALÉ'

I have mentioned the village temple, the *huna halé*, and I will here turn to a detailed description of it.

First should be mentioned two other types of ceremonial constructions which will be treated in detail elsewhere. The first of these are the ritual houses of each of the clans, *huna wowo* or *huna suku*. All ten of the original clans of Léuwajang may have their *huna suku* within *léu tuan*, and several still do. Only the three clans which have immigrated from other villages must build the *huna suku* outside the walls of *léu tuan*.

The second construction consists of a small representation of a house, which for a long time I mistakenly thought was called *letéq huna* (actually *letéq* is a verb and means as much as to erect such a house). These may be put up anywhere and represent the houses of female ancestors see (Vatter 1932: pl. 42, 2 and below pl. 3*a* for such constructions). The only name for these buildings is *huna lélang* ('ancient house', compare *tuan-lélang*, 'the ancestors'). It is of use to introduce this here because the term *huna lélang* seems to be appropriately applied to the other types as well: not only to the clan temple, but also to that for the village, and even to the stone constructions at *tuén tubar* and *léu rian*. Thus, though they are differentiated as to the generality of their application, they are all of fundamentally the same type: they are houses for the ancestors.

Evidently there is no *huna halé* still standing in Kédang. The Catholic mission agitates for the destruction of these buildings and it seems that some missionaries have caused them to be burned in other nearby areas, but so far as I know nothing of the sort has ever been done in Kédang. I have been told that there are none standing because they were all burnt during the invasion of the Amfoan (*méo*), but careful inquiry shows this to be incorrect. In fact I think that no single factor explains their disappearance. It seems that Léuwajang's temple suffered a gradual reduction in size and elaboration, as it was rebuilt on various occasions in recent history. There was standing a fairly small building of recent construction which substituted for it when we arrived in Léuwajang, but this decayed and collapsed before we left. I think, without being able to prove it, that the loss of the ritual house is to be attributed to nothing more specific than a turning of interest from within the village towards influences from the outside (and therefore to the loss of availability of concentrated community effort), resulting from the opening up of the area by the Dutch. The ending of warfare may well have been an important initial factor. The numerous conversions to Islam and Catholicism have finally sealed the doom of any important community ritual effort. Kédang contrasts in this regard quite strongly with several of the villages of East Flores, which—although subjected to the same influences, in some cases even more strongly—have not succumbed to the same extent. This contrast is itself a problem requiring comparative attention.

It may be useful to mention that according to Vatter (1932: 93) the *koke* in the villages west of Ili Mandiri in East Flores, which are by far the most elaborate, do not belong to the traditional culture, but were introduced from the west—a report I also heard. This suggests that the village temples in these islands were originally somewhat modest in form.

It will be clear to the reader that my ethnographic treatment of the *huna halé* can only be a reconstruction from various reports. As I have not had the benefit of observation, the description I give here can hardly be complete and it can all too easily be inaccurate.

The name is composed of *huna* ('house') and *halé*. No one could translate the last word, but I think there is no difficulty in finding its meaning in the Indonesian *berhala* ('idol') which is sometimes used with the sense of 'homage' or 'worship' (cf. Ind., *rumah berhala*, 'temple'). As such, it may be a direct loan word from Malay. (Dr. Needham has drawn my attention to a possible relation to Sumbanese *hári*, 'sacred', 'prohibited'.) Another name for this building is *huna mier*, and it may also be called *huna marén*.

As is clear from its various usages, *marén* has the meaning of 'marked', 'prohibited'; it has something in common, perhaps, with the Polynesian word *tabu*, but there is no very marked fear shown in connection with the *huna marén* or its location.

The original *huna halé* seems to have had twelve posts; a more recent version appears to have had six. We observed the remaining posts of the *huna halé* of Léutubung which had traces of carving on them. We were told that when it was built the workmen carved superficial patterns on the posts, but that during the night after the work was finished the deeper carvings appeared by themselves. The village head explained that this was possibly caused by the fact that the (spiritual) strength of the workman was 'too great'. The carvings on the posts of the village temple of Léuwajang were described to me by a man who claimed to remember seeing them. They included numerous animals such as iguanas and snakes. At the top was a full moon, at the bottom a new moon. Another old man told me that when it had twelve posts the 'right post' (*lili wana.* N.B. this is the corner post towards the mountain and on the same side as the right of *léu tuan*.) was marked with the carving of a full moon, and the diagonally opposite corner post was carved with a new moon. In Léuwajang, this association corresponds with their view of the course of the moon. For them the full moon rises over the mountain, while the new moon (*ula werun*, in Kédangese, the moon during the first and most of the second quarters) rises at sea. The house posts of the village temple should be made of hard and very durable wood of the tree *ai naré* (Ind., *kaju ansana*). Otherwise, the material and method of construction seems to have been like that of any other building. Because it was a special building, the black fibre of the areng palm (*poléq*), rather than some inferior material, would be used to tie its parts. Like other buildings in *léu tuan*, wood from the lontar palm could not be used in it, nor would the ridge of the roof be covered with lontar leaves. It is likely that the trouble would be taken to roof it with a durable covering of grass rather than rapidly decaying coconut leaves.

It has already been mentioned that the *huna halé* is located in the centre of the village. I was not told that it was supposed to stand next to the house of the lord of the land, as is the case in East Flores (Arndt 1951: 79), but it has already been mentioned that the mythical lord of the land, Hoéq Rian, lived in the building.

In East Flores the *koke*, or village temple, is regarded as masculine and the clan temple as feminine (Arndt 1951: 98). I found no such explicit distinction in Kédang. The granary in Kédang is clearly associated with the woman. In contrast the clan temple may be associated with males. I have been told that nothing sacrificed at the village temple may be eaten by women; and I think, though I am not certain, that women may have been prohibited from entering it. In East Flores if the village temple is completely rebuilt, a man from an enemy village must be killed and his head placed under the main post (Arndt 1951: 79). Though it is nowhere said in the published ethnography, this is the *rié wana* ('the right post'), which corresponds structurally to the *lili wana* in Kédang and is positioned in the same way. The taking of a human head for this purpose seems not to have been done in Kédang.

In Léuwajang if a new village temple were built, people from the villages Léutoan, Léudanun, Léuhoéq, and Kalikur would attend the festivities. The first three villages descend from the same ancestor as Léuwajang (Beni Abé) and are regarded for these purposes as brothers, *kangaring*. The village Kalikur (particularly the clan Léu Tuang, the clan of the Kapitan) are regarded as wife-takers, *maqing-anaq*.

Upon completing the construction of the village temple, gongs would be beaten. Then a goat and a pig would be offered. The goat, which had to have very long horns, would be taken up to the ridge of the roof (*wolar bala*). There its head would be cut off with a sword. The head had to be severed with one blow. The body would then be allowed to fall down the sides of the roof. The blood from this animal would then be sprinkled on the parts of the building (the beams, *atang*, house posts, *lili*, etc.), always starting at the right house post, *lili wana*, and proceeding around the building in a counter-clockwise direction according to the prescription to 'travel to the right', *wana pan*. A pig would then be killed in the same manner inside the building. While the construction of the building and the associated festivities are apparently under the supervision of the lord of the land, the tasks of killing the goat and pig are in the hands of men from the clan Apé Labi— which also has responsibility for temporal affairs and contains within it the office of village head. The same man must not, however, kill both animals. The task of killing the goat is assigned a line of descendants of a younger son of the anciently famous war-leader Boli Talé; that of killing the pig is assigned a line descending from an older son.

At this point I must anticipate somewhat to give a bare sketch of the meanings necessary for understanding the symbolism in what I have just related. First of all the goat and pig are symbolically opposed as high and low, which is most directly expressed in a euphemism employed at feasts. There are now many Muslims, who do not eat pork, and many people in Kédang may not eat goat (for reasons having to do with Kédangese ideas of health). At feasts both goat and pig are usually available, and those serving commonly ask which is preferred by simply asking 'high or low' (*laqi pa wehéq*). The goat is high (*laqi*), the pig low (*wehéq*). Additionally, one of the phrases for the younger sibling is *laqi-utun*, which means in fact the tip of a plant. It seems from this that the younger sibling is symbolically considered high and opposed to the older who would correspondingly be symbolically associated with the base of the plant. Such then is my interpretation of the assignments of the tasks of killing these two animals within the clan Apé Labi.

The word *laqi* means not only 'high', but also 'male'. This context provides one of the instances for thinking that the Kédangese associate high with maleness and with the goat. It will later be shown why the inside of a building (particularly the granary) is to be seen as associated with the female. If the goat, the male and the high are associated, then the pig, the female and the low must be associated. Later I will give other instances of these correspondences. For the moment, this should be enough information to understand why the goat is killed at the top of the roof (both high and outside), while the pig is killed inside the building (both low and inside).

In addition to these two animals, numerous chickens brought by the people attending may have been offered in subsidiary ceremonies, but I can give no account of these. These animals would have been added to the food eaten in the feast. There are small altar stones associated with the *huna halé*, two in number, called *pikan rian* ('large *pikan*') and *pikan éhoq* ('small *pikan*'). I could get no translation of *pikan*; so far as I know it occurs in no other context and above all is not applied to the altar stones (*lapaq*) used at other locations.

At any ceremony at the *huna halé*, banana of the type *muqu erun léqi* and fish of the type *ia ajang* are placed on the *pikan*. The type of banana *muqu erun* ('sweet banana') is used in many ceremonies, but *muqu erun léqi*[2] is used only at the *huna halé*. If fifteen pieces of banana or fish are put on the large *pikan*, eleven must be put on the small *pikan*. If nine are put on the first, seven must be put on the second.

When the *huna halé* is newly built, a priest (*molan maran*) must sit in it for a day and a night and recite *nukun*; that is, he must recite the descent lines from God (Lojo Bujaq) down to the living children of each clan—a clan at a time, not forgetting the wives of each of the men in the genealogies and not leaving out any line. This must be done so that there would be no deaths or illness in the village. Unfortunately, the last person who could possibly undertake to perform this feat (and also historically the last person to do so) died just a few months before I arrived. This recital would occur, I think, on the night after the ceremony for completing the building; and on that night the members of the village and their guests would circle-dance throughout the night. I think this corresponds to the night of watching when a house of the new type (*huna hering*) is erected at the beach. There is no subsequent period of quiet, or closing the village, as there is when they have the village ceremony *nu néjéng*. The actual feasting, it was said, would last for about two weeks.

The substitute building contained various treasures of great antiquity handed down from the ancestors. These included the rusted remains of an old sword blade, two ancient Chinese bowls, a smaller, no doubt Buginese, bowl, the remains of a huge old clay pot, and two old conch shells. The conch shells were said to have been brought down from the top of the mountain when the ancestors descended from *léu rian*. The history of the rest of the collection was not known.

4. 'SAJIN-BAJAN'

There is one final ceremonial object in *léu tuan* which I have not yet mentioned. This is a large boulder near the bottom of the village, designated as *waq sajin* ('the *sajin* stone'). This commemorates the institution *sajin-bajan* which is based on an agree-

---

[2] It is a variety of *muqu erun* and like it in leaf, trunk, colour, and taste of the fruit; but it is like *muqu léqi* (a banana with a reddish tint) in that the bottom of the fruit is rounded (bullet-shaped), whereas *muqu erun* is pointed.

ment made in the early part of this century between Léuwajang and villages on the other side of the mountain. According to this agreement, people travelling outside their own territory may take a coconut or bananas as refreshment without asking permission from the owner. If the owner were to cause trouble to a stranger availing himself of *sajin-bajan*, he would be liable to pay as fine *woiq dokur eliq* (a goat whose horns reach to the armpit) plus a gong so large that its sound might be heard on the other side of the mountain. Additionally, he would have to pay enough liquid from the fruit of the lontar palm to fill a large earthen jug (*auq-oli werén kué udéq*) and enough liquid from the pinang nut to fill a similar jug (*ué werén kué udéq*). Naturally none of these things could be obtained.

Another part of the *sajin-bajan* agreement was *nobol-sajin*. If someone from a strange village were to molest a man's wife, he would be liable to a fine of *laong butil* (an ear ring small enough to be hidden in the hand), *wawi lowoq* (a pig small enough to be hidden in one's garments, i.e. a baby pig). If he molested an unmarried girl, there was no fine. Unfortunately, this agreement seems to be very much of a dead letter. The Indonesian government now insists that they impose more substantial fines on molesting women; and, although I have often heard them speak of how much better it is that they have the agreement concerning travelling, I have observed that they are extremely reluctant to avail themselves of it.

There is another stone (*waq sajin*) at the beach which commemorates a similar agreement made about the same time between Kédang and the Lewotolo or Gunung Api region. The consequence of disturbing a stranger taking advantage of this agreement is somewhat different. He may return home and take the leaves of the *tulur*, a tree with leaves like those of a locust tree, and strip them from the spine of the leaf, and he may take a grasshopper and strip off its legs (*holaq tulur lolon, ruka waiq palun*). If he does this the whole clan of the person who offended him will die out; just as all the leaves fell from the twig.

Sajin may be the Indonesian word *sajang* which means 'sorrow', 'pity', 'love', and which can be used in the form *penjajang* meaning 'charitable' or 'merciful'. Thus, *sajin-bajan* would be an agreed institution of mutual charity, and *waq sajin* the stone of love.

5. THE SPRING 'WEI RAWÉ'

Although it could have been introduced before, I have not yet mentioned the spring *wei rawé*. Adequate water is very hard to find on the mountain, and many villages characteristically must carry their water from a distance of several kilometres. The inhabitants of some mountain hamlets, or people who have fields high on the mountain, sometimes must obtain water by tapping the trunk of a sort of wild banana. By far one of the most shocking and difficult experiences to a European upon first arriving in Kédang is the necessity of adjusting his daily consumption of water, for all purposes, to less than he might employ at home to wash a moderate stack of dishes. Léuwajang is in this regard one of the most favoured villages in Kédang (one of my grounds for choosing to live there). It has—at a distance of under a kilometre— perhaps the best spring to be found anywhere in Kédang so high on the mountain. This runs throughout the year, even in years of extreme drought. During the dry season, its small canyon with its tall stand of bamboo, candlenut trees, coconut, pinang, and areng palms provides one of the few cool, green spots in the vicinity. It has, quite understandably, a correspondingly important place in the life of Léuwajang.

We can most directly arrive at an understanding of this importance by beginning with the following account of the origin of the spring.

Its ritual name is Rawé Rian, Kila Rian—names which do not really yield to translation or analysis. According to the account which I was given, there were two large pots (*tajong*) at *léu rian*. These pots were said to have originated from Pulau Lama Léqang, who got them apparently from God (*Ula-Lojo*). Both pots were made of gold. The villagers of *léu rian* observed that one was shedding water from around the rim as though it were crying. When they picked it up they found the ground beneath wet. Although to others it appeared a golden pot, Lalé Ramuq (see the genealogy in Appendix II) recognized in it a girl who was crying. This pot was brought along during the descent from *léu rian* and placed near *léu tuan* where it took the form of a spring.

This location is a small ravine which does in fact look very much like a good place for a spring, though there is none there now.

According to tradition, *wei rawé* fled from this spot to its present location because the village pigs used to wallow in it and make it dirty. Lemur Lalé (see Appendix II) took a loincloth from Labala (*tariq léwo bala*) and a woman's sarong from Mau Behiq (*wéla mau behiq*) to the spring on this occasion as an offering to keep it from running farther. The original pot, which became *wei rawé*, was the woman Rawé Rian, and it is now located at the source of *wei rawé*, though it cannot be seen.

The second pot was, according to the man who told me the above, a man named Kila Rian. It was also brought down to *léu tuan* and is kept in the village temple—if this is so, I was not able to identify which of the pots it was. Supposedly this pot, Kila Rian, used to be kept tied in the temple with a rope made from the fibres of the areng palm to keep it from going to *wei rawé* to cohabit with Rawé Rian. One of the pots in the temple, according to this tradition, is called *anaq meker* ('oldest child') and is the child of Rawé Rian. Another child is *molé buq, wei teper*, a spring above *wei rawé*.

Unfortunately, there is very marked disagreement about one aspect of this tradition. A priest (*molan maran*) whose opinion is often reliable, although traditional history is not one of his stronger points, insists that Kila Rian is not kept in the temple, that it is not male and that it is identical with Rawé Rian. Since he is, at least now, the person most likely to conduct ceremonies in *léu tuan* (although there is absolutely no restriction on other *molan maran* doing so), his authority would be very difficult to controvert. Furthermore, there are no general principles to be drawn from Kédangese culture to suggest that he is wrong: that the double name Rawé Rian, Kila Rian stands for one thing is rather to be expected, and there is no necessity for the names to be distinguished as male and female. We do not need to resolve such difficulties. I found variations of this sort concerning oral traditions rather common in Kédang. Both versions are authentically examples of Kédangese thinking and are useful as such.

For purposes of interpretation it is essential to note the following points. The water originated at the top of the mountain, which otherwise has been shown to be the source of life. It was then flowing from a golden pot which was actually a woman. When the spring was moved from place to place, it was this pot which was actually moved, and it continues to be the source of the spring. When the ancestors left the top of the mountain, they brought the pot with them, and it has always accompanied them on the stages of the descent. When it was defiled it fled, and the villagers found it important to propitiate it to keep it from going farther.

As a matter of fact gold is one of the keys to interpretation of Kédangese culture and will be dealt with later as well.[3] For the moment I want to introduce some considerations of a linguistic nature which are of direct use in understanding the connection between the golden pot and the waters which it emits. The Kédangese word for gold is *werén*. On the face of it, it is strange that they would have their own word. It has nothing to do with Indonesian *emas*, and I can find no related word in neighbouring languages. Gold is certainly not a metal which can be obtained in a raw form in Kédang itself, and it is known only from the jewellery introduced by foreign traders. However, it must have been available in this form for centuries, and I would hesitate to suggest a historical point before which it would have been unknown. A clue to understanding gold is that it is quite explicitly described in Kédang as something which comes out of the ground. One soon learns that most Kédangese, when speaking Indonesian, apply the word for gold, *emas*, quite indiscriminately to all metals, which are also subject to interpretation as 'things which come out of the ground'. Furthermore, the prohibitions concerning gold apply equally to any other metal. Endicott has uncovered much the same thing in his analysis of Malay magic, about which he says, 'Gold and silver seem to have the same kind of power in ritual as iron . . .' (1970: 133) and observes that 'as ritual materials they seem to form a set' (1970: 134). Although these metals are used somewhat differently by the Malays, for whom they represent according to Endicott's interpretation means to seal boundaries or to block off points of transition, Malay ideas about them are clearly related to those of Kédang.

The word *werén*, however, really tells us all that we need to know. Its other meanings include the liquid which may be gotten from any plant, the liquid of the coconut, soup, the water which

---

[3] Kédangese conceptions on this and other issues may usefully be compared to the ideas revealed in Bosch's study of Indian symbolism. At the moment the reader is directed particularly to the *hiranyagarbha*, 'the golden germ' or 'the golden womb' (1960: 53) and *rasa*, life-giving essence (p. 60).

condenses in salt, and so on. Its root is *weré*, which is used in such expressions as *tuaq weré*, which indicates the period when the lontar palms (*tuaq*) give the most wine. The full phrase as a dyadic pair is *werén-lalan*, a term which occurs in the ceremonial phrase for the fertile fluids of men and women (semen and blood).[4] The root of *lalan* is *lala* which means 'path', 'road'. We can derive, then, a conclusion about the meaning of gold which might at first seem surprising: gold is like a fluid which emerges from things, it crosses the boundaries of bodies.[5] In fact gold emerges from the ground. In the previous chapter, mention was made of *neda* in the phrase *neda bua, hari belé*, concerning the origin of life, and that *neda* was interpreted as the mountain and more particularly the water which comes from below the surface of the earth. This seems to confirm that gold and the other things subsumed under the term *werén* are in their various aspects waters of life. Gold will come into more discussion later but in ways which will confirm this association.

In this regard it might be of interest to mention a gold goblet (originating from Dili, Timor) which was once owned by one of the former village heads of Léuwajang. When this was being described to me, great emphasis was given to the fact that (owing naturally to its reflecting surface) it looked like water inside, but when one turned it upside-down this water did not flow out.

The golden pot is now the source of the spring (*wei matan*) and the fluid which emerges from it is *wei weré*. *Wei* means 'water', and *weré* has been explained. After the preceding review, it is easily seen that the spring represents the life waters of the village. In the thirties the Dutch ordered the entire village to move to the beach, and *léu tuan* was abandoned. During that year the drought was so bad that the spring nearly dried up; and, observing that the spring must always follow the village, the village government became alarmed that it was preparing to move to the beach. In

---

[4] 'Rasa is purest in the sap of plants for plants are the "embryo of the waters"' . . . The sap of each plant is rasa but the sap of Soma, the king of plants, is rasa in its strongest concentration, its purest essence. The same substance is moreover found in cow's milk, in rain, dew, mead (*madhu*), blood, semen virile, and liquor (*surā*)' (Bosch 1960: 60). In Kédang *ai soma* ('the *soma* tree') is any tree in which there are bees' nests containing honey.

[5] 'The properties of the substances, however, make less difference than might be expected. Gold is neither edible nor soluble, yet it is drunk in India and Siam' (Hocart 1952: 159). In alchemy the waters of life were called *aurum potabile*, 'potable gold'.

order to forestall this eventuality, they ordered the old men to move back up to *léu tuan*. This incident will later play a role in my interpretation of the meaning of age and adds in this way more to our understanding both of the spring and of *léu tuan*.

No snake seen near the spring may be killed. This is because it may be the guardian spirit of the spring, *wei nimon* or *wei murun*—both phrases conveying the meaning of the proprietor or protector of the water. Although any snake found there may be this spirit, the characteristic form for it to take is the snake called *ular réta-rading*, a snake which sounds to me very much like a python (Vatter 1934: 121 says python occur in East Flores). It is not poisonous but very large, in width like the type of large bamboo known as *perung*. It was said that it will lie quietly if it knows a human is around and will not move until someone prods it with a stick to get it to go away. A rainbow (*nado-tado*) seen near the spring is this snake. Rainbows are particularly associated with gold and are one of the forms which may be taken by the snake-like guardian spirit within gold. Therefore, the golden pot at the source of the spring is an origin of rainbows.[6]

There are quite a number of additional prohibitions associated with the spring, some of which we unknowingly violated when we first arrived, but ceased to do when we were told about them. It was said for example that strangers were formerly forbidden to use the water, but this restriction has long disappeared. Most strongly prohibited—as I was told several times because regrettably it represented one of our most serious mistakes during the first weeks in Léuwajang—is to use soap at the spring. This is practically a very wise rule, and it derives its religious as well as practical importance from the fact that it dirties the water. Equally strong is the prohibition on putting gold (that is, metal of any kind) in the water at the spring. One must not get one's clothing wet while bathing there. A woman must remove all jewellery, bracelets, and similar external decoration before bathing there, and above all she may not get her hair wet. In this regard a woman stands in marked contrast to the man, for there is no restriction on a man washing his hair there. Should a woman do so she stands in danger of being married by the spirit of the spring and therefore being driven insane. We shall later encounter more evidence of the

---

[6] Concerning the association of snakes and rainbows see Hooykaas 1956b and Pleyte 1894: 97–8.

1*a*. View of *Léu Tuan*

1*b*. Napoq Wala

2a. The frame of a granary,
wetaq rian

2b. Ceremony at a clan temple

3a. Two *huna lélang*, houses of female ancestors

3b. Molan Bala and Péu Atuq

4a. Bala Béjéng

4b. *A-weru*, new food ceremony at clan temple

symbolic importance of a woman's hair. For the moment, I will remark that the context suggests a comparison with gold, and an interpretation may rest on the assumption that for a woman to put her hair in the spring is a sort of confusion like that of incest. The consequences of violating most of the other prohibitions are either that there will be a huge flash-flood, or that the frogs and snakes at the spring, i.e. the guardian spirit, will die and that this will cause a drought or prevent the rains from coming and the spring will dry up. That is, there will either be a superabundance or an inadequate amount of water. One might compare the consequence of drought with the use of metal in Malay magic to stop up points of transition and ask if there may not be cases where for the Malays metal might have the opposite effect. The things prohibited in Kédang seem not always of the same type. Putting gold or a woman's hair into the spring might be interpreted as putting like into like, that is, confusing things which should be kept separated because they are alike. Other things seem to have the opposite effect of confusing things which should be kept separated because they are unlike. For example, strangers were once prevented from using the water. Clothing may not get wet, and clothing is in that category of things which have been introduced from outside. Another prohibition, which according to an argument made earlier may be of this type, is that on bringing the fruit of the lontar palm to the spring. A final example which is clearly of the type concerns the bamboo container (*hau*) used to carry water. The inhabitants of the hamlet Édang live about equal distance from two sources of water, the one being *wei rawé* and the other a spring at the shore. They take water from both of these springs. It is prohibited, however, to use bamboo containers to carry water from *wei rawé* which have previously been used to carry water from the beach.

Though there is a heterogeneous set of things prohibited at the spring and though the consequences of violating these prohibitions sometimes seem to have the opposite effect, what is common to all violations is a categorical confusion of things which should be kept apart, and what is common to the results of such violations is that a source of life is impaired.

These restrictions apply only at the spring. The water may be used for bathing with soap or for washing clothing if it has been carried away from the spring.

As an addendum to this discussion of *wei rawé*, it may be mentioned that the various springs near the *léu tuan* of Léudanun are thought to be descendants of *wei rawé*. The most important of these is *wei noel* (the name of which derives from the verb *doel*, which means to carry on one's shoulder). The tradition goes that some people working fields near the present site of *wei noel* brought drinking water in a bamboo from *wei rawé*. When they were finished for the day, they left the bamboo and the remainder of the water on the spot. The bamboo became a grove and the water became *wei noel*. The prohibitions on *wei noel* are of the same type as those on *wei rawé*. Within the grove, one may not let the iron of a field-knife or a digging-stick touch the ground. If one wishes to bathe, one must take the water out of the grove. When at the water, one must remove all jewellery and external adornments. Metal of no type may be put in the water. On the other hand, during the period of seclusion after birth when a woman must (as in Léuwajang) drink only water from *wei rawé*, this water may be taken from one of the springs, such as *wei noel*, which derive from *wei rawé*, for it is of the same essence.

III

THE HOUSE

As an organic unit, the structure, significance, and function of the home is dictated by the same fundamental principles of belief that rule the village (Covarrubias 1937: 88).

A FTER a description of the mountain and the old village, it is in certain ways a logical step to proceed to a description of the buildings used in everyday living. I include in this chapter the granary because it is not separable from the ordinary dwelling, and is actually of more importance. This chapter will, in fact, usually be concerned in the first instance with the granary; yet it is no misnomer to entitle the discussion 'The House', because in the language of Kédang the granary is a 'house' (*wetaq*) and the dwelling is in several ways derived from it. Most symbolically important rules for the construction of this building are equally binding for any other building, and for that reason I have passed over for the moment the clan temple and reserved it for a later chapter where its role in the ceremonial of the clan will be described.

1. RELATION OF THE DWELLING TO THE GRANARY

Of principal interest now are two buildings: the granary (*wetaq rian* or *ébang*) and the dwelling (*wetaq rongoq* or *huna-wetaq*). *Wetaq* is a synonym of *huna* and means 'house'. *Rongoq* specifies that it is a dwelling, and I know no other translation for this word. *Wetaq rian* is the name used for the granary in the northern part of Kédang, while *ébang* is used in the south; and I have been told that the two terms may be combined to form a dyadic pair in ceremonial language, though I have never encountered the usage otherwise. The *wetaq rian* could be translated as 'the great house'; the name makes clear immediately that the granary has superior significance to the common dwelling.

There are two approaches to this inequality, and I will begin with what is primarily the historical side. I have been told that formerly everyone lived in his granary, but this statement was

explicitly contradicted by an older man when it was made. The
latter was of the opinion that there had always been some who had
their dwellings separate. Another person told me that when
granaries were used as dwellings, there was a platform built
beneath the granary which was enclosed with walls, and this was
where its inhabitants lived. It was usually said that granaries had
been used as dwellings because they were safer from attack. The
granary is built on posts (usually four but sometimes six). The
most common residence, although its frame is almost identical with
the granary, has walls which rise from the ground and a dirt floor.
There are still a few, normally quite small, dwelling-houses which
likewise rest on posts. This form is probably quite ancient and
may once have been more popular, for it would have the same
advantages of defence—whatever they may be—that a granary
has. The normal residence also has house posts, but they simply
support the framework for the roof.

No one now lives in his granary in Kédang. I think this is not
a new condition, but there is absolutely no historical information.
At the latest, the change probably came about with the ending of
warfare. However, it seems quite probable that this form of
dwelling was once used. Vatter (1932: 208) reports it from Lerek,
which lies on the southern part of Lembata in the district of
Labala. The term for these dwelling-granaries, as Vatter calls them,
is *wétaq*, the same as the Kédangese word. They are also very
common on Alor (cf. DuBois 1944: 19–20, Vatter 1932: 232).

The present dwelling seems, then, to be historically secondary
to the granary. It is a convenience, created when the family moved
out of the granary; but in a society such as Kédang such practical
but derivative manifestations are not likely to supersede in ideological importance what preceded them.

The second name of the granary, *ébang*, also means 'gizzard', an
analogy possibly based on the fact that both contain grain. In
Lamaholot the word appears in the form *kébang*. In East Flores
the granary, *kébang*, is of especially marked ceremonial significance (Vatter 1932: 110–13), particularly in connection with
agricultural ritual; and Arndt refers to the *korke* (village temple)
and the *kébang* as the two sacrificial houses (Arndt 1940: 48).
To the west of Ili Mandiri there were formerly special buildings
in which the young girls slept, and these too were called *kébang*.

In Kédang, where agricultural ritual has nowhere near the

development it has in East Flores, the granary does not figure in such ceremonial prominence. Nevertheless, the 'soul of the maize' is kept there as are the navel cords of the members of the house and various other ritual objects. These things may be kept in the dwelling, but this will be done only if there is no granary.

Normally only one married couple and dependants live in a house. There are no houses for extended families or lineages, and married children move out immediately. The Kédangese seem very reluctant to live with two or more families under one roof, and even very old people will have a house of their own, especially when both husband and wife are still living. Only during the short period just after marriage when a man goes to live with his wife's parents will there ever be two married couples in the same house.

The house and the granary are inherited patrilineally, but there seems no clear rule as to whether the elder or younger son inherits. I was told that the older son 'goes out', while the younger son 'guards the door', but this was not explicitly related to the possession of the house—it concerned who may leave the family and the island to seek work in other parts of Indonesia—and I was also told that if the older son wants the house he may have it. It is felt that the granary should be kept up, although it may be moved; and if it is not, as sometimes occurs, it could happen that this would later be interpreted as the cause of some illness or misfortune. It is generally thought that the ancestors do not want the granary to disappear. There is no such concern for the dwelling.

2. ORIENTATION

Neither the dwelling nor the granary is oriented in its internal construction, as are the houses of several other eastern Indonesian societies, such as the Ngada of Flores (Arndt 1954: 176), Atimelang on Alor (DuBois 1944: 20), or the Atoni of Timor (Cunningham 1964: 47). However, the way in which it is put together is of great importance. The major parts of the house must be placed in a prescribed way; to fail to follow the rule would cause disaster. These rules are the same for all buildings and also for the bamboo platforms (*lipu*; Ind., *balai*) which serve in one as bed, chair, and table. If the granary is not built properly it is said that the rats will be able to climb up the poles—despite the heavy wooden rat guards—and then eat the stored grain. In a dwelling which was not built according to rule, the inhabitants would be liable to illness and even death.

The first rule is that the house posts (*lili*) must stand in the ground in the same position as that in which the trees grew from which they are made. One of the phrases for incest, *hunéq-koloq*, which means 'to turn upside down', is also applied to putting a house post in the ground in the reverse position from that in which it grew. Another part of this rule is that all other major vertical beams and rafters in the building must also preserve the natural orientation of the piece from which they are made; and major parts lying horizontally must be put in place according to the imperative *wana pan*, 'travel to the right'. By this last phrase is meant that the tips of the boards and poles must all point counter-clockwise around the rectangle of the building (as in Figure 3).

FIG. 3. Orientation of the parts of a building.

A rule of this type must be very widespread in Indonesia, but it is subject to variations. When I was in the west of the island in the region of Lewuka, I was told that it only mattered that the horizontal pieces point in the same direction, whichever that was; and a resident of Lerek told me that this rule was only observed in fences. However, I found it again equally strongly in Wailolong, East Flores. In Lamalerap, Lembata, the whaling-boats (*pĕlédang*) are constructed according to a version of this rule. All planks and poles must be so placed that the original base lies towards the prow, the tip towards the stern, and the two bamboo poles which form the mast must stand with their original bases in the boat. In this case, although the boat is divided into left and right sides, the pieces do not describe a rectangle—the boat being conceived appropriately as a pointed object. All over Lembata, I think, the house posts are erected as in Kédang, and this must be the last part of the rule which would disappear. Covarrubias (1937: 94) reports it from Bali.

The spars which form the sloping framework on the roof, and to which the grass or palm-leaf roofing is tied, must be, on each of the four sides, of an uneven number. In the dwelling there is no fixed rule for the placing of the doors, but a granary, in which they have the form of an opening in the floor—though it may have several entrances—must have one on the side facing the slope on which it is built (see Figure 4). It is this side which is considered the front. What was said to be the old style of granary was once described to me as having doors as well at each corner, but I have never seen this type.

Doors in a dwelling may not, however, be placed directly opposite to pieces of the framework called the *manuq leténg* ('chicken strut') and the *nuar*. The former of these runs through the centre of the house just above head level and forms a support for the ridge pole (*wolar bala*) to which it is connected by two vertical poles (*nubu*). The *nuar* are on either side of this just below the roof, and give lateral support to the ridge pole, to which they are tied. They rest in the *kawanang lawan*, a large beam just under the eaves of the roof. The ends of the *nuar* and the *manuq leténg* thus form centre points in the structure of the house, and the rules concerning them were described to me by way of analogy to a birthmark. Birthmarks are bad signs, but only if they occur in the centre of the face or on the front of the body. Doors, then, must not break the boundaries of the house opposite these centre points.

It has already been mentioned that the ladder to the village temple was traditionally supposed to have seven rungs. I have been told by several people that the ladder of a granary must have rungs of an uneven number. This seems to be correct, although one of my friends, whose ladder had four rungs, repeatedly denied it.

The building is, furthermore, oriented to the slope on which it sits. This is to be seen from the names given to the various sides of the roof, the location of the right house post (*lili wana*) and the orientation of the ridge pole. The *lili wana* stands on the upper side of the slope and on what would be the right side of a person who was facing away from it. The ridge pole must run from side to side (*oté-oléq*) in relation to the slope rather than towards it, or up and down (*bunuq-dau*). There are a few houses which do not accord with this latter rule, but by far the majority (over ninety per cent) do. The side of the roof on the 'up' side is called *wajan*. That opposite it on the 'down' side is *unéq*, while the two lateral sides are called *bubun* ('fontanelle'). The four corner ridges are called *mutung*. These terms will come into consideration in a more general treatment of orientation in space. For the moment the above rules are demonstrated in Figure 4.

Divination is not used to find the location for a building, and there is usually no ceremony connected with the construction of a dwelling. There is a ceremony, however, when one builds a granary. Unfortunately I never saw such a ceremony, and my description is a reconstruction from hearsay.

It would seem that if the granary is completely rebuilt, one will ask a priest (*molan maran*) to perform a ceremony in which he

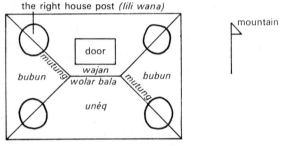

FIG. 4. Sections of the roof.

scrapes a little wood at each corner, starting at the *lili wana* and going from there counter-clockwise (*wana pan*) around the building.[1] This is called the *mutung-alé*—from the corner ridges, *mutung*, and *alé*, a word which seems to be related to Lamaholot *aleng*, 'navel' (cf. Krol n.d.) and from which Kédangese *alén*, 'intestines', may be derived. This is wrapped in leaves and thrown away in the canyon, later to be carried away to sea by the rains. A ceremonial phrase associated with this is *ai déjéq, waq dolan* ('sharp wood, sharp stone'); *ai utuq-alé pan belé* ('the tips of the wood go away'). The point of the ceremony is said to be to take away the sharpness of the wood used in building the granary.

If the granary has been moved, part of the ceremony will have to be a ritual closing of the old holes in which the house posts set. This is called *bata lili, oang lawel, loiq-bawo* ('to dig out the post,

---

[1] The scraping is taken from the outside, under the floor, at the four corners, specifically, from the end of the outermost *noruq*, from the end of the *nobol* and from the tip of the peg which joins them.

take down the *lawel* [spars of the roof], fill in the holes'). If the ground is not closed, the rats will destroy the owner's maize. The ceremony for closing the ground will also be used on other occasions, as, for instance, when a large boulder is moved.

If the granary is not entirely rebuilt, but only certain parts of it replaced, the above procedures are not necessary. But there are certain small ceremonies, requiring no priest, which are carried out on these occasions. Once when we were replacing the posts of a granary, I observed that they put broken candlenut shells in the bottom of the hole before placing the post in it. This was very casually done, they missed one post—in fact, the most important, the *lili wana*—because, as they explained, the nuts had not been prepared and brought out in time. The reason for doing this was to keep the termites from eating the new posts. This custom is very reminiscent of that of the Malays described by Skeat, where candlenut and scrap-iron are put in the bottom of the hole before erecting the central house post (Skeat 1900: 143–4).

Endicott (1970: 133) interprets this as a means of sealing the boundary between the earth and the house, and he classes the candlenut as a boundary strengthener. I do not wish to say that this may not be a correct interpretation for the Malays, but a very similar set of ideas and procedures have a different significance in Kédang. Actually the ceremony described by Skeat includes several things which are clearly offerings, which is indeed what he calls them. This is what the candlenut represents in the rite which I have just described. The fact that it is broken up and is thus prepared for consumption shows that it is not a boundary strengthener *per se*. Though the goal is in a sense to strengthen the boundary, the nuts are not a threat to the termites but are a means to propitiate them. This is clearly seen in a very similar instance. One of the posts in the granary belonging to one of my friends had a rectangular hole chiselled in it. I asked what its purpose was, and it was explained that the post was hollow, as it had been when first erected. They had chiselled the hole in the post when they set it up so they could pour palm wine into it to keep the termites from climbing up inside. In this case, it seems to have worked, for the post has stood for over forty years. As will be shown below, an absolute sealing of the boundary between the house and the earth is something the Kédangese would not want. I think Endicott is right in the emphasis he places on boundary weakeners and strengtheners in his interpretation of Malay magic, but I think some of the things which he classifies as boundary strengtheners may sometimes have other uses.

When work is done on repairing a building, it is customary that the owner provide a meal to those who have helped him. Just before serving the meal after we had changed the house posts, the wife of the owner placed a small offering of food, palm wine, and sirih-pinang on a stone near the house. This offering is called *wajaq-doping* and is observed on many other occasions. The recipients are the ancestors (*tuan-woq*), and the food might more directly be regarded as their share of the meal rather than as a gift or sacrifice. This they must receive before the meal and it must be given them by a woman. It is not required if work is done on the dwelling, but it follows other work on the granary, such as roofing.

3. THE 'HUNA HERING'

I have said that the dwelling requires no ceremony when it is built. There is an exception to this, which proves in a surprising way to be of very great use in understanding the significance of the house. This exception is a new form of house favoured by the people living in the new hamlet at the beach. These are usually constructed with the help of mission-trained carpenters, and consist of board frames on to which walls of split bamboo sheets are tied. To my taste they are aesthetically very unpleasing. They differ from the ordinary *wetaq rongoq* principally in that they do not require house posts. This is shown already in their name (*huna hering*) which indicates that they have been just set up or rested on the ground in the same way that something would be put on a shelf.

Such a house requires a night of guarding before it is erected, much like the night spent guarding the corpse before the funeral. Interestingly, the granary need not be guarded in this manner. When the building is erected, water must first be sprinkled (*pauq*) on the part of the frame which corresponds structurally to the right house post, *lili wana*. Then grasping this part and assisted by others, the wife-giver (*epu-bapa*) raises this section of the framework into position. The intention of putting water on the house post is to cool the house, so that its inhabitants will not suffer from misfortune and illness. The heat which must be removed is produced by boring holes. The holes are said to be so small that the *bowol*, which could be compared to breath, could not get out. This custom will later be used in discussion of certain traditional methods of treating illness with which it has a close similarity. The reason these ceremonial observances are not required for the granary or the *wetaq rongoq* is that they have house posts and the cool can rise through them from the ground. Because the *huna hering* has no house post and therefore lacks connection with the ground a piece of 'gold', which could be for example a silver or copper coin, must be put in what passes for the right house post. This is provision for the spirit (*sehar metung*, they said) which can then dwell in the house, as it could in a building with house posts, and can, therefore, guard it. It must be made explicit that this gold substitutes for the gold already indwelling in the ground and connection to which is provided by the house posts.

The ceremonial procedures just described deserve extended attention. First of all the *huna hering* provides one of the few instances in Kédangese culture where a night of guarding precedes a major transition. From the two instances mentioned (the erecting of the *huna hering* and the funeral) it can be seen that such guarding is associated with a major passage of spirit: in the one case a coming into life in a sense, in the other a passing out of life. The custom is very common in Indonesia; Vatter, for example, mentions it for the *pĕlédang* of Lamalerap (1932: 203). Hocart seems to find such customs nearly universal; as he remarks, 'Ritual almost invariably involves a period of quiescence like the vigil of the knight before his investiture' (Hocart 1933: 155). Stated in this form, it might be taken to include periods of confinement, called *iréng*, which follow certain important ceremonies or periods of transition in Kédang.

A second point of interest is that hot and cool play a ceremonial role. In the culture of the neighbouring Lamaholot the categorical distinction between hot and cool is of major importance, and the very nearly complete lack of attention given to this opposition is one of the main ways in which Kédang contrasts with Lamaholot. It is gratifying, nevertheless, to find it here, because it shows that it must be taken into consideration in an analysis of Kédangese thought, and if it were not so Kédang might to that extent appear very un-Indonesian.

Cunningham says for the Atoni of Timor the construction and cooling of the roof of the house is one of the responsibilities of the wife-giving group and for which they are essential (1964: 60–1). This is not true in Kédang, but the example of the *huna hering* shows that the wife-givers have a very similar role. There would seem to be reasons for associating the wife-givers with spiritual authority, and these reasons will be examined later. For the moment I will suggest that the wife-giver is called upon because he is in some way analogous to the house post. Least this assertion seem too obscure, I will mention that this analogy lies in the imagery of the tree, for the mother's brother is called *epu puén*, *puén* meaning the 'trunk' of a tree; and the mother's brother is by categorical prescription the wife's father. Fox (1968: 291; 1971b) mentions that the same metaphor of planting and growing dominates the Rotinese conception of affinity.

In a certain sense, the house posts are planted; this is shown by the way in which care is taken that the original root end is placed in the ground. However, some Kédangese idiom would seem to contradict the idea that the posts, and therefore the house, are alive. House posts which are set in holes in the ground and cannot be moved are called *lili maté* ('dead posts'), while the posts of platforms (*lipu*) which are simply set on the ground and can be moved are called *lili bita* ('living posts'). This idiom is parallel to that by which they describe the protected waters of bays and inlets as *tahiq maté* ('dead sea') while the open ocean is *tahiq bita* ('living sea'). I think though that these usages are determined by situation, in the same way that water is called 'black' (*miténg*), i.e. clear, in opposition to palm wine which is 'white' (*bujaq*); and such wider implications possibly cannot be drawn from them. It should be kept in mind, however, that the Indonesian word meaning 'to plant' (*tanam*, to which Kédangese *tanéng*, 'to bury', may be related) also means 'to bury'. Comparatively, planting and death may not prove such distinct ideas. Many Indonesian stories of the origin of rice or other grains characteristically turn upon the equation.

4. ANALYSIS

Whether or not the house is alive in the sense of humans or animals, it is inhabited by a spirit. The house posts are the means by which the spirit has access to the building. They are means or points of transition. Most important of them is that which is designated as the right post, *lili wana*. It has been mentioned that various ceremonial objects are characteristically stored there. Though the actual orientation in the house is different from that of the Kédangese *lili wana*, the main house post of other peoples, for example the 'head mother post' (*nakaf*) of the Atoni or the *lor* of the Belu of Timor, serves as an altar for offerings to the ancestors (Cunningham 1964: 42; Vroklage 1952: 2: 106). Such customs as hanging a basket for the ancestors with sirih-pinang, etc. at the *lili wana*, do not exist in Kédang, but this post is nevertheless conceptually associated with the ancestors. In fact in some versions of the short chant made during the conventional offering to the ancestors before the meal (*maran*), in which they are requested to leave and stay away, they are explicitly told not to stand at the *lili wana*.

In addition to house posts and doors, I think other points of transition may be identified in the house. Important among these are the corner-ridges, *mutung*, of the roof. In certain ceremonies where the house is being ceremonially closed to a spirit or dead soul, markers of prohibition (or boundary strengtheners) are placed at the doors and at the *mutung* of the roof. This would not seem necessary if the corners and corner-ridges were not possible points of entrance to the spirits. The ridge poles of the Atoni house seem in certain ways to block off an entrance (Cunningham 1964: 50-1), and the roof ridge of the Kédangese house is similar to the *mutung* in that it is a possible point of entrance for the soul (*éqong*) of a witch (*maq-molan*). The name of the bamboo rain guard which covers the ridge is called *bowong wolar*. *Bowong* curiously means to 'bark', and I have heard it used in the sense to 'trick'. *Wolar* is the ridge. I think it possible that the symbolic function of this piece may be to deceive spirits who might otherwise use it as access to the house.

The interpretation which I am putting forward here is that the house is for the Kédangese regularly divided into solid portions and interlinking points of transition, that it is articulated and segmented like, for example, bamboo. I will return to this idea on later occasions and eventually attempt to demonstrate that this is the characteristic of all bodies which have form or structure. There are various linguistic clues which lend support to this idea, but for the moment I wish to show what we can learn from the use of numbers.

The major points of transition, as I have identified them, are the ridge at the top of the roof, which is structurally equivalent, for example, to the centre of the village, the house posts and the corners and corner-ridges of the roof. There are four house posts (if not six) and four corners. This may seem such an unavoidable consequence of the practical requirements of constructing a house that it deserves no mention. But I want to show that there is, nevertheless, something to be learned from it. The word used for even numbers in Kédangese is *anaq*, meaning 'complete'. It is also, I think, etymologically identical with the word for 'child'. Even numbers, then, are complete numbers. It would seem that an association is made between even numbers, and hence completion, and points of transition in the construction of the house. This may not seem so convincingly present, but we should recall that in certain cases it was prescribed that sections of the building be made up of parts of an uneven number. The rungs of the ladder in the granary and the spars in each side of the roof must be of an uneven number. Parts which are structurally less significant, such as the walls of the dwelling, are under no prescription. This rule suggests that what has structure or body, in this case the solid sections between points of articulation, are associated with uneven numbers and hence necessarily with incompletion. The way they sometimes state this rule, *ohaq bisa anaq*, can literally be rendered, 'it may not be complete'. We are presented here with one of the most important categorical distinctions in Kédangese thought and one which allows the widest comparisons, not only with tangible entities such as the human body, certain games, bamboo, even the universe, but also with the very structure of duration itself.

I have said that I would present evidence of a symbolic association between women and the granary. This is clearly seen in Lamaholot where the young girl acting the role of 'rice maiden', *Tono-Wudjo*, must spend a night of vigil in the granary prior to planting (Vatter 1932: 110–11) and where in a certain area a special building for young girls is called a 'granary'. In Kédang the association is shown most directly by the rule that only women may take the grain out of the inner compartments of the granary. This means a man's wife or mother may do so. His children, even if female, may not. If his mother is dead, but his father (an old man) still lives, his father may take the grain out. If the man stays at home by himself, his wife should take the grain out for him before she leaves. This can be left in the outer compartments of the granary where the man can then get it. I was told that if the granary is full, the prohibitions apply even to the outer compartments. If an old man or woman is living, the grain for their meal should be removed first. The old people may eat first. There seems to be some practical flexibility in the application of these prohibitions. My neighbour who was still an active head of a family, although he was already an old man, said he could get the grain himself if his wife were not there. However, most strongly affected are children, who may in no circumstances remove grain from the inner compartments.

This rule not only indicates an association of the granary with women, but also provides an example, as promised, of the equations of the woman with the inside and the male with the outside. By the strict prohibition placed on children and the relaxing of the prohibition in the case of old men, it demonstrates a similar association in the matter of age. Age will have to be taken up later, as it requires an extensive examination of its own. If the granary is symbolically associated with the woman, it would seem that the dwelling must necessarily also be associated with the woman. I uncovered no evidence on this question, and it seems that the dwelling is marked primarily by the lack of symbolic attention which is given it.

I have shown that a building is oriented in relation to the slope on which it is constructed. For those buildings located high on the slopes of the mountain, this orientation is identical to that of *léu tuan*, and for practical purposes it may be said that the building is oriented to the mountain. In view of the importance of the mountain in the traditional history of Kédang, this is to be expected, and it provides a pleasing correspondence between the situation of buildings and historical ideas concerning the descent from the summit. The question of spatial orientation has only been introduced in these chapters and it requires extensive treatment of its own. In the following chapter I attempt to give a comprehensive account of this most complicated question.

IV

ORIENTATION IN SPACE

KÉDANG presents problems to the ethnographer or linguist which are perhaps not entirely familiar to scholars dealing with other areas of Indonesia. These derive from the fact that the Kédangese quadrant of cardinal points is not fixed in the way familiar to us. Western conceptions of orientation in space—which are tied to the idea that one always moves within a world conceived as a plane held constant by four fixed poles—must be abandoned when one attempts to adopt the categories of the Kédang language. On Timor the cardinal points are oriented to the direction of the sun (Cunningham 1964: 36), and seemingly they do not there present these problems to analysis. In Borneo orientation is usually to the course of rivers and to the path of the sun (cf. Schärer 1963: 66; 1966: 926–30). While orientation of space in these societies is very different from that which prevails in the West, the reference point in each case may be so singularly and immediately obvious that no particular interpretative difficulty is offered.

In Kédang the situation is different, and I had to free myself from a number of misconceptions before I could obtain my present understanding of the question. The process lasted most of my stay in the field, during which I found that I repeatedly came to premature solutions. I hope now that I am at last in the position to present a satisfactory account of the matter.

1. THE PROBLEM

As one might expect, it appears that in Lamaholot one is faced with essentially the same problem as in Kédang. Although in his discussion of direction adverbs, which he says also serve to indicate the cardinal points, Arndt attempts to give simple and straightforward definitions (1937: 90, 106), he appends a number of examples of particular applications to show with what difficulty one is faced when attempting to employ the terms as defined. His explanation is followed by this important qualification.

However, he who is unfamiliar with the features of a particular location must avoid carrying his own conception of direction over into Solorese. Sometimes many of the applications by the natives of these direction adverbs are unintelligible, almost inconceivable; one does not know quite what the native does or does not take into consideration with these expressions or what he had once taken into consideration and then allowed to become firm expressions. Therefore, if in a particular location one wants always to use the correct expressions for its situation, one must enquire with the people of the village.

This fairly characterizes the plight of the half-initiated European. One simply cannot proceed from a translation of the terms by a native speaker to a sure application of them in all occasions.

What is of principal concern to us are not such simple terms as those which translate our 'here', 'there'; 'in', 'out'; 'high', 'low'; and so on, but the words which serve the same purpose as our 'north', 'south', 'east', 'west'. As in many other Indonesian languages, so in Kédang there are no words meaning 'north' and 'south'. Those for 'east' and 'west' are the common *timur* and *waraq*. These are related not only to the course of the sun but also to the direction from which the winds blow during the two great monsoons of the year. The rainy season is called, in fact, *uja-waraq* (as good as, though not literally, 'west rains').

However, *timur* and *waraq*, though comparable to our 'east' and 'west', are not terms of primary importance in spatial orientation. This role is reserved for the following set and their dyadic extensions: *oté/olé, oli/owé* and *ojo*. These have adverbial, prepositional, and even verbal applications. If one asks for a translation, one will be told that *oté* means 'up' and *olé* 'down'. *Oli* also means 'up' and *owé* 'down'. *Ojo* means 'to the side'. If one asks what distinguishes the first two pairs, one will be told that *oté* is higher than *oli*. If one proceeds from this to examine particular applications, one will soon find that the definitions are inadequate.

In Indonesia, when one travels one is constantly greeted with the question, 'Where are you going?' In Kédang this question may also be phrased in the above terms and have the form, 'Are you going in such and such direction?', where one is essentially asked if one is going in the direction where one can be seen to be heading. The question may be answered either with an explicit destination or with one of the above direction indicators or one of their derivative forms. For example: '*Oliq o?*' ('Are you going up?'). '*É, éi pan oté wéla.*' ('Yes, I am going up the mountain.')

Thus, one is constantly reminded of these terms, and their proper use becomes a matter of daily concern.

As I was living on the mountain and began to investigate this question by learning the application of the terms appropriate for the hamlet in which I lived, I first learned to use them in relation to the slope of the mountain. In fact it was one of my most persistent mistakes to think that the terms were actually defined in relation to the mountain itself. From my previous discussion of the mountain, this may seem a natural surmise. It has been shown that the opposition between the mountain and the sea or the mountain and the beach is an important categorical distinction. Where this is not possible on the southwest side of the mountain, the distinction becomes one between the mountain and the outlying terrain. Covarrubias says that on Bali the mountain and the sea are equivalent to our north and south (1937: 40), and further that 'The principle of orientation—the relation of the mountains to the sea, high and low, right and left—that constitutes the ever present Balinese Rose of the Winds (*nawa ganggah*), rules the orientation and distribution of the temple units' (1937: 267). It would be easy to assume on comparative grounds, then, that the mountain/sea opposition is in Kédang the basis of orientation and therefore corresponds to the opposition as used on Bali, taking a role similar to the land/sea distinction of Roti (cf. Fox 1968: 41–6) or the upstream/downstream opposition of Borneo.

I did make a certain amount of progress with this assumption, but quite early it appeared that this was not all there was to it. From the hamlet Napoq Wala, one would use *oté* for a climb to a much higher point on the mountain, but *oli* for the relatively short climb to the spring at *wei rawé*. This fitted well enough with the definitions I was given; But I could find no immediate way to reconcile the use of *oté* to refer to the village Kalikur (*oté Aliur*) or even worse to the beach at *rauq utuq*. If *oté* meant even higher than *oli* how could it be applied to these places located at the beach and therefore decidedly lower than Napoq Wala?

2. EVIDENCE

I will not give a chronological account of the path I took in unravelling this problem but go directly to the information, some of which I found quite late, which allows the first interpretative advance. It has already been mentioned that the right in several

particular cases has a symbolic pre-eminence and that in the building the *lili wana* is not only on the right side but also on the 'up'
side of the slope. It may also be remembered that if the body of
the fallen enemy is not retrievable, then it is sufficient to bring
back the head or right hand. There are two instances, then, where
the up or the head are associated or equated with the right. I had
begun to suspect that this might also be true in the case of direction
indicators, but I did not happen across conclusive proof of this
until my second year. I first encountered the expression *oté-
olé(q)* referring explicitly to laterality in a case where it was
applied to the inner compartments of the granary. This allowed
immediate tangible confirmation of its application. *Oté* was applied
to the side which from the previous discussion of the house will be
recognized as the right, *olé* to the left. After this discovery, I later
encountered parallel examples which I could interpret with
confidence. One of these came when I found that the roof ridge
was oriented to the slope on which the house stood. It will be
remembered that the roof ridge must run in a lateral direction in
relation to the slope, *oté-oléq* (the use of the final glottal stop is
variable for these terms).

With this point secured, it could be seen that *oté* can be used to
mean 'high' (higher than *olí*) and also to mean 'to the right'. Its use
in the case of the market and the village Kalikur is an example of
its use meaning 'to the right'. From Léuwajang, one uses *oté* in
reference to all villages round the mountain in the direction of
Kalikur and past to Wairiang. I soon came to the conclusion that
this was because they were to the right, round the mountain from
Léuwajang.

When I asked if this were so, I was always answered, 'No. It is
because we have to go up a slope.' In some instances this may well
be true, but it did not seem to be so in this case. In the first place,
given even that one starts from the beach and not from the
mountain hamlets, one mounts no appreciable slope to reach the
market at *rauq utuq*. Secondly, when I was in Léuwutun and inquired about the use of these terms, I found that for Wairiang
and beyond one also uses *oté*. Now, Wairiang continues round the
mountain to the right, but it lies lower than Léuwutun and one
descends to get there. Thirdly, for villages lying in other directions
from Léuwajang, one uses other terms, although there are certainly places where one mounts before one reaches them. One says

ojo (the undifferentiated lateral term) Péusawa and *olé* Balaurin. That the association between the right and the word *oté* plays an important part in these particular applications seems an unavoidable conclusion. It must be admitted, however, that a rule stating that *oté* is always used for villages lying to the right round the mountain and some other term for those lying to the left will hardly be of more practical use to the outsider than the definition of *oté* as meaning 'up'.

I am sure that in some cases this is actually what occurs, but the problem lies in the fact that the mountain is not exclusively the object in relation to which these terms are defined. This one can discover when one moves off the slope of the mountain far enough to encounter the terms being used quite independently of it. Perhaps this was more difficult for me to see than it would have been to another because I was living on the mountain itself, and it so dominated the physical situation in which I lived and the ethnographic material which I was collecting. It might have been thought that I could have seen through this difficulty whenever I travelled, and though this is true enough, that it was a long time before I did, is due first to the fact that it took a long process to conceive the problem in a way which would make such testing useful and secondly to the fact that one does not really escape the mountain so easily in travelling. When one is going round it, particularly, or in travelling away from it and then back, it remains a major reference point of orientation. One only frees oneself from the dominance it has on one's imagination when one has a chance to examine the orientation of a particular place which is so situated that it forces one to abandon one's preconceptions.

There are certain unexpected clues which are a great aid in this and which allow one to break away from doubts about what is really intended, which as Arndt mentioned are inherent in purely oral communication. These have to do with the construction of the house, and principal among them is the orientation of the ridge of the roof. If one can find a spot high enough to overlook a hamlet or village, one can see immediately from the arrangement of the roofs how the direction indicators will be applied within that immediate area. Many houses in the new hamlet of Léuwajang are built on the sides of slopes which face in a different direction from that of the over-all slope of the mountain, and it is to these slopes which the houses are oriented, not to the mountain.

Once this point has been cleared up, we can see that the direction indicators are truly abstract terms for ordering space. Their application depends on no particular feature of the landscape. Nor, as I have said, are they fixed to the course of the sun. This requires demonstration which will be given just below. Their application in an immediate context may seem inconsistent with their use in another, but this is because reference points change. Because the mountain physically dominates the terrain of Kédang to such a great extent, there is a tendency, where immediate relations no longer apply, for the terms to revert back to it for definition.

The first analytic question I set myself in the field was phrased in the form, 'Does the mountain define these terms, or does the course of the sun do so?' This I think I have satisfactorily settled. I made three trips to the southern side of the mountain. The first of these was during my preliminary visit to Kédang, when the village head of Léuwajang kindly guided me on a walk round the mountain. The second was a month later, when I still did not know the language. On the third trip, however, I was in the position to supplement observations made on the first two and usefully to phrase questions related to the use of direction indicators. If the direction indicators were determined by the course of the sun, it would seem that the orientation of the buildings and the villages would similarly be determined by the sun's course. Observation has shown in all cases on the north slope of the mountain that the right is to the east. If the sun was of primary importance in determining the Kédangese cardinal points, the right would necessarily also be to the east on the southern slope of the mountain. In fact, it seems that in *léu tuan*, houses on the slope of the mountain and in the funeral, on the south slope of the mountain the right is to the west. This rules out the possibility that the sun determines the cardinal points.[1]

After this lengthy consideration of the role of the mountain in determining the use of direction indicators, it may be useful to

---

[1] Hooykaas (1956a: 85) says of Bali that they 'only distinguish two absolute directions: East and West, the two others being *to the Sea* and to the *Mountains*, which notions are opposite in North- and South-Bali, the mountain range crossing the island roughly East–West'. The east–west direction seems more important in Bali than in Kédang. Swellengrebel (1960: 37–40) gives an excellent summary of the question on Bali with instructive reference, as well, to Celebes. He points out (p. 38) that east and west may once not have been linked to the Balinese terms *kaja* and *kělod*. Goris (1960: 377, n. 16) says, 'in the mountain areas the local situation serves to determine usage'.

report some related facts which demonstrate the curious grip the mountain has on the Kédangese imagination. I was greatly astonished after successfully completing the circuit of the mountain when my guide pointed to the mountain and said, 'See, it's not possible to go round it.' I did not yet know Indonesian very well at this time and had no knowledge of the Kédang language, so I simply assumed that I did not understand. But I later encountered this idea repeatedly, and on two or three occasions an animated group attempted to explain it at great length. Since it is a paradox and seems to turn to some extent on the use of language and since the explanations depended a great deal on gesturing with the hands, it is no wonder that I found them hard to fathom. One thing they always succeeded in making clear is that they did not mean that it was a hopeless enterprise to set out on the Dutch road encircling the mountain in one direction with the hope of eventually returning to the starting-point from the other. The practical feasibility of going round the mountain was very clear to them. What perturbed them was that the mountain always stayed on the same side. Now to some this may seem an elementary mistake of the imagination; but I think it is a problem inherent in the language itself. They say that other mountains do not present these (conceptual) problems of being encircled.

Now, in encircling the mountain, one's prime reference point is naturally the mountain itself (this is even more true, if, instead of taking the Dutch road, one takes the far shorter and much more pleasant and scenic mountain trails). This has the effect that instead of moving within a fixed field determined by the cardinal points as we comfortably do, one has the sensation that this field also moves. It swivels, so to speak, with one; so that only the top of the mountain appears to provide a fixed point of reference. To show the consequence of this, we may compare what it is possible to say about going round the mountain in English. If we set out in Léuwajang, the mountain is to the south of us (actually southeast). We walk east until the mountain is to the west of us; when we have completed half of the journey, the mountain is to the north; and so on it goes until we have returned and the mountain is again to the south. Our terms support a sense of accomplishment. However, in Kédangese all one can ever say in any stage of the trip is that the mountain stands *oté*. This is a real conceptual difficulty and one which apparently only the mountain causes them. Going round a house or a tree is conceptually an undertaking of exactly the same nature as it would be to us. We are comfortably secure in the knowledge that going round a mountain is essentially no different from going round a tree. For someone using the language of Kédang, going round at least one mountain seems to be an entirely different proposition from going round a tree.

Related to this fact is the conviction which many have that an aeroplane cannot fly over the top of the mountain. During World War II they observed that Japanese and American planes always flew round the mountain rather than directly over it. I do not know if this was because they were avoiding detection by radar or because they were taking bearings on the mountain, but the fact was readily perceived by the people of Kédang, and to it was attributed an importance in relation to the conceptual problem just described. In terms of the Kédangese culture it makes a great deal of sense that an aeroplane cannot fly over the top of the mountain. To do so would be to fly right out of ordered space. It would be very much like finding a hole in the universe and going through it. Perhaps this seems too fanciful, but the discussion of encircling the mountain has demonstrated another instance of the lack of categorical differentiation which has previously been shown to be characteristic of the top of the mountain. It is, after all, an origin of life.

3. A STRUCTURAL ACCOUNT OF TERMS OF DIRECTION

I can now return to the terms used for the cardinal directions and attempt to give a structural account of them. It seems that the terms *ojo* and *oli/owé* are straightforward enough and do not pose great problems either of translation or analysis. *Ojo* is an undifferentiated lateral term; it means to the left or the right, but not up or down. *Oli* is adequately translated 'up' and *owé* 'down'. Taken together they form the quadrant shown in Figure 5c. In certain cases *ojo* may be replaced by the differentiated lateral opposition, *oté/olé*. These then may serve in opposition to *oli/owé* meaning 'up' and 'down' (otherwise *oli/owé* may be replaced by the verbal opposition *bunuq*, 'to climb down'/*dau*, 'to climb up'). Figure 5b shows this version. Finally *oté/olé* may subsume both the lateral distinctions and the opposition of up and down—as in Figure 5a. Once the orientation is given, all terms may be used to refer to directions which occasionally are perfectly horizontal. Thus, if the mountain is the prime reference point, one could use *oté* to mean across a yard in the direction of the mountain.

There are terms which complete the dyadic pair for each of these words, and the full forms are shown in Figures 5d through 5f. It will be seen that when *oté/olé* are employed for laterality they are completed by the word *apan*, otherwise linked to *ojo*.

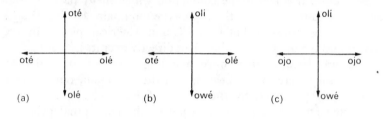

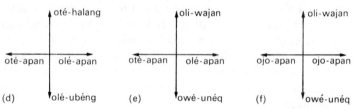

FIG. 5. Direction terms in the language of Kédang.

However, when they are used for 'up' and 'down', they do not take the completing words for *oli/owé*. The first of these facts allows a distinction of sense to be introduced (shown in Figure 5d), which is not present when the full dyadic pairs are not used (as in Figure 5a). The second fact seems to emphasize the distinction in sense between *oté/olé* and *oli/owé*.

Of the words used to complete the pairs, only *ubéng* has any wide usage outside of this context. It means 'under', and appears in contexts where *olé* is not employed. *Wajan* and *unéq*, it will be remembered, are the names of the sides of the roof which are on the 'up' and 'down' side of the slope, respectively. *Wajan*, which also occurs in the name of the village, may be related to the western Indonesian homonym which gave the Javanese and Balinese shadow-puppets their name. It has been suggested that it may originally have had a meaning in relation to the cult of the ancestors (cf. Covarrubias 1937: 316, 412). It has no such application in the language of Kédang, but its actual present use would certainly not conflict with such an interpretation. The form of the terms can be slightly changed by adding an initial *b* or *m*, but this involves no change of meaning. There are also special words added to describe movement towards the speaker; thus *oté* (or *oli*) *né*, 'from above down', *olé* (or *owé*) *aq*, 'from below up', and *ojo ma*, 'from the side here'.

In addition, these words often have by themselves or in combination with other terms quite different meanings, and the connection thus drawn between different spheres of meaning can be of great interest. I will give here some examples. The word *oté(q)*, meaning 'up', also occurs in the form *otéq* with the meaning 'hair'; and the *otéq-noloq* is a stage in the bridewealth exchange paid to the mother's clan at the death of a sister's son. *Binin-otéq* occurs in the ceremonial language meaning the clan's possessions and refers to the clan sisters (and, I think, their hair). *Baraq-beté* (*beté* is identical with *oté*) means 'heavy' and can also mean 'illness'. *Belé* (identical with *olé*, 'down') also means to 'let loose', 'let down', 'free'. It can be used too to mean 'fishing', something one has to descend the mountain to do.

Though the application of the direction indicators poses a difficult interpretative problem to the linguist or ethnographer, their form is actually quite simple. Initially a single pair of complementary opposites, *oté/olé*, subsumes all distinctions to be made in space. Further differentiation is achieved by adding the second pair of complementary opposites *oli/owé* and finally the undifferentiated lateral term *ojo*. The apparent paradox that increased differentiation is provided by an undifferentiated term like *ojo* is explained by the fact that it is used in prosaic circumstances where the ideas otherwise associated with laterality are unimportant. Differentiation in this case lies in its dissociation from a wider realm of references.

It is just this wider range of reference which makes the terms *oté/olé* important. They do not simply tell direction, they fix buildings and even persons in a global conception of space. They determine a building code in a way no longer common to us which relates the situation of a house to the cardinal directions. It would seem strange to us to think of the objects and person around us in terms of north, south, east, and west; but this is just the usage which is given to the direction indicators in Kédang. Where up and down, right and left, and north and south are different words in English, in Kédangese there are words which combine all these connotations. There are also words to separate them, which shows that categorical association by no means implies confusion. Furthermore, these terms define a system of relations which does not recognize the conceptual distinctions which we make between space and religion or the material and the social. This is shown not only by all the various echoes to be found for the rules orienting a building, but also by the rather far-reaching usages described above for the two words *oté* and *olé* themselves. Spatial orientation in Kédang is then a perfect example of a *total* social phenomenon in Mauss's terms, in which moral, religious, economic, and legal features find expression.

V

VILLAGE OFFICIALS, ELDERS, AND PRIESTS

MY aim in this chapter is to examine the traditional structure of authority. This is to a certain extent a reconstruction, and one lacks the rich material on this subject that
one might have in another society; but this is due to the fact, I
think, that Kédangese ideas on authority, which are of a familiar
Indonesian character, have never received the practical elaboration
which one finds elsewhere. It is best to begin at the most general
level with the distinction between the *léu-auq wala* or 'lord of the
land' and the head of the village.

I. THE LORD OF THE LAND AND THE VILLAGE HEAD

A division of this sort between an office held by the presumed
owner of the village land, invested with ultimate ceremonial
authority, on the one hand and on the other a head of the village,
invested with administrative responsibility, is a common Indonesian feature.[1] In parts of Lamaholot, the system is nearly as
fundamental and as thoroughly developed as it ever appears. In
East Flores the institution is not only an inherent and coherently
related part of the collective representations, as it also is in Kédang,
but it is also essential to the ceremonial procedures and the
definition of land right.

Lord of the Land

In this way East Flores contrasts very usefully with Kédang.
There the head of what is regarded as the original clan, which has
at least nominal rights to all the land, is the lord of the land (*tana
alat*)—in some cases there may be several land-owning clans with
as many lords of the land. All land in possession of this original
clan is called the *tana ekan*, which might best be translated in this
case as 'domain' (*Tana Ekan* is, in fact, the earth goddess in
Lamaholot). Not all the land in this domain will be utilized, but,
nevertheless, any stranger must ask permission before he may

[1] For a review see Scholz 1962.

occupy any part of it. It is usually over 25 sq. km. in size and is bounded in most places by natural barriers. Each domain is divided into a number of *etang*, each of which is a collection of individual fields with a specific name. These *etang* are cultivated in rotation according to the choice of the lord of the land. Almost all of the land in cultivation is in the communal possession of the clan and can be alienated only with the permission of the lord of the land (Arndt 1951: 140–50).

Agriculture ceremonial involves an intricate series of rites which are organized and conducted by the land-owning clan under the direction of its head. Each year he chooses a field which is worked communally by all the clans in the village following strictly prescribed procedures. The communal work on this field serves to insure a good harvest on the others and makes individual rituals at each field superfluous (Vatter 1932: 99–113).

Kédang provides an almost complete contrast to East Flores. In Kédang, as in East Flores, the office of lord of the land in each village is found in the original or eldest clan. Agricultural ceremonial, however, is not communal and the rights of the *léu-auq wala* in the land are entirely nominal. Land-right in Kédang is very similar to that which Arndt describes in Lewo Lein and Wulu Belolong on Solor (1940: 235–8). A person is free to open new land wherever he chooses (subject to certain restrictions imposed by the Department of Agriculture and Forestry). His right in the land is established by clearing it and remains after it has been abandoned, even after years when it is overgrown again by trees and bushes. If another person wishes to use this land, he must ask the owner. The lord of the land has no say of any sort in the question.

The *léu-auq wala* does not receive as tribute a part of the animal offered in an agricultural ceremony, and it appears that he never did, nor does he receive tribute from any other ceremony of a purely individual or clan nature. However, he has the right to receive the head of a turtle, whale or large fish stranded on the beach in his area or the head of a deer which might die on the land in his domain. If a large-scale hunt is organized in his area he may expect to receive a portion of the game. While this is of practical significance in some parts of Kédang, such as the southern and western regions, in Léuwajang there is no good hunting land, and the *léu-auq wala* can expect no hunting tribute.

The only game (other than birds) on the mountain itself now are wild pigs, and these are here subjected to only small-scale hunts, for which no tribute is usually made. The lord of the land will receive a part of the animal offered in a ceremony of village-wide significance. Large community ceremonies are now no longer made, but rain ceremonies are still carried out on a very reduced scale; so, in Léuwajang at least, he does still receive some tribute.

The division of the animal offered in a village ceremony should follow a prescribed form which is itself a symbolic representation of the social order. As an introduction to this question, the opposition between the *léu-auq wala* and the *kapitan dulin* should be mentioned. The office of lord of the land lies in the clan Apé Utung. Though all ten original clans of Léuwajang claim descent from a common ancestor (Telu Beni), Apé Utung is considered the senior. The clan Amun Toda may be traditionally the most junior, though I must admit that I could obtain no firm evidence on this point. *Dulin* is the region stretching from the lower border of *léu tuan* to the beach. Within this region, Amun Toda has certain rights and privileges which Apé Utung has within *léu tuan*. This derives from the fact that traditionally Amun Toda was assigned the task of guarding the door to the village. This clan opens the door for the village going out to war, waits for them to go out and then follows. It comes back first, opens the door, and waits for them to go back in. Presumably because of this role the office held by the clan has been given the (ultimately Portuguese) title *kapitan*. Other than *kapitan dulin*, the office may be called *kapitan aur-mier*. This may be derived from the stand of bamboo (*aur boher*) just below the lower door to *léu tuan*. If this is so, then obviously the term *aur mier* is not confined to the stand of bamboo in the centre of the old village and, reasonably enough, *aur boher* must be a dwelling of the village spirit (*mier-ringa*).

Amun Toda provides the one clear case of a clan being assigned a specific place in the village. (Seegeler 1931: 8 reports a similar office in the traditional structure of the government of the Radja of Larantuka.) Traditionally the clan had to live just outside the walls of *léu tuan*, where it could exercise its function of guarding the door. In fact one very traditional and prominent family of Amun Toda still maintained their residence just outside the wall of the village near the lower door during my stay.

The office of *kapitan dulin* is said to exist in all villages. It carries the right at a burial to break the ground first when the grave is dug. This is done only slightly, and then the work of digging the grave is taken over by others. For this service, the *kapitan dulin* was traditionally paid with a piece of silver or a small coin. It will be remembered that burials are not allowed within *léu tuan*, so this privilege necessarily falls to the *kapitan dulin*.

The present lord of the land told me that at a large scale ceremony at *léu tuan* of village-wide significance, the animals used in the offerings would be divided among the clans of the village in the following manner. Apé Utung, as *léu-auq wala*, receives what is known as the *utu-alé*. These are extremities from various parts of the body, including the jaw (*imin*). Boli Leraq receives the tail, Apé Labi the chest, Hiang Leraq the right side of the head, which it shares with Buang Leraq. Apé Worén gets the left side of the head, which it shares with Apé Liling. Apé Nobé receives a section of the back on the right side, Apé Tatu a section on the left. Amun Toda would receive nothing: however, if there is a large scale village ceremony at the beach, it will receive the portion otherwise reserved for Apé Utung and Apé Utung will get nothing. In either case the three clans which descended from outsiders (*tudéq erun*, 'new arrivals') get nothing particular because they are considered new to the earth (*auq tangén*, 'unripe earth'). This does not mean that they may not share in the feast, but they receive undifferentiated portions in common with other guests. Practically this division means little. No one at such a feast eats less or worse than another.

It is useful at this point to review the symbolic significance of the lord of the land ('lord' more nearly translates the Indonesian *Tuan* than it does the Kédangese *wala* which is a less exalted possessive, but I retain it because it is close to the intention). It has been shown above that he is associated with the inside of the village, as opposed to the *kapitan dulin* who is associated with the outside. Earlier a traditional history was recorded which indicated that the lord of the land lived in the village temple. This indicates an association with the inside in two ways: first with the centre of the village because this is where the temple is located and secondly with the inside of the temple itself. His association with the temple and with the inside indicates that his authority is of a spiritual kind, which is the general significance of this office in Indonesia, and which is in keeping with his role in Kédang within the village government. Finally it has been seen that the clan is ascribed seniority in age, which further reinforces the association with spiritual authority and with the inside.

Village Head

In Léuwajang, the responsibility for the everyday affairs of government lies not with Apé Utung but with the clan Apé Labi. It is characteristic that these two offices be divided in some manner, though this is sometimes (in Lamaholot) effected by assigning them to different lineages of the same clan. It is often recorded in the ethnography of eastern Indonesia that the division is of recent origin and was effected by the colonial government. A review of the information recorded by Arndt from Lamaholot discloses a number of instances where the division is attributed in clearly mythical histories to some form of deceit or trickery. On the other hand, I was told in Wailolong, East Flores that the division was absolutely essential to the well-being of the community. Whatever the particular history of the two offices in any region, the conceptual distinction between them seems to be of fundamental importance, and this may very well be true even in those villages where the offices are in the same clan.

Today the village head bears the title Kepala Desa Gaja Baru, or Head of the New Form Village. Before the administrative re-arrangement of the villages in 1968, the title was Kepala Desa Peradja, Head of the State Village. During the Dutch period, and until 1960, he seems to have borne the title Kepala Kampung, which means simply 'Village Head'. These are all Indonesian terms and are of external imposition. The title as such seems to have no equivalent in the indigenous language, and the office itself seems not to have existed in former times. Its historical ante-cedents are now difficult to trace with certainty. Before the Dutch take-over the men who exercised power similar to that of the village head were war-leaders and designated by the term *mier rian*. The word *mier* is by now familiar, particularly in connection with the *mier-ringa*, the snake-like spirit of the village. The war-leader of the Belu (*meo*) is simply a brave man who gathers a group of younger men around him (Vroklage 1952: 1: 646); and the equivalent in East Flores (*ata běrkint*) is a person of singular aggressiveness and bravery, not an inherited status. There is comparative reason, then, to question whether the office of *mier rian* was necessarily always in the same clan.

In answer to this, there is very little information. The only *mier rian* now remembered in Léuwajang were the last two and they both were in Apé Labi. The second of these seems even to have been appointed to the position, and the first seems to have had an authority in village affairs not confined to times of war. He once even placed himself bodily in the way to obstruct an attack by clans of Léuwajang on the village Atarodang Édang. On the other hand, I would not rule out the possibility that particularly brave men in other clans may formerly have on occasion led war parties and been designated by the term *mier rian*. I have, in any case, been told that the *mier rian*, in at least this sense, need not be in the same clan.

Given then that the historical problems cannot be solved, I would like to suggest the following speculative reconstruction. No certainty is claimed for it however. To introduce it, I will record a report which I received from the present village head of Léudanung, and which is similar to reports received from other areas. In that village the office of village head has recently come into the hands of the largest clan Bunga Laléng (through election, I think). This clan happens also to be regarded as the lord of the land. When I inquired why both offices were in the same clan, I was told that that had been the original arrangement. It may be relevant that in Léudanung, unlike Léuwajang, only one clan claims descent from the original inhabitants, the rest being out-siders. The lord of the land then, according to this version, em-ployed members of the other clans as delegates to arrange external affairs. When the Dutch came in, they misunderstood the situa-tion and appointed these delegates as village head (cf. Vroklage 1952: 1: 555–6, Vatter 1932: 81, Arndt 1940: 233 and van Wouden 1968: 140–1 for very similar reports).

I suggest then that in Kédang the *léu-auq wala* formerly had primary authority in affairs concerning the welfare of the village, but that he was devoid of executive responsibility. His authority was, we have seen, primarily spiritual. Nevertheless, ultimately executive power may have been answerable to him in a way that it is not now. The distinction between the two corresponded, as it does in East Flores, to the distinction between the inside and the outside. Though internal, spiritual authority was clearly invested in a single, hereditarily transmitted office, responsibility for temporal affairs may not have been so specifically attached to a single office or clan. The primary problem of temporal government may well have been the successful prosecution of war. It is unthinkable that the *léu-auq wala* should actually serve as war-leader. That task was left then to men who showed especial strength of body and personality. These may well have appeared in any clan. As war-leader they were clearly delegates of the lord of the land; a war undertaken by the village should be under his ultimate direction. Temporal matters other than war would easily enough be delegated to those who had distinguished themselves by their leadership in war. Thus, a distinction between internal authority and external execution should have led to a more or less enduring investment of temporal power in a given individual.

In Léuwajang, in the last century, one such leader led the village in a highly successful war in aid of Kalikur. His reward was to be sent to Timor to be appointed *fettor*, a sort of lieutenant to the *kapitan*. He chose, on grounds of age, to transmit the privilege and office to another member of the clan (Apé Labi). This led to a situation where the responsibilities of village head were already quite firmly ascribed to Apé Labi when the Dutch arrived. The Dutch were too, after all, only looking for a delegate. What really changed, then, was not so much that the lord of the land lost power to the village head, but that he lost authority itself to the colonial, and later to the Indonesian government.

The office of village head has been kept within Apé Labi during this century except for one short period when it was filled on a temporary and acting basis by a man of another clan. It was not usually passed from father to son, but alternated in an irregular manner between two rather distant lineages. Appointment to office depended upon having the suitable personal qualities and receiving the approval first of the members of Apé Labi, secondly of the village elders, and finally and most importantly of the *kapitan* of Kédang and latterly of the Tjamat. At present, when the office is vacated, a village-wide election must be held in which candidates from any clan are eligible. Such an election has not yet been held in Léuwajang, but it is expected before very long. In other villages, especially those where two villages were combined to make a 'new form' village, where the elections have been held, they have often resulted in the office passing out of the hands of the clan which traditionally held it and into those of the largest clan.

The responsibilities of government figures such as the head of the village are represented in the following ceremonial lines:

> *Uben, kapung oroq-laléng*;   Night, cradle within the chest;
> *Lojo, dongo obi-lolo.*   Day, carry on the back.

He must both shelter the village and carry out the burdensome tasks of government. At present this means that in addition to implementing the directives of the Indonesian government, he must preside over trials for small suits and petty delicts, oversee bridewealth transactions, adjust questions of traditional custom, and represent the village in inter-village cases, bridewealth negotiations, and at feasts. I was rather awed by the amount of work the head of Léuwajang had to accomplish, including supervision of the village census, overseeing the construction of a market, and extensive preparations for the elections of 1971, while still having to support his family in the same manner as everyone else. The job demands character and intelligence, and not every village was so fortunate in its village head as Léuwajang.

These tasks are carried out with the assistance of a set of village officers which include a deputy (*wakil*), several assistants (*pamong*), a secretary (*djuru tulis*), and clerks for each of the clans (*pegawai suku*). This quite recently introduced set of offices has to do with the side of village government which is concerned with the place of the village in modern Indonesian life. More traditional concerns of the village government are still carried out with the assistance of the village elders.

2. ELDERS

These elders are termed *aqé-amé*, but the phrase and its use deserves extended treatment which will reveal a good deal about the social role of age in government. The phrase is made up of two words: *aqé*, which is typically applied to an elder sibling, and *amé*, applied to father and males of his genealogical level within the clan. Age is characteristically associated with authority in Kédang. One should be respectful and obedient to one's elders. The elder males (including elder siblings) in one's clan represent the group whose counsel, and in some cases whose orders, one must particularly heed. Though the term has this broad application, there is also one man (sometimes two) who is recognized as being invested with particular authority in clan matters, especially bridewealth affairs. Though he is by no means necessarily the eldest living member of the clan, he is characteristically among the elder group of still active men, and he is termed *aqé-amé*. Appointment depends upon consensus of the clan. There seems to be no competition; the correct candidate simply emerges. I will later discuss the ceremonial roles ideally—but practically not now (and perhaps never) typically—associated with this figure. All elders of the village are called *aqé-amé léu*; but a more particular use of this term is to apply to the assembled group of these clan leaders (*aqé-amé suku*).

Just as affairs of the clan are managed by careful consultation within the clan and the arrangement of consensus to which all adhere, village affairs are handled by an arranged consensus among the clans. The village head does not impose his will on the village so long as he wishes to remain secure in his position. Although this is the traditional, and very Indonesian, technique of government in Kédang, there have been in this century some extremely headstrong and individualistic village heads in Léuwa-jang; and their reigns were characterized by rebellion and eventually their own deposition. Bridewealth affairs must be arranged in the presence of the assembled *aqé-amé léu* and the principal members of the village government. When there is a case to be settled between two villages, representatives of the *aqé-amé* must be included in the village delegation. Commonly included by tradition in the fine for theft, violence, or the violation of some village-imposed prohibition is the payment of a goat and a quantity (forty litres) of rice. This never goes to the plaintiff (his recompense is a separate part of the fine), but is eaten in a feast attended by the village officials and the *aqé-amé* of all the clans.

3. PRIESTS

There are two additional figures who, though they have no part in the village government, deserve a place in the examination of the traditional structure of authority. These are the two forms of *molan-maran*. The first is the priest, *molan-maran poan-kémir*, and the second is the adept in healing and traditional medicine, *molan-maran potaq-puiq*. In Lamaholot, the term *molan* is applied to the latter of these, the healer. *Marang* is one of four offices among which both ceremonial and governmental functions are distributed. The system is most consistently followed in East Flores, where *koten* ('head') is assigned the lord of the land, who holds the sacrificial animal at the head; *kelen*, who holds its feet, is the village head and war-leader and is responsible for external affairs, *hurit* kills the animal; and *marang* recites the ceremonial chant (Vatter 1932: 81–3; Arndt 1940: 101–2; Ouwehand 1950: 57–8). This system is quite variously applied in other parts of Lamaholot, and on Lembata it became known only because the Dutch introduced it in some regions (Vatter 1932: 82). In Kédang it is not known at all.

The term *marang* (in the form *maran*) is, however, known; as it is also on Alor, where according to Vatter (1932: 237) it means 'priest'. Vatter even suggests that the word is etymologically related to the Lamaholot *molan*, the difference in form being attributed to the *r/l* shift. However that may be, *marang* is related by Arndt to the verb *maring* meaning 'to speak', 'to pray'. Though this verb does not exist in the language of Kédang, it is clear that the word *maran* contains the same idea. One might even give it the gloss 'to speak to the ancestors', if this were not in some ways too restrictive. When making the small conventional offering of food to the ancestors before beginning a meal, one begins the chant with the word *maran*, which by itself is also sufficient.

Etymologically or comparatively, there is little more to find. I will suggest for Kédang that the term *molan* means 'adept in dealing with the spirits'. *Maran* being the means by which one communicates with them, it has been added to complete the name in the traditional form of a dyadic pair. The form of the name for the priest is further qualified by the term *poan-kémir*. The words of this phrase do not yield to analysis either in relation to other words in the language of Kédang or comparatively. It means, however, a ceremonial offering by the priest accompanied by a chant. Another term for the priest is *molan-maran mahu-manuq*. The word *mahu* is conceivably related to the verb *ahu* (which is conjugated), meaning 'to bring something'. I am not certain that this is so, but the context of use makes it appear very plausible. *Mahu-manuq* is used for the throttling of a chicken during the ceremony. A bird (*manuq*) is a common image of the soul in Indonesia (cf. Endicott 1970: 38), and the principal technique of the offering is the calling of the spirits and souls of the ancestors to gather at the site of the ceremony. The killing of the chicken is the climax of this procedure. So I might suggest a translation of this phrase as 'the adept in gathering soul or spirit'.

It is expected that a priest will be an old man. One does not learn to be a priest by taking instruction from other priests; rather one receives one's instruction in dreams. This is normally a long process, lasting over years and proceeding in stages. The priest cannot practise augury with bamboo sticks until he has been instructed in dreams to acquire the sticks. He then goes to the stand of bamboo below *léu tuan* (*aur boher*) and cuts his sticks, which must be of this type of bamboo (*aur*). He cannot then practise the augury (also called *mahu-manuq*) until he has received instruction in its use in dreams. Having received this instruction, he may then be consulted in the search for the causes of ill fortune, but he is not yet prepared to conduct the ceremony necessary to set them right. He must wait until he receives instruction stage by stage in the throttling of a chicken, chanting, inspecting entrails, and so on. The whole collection of techniques and types of ceremony that a really accomplished priest would command is very long.

Concerning instruction in dreams, it must be realized that a member of the community will have witnessed so many ceremonies in his life that without ever being taught he will, if he is intelligent, already have most of what it is needed to know in the back of his mind by the time he may ever begin to act as a priest. Most men, and even many women, can recite a certain amount of the ceremonial language. So the priest does not command an esoteric or secret body of knowledge; and he does not require a lengthy practical training. When he learns through dreaming to become a priest, he simply realizes something equally available to everyone else. I have been told that certain priests, who as individuals are not well liked, did not really dream but only learned by copying others; and an accusation of this sort implies that the priest is not authentically qualified to do his job. It was notable though that these claims did not diminish the demand for their services; and I think it would be impossible as a practical matter to distinguish by means of this criterion between a real priest and a cheat. As the ability to act as a priest is not limited by inheritance, nor is it an arcanum jealously guarded and passed from father to son, dreaming is really the only available means of acquiring the skill; and no one can say what another dreams.

Indeed, I found that there were men who were sufficiently initiated through dreaming to become priests, or nearly so, but who were reluctant to take upon themselves the position. I assume there may be any number of factors of personality (shyness for example) which might lead a man to avoid becoming a priest, but I wish here to recount some of the practical reasons why it is avoided or delayed. Commonly a man will not begin to conduct ceremonies until his children are married and self-sufficient. There are exceptions to this, and I think there are other reasons than those which I here call 'practical', but I will discuss these later. Being a priest is very demanding on one's time and makes it very difficult to work one's own fields. In certain seasons, the priest will be called to perform ceremonies day after day for several weeks. This sometimes occurs just at the time when the fields demand the most attention. Under these conditions it is difficult or impossible to support a family, and some have given this difficulty as the reason why they were actually afraid, as they said, of their dreams and of carrying them to the point of conducting ceremonies.

The second figure is the healer, the *molan-maran potaq-puiq*. In a certain sense, at least in Kédangese terms, he might also deserve to be called a priest. He is also an adept in dealing with the spirits, as his name indicates; and his techniques may include speaking to them. However, he does not chant in a regular manner, nor does he conduct ceremonies. There is no reason why a priest may not also be a healer, but the roles are commonly found separated. It is probably less convenient to combine them; and there is no inherent necessity for doing so. As with the priest, the healer learns his skills through dreaming, although I have been told that in some cases he may receive instruction from another healer. Like the priest's, the office of the healer is not an appointed one, nor is it hereditary. In addition to those men who are recognized adepts, there are many men who possess to a lesser extent some of the same powers. While a woman may not be a priest, *molan-maran poan kémir*, there are recognized women healers. The skill seems also to be less restricted to the elderly.

The term *potaq-puiq* which qualifies this kind of *molan-maran* refers to the technique which this adept employs. *Potaq* means 'to spit' and *puiq* 'to blow'. Each practitioner has his own medicine, which has been revealed to him in his dreams, and other people do not know what it is, even if they see it. In one case (a Muslim), one healer professed not even to know what his root was. He had been told in his dream where to look for it and had gone there and dug his medicine up without recognizing what plant it belonged to. I found another man (not a Muslim) much less secretive. The latter was in fact somewhat of a herbalist and would prepare concoctions about the contents of which he made no secret. Since herbalism is general knowledge anyway, I think there may be reason to keep that separate from this special knowledge of the healer which represents his own relation to this guardian spirit and is by definition individual. Because of their relation to this guardian spirit, they may find the seat of the disease by feeling with the hand. The Muslim practitioner mumbled during his operations, this representing an individual language for communicating with God (in his case). I once overheard him at a stage when I was familiar with the language, and realized that he employed a certain admixture of standard ceremonial language, but the rest was just gibberish. The important point was that no one could understand it, but I found that practitioners who were not Muslim made no use of this secret language. After the seat of the illness has been found the healer then blows and spits all over the body of his patient. The purpose of this procedure could not be readily explained to me, and it will have to be examined in a later section on illness. The healer regards himself, however, as only the agent through which his guardian spirit, or God, cures the patient. They expressly do not guarantee that the patient will be cured; one just has to see if one has had the desired effect.

After this very brief introduction to the two roles, it may be useful to conclude with a consideration of how they are related in the structure of authority. It is first to be remarked that the priest is to a certain extent another of the delegates of the lord of the land. At village ceremonies, it is not the lord of the land who conducts the offerings but a *molan-maran*. Like the war-leader, the priest does not hold an ascribed status, but attains the position through his own personal qualities. The *molan-maran*, however, has nothing (in this capacity at least) to do with the temporal affairs of the village. His realm is unquestionably the spiritual. The healer, however, has none of the qualities of a delegate or official. His clients are always individuals. Though his means of acquiring his skills are very similar to those of the priest, his relation to the world of the spirit is rather different. I think both derive their skill from their guardian spirit, but the priest is in the position to enlist the aid, and temporarily to control, the whole range of the world of the spirit—from the souls of the ancestors to Deity. This he does by means of formal ceremonial and chants. The healer, however, is himself an instrument through which a single spirit works, his own guardian spirit.

VI
DIVINITY, EARTH, AND THE HEAVENLY BODIES

THE people of Kédang have very little which could serve the purposes of a formal theology. When one asks for details concerning the personal characteristics, habitation, intentions of God or of the role He takes in human life, one receives almost nothing in answer. Only rarely are any of the names of God mentioned in the ceremonial chants, and one never encounters in the chants the lengthy accounts of His features and powers and the reasons of His actions which Arndt has recorded from Lamaholot (1951). Generally God is remote, and only rarely does He manifest Himself directly. Lacking, then, any detailed description to start out with, the investigation of Divinity in Kédang will have to consist of a lengthy examination of a variety of evidence, and only after having reached the end of this can it be hoped that we can know what it represents for Kédang.

The name for God, as in the languages of so many other eastern Indonesian peoples, is made up of the words for the sun and the moon: *Ula-Lojo*. Even in this Kédang distinguishes itself from its neighbours in Lamaholot. There the word for sun precedes that for moon (*Lera Wulan*), whereas in Kédang *Ula-Lojo* would have to be translated 'moon-sun'. Furthermore, in Lamaholot *Lera Wulan*, who represents the firmament or the upper regions, is opposed to *Tana Ekan*, representing the earth and the lower world. *Lera Wulan* and *Tana Ekan* appear to represent the two aspects of a single, unitary Godhead, rather than two quite distinct divinities. In this way Lamaholot concepts of Divinity appear to be very similar to those of the Ngadju Dayak of Borneo, described by Schärer (1963). In Kédang, however, there is no equivalent to *Tana Ekan*. Indeed, when I asked for the equivalent, I was told that it must be *léu-auq*, but though this does show some similarity in idea, it is never used to refer to a deity.

I was once told that in Kédang they prefer to ask help from the land because it is close and familiar and they can get what they ask very soon. If they ask the sky, it would take much longer, perhaps a year, to get it. On this ground, I will reverse what might otherwise seem the logical procedure, and try to give an account of what the earth means to them before I turn to *Ula-Lojo* and the heavenly aspects of Divinity.

I. THE EARTH

The Lamaholot name *Tana Ekan* consists of *tana* which means 'land', 'fields', 'earth', and *ekan*, which is often employed in the same sense; it also means 'evening', 'darkness', 'obscurity' (Leemker 1893: 431, 456; Vatter 1932: 92). *Tana Ekan* herself is described as a blood-sucker and a corpse-eater (Arndt 1951: 247), and blood offerings are made to her. She is at the same time the provider of the riches of the field, and her fertile and macabre sides are directly linked in ceremonial.

The Kédangese *léu-auq*, as has been shown, refers to the land and in a more restricted sense to the village. Although the term is never used to address or refer to Deity, it can be shown that in some ways similar ideas are associated with it. I have already mentioned that the spirit of the village takes the form of a snake and that when an enemy is killed he may be taken back to the village to feed this spirit. I will later describe a ceremony performed at the beginning of the rainy season in which the *léu tuan* is sealed and cleaned in order to ensure the fertility of the crops. It has also been shown that the mountain is considered a source of life and that the original men are said to have emerged from the earth, and mention has been made of the association between life and death to be found at the top of the mountain, particularly in the shaft or hole *wélong*.

There is a word, *uhé*, which means 'the inside of the earth' and is particularly evocative of the earth's life-giving powers. This occurs in the traditional account of the structure of the universe. In Kédang it is said that there are seven levels above the earth and five below. Each level is an earth like our own. When someone dies on this earth, he is reborn on the earth below; when he dies there, he is reborn on the earth below that. This continues until he reaches the bottom level. When he dies there, his body becomes a fish and his soul goes back up to heaven. It is thought that he then repeats the cycle starting at the top layer. (Arndt reports a very similar tradition in Lamaholot 1951: 57, 193). This tradition is formulated in the following lines:

Uhé dan pitu,	Core of the earth, seven levels,
Ara dan lemé	Heart of the earth, five levels.

An earthquake (*néju-déju*) is said to be caused when a bird flies under the earth and tells the man who is holding up the earth that all the men above are dead. The man then shakes the stalk (*auq puén,* 'trunk of the earth') which supports the earth to see if this is true. Arndt says that the Lamaholot tradition is that the earth is supported by *Tana Ekan* or by a snake. When there is an earthquake everyone shouts (as we, ourselves, witnessed), '*É beq, é beq!*', 'We are here, we are here!' This then is to let the being below who is shaking the earth know that mankind is still alive.

I have already dealt at some length with gold (*werén*) and its connection with the waters of life. I want now to elaborate on this theme to show that life, fertility, and wealth are in many ways equated in Kédang, all being gifts from the earth. I was told on one occasion that the ancestors believed that there is a great treasure of gold hidden beneath the earth. There is every reason to think that the guardian spirit (*mier-ringa*) of *léu tuan* is associated with this treasure. I was told that this snake may *nado-tado*, that is, he may open his mouth and the gold inside will rise up in the form of a rainbow. It has been mentioned that a rainbow may rise from the golden pot at the source of the spring *wei rawé*, and there are other possible golden sources of rainbows. In addition to *nado-tado*, there are several synonymous phrases for this sort of radiant luminosity, and they each provide a key to interpretation. It is not, however, just a rainbow in our terms which is in question, but any form of resplendent light, such as the yellow light sometimes seen on stormy days. The full set is *nado-tado, lair-kéu, ihin-werén, matan-méan.*

Nado-tado has been translated. Unfortunately, there is no immediately obvious translation for the word *lair*. I at first mistook the word for *laqin*, meaning 'high'; and I am not yet convinced that there is no connection between the two, as the latter form would make a good deal of sense. It is just barely possible that it is related to the Lamaholot word meaning 'pure' (spelled variously by the sources *lae, laien, lain*). *Kéu* means 'to climb', 'rise'; and this is the essential meaning of this term; it is the rising effulgence into which any guardian snake may transform itself. *Ihin* is the Indonesian *isi*, meaning 'contents'. In Kédangese it means particularly 'meat'; and *werén* ('gold', etc.) is the regular dyadic completion. *Matan* will later receive particular attention in connection with the word *puén* ('trunk', 'base', 'source'). It means 'eye', 'source', 'origin', and occurs in an extremely wide number of contexts. *Méan* in Kédangese is a superlative, as in the phrase *alu méan* ('extraordinarily good', i.e. better than just *alu rasa*, 'very good'). It seems to be found in many neighbouring languages, but surprisingly rarely with exactly the same meaning. In Lamaholot it means 'red', but a *kewatek mean* is the finest form of woman's sarong (Vatter 1932: 52). Not only is the word unrelated to the Kédangese *putuq* ('red'); but in Lamaholot red has an entirely different cultural meaning from that which it has in Kédang. In any case it often seems associated there with extraordinary powers (such as bravery) or wealth. The Lionese word seems to mean 'to grow' (Arndt 1933); in Ngada it means, among other things, 'extraordinary' (Arndt 1961). In Tetun, the language of the Belu of Timor, it means 'golden', 'valuable' (Vroklage 1952: 1: 576), 'red', 'strong', 'robust', 'healthy'. 'Indeed, God, Himself, is also called *mean*' (1952: 2: 7). *Matan-méan* are all forms of extraordinary wealth of which golden objects are particularly representative. It includes also the products of the fields, *tawan-méan* (*tawan* derives from *tawé*, 'to grow', 'to laugh').

This set of synonymous phrases allow the establishment of the following equations: wealth of all forms (clothing, jewellery, ivory tusks, and so on) = products of the field = meat = gold = fluids of life. In addition, this set is associated with snakes, luminosity, and spirit.

These connections are also demonstrated by a certain class of found objects, *talu-beru*. These come to people particularly when they are elderly. They are usually presaged by a dream, in which the person is visited by a spirit (such as Laba Lia, Divinity in the form of the morning star) and told where to look. I have seen many of these things and they are characteristically very ordinary objects. Their significance is, however, far from ordinary; it was always emphasized that they were things, 'gotten oneself' (Ind., *dapat sendiri*); they just suddenly appear without warning in one's tobacco pouch, in a bowl of rice, or between one's toes while walking. A representative group of items would include perhaps a candlenut, a highly polished pebble, a lead ball for a muzzle-loading rifle, a piece of broken bottle glass, an old ear-ring.

However, no matter how ordinary the type, what is important is that the particular object is thought entirely unique and extra-ordinary for its class. Finding these things is commonly associated with certain changes of a spiritual character and the adopting of a range of food prohibitions and ceremonial obligations. These will be described later. What is of especial interest now is that these things which just materialize are thought of as emerging from the earth, and gold is considered particularly representative for the whole class.

One of my friends had a Chinese plate which had been found by his grandmother and which depicted a dragon. This would *nado-tado* ('emit a rainbow') if it were rained on. Particularly apt to do this is a sort of chain made of plaited copper or golden wire, which seems once to have been brought in by traders. I have seen one of these on Flores, and they appear to be common on Sumba (Onvlee 1949: 448). On Sumba they are thought of as snakes (Adams 1969: 38), as they are also in Kédang. They are called *aba*, and they can also *nado-tado* if put in the house. If one allows it to do so, it will eat the grain stored in the house, but only rice or millet, not maize. It can be killed by being put in a bamboo container and roasted (*dajuq*) in the fire (as they do meat). That it will not harm maize is a sign that maize remains, even in Kédang, something of a foreign object. It also indicates that traces of familiar Indonesian ideas about the soul of rice are still to be found in Kédang, and suggests that the spirit of *aba* is connected with it.

Many of these ideas associated with gold are demonstrated in the Kédang version of the myth of the tree of wealth, which I give here.

The Tree of Wealth

There were once two orphans, a girl named Tuéng Lélu ('To Spin Thread') and a boy Hau Kaéq ('To Shave a Bamboo Water-Container'), who were abandoned as infants to be raised by other people.

When they were old enough to walk, they went out into the forest where they found a civet cat. This they raised and kept until it died. When it was dead, they took the pupils of its eyes (*mato uluq*) and buried them in front of the door of their house (*wetaq maqur-matan*); the rest of the body they threw away.

In four days, the pupils of the eyes grew into a tree (*ai naré*, Ind., *kaju ansana*). The tree's blossoms were golden chains (*abalodon*), its fruits were golden ear-rings (*laong werén*), its leaves were cloth (*tola*, i.e. expensive sarongs), its trunk and branches were elephant tusks (*bala*).

At this time traders from Lamahala (on Adonara) came to sell their wares in the market. But the two children would not buy because their own clothing was much finer.

The traders asked to be taken to see the tree, where they saw that it bore goods far finer than their own and were humiliated. They decided then to destroy it so that they could again sell their goods. But their axes would not cut it, nor could they dig it up. Therefore, they returned and got their billows. They then built a huge fire at the base of the tree and kept it hot with the billows. In this way they burned the tree in two. The top fell to the west and landed in Europe, while the base remained in Kédang.

The Europeans ran to strip the tree of its branches and leaves, therefore the people of *Sina Puén, Sawa Matan* ('China the trunk, Java the source'; i.e. the West including Asia and Europe) became rich because of this tree. The base remains at *wei laong* ('ear-ring stream', just below the hamlet, Édang), where it is guarded by the *ular naga* and the *ara bora*. The roots of the tree reach into the sea where they remain today. At night when passing in a boat, one may see the roots glowing on the bottom of the sea, and in order to pass one must make an offering (*wajaq doping*) to the *ara bora*. If the boat is carrying rice or maize, then a little must be dropped in the water. If the offering is not made, then the boat will not reach the land.

This tree is sometimes referred to as the 'tree of gold' (*ai werén*). The myth of a tree of wealth or gold is common on Flores (cf. Piet Pitu 1969: 177–82), but this version is easily interpreted in terms of Kédangese concepts. It is particularly interesting that the tree springs from the pupils of the cat's eyes (*mato uluq*); *uluq* actually means 'seed', and *matan* (to which *mato* is related) commonly means 'source' or point of transition. We have here both a linguistic and a mythical analogy drawn between the eye and the origin of wealth. Secondly, the image of the tree is employed, which means that these kinds of wealth are—like the products of the field—organically connected with the earth. Of course it should be noted that the story provides a convenient rationale for the superior wealth of foreigners (not just Europeans, Javanese, and Chinese, but also the traders from Lamahala), and points out that the source of that wealth is still Kédang, even if the people of Kédang are poor.

2. THE HEAVENS

If the earth then is the source of wealth and fertility, which means that it is primarily concerned with bringing into being, the heavens are principally concerned with regulating events. Before I demonstrate this, I should mention certain traditions about the separation of the two. It is said that at first the sky was close to the earth: *auq werun*, 'when the earth was new', *eléng déhiq*, 'the sky was close'. They used to climb the pinang palm or the aerial roots of the banyan to *eléng ajaq* ('the centre of the sky') to get fire. For some reason (which could not be remembered), these roots were cut, and the earth and sky separated.

The banyan at the top of *léu tuan*, called *béu ula-lojo*, has been mentioned. This represents the banyan in the moon. Formerly when the sky was much lower it seems to have been this banyan which provided access to the sky. It is disappointing that very little more is known of this tradition in Léuwajang. Such a tradition seems to be common in eastern Indonesia in association with a tradition that the rain from the sky which fertilizes the land is the sky's semen. I could uncover absolutely no overt evidence of the presence of this idea of sexual intercourse between the sky and the earth. When I asked about it, it was expressly denied; and agricultural ritual revealed no sign of it. However, the idea that the sky was formerly close to the earth plays an important part in the ceremony for erasing the consequences of incest. *Ula-lojo* in fact is a very coarse term for incest, which can be understood as an elliptical way of saying that incest is like bringing the sky down to earth. The symbolism of the incest ceremony turns on this idea, and consists of reconnecting the sky and earth (through the agency of a piece of aerial root from a banyan standing for *béu ula-lojo*) and then severing the connection.

The only account which I could get of this tradition was a brief summary of a myth said to be characteristically associated with the village Léuhoéq. According to this account, during one rainy season the village had no maize to eat and the clouds lay low over the village (as they do every year at this time). The villagers thought *ula-lojo* had descended, and in order to get it to go back up, they took an arrow, the point of which was made of the bone of a dead ancestor and the shaft from a stalk of millet (*weréq*). This they shot into the sky, which then returned to its proper position.

The myth in its original form surely must be rich in useful symbolic associations; and it is sad that the present version is so inadequate. Nevertheless, we have enough to know that the separation of the earth and the sky was necessary for the coming into being of the world, and the original state is comparable to incest. This presents a conceptual situation like that which has been demonstrated for the summit of the mountain. It also suggests that we may find that the heavenly bodies will stand in many ways in opposition to the earth.

The school of Christian ethnology deriving from Father Schmidt adheres to the doctrine of original monotheism, and there have been a number of studies devoted to the High God of particular Indonesian peoples. It is more difficult to impose this conception of Divinity in Kédang than it is in Lamaholot, where a good deal of enthusiasm is commonly shown for equating Lera Wulan with the Christian or Muslim God. While this is also done to some extent in Kédang, the material one has to rely on tends rather to leave this conception unemphasized. The Arabic name for God is sometimes employed in Kédang as in many other parts of Indonesia. Here it occurs in the full form *Tuhan Allah, Lahatala*. Otherwise, traditional names are employed, and these are characteristically made from the names for the sun, moon, and morning star. Most prominent of course is *Ula-Lojo* ('Moon-Sun'). Among others are *Lojo Rian* ('Great Sun'); *Lojo Bujaq* ('White Sun'); *Lia-Lojo* ('Morning Star-Sun'); *Lia Rian* ('Great Morning Star'). Although these terms are considered in some contexts as identical, in others they may be treated as being different. Even the term *Ula-Lojo* may be broken into its parts, and each treated as having opposed characteristics to the other.

This is seen for instance in the contest between the sun and the moon recounted in the beginning of the story of Pulau Lama Léqang. There it is shown that the moon, as distinct from the sun, is a witch and an eater of corpses. I was once told that the sun raises and cares for man (*lojo paro até-diqén*), whereas the moon, which eats fish, may also eat men when the fish are finished.

It should be noted that the fish are sometimes said to be the form taken by corpses and lost souls. In the contest between the sun and the moon, just mentioned, the sun argues that the moon is a witch for the following reasons. The moon is half blossom (i.e. human), half witch; now full, now new. The sun claims he rises in the east and sets in the west (*bohor beli*, 'rises over the mountain', *béuq bewé*, 'sets at sea'); by this he means that he always rises and sets in the same place, whereas the moon constantly changes his place of rising, appearing sometimes in the evening first over the mountain, sometimes over the sea. Sometimes the moon is old, sometimes young, whereas the sun is never older and never younger. Since these claims are true, when the moon drops a woman down to the earth (attempting an act of creation), his woman lands in the centre of the sky and shatters into mosquitoes, gnats, ants, lizards, snakes, and other such vermin. The sun, however, wins the contest, and in his attempt at creation, his woman proves to be a true object of gold (*ihin-werén, matan-méan*) and lands safely on earth in the top of a banana tree. The sun, that is, could draw from his granary, which at the beginning of the story the moon had inspected and seen to be full of golden riches and products of the field (*ihin-werén, matan-méan, utan-watar*; the latter is 'beans and maize'). The moon though is devoid of creative potential, and when the sun inspected the moon's granary, he found nothing but skeletons (*matén lurin*) stacked high like the ears of maize. The moon's granary, instead of being full of life-giving wealth, products of care and labour, held nothing but the useless remains of victims of the moon's destructive rapaciousness.

There are no stories of the origin of the sun and the moon, and I could get no opinions on this question. I also found no clear idea of the sex of the moon. The sun is male (cf. Appendix I). From this can be inferred that in so far as the moon stands in opposition to the sun, it must be female. In Lamaholot, there seems to be no definite doctrine on this question, and it is once mentioned that the sun is a woman and the moon a man (Arndt 1951: 59). Perhaps there is really no reason why an invariable association should be made. They are both manifestations of Divinity, and when taken together in one phrase form a name for Him. I think we can conclude that for the Kédangese there are really a number of different levels of reference which can be found for the words sun and moon. Taken at the most undifferentiated level, as in the phrase *Ula-Lojo*, they mean simply Divinity; I found no more inclusive term than this for the Godhead. At this stage, *Ula-Lojo* also represents the heavens as opposed to the earth. This seems then to introduce the first distinction within Divinity itself. I have dealt at some length with the fact that the earth is concerned with bringing into being, that is, with the execution of becoming. Through the association of gold and the waters of life with the woman, and on the model of neighbouring Lamaholot, we may assume that the earth is, for the people of Kédang, feminine. The heavens on the other hand can be shown to be concerned with governing this process of becoming, and God appears on occasion as an old man, indicating that the heavens are masculine (it has already been shown that the above and maleness are equated, and the below and femininity). Events are regulated by the heavens. Various of the heavenly bodies are involved in the several means of observing change which would come under our word 'time'. This introduces further distinctions, which are paralleled by divisions in the manifestations of Divinity.

The Sun

In this the sun remains concerned primarily only in the eternally constant changes which make up the course of the day. The yearly motion of the sun along the horizon between the two solstices is observed, but neither the solstices nor the equinoxes are marked or associated with any stage of the calendar. Only in one way does this motion serve to mark time, and this only in an approximate way. In Léuwajang, when the sun has moved so far south in its rising that it comes up over the mountain, it is considered about the time to begin planting; but the sun is only one of the signs observed in this connection, and not the most important. This is not a solstice, it should be noted, as it occurs almost a month earlier.

I give here a table showing the recognized stages of the day and night. This table shows, by the way, that Nilsson (1920: 17) is wrong when he says the sleeping time 'has no separate parts' and that it 'appears as an undivided unit, a point'.

The right-hand column gives approximate times by the clock. This is to serve only to orient the reader and does not define Kédangese terms. It will be realized that the categories of time in Kédang in no way imply a mechanical precision.

TABLE I

Stages of the day in Kédang

Tutun padu noléq udéq	The first stick of a resin torch is lit	Around 7.00 p.m., before the evening meal
Tutun padu noléq sué	The second stick of a resin torch is lit	Perhaps 9.00 or 10.00 p.m.
(*Tutun paelu noléq telu*)	(The third stick of a resin torch is lit)	(Later)
Uben doa; manuq kokoq wowo udéq	Late evening, the first cock's crow	Around 11.00 p.m.
Uben ajaq	Midnight	12.00
Manuq kokoq wowo suéq	The second cock's crow	Perhaps 2.00 a.m.
Manuq kokoq wowo telu, etc.	The third cock's crow, etc.	
Éqa naun; ribo-rabo	Day soon; twilight	Between 4.00 and 5.00 a.m.
Manuq kokoq rotaq	The cocks crow continually	About 5.00 a.m.
Manuq doq; éqa nihon huang	The chickens descend, the day is clear, but the sun has not yet appeared (lit., 'the day plays at lighting')	Before 6.00 a.m., by now everyone is up
Lojo bohor	Sunrise	Between 6.00 and 7.00 a.m.
Lojo bohor laqi	The sun has risen high	Perhaps 8.00 to 10.00 a.m.
Lojo panan	The sun is hot	About 10.00 a.m. to 2.00 p.m.
Lojo ajaq	The sun is in the centre of the sky	Noon
Lojo hepaq	The sun descends slightly	About 1.00 p.m.
Lojo wehéq	The sun is low	After 3.00 p.m.
Lojo wehéq emi; lojo béuq	The sun is low and cold, the sun is descending	After 5.00 p.m.
Lojo wehéq uma	The sun is low and the light is getting yellow	Just before sunset
Lojo heléng	Sunset	Around 6.00 p.m.
Wau aruq	Faces can no longer be recognized	After 6.30 p.m.

The table speaks for itself and requires very little analysis. It can be seen that the passage of time within the twenty-four-hour period is observed by reference to a quite various collection of events. These are drawn from the animal and human realms as well as from the course of the sun. Even though it is very nearly true, it is still not quite enough to say that time is told by reference to natural signs. It may be noted that the Kédangese can also estimate the passage of time at night by observing the apparent motion of the heavens.

The Moon

Nilsson remarks that, 'The moon is indeed the first chronometer . . .' (1920: 148). In Kédang the moon is, before any other heavenly body, associated with change. This is shown not only by its role in the yearly calendar, but in a number of expressions connecting it with human activities and biological processes. The name for moon is *ula* or *wula*; it is the same as in many other Indonesian languages (e.g. Lamaholot, *wulan*, Ind., *bulan*). It lends its name to menstruation, and in the form *meti ula* ('stage of the moon'), applies to any important physical change a person may undergo. Before going into these usages, I think it may be useful to describe how the stages of the moon are actually figured.

Nilsson says that the quadripartite division of the month is practically non-existent among primitive peoples (1920: 171). Indeed, in Kédang the moon is essentially divided into just two phases, these being the waxing and the waning moon. What the Kédangese call 'the new moon' (*ula werun*) refers to the entire period of the waxing moon. The full phrase is *ula werun kéu katiq déi uliq*, 'the moon is new and changing the starting-point of its path to a higher one'. The waning moon is called *ula halaq*, which means the moon has been 'put up'. I was told that the waning moon is called *ula halaq* because it is still visible after sun-up. Each phase is considered to consist of fifteen days, and the full month consists of thirty. Each of these thirty days is reckoned a sort of stage itself, for which the word *léu*, otherwise meaning 'village', is employed. Thus, the ninth day of the waxing moon is called *ula werun kéu léu lemé-apaq* ('the ninth stage or village of the new and rising moon'). Similarly the fourth day of the waning moon is *ula halaq léu apaq* ('the fourth stage of the moon which has been put up').

The full moon is *ula opol-tudaq* ('round'). When the moon rises after sunset, this is called *ula peréng*. When it begins to get small it is called *meti utu* ('becoming small') or *meti éhoq auq laléng* ('getting smaller and [disappearing] into the ground'). When the moon disappears it is called *ula miténg* ('black moon').

Any of these stages may be called *meti ula*, and for this reason I translate the term 'stage of the moon'. It also may mean the tides; high tide is *meti kéu* ('in the stage of rising'), low tide *meti majaq* ('in the stage of dryness'). They recognize that the tides follow the moon and that there are two tides a day. *Meti ula* or *tada meti* ('sign of the stage', cf. Ind., *tanda*) may also mean 'to fish'. This comes from the fact that fishing is best during the two biggest tides of the month (cf. Fox 1968: 66; on Roti *meti* means 'tide').

Meti ula is also a euphemism for pregnancy. This though derives from a much broader usage. Each stage of pregnancy from conception to parturition is *meti ula*, as is also each stage of the child's growth. Even any illness one may have in life (whether one is an adult or child) and eventually death may be designated by this term. It is clear that this wide range of uses is not fortuitous; behind it lies the conception that all changes are directly related to the changes undergone by the moon. It is hardly surprising then that one of the terms for menstruation is *ula-malé adan* ('the coming of the moon-star').

The direct relation between the moon and human development was made clear to me in two instances. One of these which will be more fully described later concerns the fact that the soul of an infant (*nawaq*) is likened to a young shoot, which grows higher in the body as the moon changes, thus bringing about the developments by which he acquires teeth, learns to crawl, walk, speak, and so on. The second is that the moon during an eclipse is said to take the soul (*ku nawaq*) of an important man. This is the common idea that an eclipse or other such unusual happening will be followed by the death of a rich or powerful person. The word for the eclipse (*ula maté*) means in fact that the moon dies.

In Kédang as elsewhere, a moon eclipse will be accompanied by beating gongs and making loud noises. I never heard that it is explicitly thought of as the death of God, as is to be concluded from a song Arndt recorded on Solor (1951: 196–7). In Kédang they sing a song at this time requesting the moon to return to life and to awaken, but it is accompanied by such a cheerful and lilting melody, that it is hard to imagine that they are ever really frightened by an eclipse.

Ula bita hokoq,	Moon live awaken,
Ula mori mari ko, mari ko,	Moon come back, come back,
Ula mori mari ko.	Moon came back.

It is known that eclipses of the sun occur, but most people insisted that nothing would be done and no gongs would be beaten on such an occasion. It seems puzzling that so little attention would be given such an eclipse, but that this is actually so would seem to be supported by Mallinckrodt who witnessed the eclipse of the sun of 21 September 1922 in Borneo. He says that it made hardly any impression on the population; there was some beating of gongs, but to nowhere near the extent as during a moon eclipse he had witnessed during 1920 (1924: 579).

The role of the moon in regulating the calendar will be described below in connection with the Pleiades and Antares. The following are brief introductions to other significant objects in the sky.

'Malé Tené' (Ursa Major)

This name means literally 'the boat star', a name it has in other Indonesian languages as well. Only the four bright stars which form the torso of the Great Bear are recognized, and they are conceived to be a boat. In the southern hemisphere Ursa Major is visible along the northern horizon, where, during the course of a night (during the period when it rises in the evening, from January to March), as it moves across the sky it appears to turn upside-down. The fact that it appears in inverted positions in the sky gives rise to the tradition that there are two *malé tené: malé tené diqén*, 'the good boat star', that is, when it stands upright as during the evening rising, and *malé tené datén*, 'the bad boat star', the inverted position. These two versions of *malé tené* are sometimes equated with the good and bad aspects of the personal guardian spirit (*nimon-narin diqén* and *nimon-narin datén*).

At the beginning of December, the rising *malé tené* is just visible in the early morning sky. Throughout December it rises earlier each night, until in the middle of January it begins to appear before midnight. Its reappearance is therefore approximately associated with the early stages of the rainy season, and it is thought that it disturbs children at this time and causes them to cry. It does coincide with the period of worst weather and greatest hunger, and it did seem to us that the children in the village cried more often at this time.

It is also feared that *malé tené*, which is sometimes considered bad in itself, and is not distinguished into good and bad, will disturb a pregnant woman by making her dream or not allowing her to sleep. For this reason (as well as the fear of witches), she may not sleep alone. If one sees *malé tené datén* ('the bad boat star'), especially while tapping palm wine, while in a boat or if one is pregnant, one must not point at it (*karéq*). If one does so, one will fall from the trees, have a disaster at sea or the birth will be unfortunate.

'*Popoq*' (*the Pleiades*) and '*Pari*' (*Antares*)

Andree (1893: 362) in his study of the Pleiades remarks that no other constellation is so significant; they are associated with planting and the yearly calendar in Oceania, Asia, Africa, and South America. It is reported that certain tribes in South America observe both the Pleiades and the constellation Scorpion for determining the seasons of the year (Lévi-Strauss 1964: 249), and the same is reported of Atjèh and the Toba Batak on Sumatra (Snouck Hurgronje 1893: 1: 267–78; Winkler 1913). The traditional calendar of Sumatra is, in fact, very similar to that of Kédang.

The Pleiades stand opposite the sun in the sky during the second half of November; this means that they rise in the evening just after sunset. From then on they rise earlier, so that at sunset they appear higher in the sky each night. Simultaneously they set earlier in the morning, until at the end of February they set about midnight. In the second half of May, the Pleiades stand near the sun, and therefore rise and set with the sun. They are then completely invisible. After this point they rise earlier and earlier in the morning before sun-up, until by the end of August they stand midway in the sky when the morning sun appears. The constellation Scorpion stands almost directly opposite the Pleiades in the sky, and it rises in the evening in May just as the Pleiades disappear from the sky. Its period of best visibility is during our summer months, and it finally disappears at the end of November, just as the Pleiades begin to rise again at sunset.

This pattern is recognized in Indonesia and is the basis of a number of myths explaining why the two are separated (cf. Arndt 1951: 62–5). I did not get a version of this myth in Kédang, but I was told that *popoq* (the Pleiades) and *pari* (Antares) were ordered not to rise and set together, for reasons which my informant did not remember. There is in fact an aphorism in which the opposition of the morning and evening star is compared to that of the Pleiades and Antares:

Uno kéu, lia heléng;	The evening star rises, the morning star sets;
Popoq kéu, pari heléng.	Pleiades rise, Antares sets.

Curiously the Pleiades are called *Wuno* in Lamaholot, a word which in Kédang is used for the evening star.

That the Pleiades and the morning star, and by implication also Antares and the evening star, are manifestations of God is indicated by the following line from the ceremonial language: *Lia huraq manusia, Popoq libur até-diqén*, '*Lia* (the morning star) created mankind, *Popoq* (the Pleiades) protects humanity.' The acts of creating and protecting are separated to fit the structural parallelism of the ceremonial language, but the intention is that they are two aspects of the same thing. In the same way, this line indicates that the Pleiades and the morning star are two aspects of the same thing; and the context shows that they are in fact aspects of Divinity.

The rising of the Pleiades at sunset in late November is the most important sign that the rainy season is approaching and that the time for planting is nearing. This is expressed in the phrases *lojo heléng, popoq hering* ('the sun sets, the Pleiades rise'). This marks the beginning of planting season. Later when the Pleiades rise about an hour before sunset, it is time to stop planting:

Popoq kéu eréng-pehé,	the Pleiades rise before sunset,
Miwaq mai, baing mai.	Planting is over, seeding [rice] is over.

The Pleiades are said to have the rainy season to themselves; while Antares has the dry season. The last rain of the rainy season is called *popoq heléng* ('the Pleiades set'). When Antares first rises in the evening, it is time for picking the beans and the new food ceremonies (*a weru-wéhar*).

During the rainy season, the passage of time is not reckoned in months (the moon is not easily observed), but through the very approximate method of observing the various storms, for which there are a series of names. The dry season, however, allows the observation of the passing months, and each month is reckoned (as on Sumatra) by the stage in which the moon comes in conjunction with Antares (actually, when it appears in the constellation scorpion—cf. Snouck Hurgronje 1893: 1: 273). This means that the Kédangese have a calendar based on the sidereal year. Nilsson remarks that when the rising of the Pleiades is used to mark the beginning of the year, this sidereal year 'is obtained at once with the greatest accuracy that is possible without scientific observation' (1920: 274). It is true too when Antares is employed. In Kédang it is not the exact number of months in a year (which they recognize as twelve), but the annual passage of the stars which regulates their calendar. For this reason, the intercalation of the calendar is of no concern to them. Both the Pleiades and Antares serve to mark the two *nu néjéng* (translated for me as 'time boundary', Ind., *batas waktu*) which divide the year in half. In this regard, Leach must be wrong when he says, 'Most primitive peoples can have no feeling that the stars in their courses provide a fixed chronometer by which to measure all the affairs of life' (1961: 133).

Antares, then, is used to keep track of the months of the dry season in this manner. The synodic month, or the interval between two new moons, averages over 29 days and 12 hours. The sidereal month, or the interval between two successive moments at which the moon culminates in the same spot and at the same time as the same star, is over 27 days and 7 hours. There is a difference then of about 2 days between these two types of month. This means then that the moon comes in conjunction with a specific star a little more than 2 days earlier each synodic month, or that the moon appears to be 2 days younger each time it does so. The path of Antares through the sky is near the heavenly equator; thus the moon travels very much the same path and is enabled to arrive at the same spot in the sky once every sidereal month (or about 13 times a year). During the end of May, Antares rises about sunset; this means that the moon will come in conjunction with it just about the point at which it is full. The next month Antares rises a little before sunset and will then appear higher in the sky. The moon will then come into conjunction with it before its own evening rising, and will thus appear (2 days) newer. This proceeds for 7 months, until Antares disappears in late November. I have described how for the Kédangese each day of the moon has a number. By their reckoning then each month of the dry season is characterized by the number of the day in which the moon comes in conjunction with Antares. Thus our May is called *pulaq-lemé ka* ('fifteenth stage of the waxing moon'). *Ka*, which otherwise means 'to eat' or 'bite', is always used for measurement; thus, there is no clear allusion to the moon eating Antares, as one might otherwise think. This proceeds by a regular reduction of number until *telu* or *udéq ka* ('third or first stage of the waxing moon'),[1] which is a sign of the time to begin planting.

The facts of nature themselves assure that there will be a regular reduction of between 2 to 3 days in the stage of the moon, but there is nothing which entails the counting by odd numbers. The estimation of the stage of the moon in conjunction with the star is not so precise that it is possible to say (at least when measuring with the naked eye) that it is the fifteenth and not the fourteenth day on which the conjunction occurs, and the conjunctions do not as a matter of fact always occur on uneven days. This then is a factor, completely extraneous to the workings of nature, which is introduced for purely cultural reasons. It will constitute an important piece of evidence for the eventual discussion of the meaning of odd and even numbers.

The regulation of the calendar of Atjèh by the conjunction of Antares with the moon has been superbly described and explained by Snouck Hurgronje (1893: 1: 267–79), and the reader is recommended to consult his monograph. Of interest are his tables giving the dates of the conjunctions (in the language of Atjèh, *keunòngs*) for the years 1892 and 1893 (pp. 269–70). In Atjèh, they begin their reckoning of the calendar (in January) with what they consider the conjunction of Antares with the moon on its twenty-third day. In Kédang, they do not regard conjunctions before the simultaneous rising of the full moon and Antares around May. Therefore, they are not faced with the problem of adjusting the number of conjunctions in a sun-year to those in a moon-year. What is of particular interest in the comparison is that the people of Atjèh too reckon the successive conjunctions only in terms of uneven numbers (pp. 272–3).[2]

---

[1] The actual conjunction of Antares with the full moon is in late May or early June. It sometimes occurs that there are 8 rather than 7 conjunctions from May through November, and the November conjunction may be regarded in Kédang as on either the third or first day of the waxing moon.

[2] It can be concluded from the fact that the conjunction which marks the beginning of planting is called *gan toü*, which Arndt misleadingly translates 'eats one', that in Lamaholot the conjunctions are also counted with only odd numbers (Arndt 1951: 148).

The names for the Pleiades and Antares are used in other connections which are interesting. *Popoq* also is used for several types
of beggars' lice, a usage which I suggest is based on the idea that
the star is influential in affecting one's life. *Pari* means, as it does
in Indonesian and other languages, 'the manta ray'. It can also
be used to mean 'to dry something in the sun'. This also might be
related to the belief that the heavens affect life.

'Uno' (The Evening Star) and 'Lia' (The Morning Star)

I have already reported the aphorism concerning the rising and
setting of Venus. I give here another:

Uno nulo eréng-pehé,	The evening star precedes at dusk,
Lia kéu éqa-bia.	The morning star follows at dawn.

The two forms of Venus are unmistakably paired. I am not certain
that they are regarded as the same star, but it is possible that in a
different sense they are regarded as identical. I have mentioned
that Lia Rian is an aspect of Divinity. I have a rather fragmentary
story which makes this clear (versions of this from Lamaholot are
also recorded by Arndt). This is called *Lia kéu paiq tuaq* ('The
Morning Star rises and taps palm wine'), and concerns an ancestor
of some of the clans of Léuwajang. It appears that a member of
the village (Lemur Lalé, ancestor of the clans Hiang Leraq,
Buang Leraq, and Boli Leraq) was angered because each morning
when he climbed his coconut tree he found his palm wine containers empty. Deciding then to find the cause, he waited one
night and watched the tree. He then trapped Lia in the top of
the tree tapping his palm wine. Grabbing Lia's beard, which was
so long that it reached down to the ground, he threatened to pull
Lia down. Lia promised him that if he would let him go, he would
bring back something valuable to give him the next night. The
next night he returned and gave the man a golden pot called *uluq*
('seed'). This seems actually to have existed, and was in the
possession of the village until one of the former *kapitan* of Kalikur
gathered all the gold valuables in Kédang to send his son on a
pilgrimage to Mecca.

This story represents God as a man with a long beard (cf. Arndt
1951: 1). It also turns on his creative powers (the golden pot or
germ, *uluq*) and associates him with palm wine tapping. This idea
is effective in other areas of the culture than just the myth. One

of my neighbours taps trees which still give some palm wine during the season when the other trees go dry. This ability to tap throughout the year he acquired from Laba Lia (or Lia Rian) who visited him in his dream and instructed him how to do so. Connected with this dream was the finding of one of the objects called *talu*, described above, and eventually the assumption of restrictions on eating young maize and so on which go with such objects.

The various names given the evening star show that it is a woman: *Nari Uno, Peni Uno, Uno Pito, Aran Dikéq*. Nari and Peni are human names; the latter is frequently used in myths in Kédang and Lamaholot as a typical name for a woman. *Uno*, of course, means 'the evening star'. *Dikéq* is Lamaholot and means 'good' (cf. Kédangese *diqén*); *aran* means 'bright' in Kédangese; so I interpret this name as meaning 'shining well' or 'bright'. *Pito* is Lamaholot for 'seven' (cf. Kédangese *pitu*). Peni Uno is the wife of the morning star, *Lia Rian* ('Great *Lia*') or *Laba Lia*, *Laba Dong*. *Laba* is a common man's name; if there is a translation for *dong* it may indicate the sound of a gong (the verb for beating a percussive instrument is *dang*; *laba* otherwise means 'to chisel'). Additional names for the morning star are *Malé Rian Paiq Tuaq* ('Great Star Who Taps Palm Wine') and *Malé Anaq Kuéq Ejéng* ('Star [of] Children Who Cry in the Morning'). There is a fish named *uno*; and the hearth is called *lia matan*. This latter term is a name for the sun on Seran (cf. Maass 1920/21: 60).

Other

The southern cross is known as *malé taq*, 'the coconut palm star'. The milky way is called *wei boroq* or *wei nawar*. *Boroq* is a kind of breadfruit, which has a covering consisting of hundreds of small nibs, which could be taken to resemble the thousands of stars of the milky way. The first phrase means then 'the breadfruit river'. *Nawar* is the bamboo skewer on to which lontar leaf roofing is threaded. This name seems to refer to the long straight path of the milky way.

The belt of Orion is called *teté wawi* or 'to carry the pig', as is done when a pig is tied to a long pole and carried by several people. The sword of Orion is called *teduq witing*, 'to lead a goat on a rope'. The head of Taurus is called *popoq né huna*, 'Pleiades' house'.

Comets are a sign that someone prominent will die. There is no particular name for a comet other than *malé noré né ebon* ('star with a tail'). Shooting stars are *malé hepuq*. When they see one they chant *ia ka o, buhu ka o*, 'fish eat you, the *buhu* (fish) eat you'. The chant is self-explanatory. They think the shooting stars fall into the sea and are eaten by fish.

There is a snake called *ular malé manuq* ('the chicken star snake', perhaps *Chrysopelea paradisi*). It is said to eat eggs and lives in the tops of trees. It is supposed to have wings which fold out like a bat's with which it sails from tree to tree at night. However, the wings cannot be seen. It is paired with a bird called *boréq*. This is a very small bird which never flies. They believe that *ular malé manuq* may never touch the ground or it will die, while the bird *boréq* may never fly into a tree for in that case it too would die.

3. SUMMARY CONSIDERATION OF DIVINITY IN KÉDANG

The view of Divinity which one draws from this review is that of a total, unitary Godhead which is simultaneously differentiated and capable of a variety of manifestations. The primary division in Kédangese conceptions of Divinity is between the distantly regulatory aspect and the immediate, life-giving aspect. This distinction corresponds to the division between the heavens and the earth, and to a degree to that between male and female. This latter correspondence is only partial, and the distinction between male and female appears within the heavenly bodies themselves. Each of the heavenly bodies is regarded as a manifestation of Divinity, and they show a tendency to form wholes consisting of complementary and opposed parts. A direct conceptual connection between God and the personal guardian spirit is made through the stars. In certain ceremonies, the priest may conduct an augury to find the name of the client's guardian spirit. The names are always taken from the stars: such as, in one case I witnessed, *Uno Lia*. The genealogical connection between God and man is displayed in the names found at the origin of mythical genealogies, which are characteristically those of the sun, moon, and morning star. One wonders then if other free or even malevolent spiritual beings are not to be traced back to Divinity, as they are also genealogically related to man. It is clear that the Christian conception of a purely good God is not found here, and there is no fallen angel. The incipient form of such a concept is present, as is shown in the story of Pulau Lama Léqang; but it is quickly seen that this conception turns on the theme of complementary opposites and not rational antithesis.

VII

YEARLY CYCLE

NILSSON thinks that primitives cannot conceive of such whole time units as the year and the twenty-four-hour day. Systems of time-reckoning based on what he calls time-indications, 'related to the concrete phenomena of the heavens and Nature' (1920: 9), proceed by the *pars pro toto* method in which some concrete phenomenon recurring only once within the unit is counted rather than the unit itself which has not yet been conceived. In line with this he claims that 'The primitive intellect proceeds upon immediate perceptions and regards day and night separately' (1920: 11) and also thinks it can be shown that 'the uniting of the seasons into the year is only a late and incomplete development . . . originally the year does not exist as a numerical quantity . . .' (1920: 86).

1. PRELIMINARY CONSIDERATIONS OF TIME IN KÉDANG

Misconceptions of this order are not uncommon, and they require that we begin with some general remarks about the nature of time in Kédang.

Finding out how a people conceive the passage of time is obviously one of the most fundamental problems in understanding their system of thought, and if it is not adequately solved the whole project may well fail. Leach (1961: 124–5) usefully shows what a variety of words will be found in another language in contexts where the English word *time* may appear. It may even be thought that to introduce the word into an ethnographic study would bring so many misconceptions with it that it is best avoided, but *time* seems to be one of those words without which it is not possible to think, and it is at any rate useful for alerting the reader to the sort of questions that are going to be considered. If it later proves that the material is best sorted into different categories, perhaps the initial phrasing of the problem may not nevertheless have been so inhibiting.

In Kédang, and contrary to Nilsson, there are words for the twenty-four-hour day, and for the year. *Weng*, in fact, has no other use than in counting days; and in this it is unlike other words (*lojo*, 'sun'; *éqa*, 'daytime') which are sometimes used to mean 'day'. The Kédangese also do not count by nights, which Nilsson thinks is the most general version of the *pars pro toto* method of keeping track of the passage of days. Nilsson (1920: 96) claims that the Malay *tahun* ('year') originally means 'season', and that the years are originally counted by seasons. Even if this is so the related word in Kédang, *tun*, means 'year' and is never used to mean a season or part of a year. I think we shall immediately fall into misunderstanding if we think that time for the Kédangese is only a collection of odd events and incapable of any holistic representation.

It is also often held against similar cultures that they have a very imperfect cumulative conception of time; that is, dates are rapidly forgotten, the number of years since a certain event cannot be accurately recalled after perhaps four or five years, and that, in short, there is no history. This is of course true in Kédang too and for the familiar reasons; but of course this way of looking at the problem sometimes overlooks the fact that there are no mechanical contrivances or other technical means of keeping accurate track of time and that there is further no pressing need to do so. The problems of explanation lie not really with time conceived in this natural manner, but with the Western time concept. Here, of course, a great part of the answer is to be found in the history of the technical developments upon which not only our means of telling time depend but also our very unusual, socially and technologically determined *sense* of time. But more basic even than this is the history of the change of the time concept brought about in the Hebraic and early Christian religions.[1]

Telling time in Kédang is based on the eternally recurrent. The calendar consists of a cycle of events, predominantly natural, which can be expected to occur more or less at the same time each year. The other two time units, the month and the day, as has been shown, are of the same nature. Perhaps this recurrent conception of time is as important as are the technological deficiencies in the fact that no accurate record is kept of the passage of the years. Although it is perfectly possible in the language of Kédang to say that something happened so many years or months in the

---

[1] See Duhem (1913–17: 2: 447–77) and Eliade (1949: 198–205, 214) among others on this point.

past or will happen so many years or months in the future, it is characteristic that when no particular need for precision is felt it is enough to say simply *tun weén* or *ula weén*, which terms could be translated merely 'another year' or 'another month'. These terms refer equally well to the past or the future, and the grammar of the language is such that it will also give no clue unless special effort is made to do so. Context alone is usually all that indicates whether the event is in the past or future or whether it is in an adjacent month or year or separated by several such units. Perhaps it would be argued that this shows a primitive failing of imagination, an inability to abstract from one's present state to form an over-all image of time, but I will argue that there are in fact several such over-all images of time employed in Kédang, and that the feature just mentioned is related to their common, essentially cyclic character. One moves through an invariable series of stages, which eventually repeat themselves. Each stage then is like the same stage in previous or later cycles, but different from the other stages of the same series. For this reason, logically the most primitive distinction to be made, and evidently the most frequently useful in Kédang, is that between the present stage and the others. Lacking special reason to specify where some event lies in the series, they will fall back on this. Furthermore, given that such specification is required, they will not necessarily resort to numbers, even though this can be done, but will characteristically choose some event for which a given stage is known and employ this for a more direct and in their terms frequently more precise determination.

Before turning then to the details of their system, it is worth remarking that Leach has explicitly questioned the propriety of using the term 'cycle' in connection with the concepts of time in what he calls primitive, unsophisticated communities, and says, 'Only mathematicians are ordinarily inclined to think of repetition as an aspect of motion in a circle' (Leach 1961: 126). First of all, it is not entailed that the word 'cycle' refers to a geometrical circle. Webster's first definition refers only to time: 'an interval or space of time in which is completed one round of events or phenomena that recur regularly and in the same sequence; as, the *cycle* of seasons'.[2] It is of course a question not to be assumed,

---

[2] Webster's New Collegiate Dictionary. According to Grandsaignes d'Hauterive, the words 'cycle' and 'circle' derive from different roots. The Greek

whether a drawn circle will be used to represent time in any given culture. In Kédang, which has almost no material art, it is even very unlikely. I am afraid I never asked if they thought of time as being like a circle, but I can report that I have never seen a material image made of time. It is questionable, though, whether Leach's zig-zag is any more likely to be employed as an image of time, and in introducing it he commits the same error, that of imposing a geometric metaphor, which he imputes to those who use the term cycle.

Although it is not possible at present to know whether the people of Kédang would recognize a circle as corresponding to their image of time, it is possible to state what the defining feature of that image is which justifies the use of the word cycle. This is that a sequence of events is completed, that it returns to the original state. In the case of the year, the month and the day, the events are characteristically regular and they occur in the same sequence. Of course, the stages of the year are subject to more irregularity than those of the moon and day. It must be emphasized though that the sequence is still sure enough, and even if certain primarily meteorological events sometimes get out of place, the over-all motion is in one direction and irreversible. Time, as it is represented in Kédang, is oriented, irreversible, and repetitive.

The idea that things should proceed regularly along their path and not reverse their direction occurs in a number of areas of their culture. The first of these is that one should always hand things with the right hand; to do so with the left hand is an offence. I have shown how this principle appears in the construction of the house where the parts must cycle through the house to the right (*wana pan*). To reverse this would bring disaster. Likewise, the souls of the dead are told to go on to their new village and not to return, and in a variety of instances measures are taken to block the path to them. If they return this is obviously a reversal of direction, comparable to the others just mentioned. When the souls of the ancestors are called back, it is in controlled ceremonies and at special portals or points of origin, which allow

kuklos does mean a circle, but it may also mean the regular return of related events. The sense of the root from which it derives is 'to turn around'. Another sense of this same root eventually gives us our words 'cult', 'culture', and to 'cultivate'. The Toba Batak image of the year seems to be circular (Tobing 1956: 107–29). Tobing must be misled however, when he says, 'The Tobanese can only state the course of time from changes in space' (p. 129).

their orderly and temporary presence. All of these ideas have in common the conviction that the orderly way to return to the starting-point is by proceeding through a sequence to its completion without ever reversing the direction.

This characteristic ties in with their feeling that someone so fortunate as to be cared for by God until he reaches old age will then not die until the day of his birth (or as they say 'his mother's time', when she gave birth to him); of course the date is no longer remembered; so they find out again only when he dies. It also lies behind their belief that the universe consists of a series of levels, through which one cycles in a series of lives; and it also corresponds to their ideas about descent and marriage as will be shown later.

2. DIVISIONS OF THE YEAR

The stages of the moon and the day have already been described. Here I will give the principal divisions of the year.

The first division in the year is that between the two seasons, the rainy season, which lasts from the end of November or early December until May or June, and the dry season, comprising the rest of the year. The rainy season is a time of winds and storms coming primarily from the west; as in Indonesian, the same word is used for this period as means 'west' (*waraq*). The fuller term is formed by joining this word with that which means 'rain' (*uja*): *uja-waraq*. The dry season is called *lojo matan*. It is very common in Indonesian languages that a word for sun is joined with *matan* to form a combination sometimes translated 'the eye of the sun'. This form is commonly a name for the sun itself (cf. Ind. *mata hari*, Lamaholot *lera matan*). Curiously, in Kédang it is not used for the sun, but for the period when the sun is apparently at its strongest (because of meteorological factors, this occurs during their winter).

Burning off the fields begins in August, and in October and early November full attention is given to clearing them and preparing for planting. During this time, increasing attention is given to natural signs presaging the beginning of the rainy season. The first of these occurs in early September and is a small shower called *uja lang*, *péu tuaq*, or the rain which sprinkles the land, allowing the mango blossoms to turn into fruit and the lontar palms to give sap. This marks the beginning of the second period of palm wine tapping, called *tuaq apé* ('the cotton palm wine') because it coincides with the period to pick cotton. From then until the rainy season has really started, palm wine and (unripe) mangoes are available, which, taken together, are highly valued delicacies. The next shower is called 'the locust rain' (*uja ioq*). This is the last rain before the onset of the rainy season and occurs around the first half of November. It brings out the locusts, which then make a great amount of noise in the evening, and which are collected in great numbers by the children and roasted. They too are a delicacy. With this rain, planting begins on the fields high in the mountain. After this a series of signs appear in rapid succession marking the beginning of the rainy season.

These include the conjunction of Antares with the first or third day of the waxing moon, the rising of the Pleiades at sunset, and for Léuwajang the rising of the sun over the mountain. Another sign which they observe is the passing of the sperm whale going back to the east. The sperm whale is called *ia laru* (compare Lamaholot *kalaru*); *ia* is 'fish' and *laru* is the section of the limbs (of, for example, the human body) between joints or the sections of bamboo between nodes. Because of its connection with the rains, however, the sperm whale is sometimes called *uja laru*; *uja* means 'rain' and *laru* may well be related to Ind. *lalu*, meaning 'to pass', or it may at least be used in this case as if it were the same word; for the phrase seems to mean 'the passing (i.e. coming) of the rains'.

When the first rain comes, if it is large enough to give confidence that the season has really started, there is a rush to get the seed in the ground. From now until the maize is picked the village will largely remain deserted except for people making occasional and short trips home.

Unlike the dry season, the passage of which can be judged by accurate observation of heavenly phenomena, the passing of the rainy season is gauged by estimating the storms and observing the natural development of various plants. I was once told that there are seven storms of the rainy season. It is in fact important that there is such a tradition; but I eventually discovered that it was hopeless to try to find an exact list of seven storms. Not only could no one ever give me a consistent list with seven names in it, but more importantly the meteorological phenomena themselves do not allow this orderly classification. Nevertheless, there are names for the various storms of this season, and the first few of these do occur with a certain regularity.

The first storm, upon which planting awaits, is called *tobi lemuq* (*tobi* is lamaholot) and is named after the flowering of the tamarinde. About the middle of December is the second storm, called *nuting-maing*. This is named after the remainder from the seed not needed for planting; after this rain, there can be no more planting. The roughest and longest storm occurs in the second half of January or early February, and is called *waraq rian, mato datén* ('the great storm, eyes bad'). I got several different opinions why a reference is made to bad eyes, but the most plausible is the one which refers to the clouds which lay in the higher villages all day long for days on end. At times one can hardly see neighbouring houses. The clouds then sweep through the house, leaving a thick layer of mildew on and in everything, called *owa teé*, 'the clouds touch'. This storm is characterized by heavy winds and breakers so large that one can hear them high on the mountain (*angin ubaq* 'wind and breakers'). The wind is particularly devastating to the maize crop, as it comes when the stalks are high and vulnerable, but before the ears have developed. Sometime during the first two months of the year (as we reckon it, January and February) is a small storm called *waraq laténg* because it coincides with the appearance of caterpillars (*laténg*). At the end of February and the beginning of March is a storm called *luba-holaq, perung tiboq*. *Luba-holaq* refers to the picking of the maize which is ripe at this time; the second phrase means the shoots of the large bamboo called *perung*, which emerge from the ground in early March. From then on is a collection of names for rains and showers, which I have had trouble ordering, essentially because the rains themselves are so irregular. In April is a rain called *téhang taqé, lawaq dara*, when the sheath below the crown of the pinang palm opens, allowing the inflorescence to emerge. Another such rain about this time (or the same one) is *loton puhu, edu reheq*, when the weed *loton* flowers, and the grass *edu* falls over, blocking the trails. The last rain (or rains) is called *ué amaq balang, éba halé*. The pinang fruit (*ué*) is now ripe and its skin begins to turn bad. It is also time for the new maize ceremonies at the clan ritual houses (*éba halé*). Another term for this stage is *popoq heléng*, 'the pleiades set'. The last rains of the season occur in irregular fashion as small showers through May and into June.

The first period of tapping is from April to June and is called *tuaq watar-aur* because the maize (*watar*) is in and the shoots of the small bamboo called *aur* begin to appear when the period begins. It is soon time to pick the beans. In late May and early June, when the beans are dried and then separated from their hulls by being placed on a mat and then beaten and winnowed, is a recognized time-mark named for the job (*tutu-bung*). During these months there is a period of strong winds, which prevent tapping and therefore sometimes bring a premature end to the palm wine season. These winds are called *angin ranga* because they coincide with the blossoming of the tree called *ranga* (a tree with poisonous leaves). With the end of the rainy season, the prevailing winds shift back to the east, and there is a small shower in July called *uja timur* ('the rain from the east').

These events by no means exhaust the things which may be used by Kédangese to date something, but it gives most of those which are so regular and so generally employed that they approximate the divisions of a calendar. The line between them and the variable and irregular events which may sometimes be referred to does not exist.

Having given a summary description of the markers of the yearly calendar, it is perhaps useful if I describe briefly the human events which go with them. From the beginning of the rainy season until the maize is ripe, almost everyone is concerned entirely with the care of his fields. The chickens are tied up for several weeks during the planting to allow the seed to sprout. After planting, which must be done early enough for the crops to sprout before the weeds, continual work must be put into keeping the weeds from overrunning the fields. This means that there is an almost continual job of weeding until the ears of maize are nearly ripe. When the maize ripens, a ceremony (*poan éwaq*) must be held at the boulder which houses the guardian spirit of a man's fields. Until this is done, the products of fields within the village may not be picked. The maize and pumpkins are picked first; beans ripen a few weeks later. During these weeks the maize is hung in bundles over the hearth to be smoked to protect them from weevils. From then on the main concern in the fields is with the rice crop (for those who plant rice), which is finally harvested in May. After the maize is in, the villagers become increasingly less concerned with their fields and begin gradually to return to the village. By June almost everyone is regularly living in the village. New maize ceremonies for the clans should begin about May, but they in fact often occur as early as March because, I think, the old men are anxious to take part in the relative abundance of food which is available at this time. January and February are the months of hunger, which are then first broken (for the younger villagers) during the two weeks when the succulent young maize is available. From then on a series of foods (both cultivated and wild) become available.

Beginning in June, when everyone is in the village, the younger members begin the labour required by the village and district governments (such as road repair, roofing the school, etc.). July is traditionally the period in which the village bean festival (*a utan*) should be held. From June until November, the villagers turn their attention to things which could not be conveniently done while they were working the fields. This is the time for marriages, paying bridewealth obligations, rebuilding houses, and a variety of small ceremonies. There is a lull in festivities around August, as they wait for the palm wine season to begin again. Then things are taken up again at such a pace that many finally begin to look forward to returning to work in the fields with a sense of relief. Finally, at about the beginning of the rainy season, a ceremony should be held in the old village to clean it and to ensure the crop.

The major features of the yearly calendar I now present in tabular form, so that it can be easily viewed as a whole.

TABLE 2

Stages of the yearly calendar in Kédang

I. *Uja-waraq*:	'The rainy season'	Late November until late May
Nu-néjéng: Antares and 1st or 3rd day of the waxing moon in conjunction; the Pleiades rise at sundown; whales pass to the east; sun rises over the mountain	'Time boundary', marking the division between the rainy and the dry seasons	Late November or early December
Tobi Lemuq	'The flowering of the tamarinde', 1st storm	Late November or early December, chickens tied up

Habiq wéloq-matan	'Closing the doors', an important village ceremony to ensure the crops	Middle of December, after planting, before planting if the rains are late
Nuting-maing	'Remainder of the seed', second major storm	Latter half of December, planting ends
Waraq rian, mato datén	'Great storm, bad eyes', third and largest storm	End of January or early February; contains heavy winds which damage the maize
Waraq laténg	'Caterpillar storm', a smaller storm coinciding with the appearance of caterpillars	During January or February
Luba-holaq, perung tiboq	'Picking maize, shoots of the *perung* bamboo', a storm coinciding with the harvesting of maize and the sprouting of *perung*	End of February, beginning of March
Tuaq watar-aur	'The maize and *aur* bamboo palm wine', the first season for tapping palm wine	April through June
A weru-wehar	'Eat the new', ceremonies at the clan temples for eating the new crops (particularly maize)	April and May
Téhang taqé, lawaq dara	'The sheath below the crown of the pinang palm opens, allowing the inflorescence to emerge', a rain	March or April
Loton puhu, edu reheq	'The weed *loton* flowers, the grass *edu* falls over', a rain	April
Ué amaq balang, éba halé; popoq heléng	'The skin of the pinang fruit turns bad, ceremonies at the clan temple; the Pleiades set', the last rain or rains	May
Tutu-bung	'Shelling the beans', a period of preparing the beans after harvest	May or June
II. *Lojo-matan*	'The dry season'	Late May until late November

Nu-néjéng: Antares in conjunction with the full or nearly full moon; the Pleiades set	'Time boundary', marking the division between the rainy and dry seasons	Late May

Each month of the dry season is numbered by the stage of the waxing moon in conjunction with Antares.

Uja timur	'East rain'	July
A utan	'Eat beans', village bean ceremony	July
Uja lang, péu tuaq	'The rain which sprinkles the land [allowing the] mango [blossoms to turn to fruit and the] lontar palms [to give sap]'	Early September
Tuaq apé	'Cotton palm wine', the second period of tapping during the year, coinciding with picking cotton	Late September through December
Uja ioq	'Locust rain', bringing out the locusts	Early November, planting begins high in the mountain

3. VILLAGE CEREMONIES

It may be useful now to give a brief description of the two major village ceremonies of the year. These are no longer held, as so much of the village has been converted to Islam or Catholicism; and I have very unsatisfactory information about them. However, they are of such obvious importance that I think it necessary to put together what is possible.

I will begin with the rain ceremony. It was never clear to me whether this was associated with the ceremony in which the village was closed or not. From reports, I conclude, however, that this may have been done sometimes but not necessarily. At any rate a very small rain ceremony is still performed every year. I never got to see this, unfortunately, presumably because it was of such small scale that there was no occasion for having guests. Rain ceremonies are never held at any other time of the year than the beginning of the rainy season. There is obviously no point in asking for rain out of season, and they are perfectly aware that a ceremony at the wrong time would bring no rain. The point of such a ceremony is not to work a miracle, but to ensure that the orderly progression of the seasons is not disturbed. This is a point on which their life depends, and in expectation of which they arrange their affairs. The beginning of the rains is the most critical period of the year; if the rains are late or too little or if there is an early heavy rain and the second rain is very late, then their crops can be seriously damaged. There is also the concomitant problem that the seed must be in the ground before the weeds sprout and grow too high, and an unfortunate pattern of rain may make this very difficult.

So much turns upon the proper beginning of the rains, and this may be prevented by so much which has happened (ceremonial omissions or moral infractions) during the year that it is always necessary to conduct a ceremony. For this purpose they return to the source of water at the spring at *wei rawé*. If the rains are very late, then the steps taken become correspondingly more elaborate. In some instances it may be felt that things are so bad that a fundamental cleaning of the spring is required, and they will start at the source and clean the stream by hand of all leaves, wood, and other refuse which may have accumulated there. They then take a young coconut at the stage before the meat has developed (*taq mutiq*—this is also the name for the heart) and cut a circular hole through the skin and shell at the end by which it was attached to the stem (*matan*). This is done so as to leave a thin film of the undeveloped meat covering the hole. They then take a knife and pierce this thin film causing the water (*taq werén*) of the coconut to spurt up. By spurting up and falling back to the ground like rain, it will induce rain to come within a very few days. A similar ceremony may be conducted at the stone called *lado angin* at the centre of the village. The purpose of that ceremony is to call the wind (*angin*) to bring the clouds and rain. The wind is characteristically thought to have great spiritual powers in Indonesia, and in Kédang it is called in ceremonies to clean the village, remove illness, bring rain and so on, but it is also thought capable of bringing plagues and illness of all kinds. An illness is commonly attributed to the wind having entered the body. I think the word *lado* is (as I was once told) a form of *nado* (rainbow), which refers to the rising of some spiritual essence or luminosity. Thus the stone is named for the rising of the wind.

If the rains still do not come or are insufficient after these ceremonies, they may then go back up the mountain and conduct a ceremony at one of the former village sites, the most obvious and effective being *léu rian*. Some decades ago, the drought was so bad that the *kapitan* of Kalikur gave the village of Léuwajang (because of its association with *wei rawé*) two chickens, a black one to represent a pig and a red or white one to represent a goat. These were then taken up to *léu rian* as offerings in a rain ceremony.

The ceremony for cleaning the village used to be held every year. The most appropriate time for it was when the maize was about knee high. This would be held especially if the crops were not growing well. I think it is here that the connection with the rain ceremony must have come in. It seems very likely that if the rains were so bad that the crops did not do well, that in itself would be reason to clean the village and to hold another rain ceremony, which would then be combined with the village ceremony. I was told that following rain ceremonies, after finishing at the spring, they would spray themselves with water while returning to the village, and when they had reached the village they would do the same to the people there, especially to anyone they caught sleeping. They had a kind of bamboo pump which could be filled with water and the handle pressed to spray it out; it was evidently quite like a bicycle pump or a Flit gun (they do have a kind of suction pump for serving palm wine). This custom of sprinkling each other with water is still followed at the end of large feasts or ceremonies, especially when one village visits another.

In preparation for the cleaning of the village, every member would have to prepare small cotton pellets (*panga-lewéq*) into which some silver scrapings were rolled. One each of these pellets would have to be prepared for everything one had stolen during the year ('whether a cassava leaf or a chicken'). Then the whole bunch was brought to the ceremony, where the priest gathered them together. Also at this stage they would clean the village of anything bad or unclean (such as anger, guilt, moral infractions) which had accumulated during the year. This was done by walking through the village beating all the houses with sticks while shouting *doq, doq, doq* ('come down, come down, come down'). Then all of this accumulated badness would be taken up in the ceremony by an egg. This egg was likened to a buffalo, and led by its nose down the mountain to the beach. There seems also to have been two chickens offered, one representing a lamb in *léu tuan*, the other representing a buffalo at the beach. The latter was cut in two. The egg was then put on a small boat made from the sheath around the inflorescence of the coconut palm (*elir*) and let loose to drift away to sea. When the ceremony was over, a period of quiet (*iréng*) lasting four days began in the village. This was preceded by the *habiq wéloq-matan*, *belé witing-tuaq*, 'the closing of the doors to the village' (the second phrase, meaning 'to release or put down the goat and palm wine', refers to the feasting accompanying the ceremony just described). This was done so that the soul of the village could not go out and so the wind could not enter. Signs of prohibition (*marén*) were put around the old village, so that no one not a member of the village would enter. If some stranger entered, he would then have to provide bananas, palm wine, and an animal, so that the priest could perform another ceremony to reclean the village. During this period of quiet, at night one could not crush maize, sing while tapping, or make any loud noises. If anyone violated this prohibition, he would have to pay a fine of a goat or a pig, and the period might be extended.

This is the only occasion in which a period of quiet is imposed, and I interpret the whole ceremony to be related to (in a sense, to be a survival of) the restrictions and rituals associated so frequently with rice growing in other parts of Indonesia (including their neighbours in Lamaholot). Quiet is usually imposed when working in the rice fields, especially during the period of germination, in order to protect the soul of the rice. In fact, in Kédang, where otherwise there is no ceremonial associated with rice, it is still not allowed to talk to someone working in his rice fields, though this is perfectly permissible in a maize field.

Agricultural ceremonies in general are only required in Léuwajang for fields in *léu tuan* and the hamlets closely associated with it (Napoq Wala and Uru); and the purity of *léu tuan* is shown in this ceremony to be related to the health of the crops. This suggests that it is the origin of the spiritual vigour or better yet the soul of the crops. In that case the *mier ringa* must be basically the original of the snake-like guardian spirits of the fields which inhabit the altars (*éwaq-metung*) of the fields. All this leads to the conclusion that when they are dealing with the coming into life of their crops, they go back to an origin of life, the most relevant one being their village, and ensure its pure and unobstructed state. The ceremony characteristically occurs at just that critical stage when the life is coming into the plants, and the period of restriction associated with it is very similar to the one which follows the birth of a baby. It is also very interesting that the same name (*iréng*) applies to the period of equal duration following a funeral, when no work may be done on fields within the village. It is found, then, in association with major transitions of life, in some cases coming into life, in others going out.

I have mentioned the ceremonies for eating the new products of the fields. These now occur in April and May (sometimes as early as March). In some clans they are relatively elaborate and held at the clan temple; failing such a clan-wide ceremony, they are simply individual and fairly private. They now commonly include the eating of white beans as well as maize. I am not at all sure what the original relation was between these clan ceremonies and the original village-wide bean ceremony. The prohibition on eating the new maize applies only to certain, almost invariably elderly people who have received *talu*, objects which materialize to them out of the ground. The prohibition on eating white beans is, however, village-wide and applies to all adults of the village. Formerly it lasted until the village bean ceremony. Many insist that originally the clan ceremonies were separated from the village ceremony and that the eating of beans has been included in them in default of the latter. This is reasonable and, I think, correct; but it raises one difficulty. The clan ceremonies are called *a weru-wehar*, which just means 'to eat the new'; the *a weru* ceremonies, however, are supposed to be scheduled according to the rule *opol pitu, werun pitu*, that is, when seven full moons and seven new moons have passed since the beginning of planting. This is in July, the time for the bean festival.

I suggest the following solution to these difficulties. *A weru* is a very general term, and it would not be out of keeping with the language if it applied equally well to the ceremony for eating the new beans. Thus, there are two forms of *a weru*, one for the beans and one for the maize. The beans are really the last crop to be brought in, and when they may be eaten (excepting young beans eaten before they dry), the agricultural season is completely over. Anciently, before the introduction of maize from America, the staple may have been millet and rice (in this area, unlike Bali and

Java, possibly also cassava). Rice is harvested and finally brought
into the village a little after the beans, but essentially at the same
time. Therefore, once both forms of *a weru* would more easily
have fallen at the same time. Maize, however, ripens much earlier,
and since the prohibition on this staple tends to be associated with
the spiritual well-being of the clan (when it is not purely individual), there are two different kinds of possible causes which might
together work to bring a rupture in the original *a weru*: one a
natural, the other a social-structural cause. However, there
obviously was never a reason why the clan ceremonies might not
be held-up to coincide with the village bean festival, and I think
this may have been common. There was still one very ancient and
prominent old man whose ceremony was held in July, and it was
considered in some ways (essentially as a time-marker) to be a
substitute for the now defunct bean ceremony.

What transpired at the bean ceremony is not fully clear to me.
I think there would have been a ceremony at the village temple
and its two altar stones (*pikan*). There undoubtedly would have
been dancing and feasting (cf. Vatter 1932: 215); and I have been
told that someone versed in the village genealogies would sit in
the temple for a full night and recite the whole set from *Ula-Lojo*
down to each child in the village. In the minds of those who
could tell me anything about it, it was almost identical to the
ceremonies held when building the village temple itself.

4. SUMMARY CONSIDERATIONS OF TIME IN KÉDANG

In this and the preceding chapter I have described several ways
in which the Kédangese order sequences of events which I think
correspond to various aspects of what we call time, and I have
argued that they are all in Kédangese terms cyclical because they
are irreversible and they proceed through the sequences until they
return to the beginning. Such ordered sequences are: (1) the day,
(2) the month, (3) the year, (4) the life of the individual within
this world, and (5) the cycle of lives through the levels of the
universe.

Leach (1961: 126) lists among possible metaphors for repetition
'the ritual exchanges of a series of interlinking marriages'; and he
introduces similar material in his arguments about time when
he refers to Radcliffe-Brown's 'doctrine concerning the identification of alternating generations' and 'the stress which Lévi-Strauss

has placed upon marriage as a symbol of alliance between other-wise opposed groups' (1961: 131). It may appear to pose impos-sible problems of definition to try to range marriage alliances or the alternation of generation under the word *time*; but I think Leach is right in introducing them. The worst result might be that we would have to redefine 'time' or even throw it out alto-gether. What is to be gained from it is the recognition that, as will be shown in later chapters, in a society such as Kédang, marriages ideally *are* linked into self-closed cycles, showing the same feature as the various time cycles, down to the prohibition on reversibility. Ageing too seems to be represented in a similar way.

For Leach what these features have in common with time con-cepts is that they may be represented by opposed pairs linked by a zig-zag pattern, which he claims is how the Greeks conceived time. If I were to choose my own image for time in Kédang, I might more readily compare it to a wave. What lies behind Leach's view of Greek time and what provides its similarity to time concepts in Kédang is that it is an example of thinking in terms of complementary opposites. It just happens that the social order of Kédang is a much better example of a system based on complementary opposition than was that of ancient Greece. How-ever, it is not possible to represent the indirect exchange of women in an asymmetric system by a zig-zag. It is well known on the other hand that people with such systems frequently represent it by some sort of cycle (Leach 1961: 73). It is indeed a real question of interest whether time concepts in societies with direct exchange differ from those in societies with indirect exchange in the same way that the alliance system differs.

Behind Leach's theory is, as he remarks, the ideas about time presented by Hubert and Mauss (1909) and van Gennep (1960). If we take a section out of any one of the time cycles of Kédang it will look very much like Leach's diagram (p. 134) which shows the results of Hubert and Mauss's study. That, however, was based on an examination of Christian ritual, for which sacred and profane are important categories. These terms do not apply in Kédang, and it is necessary to find others.

If I were to write this study in the language of Kédang, I would choose the words *laru* and *woq*, the first referring to the long sections between joints (*woq*) in a human (or animal) body or in a piece of bamboo. As I am using English, I would substitute for the 'profane' of Hubert and Mauss the word 'segment', and for their 'sacred' the phrase 'point of transition'. I avoid using the word 'solid' in connection with segment because we are, after all, speaking of time.

The symbolic association of birth and death is so common, that almost everyone who touches on the question of time or passage rites draws attention to it.[3] In Kédang the word *woq*, meaning 'joint', but which I translate here as 'point of transition', is joined to the word *tuan* to mean 'ancestor'. *Tuan* itself derives from *tua*, 'old'; so the implication of *tuan-woq* is those old or former humans who have undergone the transition of death.

Leach (1961: 133) claims that 'the only picture of time that could make this death-birth identification logically plausible is a pendulum type concept'. What he means by this is his zig-zag or 'discontinuity of repeated contrasts'. These conclusions rest on his view that all aspects of time derive from two basic experiences: '(*a*) that certain phenomena of nature repeat themselves [and] (*b*) that life change is irreversible' (1961: 125). As I understand him, he thinks primitive time concepts tend to emphasize (*a*) and modern concepts to emphasize (*b*). Irreversibility disappears, according to Leach, from the representation of time by primitives, leaving only the discontinuous repetition of contrasts (p. 134). Now contrary to Leach I think that a holistic (that is, cyclical) concept of time may be more natural than our linear idea which leaves us literally at loose ends and therefore subject to the metaphysical problems inherent in the Judaeo-Christian tradition.[4] I claim that the Kédangese conceive time as (*a*), i.e. repetition, resulting from (*b*), i.e. irreversibility. It is easy enough to see why death falls in conjunction with birth in a cycle.

Having dealt with the day, month and year, in the next chapters I turn to that series of events from birth to death which make up the cycle of human life.

---

[3] ' "Ein Symbol alchimistischer Transmutation," fuhr Naphta fort, "war vor allem die Gruft." ' *Der Zauberberg.*

[4] For an account of the abandonment for theological reasons of the eternally cyclical conception of time of the Greek philosophers in favour of a linear and bounded time concept by the early Christian theologians, especially St. Augustine, see Duhem (1913–17: 2: 447–77).

VIII

PREGNANCY, BIRTH, AND CHILDHOOD

I. PREGNANCY

SEXUAL intercourse is known in Kédang to be essential to conception. I could uncover no theory as to what was contributed by the man and what by the woman. The soul comes from God, *Tuhan Allah* or *Lojo Rian*. The moon and the sun arrange (*atur*) births. It seems that the soul is sent down while the child is still in the womb. There is reason to associate the blood, which is the woman's fecund fluid, with spiritual influence (as is explained in the chapter on marriage alliance), but I did not find a theory that the soul came from the woman, or an idea of the differential inheritance of bone and flesh or some such. The fecundating fluids of the man and woman (semen and blood, respectively) are called by the same term, in the full ceremonial form *mijé-tén, werén-lalan*. *Werén-lalan* and its association with life-giving fluids has already been explained. *Mijé* otherwise means 'urine'. *Tén* is characteristically applied to long string-like objects, such as mucus, intestines, the navel cord, and so on.

The womb is called *nawal*, and when it contains a child it is said *nawal dawal anaq*. *Dawal* is one of those Kédangese verbs which are self-explanatory; it is what a *nawal* does. Otherwise it is said of the womb that it *oni* ('hides') *anaq* ('the child').

It is known that only women who menstruate can become pregnant. There is no name for menopause, but it is known that it occurs at the advent of old age. Menstrual flow is called *wéiq ulaq* ('filthy blood'), *wéiq datén* ('bad blood'), *ula-malé* or *ula-malé adan* ('the coming of the moon-star'). This last phrase makes clear that menstruation, like many other things, comes when the moon has returned to its proper stage (*ula anaq, malé nénin*, 'moon full,[1] star complete'). The word star occurs as the regular dyadic pair for moon. Another term for it is *uluq-nawaq* or *uliq-nawaq. Uluq*

---

[1] 'Full' in days, that is. It does not refer to the full moon (*ula opol*) nor any other particular stage, as each woman has her own time.

means 'seed', *uliq* means 'place'; *nawaq* means 'soul' (cf. *tuber-nawaq*). The substitution of *uliq* for *uluq* not only points to a possible common etymology, but shows that regardless of origin the words have an associated sense. What this idea is, is not hard to find. *Uliq* has much the same sense as *koda*, the place of origin, the top of the mountain, the old village, and so on (cf. *uli koda*, myths which explain why things are the way they are and usually refer to particular locations). The idea of the golden germ has occurred several times so far. These phrases simply bring these other origins of life into association with the womb, and therefore suggest comparison to the *garbha* or *hiranyagarbha* of India.

There are no special restrictions for a menstruating woman, nor a special house of seclusion, and she is not regarded as polluting. She wraps herself under her clothing with an old sarong which absorbs the blood. When her period is over, she washes the sarong. It must never be burned because of the remaining traces of blood. In this regard it is like any cloth or bandage used for wrapping wounds, which may not be put into the hearth but must be taken outside and preferably put in a stone terrace wall or other such place where it will be safe from the eventual burning off of the fields.

The most general term for pregnancy is *muho*. A euphemism is *meti-ula*, 'stage of the moon'. This term has been explained, as well as the fact that each stage of pregnancy and of the child's growth is thought to depend on the changes of the moon and will be called *meti-ula*. The first month approximately of pregnancy (i.e. conception) is called *putéq-liung*. Later, in the fourth or fifth month, when the swelling has become pronounced, it is said *muho aran*, 'the pregnancy is clear'. They are well informed about the stages of development of the foetus from observing miscarriages (*tiwa weq*). They claimed, however, to be ignorant of abortives, and regarded abortion as murder. Nevertheless, I was once asked to perform one. Sexual intercourse is continued up to the time of birth; then it may be stopped for up to three years to keep from having another child too soon.

If the foetus lies on the left side in the womb, this is regarded as a sign that the child is female; if it is on the right, it is male. Birth, it is known, should occur at the earliest after seven months and normally after nine. However, they sometimes say that a male child takes eleven months before birth, a female nine. The first statement represents their knowledge of natural history, but both statements are so phrased as to accord with the ideological role of uneven numbers. At birth they inspect the baby's fingernails to determine if it had completed the number of months necessary for its development (*ula anaq*). If the nails are white (i.e. clean), it is premature and its navel cord will have to be soaked in water without being severed from the placenta in order to allow the moon to complete its changes (this is described below). If it is born with black (dirty) nails, its time in the womb was complete.

Concerning the influence of the stars and moon on the birth, it is said of *malé tené diqén* (the good Ursa Major) and *malé tené datén* (the bad Ursa Major) that they create in conflict (*sé huraq awé*), which means that they struggle against each other to influence a child while still in the womb. If the bad *malé tené*, that is, the bad guardian spirit (*nimon-narin datén*), wins, then the child will be born at the wrong stage of the moon and will therefore always cry. A boy should be born when there is a new moon (*ula werun*), a girl during a full moon (*ula opol*). When I asked for more circumstantial information about the stage, I was told that a boy should be born between about the seventh day of the waning moon, and the eleventh day of the waxing moon. It will be realized, however, that this represents an attempt to provide a reasonable answer to, for them, a somewhat novel question. If the child is born during the wrong stage of the moon, it is necessary to call a priest (*molan-maran*) to perform a ceremony 'to bring back the moon' (*koloq ula*), 'return the star' (*balé malé*). In the case of a girl he will 'hang up the full moon' (*hading opol kéu*), 'drop down the new' (*lawang werun doq*). For a boy he will do the reverse.

It has been mentioned that a pregnant woman may not point at the bad *malé tené*. She also may not sit and eat under the eaves (*wido*) of a house or on the rock wall at the bottom of a field (*nanga loloq*). If she does so the child will be born with an open groove (*bubun hemuq*) running from the fontanelle to the base of the skull (*uli puén*). They say in this case that the milky way (*wei nawar*) comes down and sits on the centre of the child's fontanelle (*tebéq oté bubun ajaq*). Should this happen, they must hold a ceremony to close the groove. A pregnant woman may not sleep alone in the house, nor should she go outside at night. This is due on the one hand to the danger of being disturbed by *malé tené*. It is also because the smell (*ewé*) from her vagina is thought to be sweet at this time, and it is feared that a witch (*maq-molan*) may smell it and come and damage the child. The prohibition on leaving the house at night was said to hold whether the moon is shining or not and regardless of its stage. It is not limited to the new moon, as Arndt reports for Lamaholot. On the other hand, I was once told that the restriction only applied during the rainy season (which seems to be associated with *malé tené*) but not during the dry.

There are no food restrictions for a woman during pregnancy. However, women do have food cravings at this time (cf. Lévi-Strauss 1966: 78–9, where he questions the natural basis and the generality of cravings during pregnancy). They want sour, sweet, and salty things such as *assam* and mango. They will not eat plain foods such as unsalted maize. Food with a strong smell or which is somewhat rotten (like fish), they cannot eat. Another indication of pregnancy is that their eyes become black, that is, they get rings under their eyes.

It is usual to hold a guardian spirit ceremony for the child during the pregnancy. This is sometimes done, however, after the birth. It is always held on the occasion of the first pregnancy, and it may be repeated for subsequent ones, especially when there are accompanying bad signs or dreams or when there is a problem of repeated miscarriages. The guardian spirit is called *nimon-narin* and is acquired through the mother. If the name is analysed in order to uncover the meanings implied in it, then the first element, *nimon*, must be compared to *nimon-wala*, which means the owner or master of an animal. This latter term is not applied, however, to subsequent owners who may buy the animal, but only to the person who has raised and cared for it and to whom it may be expected to return if it breaks free. This usage reveals important meanings implied by the name of the guardian spirit. Both terms contain as indispensable parts of the thought first the idea of authority deriving from a special relationship like ownership, and second the idea of protecting, caring for, raising. The second element, *narin*, may very well derive from the word *naré*,[2] meaning 'brother' and used only by women. Children of the same mother have the same guardian spirit. *Nimon-narin* is identified with Ursa

[2] The philological issue is whether the guardian spirit is actually *nimon-narin* or *nimon-arin*, about which there is disagreement in Kédang.

Major, and like it there is a good *nimon-narin* and a bad *nimon-narin*. The guardian spirit may also be another star, such as Venus. The purpose of the guardian spirit ceremony is to send up the bad and to bring down the good. Blood from the chicken offered in the ceremony is mixed with betel and daubed on the body of the child, if already born, at various critical points so that the good *nimon-narin* may enter the body. If the ceremony is held for one child (whether already born or not), his brothers and sisters will be included in it in the same way. A piece of blood-soaked white string (called *tuéng nimon-narin*; *tuéng* means 'to twist thread'; the phrase refers then to taking up the guardian spirit as when twisting thread) which has already been consecrated in the ceremony is tied around the child's wrist to represent his tie to his guardian spirit.

2. BIRTH

The woman may give birth in her own (her husband's) home She may also, especially in difficult cases, go to her mother's, brother's, or similar relative's home. She will usually be assisted by an experienced older woman. Her husband is *not* excluded from the house during the birth. A priest will be called in to assist (ceremonially) only in very difficult cases. Birth takes place on the ground in the house. The woman sits with her legs stretched out in front of her, while she is supported by someone sitting behind her and grasping her body under her arms. An old cloth is put in front of her for the baby to fall on. They do not use baskets and she does not kneel. If the child emerges head first, the birth is easy. If it comes out feet first, it is likely to die. They do not seem to know how to reverse the position of the child in the womb (I met a man in Wailolong, East Flores who was renowned for his skill in doing this and also for successfully resetting broken bones which the hospital had wanted to amputate).

Commonly some form of percussion is associated with the moment of birth. They may use a gong, a rattle (a piece of bamboo filled with candlenuts) or they may simply strike the wooden platform in the room. It is said that this is done so that the infant will cry and begin to move. If it cries as soon as it emerges, it is not necessary to beat the gong. They are afraid that the child will die if it does not cry.

The afterbirth is known as *ulaq* ('filth'). The placenta is known as *nahaq rian* or *kaboté*. The word *nahaq* otherwise is the form of durian used for teeth blackening, *rian* means 'great'. *Kaboté* in Lamaholot means navel cord, but not in Kédang. The navel cord is *tén-botin* ('stomach string'), and the navel itself is *puhé*. The placenta is severed from the navel cord by the woman herself with the fingernails or with a bamboo knife (made from any kind of bamboo) at the connection between the navel cord and the placenta. A metal knife may not be used (perhaps because it would seal off the source of life, cf. Endicott 1970: 133–4). The navel cord itself must be left full length and may not be cut from the infant's body. It must be left and will fall off in four days. When a child is born with white (clean) fingernails, indicating that its time in the womb was incomplete, the navel cord is not severed from the placenta and the placenta and cord are placed in water in a coconut shell bowl, which the mother sets next to her on the platform (*balai*). This remains at least four days, until the navel cord has dried and drops off. The placenta is placed in a coconut shell to be disposed of and inserted in a hole in a stone terrace-wall to prevent the dogs from dragging it out to where it may be burnt during the annual period of clearing and burning the fields. The rest of the filth in the house is gathered together at the end of the period of restriction following birth and disposed of near a tree or in the woods where the ground is not worked.

The navel cord itself is carefully preserved and later, after a ceremony to gather together the navel cords of the set of siblings (*poan mawu tén-botin*), it is placed in the roof of the granary (*wetaq rian*) near the right house post (*lili wana*). If after several years the navel cord has rotted and disappeared or has otherwise been lost, there may be a ceremony called *molang katiq* to replace it. In this case a white string (*ulun duan*) is substituted. In either case the string or the actual navel cord are treated in the same way. Ashes are taken from the hearth and placed in the coconut shell, then the navel cord or its replacement is put in and covered with more ash. Another shell is placed on top and the whole is then wedged into the framework of the eaves of the roof. The ashes are supposed to fill a mouse's eyes if it bothers the cord. Supposedly the containers of the navel cords of a set of siblings must be placed in the uphill side of the roof in order of birth and with that of the oldest being at the right corner. Actually, I often saw them on the adjacent side of the roof at that corner; only one of the prominent old priests seemed especially careful about this. The ceremony of renewal for the navel cord is not performed at a regular interval, but occurs when someone has had a dream indicating the need to do so. Such a sign may be a dream of a flowing stream or a small snake. At such a renewal ceremony, the navel cords of dead members of the sibling set will not be renewed.

The *tén-botin* (navel cord) is closely allied with the *tén-déwaq*, the connection which exists among all descendants of any woman, thus the tie uniting the members of a lineage (of whatever structural order), of a clan or group of clans or villages descending from a common ancestor, or any larger segment of mankind. In this case the relationship represented by *tén-déwaq* is recognized only through the male line; so there is the interesting fact that the patrilineal principle of descent in Kédang is based on a common tie to a woman. *Déwaq* seems to mean or indicate the womb (*nawal*). Although *tén-botin* and *tén-déwaq* are probably virtually synonymous, in fact, when applied to relationships the former seems to have the more restricted use (to siblings), while the latter is more inclusive.

Sometimes a section of a clan may build a small ceremonial house in the old village (*léu tuan*) to harbour its *tén-botin*. This will in effect commemorate some female ancestor from whom all descend. Such things may be built by any section of any clan. They are occasioned by an illness, death, or other misfortune, or a dream. Whenever there is an occasion for divining the causes of some misfortune, there is the possibility (from among many others) that this procedure will turn up as the proper remedy. Such an erection in no way distinguishes that section of the clan from the rest of the clan in any corporate sense. The dream image for the *tén-déwaq* is a large snake. Such a dream could be a sign that someone within the group united by a single *tén-déwaq* has turned against the group and has got a priest to conduct a ceremony called *poan nuba-lapaq* to cause death or illness or misfortune.

Occasionally a child may be born with a large birthmark. Such a blemish is considered a good sign whether on the right or left side of the body, but not if it is on the front (including the centre of the face). The latter is a bad sign and one must have a priest perform a ceremony to move it (figuratively) to the side. If this is not done while the child is young (before it marries), then the

trouble caused by the spot may fall upon the children. The significance of the location of the spot is in the opposition of centre to the
sides. The centre-front of the body, from navel to forehead, is
the centre. I was told, as I have mentioned, that this matter of the
spot (*tada*, 'sign'; if bad *tada datén*) is comparable to the placing
of the door in the house in relation to certain important structural
parts (*manuq leténg* and *nuar*) the ends of which mark centre
points. Albinism is not considered a bad sign and requires no
ceremonial correction.

Twins are called *anaq ikang* ('fish children'). As on Adonara
(Arndt 1940: 144–5), those of the same sex are happily received,
but it is a bad thing for twins of opposite sexes to be born.[3] They
are considered to have married, that is, their union in the womb
is considered a sexual union. It is said that in a case of such twins
one will die. However, one man claimed that no such twins had
ever been born in Kédang. When I asked if they ever kill one or
let it die, as occurs sometimes in Lamaholot (as we were told by a
nurse who had saved and was caring for several such children), the
possibility was denied, and it was claimed that they must be
raised. I find it perfectly possible and in keeping with their character that many people in Kédang would raise both children. On
the other hand, I think the denial very inconclusive proof that it
never happens that one of them is allowed to die. In the event of
opposite-sex twins growing to adulthoood, the bridewealth
received for the female twin could not be used to meet her brother's
obligation (Arndt 1940: 144 reports the same for Adonara). This
is based on the thought that they are like man and wife.

The rationale behind this is worth considering. A man takes
bridewealth for his sister and gives it for his wife. If he takes
bridewealth for a twin, this is like taking it for his wife, thus
reversing the proper direction of the bridewealth exchange.
Therefore, the bridewealth received for his twin may properly
be used for meeting some other obligation in the clan where the
confusion does not exist, but his obligations can be met only with
bridewealth received for a woman of the clan who, as is normally
to be expected, does not stand in the relation wife.

When the twins are both girls, if they are married to one
husband, bridewealth may not be asked for both of them; only the

[3] There seems to be no ceremony for purifying the village following the birth
of opposite-sex twins as there is on Bali (Belo 1935).

equivalent of bridewealth for one person may be received. If they marry different husbands, bridewealth can be received for both. It needs to be mentioned in connection with twinship that if two babies are born (of different mothers) in the village at the same time, they cannot be bathed at the end of the period of seclusion at the same time; or, if it is done at the same time, one of them must be taken to another village for the bath.

3. 'AHAR-OLIQ', THE PERIOD OF RESTRICTION AFTER BIRTH

Following birth there is a period of restriction involving the child, mother, and father, known as *iréng-puting* (compare the period of restriction, *iréng*, following the ceremony for cleaning the village and that following a burial; *puting* is food restriction) or *ahar-oliq, niliq-wénaq*. After the child has been born, the mother and child move onto a *balai* (the common bamboo platform), where they stay until the end of the period of restriction, the duration of which seems to be determined primarily by the time it takes for the woman to discharge all of the blood and afterbirth. The woman has during this time her own hearth, set on the *balai* (*lipu*) in which she burns a particular type of smokeless wood (*ai bonoq*). Although the *balai* may be situated anywhere in the house, as may the hearth in normal use, and during normal times there are no prescriptions as to how or where the inhabitants of the house and their visitors sleep, during *ahar-oliq* the woman, child and hearth are very specifically oriented.

To understand this orientation properly one must refer to the system of direction indicators. I will here describe the situation where the primary point of orientation is provided by the top of the mountain (as it usually is in the old villages). The orientation assumes that one's back is to the centre of the mountain, and that one faces downhill, in most cases towards the sea. The woman must sit or sleep with her head to the mountain and her feet to the sea, the hearth being placed above her and to the left (*olé*) of her head. She may also sit with her back to the hearth (*lia-matan*), which is on the left side (*olé*) of the *balai*, and face to the right (*oté*) rather than downhill. But in no case may the hearth be below (*owé*) or to her right. The hearth serves two purposes: first, she sits with her back to it so that it warms her loins and induces (as is thought) the discharge of blood; second, she cooks on this hearth the food which she and the infant eat. During this period the woman must sleep on her right side (*wana*)—which is, indeed, implied by the rules mentioned above—although there seems to be no restrictions on how one sleeps at other times.

When she feeds the child, the woman must sit on three bamboo slats running parallel, left to right (*oté-olé*), rather than towards and away from the mountain (*oli-owé*). These three slats are made from the small type of bamboo known as *aur*, which has many other ceremonial uses; and the slats are known as *niliq-wénaq*. *Niliq-wénaq* is in fact *ahar* and is the same as the *ahar* used for the part of the funeral ceremony called *birang-kapang* when the cloth given the corpse is counted and the black cloth is shreaded. It is also the same as the *ahar* used to support the small flat altar stones (*lapaq*) at a ceremony at the clan temple (*huna suku*) or at a navel cord ceremony (*poan tén-botin*). *Oliq* means 'above' or 'on'; thus, *ahar-oliq* literally means that *ahar* has been placed on the *balai*. I think we must interpret this term *ahar* as effecting a connection between the two forms of transition: birth and death.

While the woman and child remain on the *balai*, coconut leaves are hung around the sides of the *balai* to hide from view the blood and filth which drops through on to the ground. There are no coconut leaves hung around the outside of the house or the doors to indicate that outsiders may not enter, as is done in other Indonesian societies. Indeed, there seems to be no restriction preventing outsiders from entering the dwelling during this period. There is a long list of particular prohibitions and prescriptions which apply at this time. Some of these are given in the following maxim:

Duq ai bonoq, hebu wei rawé,	Burn *bonoq* wood, bathe only in water from the spring *wei rawé,*
Obi api, tapé alén,	Back to the fire, warm the loins,
Puting ling, ingiq léi.	Restricted hands, restricted feet.

The last phrase (*puting ling, ingiq léi*) is used to refer either to this period of restriction (*ahar-oliq*) or to a prohibition on eating new maize acquired in connection with finding *talu*. *Ingiq* means 'forbidden'; *puting* means a food prohibition. The implication in both cases is that one must eat from one's own hearth (a restriction which commonly accompanies finding *talu*). During this period the members of the household may only drink water from *wei rawé.* The husband must climb to *loboq* (the former village site above *léu tuan*) and cut a bamboo from the stand of *perung* bamboo there. This he may use to carry the water from *wei rawé.* The woman may use only this water with which to bathe her loins. Other water, such as rain water, may be neither drunk nor used for bathing. Otherwise, all three are under a general prohibition on bathing, cutting their hair, or, for the husband, shaving during the period of restriction. Only when this period ends may hair be cut or may one shave. Hair clippings in this case, as generally, may be disposed of anywhere and are not given the special treatment given the filth gathered in the house. During this period the man and woman are not restricted as to what kind of food they may eat, but the infant may only be suckled (*tu i*) or fed a type of banana known as *muqu weréq.* Fruit ripened on the tree may not be used. Instead they must take the unripe fruit and boil it, making a sort of gruel. Both the woman and the infant eat from this. An earthen pot must be used for preparing this food, but not the common type bought from traders from Alor. Instead a *biar bajang waq*, an earthen pot from the village Biar Wala, must be used. Among prohibitions for women during the *ahar-oliq* are those on any work connected with making or dyeing cloth or thread.

Such prohibitions and prescriptions concerning *ahar* are said to be known from birth (*ahar beté wau bahé deq*, 'ahar is already in the forehead'). They are not learned or taught. One prescription which does not apply in Léuwajang, but which is common in other villages, concerns the use of the pin (*uréq*) which is stuck through the knot of hair which women wear on the back of the head. This is usually wooden (bamboo), but during *ahar-oliq* the women from villages in the vicinity of Péusawa must wear a metal one.

The *balai* which has been used for *ahar-oliq* (like that on which a corpse has lain) may not be burnt. If it is, the child will be covered with sores. The infant must sleep on the *balai* of its birth (i.e. that used during the period of restriction called *ahar-oliq*).

4. CHILDHOOD

When the period of *ahar-oliq* has come to an end, the father of the child must go to his wife's father or brother (*epu-bapa*) and tell him that the child is going for the first time to be fed (substantial food) and bathed. If they do these things before telling the *epu-bapa*, they will be subject to a fine payable to him and consisting of *laong* (a silver ear-ring) or *bala* (an elephant tusk). (The cutting of the placenta does not require his knowledge or permission as seems the case on Timor /Cunningham 1964: 61/.) The parents may for the first time descend the mountain and bathe at the sea. They take the clothing of the infant and wash it in the sea as well. When they return, they bathe the child with water from *wei rawé*, take him outside the house for the first time to show him the sky, and then feed him. There is no special ceremony, such as showing the infant bow and arrows or a thread spindle, connected with taking him outside. Earth is not put on the child, as is done in a ceremony for someone returning from a long absence. There is also no formal ceremony involving an offering or a feast connected with ending *ahar-oliq*. Food given an infant is sometimes masticated (*mamoq*) in advance by the parents before feeding it to the child. This would be done to crushed maize or bananas. There are no prestations associated with the birth of a child.

About the time of ending *ahar-oliq*, the child will be given a name. The 'village name', that is the traditional form of name, consists of the given name of the child and the given name of his father. Thus Péu Langun's daughter Lolo is named Lolo Péu. There are certain cases where a person is known by a name which deviates from this pattern for one reason or another, but his formal name nevertheless conforms to it. The name given follows the preference of the parents. They do not seem ever to resort to augury, nor is there a tradition of giving the child a name of an ancestor, though this may be done in individual cases. A parent (male or female) may often be addressed by the name of his child (male or female). Many people, especially school-teachers or officials, have picked up the modern Indonesian practice of using a name formed of the Christian or Muslim name, the village given name and the clan name written as one word. Either or both of the first two names are often written only as an initial. Thus, someone from the clan Amun Toda named Béda Roman and set off with the Christian appelative Urbanus might call himself Urbanus B. Amuntoda.

It is usual that the fontanelle be covered until it closes. As a minimum this is done for at least the first four days after birth. The fontanelle is called *bubun*, the same name as the sides of a roof which are not on the up or down mountain-sides; the covering is called *neneq*. This is made from cotton or from some such con-coction as a mixture of masticated leaves of the cotton and another plant, or of mixed candlenut and tumeric. The purpose of the covering is to prevent the breath (*bowol*) from escaping. They say that they can see the skin over the fontanelle vibrating when the child breathes (that is, they see the pulse). If the infant has a fever, they must remove the covering. This is, then, to let out some of the breath. It is common when anyone is ill with a fever (*weq panan*) that they put a little water on the top of the head (in the region of the fontanelle) to drive out some of the heated vapour (*panan-bowol bukaq*).

There is a custom that the mother's brother or father (*epu-bapa*) should be called to cut the child's hair when it is first cut. This is not in fact very often practised in Léuwajang. It is optional and is done only when the parents consider themselves important. One man told me that when he was a baby, his parents asked his *epu-bapa* to cut his hair for the first time. The *epu* refused to do it before a tusk of the bridewealth was paid. When this was settled, he did so. He was given in return for the service *laong-witing*, a goat and an ear-ring. The child was given by his *epu-bapa* a red fez (*songkok stanbul*, i.e. fez Istanbul) to wear. In other areas of Kédang the practice is more common. In Léuwajang it seems hardly to occur any longer; however, it was always confined to children of prominent people.

During the first four or five years of a child's life, its hair is often shaved to rid it of lice. Commonly a shock of hair is left over the fontanelle and falling over the forehead (*wau utuq*) for a boy or a long shock at the base of the skull (*uli puén*) and falling towards the shoulders for a girl. These two hair styles are in keeping with the association of the male with the above and the female with the below and also with the association between the woman and the source or trunk of life (*puén*).

It has been mentioned that the stages of development of a child's life are thought to be brought about by the changes or stages of the moon (*meti ula*). Commonly these stages are reckoned in the number of months it takes for them to appear. A child teethes in about three months; in about six months or so longer it begins to walk. They say that at each of these stages, the child develops a fever or has diarrhoea or some such disorder before it occurs. It has been mentioned that menstruation is sometimes called *uluq-nawaq* or *uliq-nawaq*, phrases which seem to mean seed, or place of origin, of the soul. I have been told that a person's *nawaq* (soul) is like a shoot (*ubuq* or *tiboq*). When one is born it is there, and when it rises (under the influence of the moon) then one's legs and arms become strong and one can crawl around, and later walk. When the limbs have thus become strong, they refer to them as *lolon paar*. *Lolon* means 'leaves'; *paar* stands in opposition to *ubuq*, the shoot or the new leaves at the top of the plant (compare in this respect *oté ili ubuq*, 'at the peak of the mountain'). *Lolon paar* are the large, old leaves at the bottom of a plant. This case provides a metaphor in which the human body (and soul) is compared to a plant. It would be mistaken though to take this in too figurative a sense or to think the comparison is solely one way. I think there are no privileged spheres of metaphor in Kédangese thought, for they perceive first what is common and then distinguish, rather than to take the distinguished and then to attempt to compare the essentially separate.

I was given this representative list of the stages of an infant's development:

(1) *katiq tawé* (responding by laughing).
(2) *iring peq* (turning over and sticking its rear in the air).
(3) *tebéq manga* (sitting up securely), *awar tawé, awar kiloq* (the teeth grow out and sparkle).
(4) *kopi-tang* (beginning to crawl).
(5) *lakaq-koqal* (taking a few steps and falling).
(6) *lédo-pan* (walking).
(7) *tutuq-nanang* (talking).

There is an expression *nara deko deq-o*, meaning the child is old enough to wear short pants. This is a recent usage. Formerly children went without clothing until they were quite large because of the difficulty of obtaining it (cf. Vroklage 1952: 1: 162–3). Today a child will usually have at least one piece of clothing by the time it is old enough to walk, but will usually go naked until about five or six (school age).

When a mother dies leaving a living new-born child (*lopi anaq*), a ceremony will be held in the infant's mother's brother's or mother's father's home. There a sign made of two posts and a crosspiece of *aur* bamboo, to which are tied grass and the leaves of lontar and coconut palms, is placed in front of the door to close it so the mother, who because of her feeling wants to take the child with her, will not come to disturb it. This ceremony is called *peting koaq, haqa*, 'To tie feathers, close the door', or *bulung huna*, 'to put a sign on a house'. I was told in one instance that the *aur* bamboo used may be split in the centre but not at the ends. Then this is pulled apart, symbolic of letting the child and people of the house pass through, after which the parts are allowed to come together, thus closing the door to the dead woman. Similar procedures may also be followed in ceremonies held in cases of illness.

IX

AGE, THE SOUL, AND ILLNESS

DIFFERENCE of age is a necessarily universal feature of human society, and the association between authority and greater age is a common topic in Indonesia. Needham (1966) has drawn attention to the conflict between relative age and social category, and has shown that where the latter weakens the former tends to come to the fore.

Kédang exhibits a society in which category is securely predominant, but for all this the factor of age is no less important here, and it is an essential part of the task to attempt to reveal just what ideas are associated with it. The main theme to be argued is that the personality is regarded in Kédang as undergoing a series of transitions associated with ageing and that these are marked in several different ways, all having the same formal effect.

The consideration of how normal transitions of personality are represented then opens the problem of Kédangese ideas concerning the soul and then finally illness.

I. TEETH-FILING AND BLACKENING

The Kédangese (other than the Muslim part of the community) do not know circumcision. There are no rites of passage associated with maturation and ageing from the period of restriction following birth until the time the teeth are blackened. This latter is not accompanied with a ceremony and is therefore not properly a rite; there also seems now to be a considerable amount of confusion about its occasion, owing perhaps to the fact that it is here as elsewhere in Indonesia such an ancient cosmetic practice that it has become considered almost necessary to beauty. It does seem, however, to be a sort of time mark, and I will try to deduce what it may signify about the meaning of age.[1]

Teeth-blackening is associated with filing them. This does not mean, though, that they necessarily occur simultaneously, or even

---

[1] Unfortunately, I have not been able to consult the articles on teeth-filing and blackening in Kédang by Lie Goan Liong.

that they derive from the same ideas. Covarrubias says that, 'The custom of filing and blackening the teeth, which is widespread throughout Malaysia, has its roots in animistic ritual, to avoid having the long, white teeth of dogs' (1937: 119). This reason is not recognized in Kédang, however interesting it may be if one turns to the question of origins. On the other hand it is true in Kédang as he says for Bali that it is done for aesthetic reasons, since it is thought that long teeth are ugly.

The filing of the teeth is not necessarily done on a single occasion, as it is a painful process. It may begin when a child is a few years old. People in their thirties may continue it, and some people occasionally wait until they are quite adult to begin. Occasionally parents will force their children to undergo it against their will, but I have the impression that it is usually voluntary.

The teeth are blackened only after they have been filed to a satisfactory level. I have been told by old people that formerly everyone blackened their teeth before they were married, even though now they do not, but this statement is in conflict with other reports from apparently equally authoritative sources, and it poses great interpretative problems. By taking all the reports together I have formed the following impression. Perhaps some men now do blacken their teeth, as is done in other Indonesian communities; and quite possibly this was once more popular. However, it has been pointed out to me several times that most men have black teeth not because they ever blacken them but because they are stained with betel. The teeth, if not regularly cleaned, will, with continual betel chewing, eventually accumulate a heavy black coating.

It seems, according to several reports, that teeth-blackening, while optional for a man, is prescribed for women. And my observations suggest that, except in coastal trading communities, this prescription has hardly relaxed. Women, however, do not blacken their teeth before marriage. It is then done only once she has had a child, quite commonly only after she has had two. This provides an essential point for interpretation and I will return to it later.

When the teeth are filed for the last time and blackened, they will hold a small private feast. This, however, is not of a ceremonial nature, but is a form of repayment for the man who has done the job. The person called in to do this need be no special relation, but is someone who is skilled in it. The substance used is taken from a durian named *nahaq* (it will be recalled that the placenta is called 'great *nahaq*'). A few twigs of this plant are put in a fire until they flame. Then they are taken out and applied to the blade of a field-knife or digging-stick until some liquid comes out. This process is repeated until enough liquid has been obtained. This then is smeared on the teeth. Among the reasons for doing this which I have heard are that it protects the teeth from the effects of betel (commonly reported from other societies) and that it shows that the woman is no longer available.

Perhaps more information can be acquired if we compare this custom with other practices. It seems that the first thing to mention is that the string used in ceremonies to represent the soul (*tuber-nawaq*) consists of two twisted strands, one black and the other white. It has been mentioned that the colour of the finger-nails indicate whether the child has been born prematurely or not. Other things are blackened after they are first made. For instance, wooden plates must be turned black (with a mixture made from indigo, I think). The red earthen pots bought from Alorese traders must be blackened by smoking before they are considered strong enough to be used (though the pots have already been fired before they are sold). There are other cases in which utensils undergo a process which blackens them; but in a number of cases my friends were able to convince me that they had primarily a utilitarian reason. At any event a number of instances show that the opposition between black and white is sometimes associated with coming into being. More detailed treatment of colours will have to wait until more of the relevant information has been presented. For the moment this result is enough.

2. FOOD RESTRICTIONS

Women as a class are subject to a number of food restrictions. Like teeth blackening, these are taken up with the birth of the first or, more commonly, the second child. It is said that these restrictions all stem from *ahar*. The woman is prohibited rice, goat, the types of bananas known as *muqu hiuq* and *muqu idin* (the first is used in a funeral and ceremony connected with a bad death; the second contains the word *idin*, which means 'orphan'), locust (*ioq*), grasshoppers (*waiq*), a kind of large worm (*tihel*) with a bright red head and a black body, which is caught in large numbers in the rainy season (about February), and egg. I was told, in the latter instance, that a woman who has food restrictions may eat eggs only if her hair is tied up in a knot behind her head (the usual way of wearing it for adults). If her hair is loose when she eats egg, it will all fall out. The general result of breaking these food restrictions is that one's knees will be weak and one will not be able to walk. The restrictions last until death; they do not end, for example, with menopause.

The problem of the reason for food restrictions is one of the weakest parts of my ethnographic findings. It sometimes seems that certain foods are forbidden because of a symbolic equivalence (as in the case of rice) and sometimes because of a symbolic opposition (as in the case of the goat). The confusion even becomes worse if one turns to comparison with other societies. For example although the woman is forbidden goat in Kédang, she is forbidden pig in Lamaholot. I think though that there is very little of interpretative use in Vatter's accusation that prohibitions of this kind represent a 'cleverly excogitated system to shorten the menue for the women and to acquire for oneself culinary advantages through the detour of religious and social prescriptions' (1932: 151). Pig meat is a highly prized food in Kédang, far preferred to goat. But I have been to feasts where, because of a shortage of animals, the men had to eat goat and the pig was reserved for the women. The two types of bananas might be forbidden because of their association with death and the inhibitory effect they would therefore have on a woman's reproductive powers, but I do not feel certain of this interpretation and I was not able to do the work on the classification of plants which is necessary to provide a definite answer. Why the insects and worm are prohibited is even more unclear.

Despite the obscurities about why each particular food is forbidden, it appears that adoption of the prohibitions as a group has much the same significance as teeth-blackening.

I have mentioned the village-wide prohibition on eating white beans before the new food ceremony; this applies to both men and women; and it too seems to be adopted about the time that the second child is born. Thus, the adoption of food restrictions of any type seems in this case to be associated with the bringing into life of children. This may be the place to refer to the apparent etymological connection between the words for child and complete (or even

numbers). The distinction in pronunciation between the two is
confined to the initial relaxing and tightening of the throat; and
this is a distinction often applied to two senses of what is clearly
the same word. Thus the most clear pronunciation of *anaq* (tight
throat) means 'complete' or 'even'; the less clear pronunciation
(loose throat) means 'child'. I will argue here that the two versions
indicate a similarity of idea.

In the chant used when offering food to the ancestors before
beginning a meal, they sometimes address among the ancestors the
oban mehun. *Oban* is a word used for an animal or person who is
unable to have offspring. It occurs in the longer form *oban watun*.
Oban mehun are the ancestors who did not have offspring, who left
no descendants. These then are those who are ancestors of no one
living, requiring a separate designation. *Oban watun* are people
(or animals) still living, but who have no brothers and who are not
able to have children themselves—whose lineage will die out. This
breaking of the ties with the living is regarded as very unfortunate;
and it is not uncommon that a person without children will undertake the ceremony to adopt fatherless children of another clan
through payment of bridewealth. This is quite often done by a
clan for a man who has long been dead and died with no offspring
(at least no male offspring). This desire to continue one's own line
of descent adds to the motivation for the (in some cases numerous)
series of ceremonies sterile couples will go through in order to
have children.

Having children then, I think, implies a form of completion for
the parents. It certainly leads to their entering a new stage in their
life, and is for that reason comparable to initiation rites. Both
parents incur restrictions in their relation to life-giving foods. For
the woman these are more elaborate than for the man because it
was she after all who brought forth. Shortly I will turn to the case
where the man catches up, but first I must make a few remarks
about age and authority.

3. AGE AND AUTHORITY

In general in Kédang an elder person must be shown respect.
This is true even for the older brother or sister. The role of the
elders in the clan has already been described. It has already
been shown that in certain respects spiritual authority is associated with the oldest clan or with advanced age in general.

Curiously enough there is very little evidence of division of two types of authority associated with the older and younger brother as is found (though inconsistently attributed) so commonly on Timor (van Wouden 1968: 115). The youngest brother is referred to as *laqi-utuq*, meaning the 'tip of a plant'. So there is evidently an association of the younger with the above and the elder with the below, but as far as I have been able to discover this is not carried farther; and on Timor these attributes are also inconsistently associated with elder and younger. Nevertheless, in general one finds a number of ideas which show great age to be associated with origins or sources of life; but this is only another instance of the coming together of death and birth.

Among these cases are the association of the oldest clan with the centre of *léu tuan* and the preference extremely aged people show for living and, especially, dying in *léu tuan* coupled with the fact that the well-being of the village even requires that elderly people live there. Another case which has been mentioned is that an old man may, like the woman, take maize from the inner compartments of the granary. In general it would seem that the image of a section of bamboo with nodes at either end (or a bone with joints at either end) is a good image of age. Active people with children would find themselves in the centre, the children and the elderly would be closer to the nodes at the ends. It has already been shown that the Kédang language suggests this image: the same word for joints and nodes (*woq*) occurs in the name of the souls of the dead (*tuan-woq*). However, in the chapter on time I have shown that such sequential progressions are thought to have a cyclic character. Birth and death are associated because they fall at the same point; the one represents a return. This is indicated by the tradition that an extremely aged person is thought to complete his span of life as other people do not and he waits until his month of birth (his mother's time) to die. This idea of completion then is found in association with the child and in association with great age. It seems here that we are approaching an explanation in Kédangese terms for what Dumont (1966: 238) calls 'the ubiquity of features which bring together in terminology as well as behaviour grandparents and grandchildren'.

However, as Fischer and Renselaar (1959: 47, 50) show, such categorical association does not necessarily imply that the grandchild enjoys the same status as the grandparent or that he need not treat his grandparent with respect and obedience. In the same way the bringing together of the idea of birth and death does not mean that these are experienced as qualitatively identical. This is shown in one instance in the fact that though an old man may remove maize from the inner part of the granary, children are under the strongest possible prohibition. To set the child as the equal of his grandparent would imply a reversal of direction of the sort which is so disliked in other areas. The aged person, after all, is approaching the ancestors; if he is in delirium in the last stages before death, it is thought that he is already holding conversations with them. The child is at the farthest remove from them.

The importance of the found objects (*talu-beru*) has been mentioned and they have been described to some extent. These may be found by men or women; and the finding of them is not confined to any one age group. Nevertheless, preponderantly they are found by mature men, or at least the ceremonial obligations and privileges associated with them are taken up usually only with maturity, and, indeed, at that stage where the man may be considered to be entering old age. Actually there may be several people in a clan who have them, but it appears that a single person in each clan is pre-eminently associated with them, and he may even be entrusted with the temporary guarding of those found by the others. At present there is a good deal of disruption of the traditional pattern; and it may never have been perfect for all the clans at all times, simply because it is not a question of appointment but of someone growing into the position. However, *talu* seems to form part of a pattern of ideas centred round the position of *aqé-amé*. As I reconstruct it, ideally the clan elder who acts as *aqé-amé* should be the one who is under the restrictions associated with *talu*. He also should live in *léu tuan* near the clan temple, which he guards just as he guards the *talu* of other clan members. He also takes the leading role in bridewealth transactions, and is specifically charged with beating down the bridewealth demands of the wife-givers. I do not think that he ever lived in the clan temple (which is very small); but just this set of responsibilities seems, according to my observations, still to be found associated in East Flores with the man who guards the clan temple, in which, in this case, he does live.

At present in Léuwajang there are several clans which no longer have a clan temple, nor anyone with *talu* restrictions who holds the new food (*a weru*) ceremonies each year. This is undoubtedly associated with the disruptive influence of Christianity and Islam, but I do not think it certain that none of those clans will ever have them again. It is still quite possible that someone will develop *talu* restrictions to the point where all the ceremonial paraphernalia, including the clan temple, will have to be renewed.

The clan temple is a small building, perhaps not even two metres on a side, constructed according to the same rules described in the chapter on the house. It stands on four posts and contains an inner room large enough for perhaps one person to sit in. The valuables of the clan are not now stored in it; and the most use it has is to keep the small altar stones used in the 'new crops' ceremony (*a weru-wehar*). The symbolic meaning of the building is that it is the house of the clan ancestors. Its names are *huna suku* ('clan house'), *huna wowo* ('spirit house'; *wowo* means 'voice' and the voice represents spirit), and *huna talu* ('house for *talu*').

One clan in Léuwajang was in the unfortunate position that the man who held its *talu* had abandoned all his restrictions and moved away from the village to live permanently at his fields. He seems to have been driven to this because his household was continually finding them. At any rate, he returned to the village and immediately fell so ill in his legs that he could not walk. One of my friends, who was in fact serving as the *aqé-amé* of the clan, told him that his *talu* had hit him back (*talu nawang*), and that if they did not have a ceremony to renew the clan temple and the *talu* he would never recover.

Talu bring a number of restrictions, among them that on eating the new maize. This lasts until the ceremony held at the clan temple (in most cases) in which the new corn is for the first time ceremonially eaten (*a weru*; the old is taken out and the new put in). Additionally, someone who has the full set of prohibitions must have a hearth of his own. In his hearth he may not burn a number of bad kinds of wood (*miréq*, candlenut tree; *uar, ewe*, and *awaq*). I cannot identify all the types nor do I know why they are forbidden. The candlenut is, however, an extremely poor burning wood. Also he may not eat anything prepared on a hearth on which food for women is prepared; and frequently women may not drink or eat from his (private) utensils. His hearth may not be lit with fire taken from another hearth which is not subjected to these restrictions. As a consequence of the prohibitions, men subjected to them frequently have their own food prepared and brought for them to feasts and they take their own cups, plates, spoons, and so on.

I have mentioned that one of my friends got his ability to tap palm wine throughout the year from Laba Lia (God in His manifestation as the morning star) in connection with finding *talu*. *Talu*, despite the inconveniences which they bring with them, are usually highly prized. It is said that they protect (*likoq*) their owners; and they represent his personal relation to Divinity. At a guardian spirit ceremony, they will cast auguries to see what the name of the guardian spirit is. They usually come up with names like Laba Lia, Peni Uno. *Talu* are in fact the Kédangese version of the philosopher's stone and are only to be understood in connection with their ideas about gold and the waters of life.

At the moment though, it is useful to draw attention to the similarities between finding *talu* and the birth of a child. First of all they are both associated with the coming into being of life in some form. In the first case the waters of life become a child. In the second they become an object which, though otherwise useless, brings advanced spiritual powers and responsibilities. They both mark a stage of transition in the owner's life. The woman is fully mature and has produced life; the owner of *talu* is beginning to pass from the stage of full productivity (his children are commonly becoming independent). They both bring a revised relation to food. Whereas a man with children may not eat white beans until the (formerly, village-wide) ceremony for removing the old and putting in the new (*a utan*), once he acquires *talu* he may also not eat new maize. Whereas the adult man seems to stand in an opposed and complementary position to the adult woman; with age this opposition becomes weakened and with the acquisition of *talu* must be symbolically strengthened. I suggest that this reflects a distinction of authority in an adult man's life. While in full vigour as head of a family, his authority is primarily temporal; when elderly, primarily spiritual.

4. THE SOUL

Although the soul is represented in offerings by a black and white thread—providing a link with those neighbouring cultures which consider that man has two souls, a black and a white one (cf. Vroklage 1952: 2: 7)—according to tradition he is supposed to have seven. In the case of a very serious illness, one of these souls may die, and death may then be brought about by the accumulating death of these souls. I was never told, however, that the seven souls had individual names or that they were assigned to particular parts of the body. Although Vroklage reports such traditions from some Belu communities, it is clear from his evidence that they do not represent the elementary doctrine but are elaborations of more basic theories. It also seems that a tradition of seven souls should not be thought in conflict with or alternative to one or two souls. The latter conception is structurally equivalent to the imagery of the golden germ or primal seed, which, it has been shown, is a recurrent theme in Kédangese culture. It represents the human soul, as made up of opposed but complementary properties.

The words for black and white are used to express colour relations in a way which may at first seem unusual to us. Thus water is said to be black when opposed to palm wine. In this usage the clear, colourless properties of water are designated as black simply because it lacks the unequivocal whiteness of palm wine. In the same way the young leaves of the lontar palm when freshly cut and still green are called black in opposition to the colourless or white leaves which have dried in the sun. Symbolically there is an essential triad of white, black, and red. White and black are used to symbolize transitions of spirit; red almost always symbolizes moral wickedness.[2]

The idea of seven souls is however an instance of the application of uneven numbers to the sections between points of transition.

In the chapter on the house I mentioned that the opposition between odd and even numbers is one of the most important categorical distinctions in Kédangese thought. Certain structurally important sections of the house must be built of uneven parts. In the same way uneven numbers occur as a structural property of duration. There are said to be seven storms of the rainy season; and the dry season is figured by the conjunction of Antares and the waxing moon on uneven days. A child must stay seven, nine

---

[2] Beyond these, there are words for green (*tangén*), which also means 'unripe', yellow (*uman*), blue (*pahélong*), and brown (*gelang*). The range of the spectrum including blue-green-yellow is called *ijo* [i.e. Ind., *hidjau*]-*pahélong*. Yellow-brown is *éor-gelang*. *Ijo-pahélong* is associated with the rainbow. Otherwise these colours are not symbolically ranked or used for other symbolic purposes. Colours are not associated with the cardinal points.

or eleven months in the womb. So we see that it is not even a question of associating uneven with the solid or tangible or with the body as opposed to the soul. Furthermore, the universe is said to consist of seven layers above and five below. As will be mentioned in the chapter on the funeral, I was once told that uneven numbers are the numbers of life, even numbers the numbers of death. Although this is in some ways inadequate, it is very close to the truth. It was also mentioned that there seems to be an association between even numbers and points of transition. Since that chapter we have encountered several instances in which the number four in particular was associated with transitions, and several of these have been in fact transitions in which life was coming into being. The period of restriction after the ceremony to clean the village (*habiq wéloq-matan*), while the crops are in a critical stage, lasts four days. So too does the period of restriction after a funeral and the period before the navel cord drops off a newborn infant. More instances will be described later.

I should like to argue then that the two conceptions of the soul are in themselves complementary. Two in this case is perhaps not to be interpreted as an instance of even in opposition to odd, but as undifferentiated or germinal as opposed to the differentiated (uneven) version of the same thing. There must be seven souls rather than four for the same reason that the spars of the roof must be uneven on each side: the even number would imply completion of the series and hence the arrival at the next transition, which in the case of life can only be death.

It is thought in Kédang that when one is ill or when one dreams the soul leaves the body. I did not encounter the idea (common elsewhere) that if one wakes a person in deep sleep too quickly it may cause him harm because his soul has not been able to return, but the above conception does provide the bases for their ideas of illness. Before turning to that question, it is necessary to consider the relation between the body and the soul.

The soul is called *tuber-nawaq, uluq-udang*. Although *tuber* and *nawaq* are apparently synonymous, *tuber* would usually be the first word given to translate 'soul'. It is clearly related to the word *tubar*, meaning 'head'; and it is evident that they associate the mental functions with the head, although it alone is not for them the seat of the soul. *Nawaq* has already been thoroughly treated. *Uluq* means 'seed', but we have seen that in the phrase *uluq-*

nawaq, which means 'menstruation', it can have the sense of 'seed of the soul'. *Udang* is a kind of dove (Ind., *perkutut*); this word then indicates the common idea that the soul is a bird. I was also told that the soul may be called *tuber-nawaq*, *ai-ongaq*. The latter phrase refers to a way prisoners or the insane used to be tied up. This involved tying round the throat and the use of large pieces of wood to confine the arms and legs. The intention in this case seems to be that the soul is retained in the body as though the throat were tied to prevent its escape.

Although they do not seem to think of the soul (or souls) as being seated in a particular place in the body, they do know that there are certain vital points where injury can bring death. In particular, the head, wrists and backs of the ankles are known to be vulnerable points, and the inner part of the wrists is called *ling tuber* ('soul of the arm'), the equivalent part of the leg *léi tuber* ('soul of the leg'). My observations of their ceremonies have led to the conclusion that these are only some of the points of the body which are associated in some way with the soul. It is not a question so much of the seat of the soul, however, as one of points of access. For example, when they daub the body with blood (*totoq manuq wéiq*) during the guardian spirit ceremony, they do so at the following points: the forehead, the cheeks, the top of the sternum, below the sternum, the navel, the nape of the neck (*uli puén*), the loins, the shoulders, elbows, wrists, tips of the fingers, knees, tops of the feet, and tips of the toes. The purpose of this procedure, according to my understanding, is to allow the guardian spirit to enter the body. The parts in the list include joints. I have argued that joints are comparable to points of transition, and I also view the points in this list as having the same significance.

5. ILLNESS

The most general term for illness is *laén-moléng*. It is a curious feature of this phrase that it is composed of words of opposite meanings. *Laén* by itself means 'to be sick'. *Moléng* means 'to heal' or 'be healthy'. Another phrase for illness is *weq baraq-betéq*. *Baraq-betéq* means 'heavy'; and the term seems to indicate that they experience illness as a state of being weighed down by something from above. In the same sense someone who is healthy may be said to be *ahaq*, 'light'. Perhaps this explains why the curious word *moléng* is used to mean healthy, although its other uses would seem to us not suited. Palm wine which is slightly weakened or watery is said to be *moléng*. A piece of wood used in some construction is *moléng* if it is weak; here the word has the opposite sense from strong, *heker*. The inside of a coconut is *moléng* if it is still soft and somewhat filmy. Later when the meat is hardened it is *leréq*. Thus *moléng* seems to be used as the opposite of a number of words meaning strong, hard, and heavy. Evidently it is the latter usage which causes it to mean healthy.

Why illness is thought to be heaviness has, perhaps, two explanations. When someone is ill his soul has gone to the land of the dead (*tuan-woq*). One must then have a ceremony to call it back, so that one's soul will be complete (*tuberanaq, nawaq nénin*). This ceremony will involve the same procedures as the guardian spirit ceremony for an infant. One will send the bad up and call the good down. By implication illness involves the bad being sent down and the good taken up. Illness is thought to come from God, and the good and bad in each case are associated with the good and bad guardian spirits. The guardian spirit is an aspect of God, and both are associated with the above. Therefore, illness is at once a form of being pressed down from above and an absence of soul, both of which seem to produce a feeling of heaviness. Wind, which is a primary symbol of spirit, can either bring illness (by entering the body) or take it away.

I have mentioned that when someone has a high fever (*weq panan*, lit., 'hot body'), water may be poured on the fontanelle to drive out some of the heated vapour and cool the body. Sweating is thought to be a way to free the body of illness, and the word for sweat seems to be the same as that for 'light', *ahaq*. Another name for good health is *weq piang bala*. *Piang* means 'to shred' or 'split'; *bala* is an elephant tusk. The image seems to indicate that the hardness of illness splits open, bringing relief.

The adept at healing, the *molan-maran potaq-puiq*, blows and spits on his patient. I could not get a direct explanation for this, but it seems that the procedure is intended to allow the guardian spirit of the healer to enter the body to find the cause of illness. Once found, then the spirit may cure it. The healer often chews some sirih-pinang and his private root and spits this on the patient; this is medicine and presumably it is carried into the body by the guardian spirit. The healer may also inspect a bowl of water to see the cause; after the session, he may then sprinkle this water around the door to seal it off, so that his guardian spirit will not return. The healer never claims success in advance; the success of the cure depends upon the will of God.

One of the obligations a man has towards his mother's brother (*epu-bapa*) is to inform him if he is sick. Were he eventually to die before the *epu-bapa* had been informed of his illness, his clan would have to pay an elephant tusk as fine. In connection with this, the *epu-bapa* is thought to hold the power of causing illness or bringing health in his hands (*laén di epu-bapa, moléng di epu-bapa*; 'sickness with the *epu-bapa*, health with the *epu-bapa*'). Therefore, if one is seriously ill, then one may enter one's *epu-bapa*'s house (*uduq-loko*). This means a man will go to the nearest relation in his mother's clan. A married woman would go in the first instance to her brother's house. My observation indicated that this procedure is quite commonly followed. The *epu-bapa* in such an instance is said to serve as *tuan ula-lojo mier*, which might just as well be translated as God. He thus protects his sister's offspring (*anaq maqing*) in the same way as a guardian spirit or God. One is especially under his protection while in his house, but that does not necessarily mean that he will do anything else while one is there. Nevertheless, if a ceremony is held to cure the illness, the *epu*'s house would be an appropriate place for it, and in any case it would include a stone for the ancestors of his clan.

It is feared that a woman may suffer from haemorrhageing if the *balai* upon which she has sat during her restriction of *ahar-oliq* is burnt. Such an illness is called *noruq-horuq, wala bai. Noruq-horuq* refers to the cross-beams under the floor of the granary. The phrase is to be distinguished from the pole (*noru*) used to pick (*horu*) mango. *Wala* refers to the tied spadices which give palm wine. *Bai* means to be stabbed from above. In explanation of the imagery, a man compared it to the way the tied spadices (*wala*) might brush against one's shoulder while climbing into the crown of the palm. A woman suffering from this disease may not burn the spadix from the male lontar palm in her fire. The only medicine is to scrape bits of wood off the poles and spars underneath the floor and roof of a granary, starting in the right-hand corner (*lili wana*), and taking from each corner in succession, going counter-clockwise and then taking more from the beams (*atang*) in the same manner, and then more from the inside compartments of the granary. This medicine is called *mutung alé*, the same term as that applied to the wood scraped from the granary when it is first built. The wood scrapings are mixed in water and drunk. After having recovered, the woman may not enter the granary for a month, after which time they will hold a guardian spirit ceremony.

Illness is not caused solely by God or one's guardian spirit, though perhaps ultimately they are always involved. One's dreams are usually investigated to determine the immediate cause or causes (*wangun-léan*); and sometimes it is found to be related to some fault of one's own or to the ill intentions of another. In either case, the immediate effects may have been brought about by an evil spirit entering the body. If one has a ceremony because of possession of this sort, one uses a young coconut (*taq mutiq*) which one then prepares in the same way as at a rain ceremony. The water this time, however, does not shoot straight up; rather it is aimed in the direction of the evil spirit; that is, against a rock or tree, if that is the location of the evil spirit.

A friend once told me a dream he had had when he was ill, which might have indicated a cause of his troubles. He said it was like he was crazy. He dreamed that he entered his mother's house (she was long dead) and broke her pot.

Leprosy is called *ai rapuq*. *Rapuq* has something to do with the bark of trees, from which the name is drawn by comparison. Anyone suffering from it may not eat large animals with blood (*wéiq ria*, 'big blood') such as goat, pig, and dog; but he may eat chicken, rice, salt, fish, and so on. A victim must live in a house by himself at a great distance from other people and will be buried far from the village or hamlet. It is said of the disease *ling bolaq*, *léi bolaq*, the hands and the feet fall off. Beri-Beri is called *babang-huréng*, and lung haemorrhage which is caused by tuberculosis is called *boor wéiq*, 'to cough blood'. Someone with the latter may also not eat anything with blood, nor may he eat rice or salt. He is prohibited rice because of the danger of the grains causing a fit of coughing. Salt will prolong the illness. He must eat only dried fish (not fresh) and maize. He may eat vegetables, but unlike a victim of leprosy, he may not eat papaya (fruit or leaves) or *motong* (*Moringa oleifera* Lam.). The same prohibitions apply to anyone ill with beri-beri. Excessive use of salt is, in general, thought to cause colds and eye infections.

Whenever a sick person is moved, as for example if he is taken to the polyclinic, they must break an egg in the middle of the walk. If the trip is far, they will do this several times. The egg is broken by a priest (*molan-maran*); then those carrying the patient each step on it. This is to prevent witches (*maq-molan*) from following.

X

DEATH AND THE FUNERAL

I. TYPES OF DEATH

THE distinction between good and bad deaths is extremely widespread in Southeast Asia.[1]

In Kédang there is a class of death called *reqé-léwun* which includes various unusual, commonly violent, forms of dying, and which requires special treatment. Always included in this class are deaths from a fall or by a weapon or a death at sea. As elsewhere, there is some disagreement whether death in childbirth or from a snakebite is included in the class, though many think they are. All such deaths were characterized as arriving suddenly; and they will entail divination to search for the cause (or causes). It is generally considered that such a death is due to some fault or sin of the victim himself; in one case it was explained that deaths of this kind are set apart because by being brought about by the victim's own fault they do not wait on God's choice.

Not everyone who dies before old age necessarily dies a bad death, however. There seems, in fact, to be a sort of middle ground. There was one woman who died in our village at middle age; and though she was given a normal burial rather than the treatment reserved for those who die a *reqé-léwun*, it was still considered that she had died before her time and the causes (*wangun-léwun*) had to be divined. It was necessary in her case to include in the funeral the use of a banana trunk to remove this badness, but the banana used was still distinguished in type from that used in the case of a bad death. Another very old woman died and the same measure was required because she had been subject to great discharges like those of cholera in the last stages; but she was certainly not thought to have died a bad death, as was shown by the festivities which accompanied her funeral. Beri-beri and lung haemorrhageing do not lead to bad deaths, nor is stillbirth in this class; but none of these are regarded as being good deaths. Leprosy on the other hand is a form of bad death, although it is by no means sudden. In this case it seems to be its ineluctable

[1] See Sell's review of this topic (Sell 1955).

quality which leads to this classification. When two people die on the same day, or if several people in the same clan die within a short span of time, this is taken to be an especially bad sign, and it sometimes causes such fright that only the closest relatives will guard the corpse and carry out the funeral.

The soul of someone who has died a *reqé-léwun* will suffer a different fate, which will be described below, from that of other people, and it is called *melo-maing* (not *mélo-main* as Vatter has it, 1932: 214).

There is no idiomatic expression in the Kédang language which would be exactly translated good or bad deaths, though they sometimes use such terms when speaking Indonesian. Idiomatically, only this especially bad form of death is singled out. The term *reqé* seems to have no use other than in this context. *Léwun* indicates, however, that it affects the well-being of the village. Among those deaths which do not fall into this category are many, usually the results of illness, which are still not good and can in fact be called *reqé datén* ('bad *reqé*'). My impression is that most deaths fall in this middle ground. They require a certain amount of correcting of faults, but they do not have the consequences for the soul that the other type has.

The only really good death is that from great age, but there is no special idiom for this type. Someone who dies in this way has been husbanded (Ind., *piara*) by God until completion of the full cycle of his life. He then dies in the month of his birth. When someone dies in this way, they will beat a gong immediately. The significance is that it is an extension of his breath. At a death, though not at a birth, it must be a gong. No other instrument is acceptable; and it will not be done for anyone but an old man or woman, or a prominent person. When one very ancient and prominent old man died in the village, they beat a single gong for a minute or so. When it was heard, everyone in the village knew what it meant, as they had been expecting it. The various gong and drum orchestras (*kong-bawa*) of the village were brought out and readied for use. They were then in constant play day and night until the burial, which took place at sundown the next evening. The gong orchestras were used in the funerals of other old men and women of prominence, but not in cases of the deaths of old people of less prominence. Dying of great age does not in itself assure that one will merit this distinction, though this is one of the important criteria.

K—G

The body of an infant is buried in the house. Whether it receives any ceremonial treatment is a matter of its parents' decision.
If it does it will receive the form of burial used in ordinary deaths.
It is in no way considered a bad death. Customs of this type are
often interpreted as indicating that the child has not yet completely
emerged into the realm of the living (cf. Hertz 1960: 84; van
Gennep 1960: 152). I regard this interpretation as being adequate
to explain why the child is buried in the house in Kédang, the
house being in this case a sort of womb or portal. I was never told
that the infant's soul is thought to return to the realm of the un-
born or that it would be reborn in another child. I was told,
though, that it is buried in the house to protect it from the rain
and heat.

Formerly, death was an occasion for the wife-giver (*epu-bapa*, in
this case the mother's clan for a man, or the brother's clan for a
woman) to demand the payment of outstanding bridewealth.
Since burial may not take place without the permission and presence of the mother's brother or present living representative of
his line (in the case where a man dies), when the bridewealth
demanded was not at hand, burial could not immediately take
place (cf. Vatter 1932: 214). Another cause for such delay was the
lack of necessary provisions for the funeral feast.[2] It was and still
is sometimes the practice to put off such a feast until those for
several lineage mates may be held together. In former times,
final burial would also be put off (cf. Beckering 1911: 199); today,
the government requires burial within twenty-four hours, a
regulation which seems to have been introduced by the Dutch.
In the cases where formerly the corpse was not immediately
buried, it would be laid out (*halaq matén*) in a specially built house
(*huna matén*). Vatter says this would be at the edge of the village;
he also says that while the corpse was there it would be provided
with rice or maize as daily provisions. Since the custom has long
disappeared, I cannot confirm this. His information in regard to
the handling of the corpse at this stage conflicts in some particulars with my own. According to him the corpse would be mourned
for four days, during which the men would become mightily

---

[2] 'We are . . . justified in believing that normally, the time which elapses
between the occurrence of death and the final ceremony corresponds to the
time judged necessary for the corpse to reach a skeletal condition . . .' (Hertz
1960: 31–2). This is not true in Kédang.

drunken. On the fifth day one of the relations—usually the wife's brother if the deceased was married—would take the corpse and shake it back and forth in front of the house until the fluids from the decaying body had all flowed out. The earth soaked by these fluids would then be enclosed by a bamboo fence; and the corpse would be set out to dry.

That the wife-giver would handle the corpse in this manner conflicts with the customs of Léuwajang. All handling of the corpse is done, in fact, by the wife-takers (*maqing*). However, the conflicting reports might well rest on a difference of custom in the vicinity of Hobamatan. The assignment of the task of handling the corpse is not uniform in eastern Indonesia. In fact, Vroklage reports for the Belu that it is precisely the wife-giving group (*uma mane*) which must make most of the preparations for the burial (1952: 2: 77). Nevertheless, the unpleasant task of removing the flesh from the corpse is not assigned to them (1952: 2: 49).

The fluid from the corpse is called *manga-pauq*. *Manga* means 'strong'; *pauq* means 'to sprinkle' or 'pour'. I was told in Léuwajang that the fence which Vatter says is built around the earth soaked with this fluid was in fact built under the house in which the corpse is set to rot. The flesh would hardly have decomposed in four days, and so I think that the custom in Léuwajang was simply to let the fluid drain to the ground below this building. They wanted to keep the dogs away from the corpse, and they were afraid of a chicken flying over a corpse so laid out because they believe it would cause the corpse to come back to life. The fence seems to have had the purpose of keeping these animals out. They also supposedly guarded the house for the purpose of keeping them away. However, this was not continuous. I was told that they had a dance one night every seven days (on a market day) while the corpse was in the house, in order to guard it. This requirement, however, was only for the older people. If a young person died it was not necessary. The guarding would last until the bones could be given temporary burial.

The spars (*nawel*) used in the roof of such a house were constructed in an unusual manner. A single pole was bent in the middle to form a spar on both the down (*unéq*) and the up (*wajan*) sides of the roof. Then on the nights in which they guarded the corpse, they could lift the up (*wajan*) section of the roof like a lid and prop it open with poles. I was told that these spars would have to be of an even number in each section of the roof in contrast to the rule for normal buildings. The rationale given in this case was that even numbers were the numbers of death, uneven the numbers of life. Other people insisted that the spars of a building of this type must also be uneven in each section. There was no possibility to check this, but the same disagreement existed concerning the construction of the platform (*nekaq-madaq*) on which the corpse is rested during an important stage of the funeral ceremony. These I could observe and I found that in most cases they were built of an uneven number of parts. It seems to me that neither point of view need be rejected; both seem plausible ways for the Kédangese to interpret their culture. Using the opposition between odd and even to represent the opposition between life and death is a possible way of employing these terms and finds parallels in other cultures. However, we have seen instances where even numbers have been associated with coming into life, so this usage would have to be considered a restricted interpretation, and it is no wonder that it does not seem to be the most frequent. It is probably more consistent for them to stay with the rule that anything built must be built according to the rule of uneven parts.

After the flesh had disappeared, the bones would be given a temporary burial (*lutur*) in or near a stone terrace wall. I was not told that the flesh would be specially removed, and I think this was not done. Later, when the bridewealth was settled, the bones could be taken out and given a full burial. If the bones or skull had disappeared, they could be replaced. Bones would be substituted by candlenut wood; the skull by a coconut or lontar fruit.

I witnessed the disinterment of a man who had been given such a temporary burial in the 1930s. His bones had been stored in a hole in a stone terrace wall, which was then rebuilt over them. They were laid out in a regular manner with the head to the right (*oté*). When they were dug out they were put in a cloth (*lipaq*) to be carried. Pains were taken to see that the larger bones, if still intact, were kept straight according to left and right. A mat, actually an old pandanus rain cape, was then tied around the bones and another cloth of the same type placed on top. There was no ceremonial connected with this. The bones were dug out, as was fitting, by his son and another close clan mate and by a man who stood in the relation wife-taker (*maqing*). He was then buried simultaneously (though in a different grave) with his newly dead wife.

When someone dies, his sister's son (*anaq maqing*) has the privilege of claiming some of his coconut trees. This he does simply by placing his arm around them and saying they are his. If he were to do so, it would be unthinkable that he shirk on his contributions to the funeral feast; and it would be expected that he bring a very large goat. On the other hand, when a very prominent man dies, his closest relations through his mother (*epu-bapa*) may demand the payment of an elephant tusk called in this case the *otéq-noloq*, or 'hair'. They then give a return called the *méi-ulé*, which means a support to protect the hair against the worms in the grave (Ind., *alasan ulat*). The hair, they see, falls out after the corpse has been exposed to the worms. The same prestation for a woman, received by her brother's clan, is called *bai-améq*, translatable as 'to call farewell'.

2. THE FUNERAL

Preliminaries (Prior to Kéu Léu)

To bury is called *tanéng matén*. By government order, a burial must now occur twenty-four hours after death. If the situation does not permit this, the burial may occur before the twenty-four hours have elapsed. Formerly a period of four days would have to elapse before the corpse could be buried. I was told by people who had experienced it that when they would wait four days before burial, the stench was ferocious and only certain people were capable of carrying the corpse, and these had to drink themselves drunk. Many people vomited. Even now I have seen small children vomit at funerals.[3]

The corpse must be guarded (even today) the night before it is buried. This is particularly the task, or privilege, of young people, those who through relationship or contiguous residence are going to be present to provide labour for whatever arrangements need to be made during the burial and subsequent feast. There are various communal games played to aid in staying awake.

On the day a man dies, his wife-takers (*maqing*) and close lineage mates come to the house to help in arranging the corpse for burial;

---

[3] 'It [the body] is an object of horror and dread' (Hertz 1960: 37). I have never seen signs of horror and dread. I think this is not a Kédangese attitude, at least so long as the corpse has not begun to decompose.

and they stay throughout the ceremony, as they have an important role in it. Someone must come from each clan into which one of the man's sisters has married. Normally, these will be the sister's husband or his close relations, but it is formally permissible for the clan to be represented by any of its members. The man's *epu-bapa* (mother's brother or equivalent) comes first on the day of burial, and he is obliged to make prestations. The funeral could not be held if he did not come and bring the piece of cloth called the *tené-uring*. If the funeral were held before he got there, he could take the *tené-uring* back home and not bring it back until he had been paid a fine of a tusk of three units (*munaq telu*), as they measure elephant tusks. It is often the case that a claim for outstanding bridewealth will be made by the *epu* before the burial. This is still done although the government does not allow the *epu* to hold up the burial; but the matter of what is owed is usually settled.

Today the head of the village or other village official, as representative of the village, must attend, as well as the clan elder (*aqé-amé*) of the deceased's clan and of the *epu*'s clan. Those from the various clans of the wife-takers (*maqing*) may well attend, but their presence is not required. When the *epu* arrives, these and others present sit down together and chew sirih-pinang. At this point the family of the deceased show the *epu* the clothing which they have provided for the corpse.

This consists, if the deceased is male, of two *lipaq* (man's sarong), a piece of black cloth (*nutaq-tawan*, *kapang* or *sitaq miténg*), a cloth to tie round the waist, known as the *mesé* when it is worn by a corpse, in which case it is made of thread, or known as *méding* and made of skin if worn while alive. This must be accompanied by a loincloth (*tariq*). Formerly, the men of Kédang wore only the *méding* and *tariq*, but in this century clothing has become available through the Chinese, and these articles are no longer worn. The clothing provided by the deceased's clan are not in the form of prestations. If he does not own a *mesé* (waist cloth) or *tariq* (loincloth),[4] his relations must buy them from someone else;

---

[4] The *mesé* is a thin white piece of cloth about a yard long and an inch and a half wide with tassels on the ends. The *tariq* is a similar, three inch wide piece of blue cloth. Blue in this case would be equivalent to black (both are produced in dyeing cloth with the use of indigo); so there is the symbolically significant presence of white and black in this clothing, which is not found in the *lipaq* and sarongs.

however, sirih-pinang is used for the purchase, not money. Although the *mesé* and *tariq* are no longer worn as normal clothing, they are still used for funerals. However, if the deceased is female, they are not used. The family of the deceased (if it is a married woman, her husband's household) provide two sarongs and the piece of black cloth. During this period (and since the corpse was first cleaned and dressed after death) the corpse lies on a *balai* in the house or under the granary, with the head pointed to the right in relation to the slope (*oté*), the feet to the left (*olé*).

The gifts brought by the *epu* are one *lipaq* (man's sarong) for a male or a sarong for a woman (in which case if she is married the *epu* in question is her brother or member of his clan), known as the *tené uring*, 'steering the boat', and a piece of black cloth known as the *tubén lala*, 'to show the way'. The *tené uring* is intended to conduct the deceased on his way so that he will not stumble during his journey: *kara koqal-hoko* ('do not fall'), *kara tipo-laléq* ('do not trip').

Next begins the stage of the ceremony known as the *ka-nin* (the last meal of the deceased). First the clothing which the corpse is wearing is removed and the clothing designated by the name of this stage (*ka-nin*) put on. For the man the clothing called *ka-nin* consists of the *mesé* and *tariq*: for the woman it is one of the sarongs given by the family. This is somewhat difficult because it is done in full view and they, therefore, must put the new clothing on underneath the old, which are removed only after the new are arranged. In the case of a male a *lipaq* (male sarong) is left on over the loincloth. Changing the clothing is known as *kelung-lodong* ('to change and drop'). This work is done by the wife-takers (*maqing*) of the deceased if male or of the husband if the deceased is a married woman. It is done under the supervision of an old person of the deceased's clan (for a woman, of her husband's clan). I was told that this old person must be of the same sex as the deceased. The old person begins the process—that is, he will place the clothing at the feet, the *maqing* then complete the task. If the deceased is a married woman, her husband's *maqing* arrange the corpse. If she is an unmarried woman or young girl, her father's *maqing* arrange the corpse, but they take none of the clothing (this will be explained later) because they regard her as *mahan*, the category from which they must take a wife.

When this change of clothing has been completed, then the

final meal (*ka-nin*) is thrown away. This food consists of a pot filled with rice and covered with a wooden plate, one plate of crushed maize, maize on the cob in a flat basket, a plate of cooked chicken mixed with coconut sauce, one glass of palm wine on a saucer, and a basket (*wajaq*) of sirih-pinang. This stage is known as the *tiwa* ('throw away') *olon-luo ahin* ('left-over food'). This is done by an old woman from the deceased's clan. It must be a woman, they say, because 'when we are alive the women arrange the food, and when we are dead they must do so too'. She takes a pot of rice and stands with it at the head of the corpse and breaks it on a stone to the right (in relation to the slope, *oté*) from the corpse. The significance is that the corpse has eaten. The other food is simultaneously poured out on the stone and is later eaten by the dogs.

Following this is a stage known as *birang kapang* or *kédaq nédaq, karéq kapang*. This consists essentially of showing and counting the cloth from the family of the deceased and from the wife-giver. For this purpose three bamboo slats of the type of bamboo known as *aur* are laid parallel on the ground next to the stone on which the food has been thrown, but above it (oli). Thus, when figured in terms of the slope, they are above (*oli*) and to the right (*oté*) of the corpse. The three slats themselves run parallel with the direction in which the corpse lies (thus, *oté-olé*). These three slats are called *nédaq*, which means, however, slats of bamboo of any sort, especially those used in making walls. When such slats are made, the verb is called *kédaq*; this stage thus gets part of its name, *kédaq nédaq*, figuratively, from the putting down of the slats. However, the slats are also called *niliq-wénaq*, the same name as the identical three slats used for the period of restriction after childbirth, *ahar-oliq*, and they are identified as *ahar*. The order in which the cloth is placed on these slats is as follows: first the two *lipaq*, or the remaining sarong, from the deceased's clan, then the black cloth (*kapang*) from the same clan.

Then this last piece is ripped. I was told that it was shredded into the same number of pieces as the deceased has same-sex siblings, except that it is cut one more time if the number is even. In the funeral of one very old man, who had previously lost four of his five brothers, instead of cutting the cloth for every sibling living, they decided to do so for the lineages of the clan. As lineages are not corporately distinguished in Léuwajang, this required a certain amount of conferring, and each time someone thought of the name of someone in any sense in an apical position, the cloth was torn. The person who does this may first make a slight cut with a knife to start the tear. Then he holds the cloth up to his mouth and blows on the cut as he at the same time rips the cloth. He blows on the cloth to heat it so that it will rip through in one go.

These pieces are carefully laid down on the *lipaq*. Then the *lipaq* or the sarong from the *epu*, the *tené uring*, and the black cloth from the *epu*, the *tubén lala*, are placed on top. Then this clothing is counted four times (*man apaq*). The clothing is taken up in the arm and counted off, putting each piece back on the platform one at a time, four times in succession. Then the two cloths from the *epu* are returned to him momentarily, and the three from the deceased's clan are put back in the flat basket containing maize. The black cloth from the deceased's clan is called, among other things, *kapang*. To count is *karéq*, hence the term *karéq kapang*. To tear is *birang*, hence the phrase *birang kapang*.

At one funeral there was a slight variation introduced at this stage. A man from the village Léudanun, who although from a different clan stood (as will be explained later) as a sort of sibling to the deceased because of a similar relationship to a third clan, brought a strip of black cloth that was included in the *kapang* for the deceased's clan. I was told that if a clan does this it makes official the recognition that the two clans are like siblings. Then if there is subsequently a marriage between them, the clan which takes the wife from the other owes the other a fine of an elephant tusk of three units in their measure and an ear-ring.

The 'Kéu Léu'

When these procedures have been completed, the corpse is wrapped in a mat and carried to a *balai* which has been built outside near the grave. This *balai* is called *nekaq-madaq*, and neither it nor the grave are oriented in relation to the house. A *madaq* is a *balai* built outside to dry coconut; but the term *nekaq-madaq* applies only to the one used in the funeral. The corpse is carried by the *maqing* (wife-takers). At one funeral of a very old woman, when they were carrying the corpse from the house to the *nekaq-madaq*, there was some horseplay in which the bystanders threatened to hit the pallbearers. It was explained to me that the members of her clan were telling their *maqing* to carry her carefully, not to drop her, otherwise they would be beaten ('*maqing*, *boté diqén. Ton, éqi paluq o!'*). This rowdiness seems equivalent to an incident I once witnessed at a later stage of the funeral and will discuss below.

The *nekaq-madaq* must be built according to a number of rules, but as in the case of the house in which the corpse is put to rot, there is considerable conflict of opinion about just what these rules are. In this case I was able to make direct observation and therefore to prove that this conflict of opinion is genuinely a part of Kédangese culture. I will begin with the most certain rule: this platform should be built with only two legs, those being on the down slope side, while the up slope side should be rested on a stone terrace wall or rocks (*dolu*). I found that this rule was often followed; but in a number of cases it was not (far more frequently in fact than the rules governing the construction of a normal house are ignored). Secondly, the main slats in the surface of the platform (*lauq*), which in a *balai* of this type run up and down (*oli-owé* or *bunuq-dau*) in relation to the slope, must be even in number. My observations showed that they were usually uneven, and many people expressly disagreed with the rule. Finally, the horizontal parts in this platform, and in the building for a corpse, must lie clockwise around the construction (*weri pan*, 'travel to the left'). I found no case where this rule was followed, and except for the person who expressed it, everyone I asked insisted that they must be built, as in the case of a normal house, according to the rule *wana pan* ('travel to the right'). I should say that the person who expressed the last two of these three rules was no more unreliable in reporting Kédangese customs than anyone else. There was no one who could be completely relied upon and no one who had nothing of genuine interest to report. As I have said before, I think the disagreement rests on honestly divergent ways of applying the principles of Kédangese culture; and I do not think it is of recent introduction. Though no enthusiasm was shown for the idea that things should be built travelling to the left; some people agreed that even parts should be used in these instances. Either case, however, is an example of a symbolic reversal of the same logical type.

The *nekaq-madaq*, itself, is oriented right and left (*oté-olé*) in relation to the slope; and the corpse, as throughout the funeral, lies with its head to the right (*oté*). When the corpse is brought here two small baskets (which would have hung above his head while he was in the house) are hung from the head end of the platform. The first of these contains white beans. The second contains tobacco, lime, and sirih-pinang and, if a man, a tiny bow and arrow or, if a woman, a small comb and knife. These are provisions for his trip. The implements are very roughly prepared from bamboo and have only representational value, as they could never be used.

At this time the corpse has a second change of clothes called the *kéu léu* or 'to enter the village'. This time the loincloth, if a man, or a sarong, if a woman, is put on the corpse. The black cloth from the *epu*, the *tubén lala* ('to show the way'), is placed under the corpse. It is not shredded like the black cloth from the deceased's clan. This latter is now placed on his chest with the sarong or *lipaq* called the *tené uring* ('steering the boat'). Following this change of clothing, the corpse is plundered. The family of the corpse may, if they wish, reserve for themselves some or all of the cloth in which the corpse is not actually buried. It is not uncommon, for instance, that they keep an expensive sarong. If they do so, this is called *utan-tolor* ('beans-eggs'); i.e. it may be used, figuratively, to shop, 'buy eggs and beans'; they would more likely use it, however, to buy a goat or repay some of the expenses of the funeral. Alternatively, they may decide that all of the cloth will be buried with the corpse. However, most often they acquiesce in the convention that those handling the corpse may take the loose pieces; and consequently, there is at this stage a free-for-all. The quickest gets the cloth. The corpse is handled at this stage, as throughout the ceremony, primarily by the *maqing*; so there is a conventional signal (which may be shouted by anyone) which begins the free-for-all: '*Maqing, maqing, suka, suka!*' This means as much as 'wife-takers, come and take what you want'. However, by this stage, the *maqing* have been joined by many whose presence is not determined by particular relationship with the deceased, so the plunder is not in fact exclusively the preserve of the *maqing*.

This plunder of the corpse must be seen as a reversal of normal decorum, especially that which is supposed to reign between the *maqing* and the *epu*, that is, wife-taker and wife-giver. I will later argue that the funeral consists of a series of ritual acts meant to mark the (progressive) separation between the spirit and the body, and such I think is the explanation for this reversal. That it is in fact a reversal of decorum, and also that it is a rupture imposed by the *maqing* and only tolerated by the clan of the deceased, is shown by the fact that I twice witnessed the head of the village stop the procedure before this stage in the case of burials of extremely old and highly respected men, and warn the partakers not, in these cases, to indulge in rowdiness which might anger the deceased's family.

I was told that in the village Léunoda they do not use a *nekaq-madaq*. The changing of clothing occurs on a mat on the ground in front of the door of the house.

After the corpse is dressed in this stage, there may be a ceremony called the *éuq wau* ('to wash the face'). This will be done in the case of a bad death or in an ordinary death in which there is still some suspicion of fault. The intention is to soak up any illness, bad feelings or sins (*wangun-léan*). In an ordinary death a banana stalk of the type *muqu erun* (lit. 'sweet banana') is used; for a bad death it is a *muqu hiuq*. The procedure is thus: a stalk of a small tree is cut, the leaves removed, and the base softened by beating it against a stone. This base is then rubbed against the forehead of the corpse. Then it is waved around the corpse four times in a counter-clockwise direction (*wana pan*). This is done carefully so that the circle circumscribes the head and feet four times. The person (who may be anyone) performing this task stands near the head but a little to the side. After the fourth circle is completed, the stalk is thrown away at the feet of the corpse. Everyone must clear away from the foot end of the grave when the banana stem is thrown away. There is danger that someone in the way might get some of the bad, fault, or illness being thrown away. I have seen that a branch of a banana tree may be substituted if the tree itself is not available.

When this procedure is over, the corpse is wrapped in a palm-leaf mat. The mat is tied by four bindings (*wadéq*), taken from the ribs of the lontar leaf. They are not tied, but as is usual with such bindings, the ends are twisted and then tucked under the cord. The four bindings are fastened by four men working in unison and on command. They first twist them four times to the right, then untwist them, then twist them four times to the left, finally tucking them under the cord to be held in place. Since this form of tying things is unknown to Westerners, it may be useful to the reader to note that it is the common practice with fastenings of this type in Indonesia to twist them and then tuck them under rather than using knots because the ribs of leaves are not suited to knots.

In this case, twisting to the right means, in our terms, clockwise, and to the left counter-clockwise. This is contrary to many other cases, such as in constructing a building, or waving the banana stalk in the *éuq wau* or other such larger-scale motions, where going to the right means counter-clockwise. The explanation for this is that going to the right (*wana pan*) means to them going away from the body to the right. In large scale motions involving changes of direction to complete a rectangle or circle, this results in a counter-clockwise motion. In this case, a counter-clockwise motion would result (since they use the right hand) from beginning with a motion towards the body. This shows that the right is not to be simply translated as counter-clockwise. In this case the point of orientation is solely in the body. In other cases, the body itself takes a place in a system which orients its environment. In this instance of the bindings, the procedure was interpreted for me as resting on the fact that the right represents life and the left death (cf. Kruyt 1941: 341, 345, 346; this interpretation would provide the rationale for building the platform used in the funeral according to the rule of travelling to the left), therefore the right must be first. On another occasion I was told that the bindings are twisted to the left the last time to make the corpse dead (Ind., *bekin mati*).

After the mat is bound, then a bamboo carrying-stick (*neté*) is laid on top and fastened by four more bindings of the same type. This stick must be of the type of bamboo known as *aur*, and supposedly it also must consist of an even number of sections. Observation showed that they are actually rather careless, and the interpretation of whether it consists of even or uneven sections depends on whether one counts incomplete sections or not. I think when they cut this piece they usually pay no attention to the number of sections. This stick serves as a handhold for the pall-bearers when the corpse is carried from the *nekaq-madaq* to the grave. It is not, however, placed on the shoulders. The four carriers grasp it palms up and hold it before them.

Interment

Although the grave (*uoq*) and the *nekaq-madaq* are not oriented in relation to the house, they are oriented in relation to each other. The *nekaq-madaq* must stand *oté* (to the right in relation to the slope), the grave *olé* (to the left). The grave may be horizontally on a level with, or offset slightly below (*owé*), the *nekaq-madaq*, but it may not be above (*oli*). On one occasion I witnessed, the terrain was such that the grave had to be dug almost directly below (*owé*), but even in this case the *nekaq-madaq* was offset slightly *oté*. That is, while the grave may be slightly below, it may not be directly below, the *nekaq-madaq*. In the case just mentioned, the grave showed signs of having been filled in at one end and extended at the other as a correction to allow for this offset; and in this case observation confirmed what I had been explicitly told on several occasions. What is at issue is that this orientation indicates that in moving from the platform to the grave, the corpse is not moving directly towards the sea. On the other hand, I have

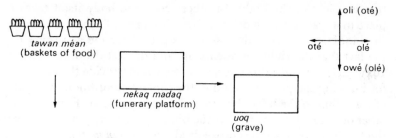

FIG. 6. Orientation of funerary platform and grave.

been told by several people that he is moving to the right (*wana pan*). Whether this is a genuine or only apparent reversal will be discussed later.

At the funeral of one very prominent old priest (*molan-maran*) when they carried him from the platform to the grave, they danced with him in and out of the house several times, while women danced in front and behind. They danced with leaves in their hands and finally some of the women fell to beating the pallbearers with their leaves. The space was constricted (it was a very steep and rocky slope), so they followed no regular pattern, but I was told that it should have been four times around the house, travelling to the right. This was to send him on his way and was a sign of his importance. It corresponds to similar rowdiness when carrying the corpse of a great man elsewhere in Indonesia (e.g. Bali, Covarrubias /1937: 374/, and Timor, Vroklage /1952: 2: 79–80/), and is of similar significance as the case reported above when the corpse was being carried *to* the platform.

There is a tradition that when the grave is dug, the first penetration of the ground must be made by a man from the clan which is *kapitan dulin* and thus guards the door to the village. I think this can be seen as being among his functions as gate-keeper, the grave being after all a form of door. I do not think this custom is frequently observed any longer in Léuwajang. No coffin is used (except in Christian and Muslim burials). The corpse is lowered into the grave and then soil and large rocks are pushed in on top. It seems that women can help in carrying stones to the grave, but they cannot take part in the actual covering of the grave. This fits with the general role of women in burial. Except for a single specific role of the old woman in feeding the last meal to the corpse (and that of changing the clothing when the deceased is a woman), women do nothing directly in handling the corpse. The grave is covered to the level of the ground, then a regular rectangle of heaped stones is made over the grave coincident with its borders and about a half metre high. This is the house (*huna-wetaq*) of the dead. In making this, they sometimes borrow stones from other graves. Before covering the grave the carrying-stick (*neté*) is untied and then placed lengthwise on the finished grave. After the grave is covered, the sides of the grave must be swept four times around, going in a counter-clockwise direction. Here it is called travelling to the right. The sweeping of the grave is called *hain dolu matén*, 'sweeping the stones of the deceased'. The broom used may be made from the leaves of three different plants, but other leaves may not be employed for this purpose. The three types are known as *mular*, *taraq méhel*, and *ai nona*. It is the female of the *taraq méhel* which may be used. I cannot identify them, but they are all types of plants which commonly are grown in terrace walls, for the purpose, I assume, of giving them stability.

After the burial is complete, the small baskets hanging at the *nekaq-madaq*, the platform itself and the *tawan-méan* (a collection of food of various kinds) are thrown away. Although this is a subsequent stage, it is actually often done while the grave is being covered over, and it is usually done by people (including women) not involved in covering the grave. The first of these three stages is the pouring out of the white beans, etc., in the small baskets. This is poured on the ground at the head of the platform. The arrow, if there is one, is then shot down (*owé*, towards the sea) and the bow, or comb, and the knife, are broken and dropped on the ground. Then the baskets are ripped down the side. Next the *nekaq-madaq* is pushed over. It, too, is pushed over towards the sea (*owé*). Later these things (especially the platform) should all be taken to the canyon where they will be safe from burning when the fields are being cleared and where they will be washed to the sea. In one case I witnessed, they were put on top of the grave itself, which served the same purpose, for they will eventually decay.

The last stage is throwing away the *tawan-méan*. During the entire period of the changing of the clothes at the *nekaq-madaq*, a row of people, usually women but including men and children, situates itself *oté* (to the right and slightly above) the *nekaq-madaq*. Before this row of people stands the *tawan-méan*. *Tawan* derives from *tawé*, 'to grow'; *méan* is a form of superlative and has been discussed. Ordinarily this phrase refers to the products of the field. In this case it consists of several baskets of maize, a dried fish, a comb of bananas, and there may be rice as well. The baskets of maize should be of an uneven number, though it does not matter how many ears each contains. Most come from the clan of the deceased. An additional number come from the lines which consider themselves siblings (*meker-éhoq*). These additional baskets are called *nahu-nohan*. The *tawan-méan* is also thrown seaward. Only a little from each basket is actually thrown away; the rest is taken home. The souls of the *tawan-méan* and of the clothing given the corpse during the funeral are considered to accompany him to the land of the dead, where they are divided by him and distributed among his relatives there. Thus a good part of the goods used in a funeral may be seen as offerings to the ancestors.

3. THE FUNERAL FEAST AND 'IRÉNG'

The traditional custom was to have the funeral feast four or eight days after burial. The feast must be given so that the deceased may enter the village of the dead. It is held simultaneously here and among the dead, and without it the deceased would not be allowed to enter his new village. The funeral feast may be seen then as being a feast of initiation.

Because the government has ruled that large feasts may not be held in the old part of the village, the family of the deceased have the choice of holding a small one in the old village or of moving

the feast down to the beach. In line with this, the village government has ruled that a funeral feast which is held in the old village
must begin the night of the burial. If it is to be postponed four
days, it must be held at the beach.

In many cases, the feast will not be held immediately. The preparations and expense for a funeral are quite considerable (but in
Kédang, not at present so large as to result in poverty or destitu-
tion of the family) and, especially if the death occurs during the
rainy season when everyone is working in the fields, the decision
may be made to put the feast off until it can be held simultaneously
with that of another close relative. When a large feast is held for a
prominent person, it may last several days. Commonly in such a
case lines standing in wife-giving or wife-taking relationships to
the line of the deceased will wish to be represented, and if these
are found in other villages, then what amounts to village delegations,
often including the village officials, teachers, and other prominent
members of the village, as well as a large segment of the clan which
has the relationship to the deceased, will be sent. Usually this
means each village delegation will have to be fed separately, and
the feast may last then up to as many days as there are delegations.

A substantial amount of the food is provided by the closely
related lines of the deceased. As for example, in one funeral the
feast was held simultaneously for the old man who had just died,
one of his brothers and one of his sons, both of whom had died
before him. His two remaining sons, his (still living) brother's
two sons, and two other men of a closely related line each provided
four cans (about forty litres) of unhusked rice (*padi*). In addition,
this group provided a can (ten litres) of kerosene and a large goat
and pig. However, the guests themselves also provide a great part
of the food used. Wife-givers are expected to bring nothing
(although members of a village delegation standing in this relation
will bring a good deal of maize and possibly rice and palm wine).
Everyone else, except especially invited prominent guests, is
expected to bring the crushed maize which they will eat. This
includes the numerous young people who help in the cooking and
other preparations and who come on the basis of a relationship
of any type, or contiguous residence, given a wide definition.
Wife-takers, however, are expected to provide if they have it, a
goat, one from each line, *padi*, and when it is in season three large
bamboos of palm wine.

When a village delegation goes to such a feast, the village group itself is considered the alliance group and goes as a unit in the given relationship of wife-giver or wife-taker (thus, potentially reversing some of the actual, but for the moment less relevant, relationships of some of its members). In travelling to the feast, the delegation walks in a long line (roughly double or triple file). The women precede, carrying large trays and baskets of rice and maize on their heads. They are followed by the young men carrying the palm wine; and the last in line are the old men and dignitaries. At the feast, the men sit separately from the women and are usually fed first. There is never at any feast a prescribed order of seating determined by age or alliance relationship.

At one feast we attended there was an incident in which an incorrectly arranged basket of sirih-pinang led the *epu* (wife-givers of the deceased) to threaten to go home. It is customary for sirih-pinang and tobacco to be passed around after everyone has been seated and before the meal is served. It is impolite not to partake at this time. At a feast of this sort, they try to provide a separate basket for each man (for a smaller feast confined to the village, these standards would be relaxed). By tradition, the baskets should contain an uneven number (three or five) of sirih peppers and an uneven number of pinang (*areca*) nuts. If an incorrectly arranged basket is set before a wife-giver, he is entitled to receive the payment of a fine of a gong or tusk of three units. If the infraction were made against a wife-taker, the fine would be two *lipaq* (men's sarongs). Infractions of this sort against anyone not standing in either of these relations, seem not to require a payment. I was told that there are some people who would take an incorrectly arranged basket and immediately throw its contents on the ground. In the same way it is forbidden for those serving at a feast to pass food with the left hand. In this case, too, there are supposedly people who will immediately strike to the ground anything served them with the wrong hand, and seemingly the infraction would be subject to a fine similar to that incurred by an incorrectly arranged sirih-pinang basket. In general, though, these matters are not now taken so seriously. The rule of course is respected, but this was the only occasion in which I witnessed anyone demanding payment for an infraction. They settled it in a characteristic manner by deciding that if there was ever a case where the clan which considered itself injured committed the same breach against the clan of the deceased, the two debts would cancel each other out.

At a funeral feast, as at a meal following work on the granary, before the food is served, an offering (*wajaq-doping*) of cooked food is placed on a rock for the ancestors. The first food to be set on the platform where the men are sitting (commonly under a specially prepared awning at large feasts, usually under a granary at smaller ones) are a number of baskets of crushed maize. These are called the *kiliq-rahaq* and must be uneven in number, three, five, or seven. One goes to the wife-giver (*epu*), one to a wife-taker (*maqing*), and the rest to lines regarded as siblings (*meker-éhoq*). The full phrase is *keran kiliq, karéq rahaq*, which is interpreted in this way. *Keran kiliq* means to set up the baskets (*kiliq*) on the *balai*. *Karéq rahaq* was said to mean to count (*karéq*) the four days of restriction (*iréng*) which follow the burial. *Rahaq* was said to be the *ahar* of the deceased (*matén né ahar*), *ahar* being in this case the synonym of *iréng* and making a verbal equation with *ahar-oliq*, the period of restriction following a birth.

There is also a parallel to the quiet period (also called *iréng*) after the village ceremony in which the village is cleaned. In the case of the restriction following death, there is no prohibition on making noise nor is there any limitation to leaving or entering the village. The sole restriction is on working the fields in the village. Those outside may be worked, and the ground may be dug within the village for other purposes, such as erecting a house post. However, this period too lasts either four days or two days and two nights (according to some eight days). The essential feature is that it last a total of four units.[5] The criterion seems to be the age of the deceased. One informant said that if an infant dies, it is still very hot and the period must be a full four days. An old man, however, is cool and two days and two nights may suffice. The child is hot because its potential life span is still long; the old man has little left.

Since the funeral feast used to follow burial by four days, the custom of placing the special basket on the *balai* could indicate

[5] 'Most often, when the deceased receives final burial without delay, it is the ideas relative to the passage of time itself which determine the end of the observances. The death will not be fully consummated . . . till a certain period of time, considered complete, has elapsed . . . Often it is the belief in the eminence and sanctity of a particular number which influences the choice . . .' (Hertz 1960: 52).

that the period of restriction is being officially brought to an
end.[6] The baskets indicate that the period has been counted and
shown to be complete. By this time, the soul of the deceased should
have completed his journey to the village of the dead, so the feast
could be held to coincide with his entering his new village. The
feast occurs simultaneously in both places. Nowadays, the feast
follows immediately on the funeral, so the period of restriction
must follow the feast. Nevertheless, it is still observed, even by
Muslims and Christians.

There are very few prescriptions or prohibitions concerning
mourning. I was told in one instance that the parents of a dead
person should not bathe, wash hair or clothing, shave or cut their
hair during the period of *iréng*. However, other reports indicated
that most of the restrictions placed on near relatives are self-
imposed and last as long as their feelings of sorrow make them
shy of seeing others.[7] Thus, according to report, a man who loses a
wife or child may not leave the neighbourhood of the house for a
month or so. A woman who loses her husband will restrict herself
in this way for three or four months. If she loses a child, it will be
much longer, up to a year. When she finally does go to the fields to
work, she will travel very early and very late to avoid meeting
people. She might cry if she saw a child. Children usually do not
restrict themselves on the loss of a parent. These restrictions and
durations are, however, in no sense customarily prescribed.
There is definitely no tradition that close female relatives of the
dead person should wear their hair loose at his funeral as a sign of
mourning, nor that his close male relatives should cut their hair
(cf. Vroklage 1952: 2: 28).[8] Only the women mourn openly. They
weep at intervals after the death and especially when guests
arrive on the day of the funeral and during the first stages of the

[6] 'We have seen that in Indonesia the feast that ends the funeral rites simultaneously releases the living from the obligation to mourn; this is a constant
feature' (Hertz 1960: 75).

[7] 'Mourning lasts normally till the second burial. Divergent customs in which
this relationship is not apparent are due, we believe, to a later relaxation of the
original custom' (Hertz 1960: 40–1). Mourning does not last until the second
burial in Kédang; whether or not this is due to relaxation of custom is unknown.

[8] 'During mourning, the living mourners and the deceased constitute a special
group, situated between the world of the living and the world of the dead, and
how soon living individuals leave that group depends on the closeness of their
relationship with the dead person' (van Gennep 1960: 147). This idea is not
explicit in Kédang.

funeral. This is done particularly by the women closely associated with the household, but during the burial itself most women present weep.

4. PROCEDURES FOR BURIAL OF THE VICTIM OF A BAD DEATH

The funeral procedures for someone who has died a *reqé-léwun* or bad death differ in a number of particulars from the ordinary funeral. The village head gave me the following list of features which he had observed in the burial of a person who had died by falling from a tree and which he said were characteristic of the treatment of people who die by falls, weapons, or in childbirth, but not those who die from snake bite or disaster at sea, who are buried normally. This effects a division within the category *reqé-léwun* for which there is no obvious explanation, and it may well be that others would not observe it. There were no cases of bad death during my stay, and I had no opportunity for independent observation.

The corpse in these cases could not be placed in the house but had to be left outside. After changing its clothing it would not be wrapped in a mat, but had to be placed in two coconut leaves which were then woven together. A platform (*nekaq-madaq*) and the bamboo carrying-stick (*neté*) were not used. The corpse was buried (not put in a tree) outside the village in a canyon. The food at the feast had to be eaten outside and could not be cooked in pots. Instead it had to be cooked in bamboo containers (*dajuq*). Returning from the burial, the people circled lontar palms or banana trees four times (travelling to the right), in order to prevent the soul of the deceased from following.

I found that small scraps of red cloth are invariably saved by sticking them in the wall or some other casual place. This is done because a person who dies a *reqé-léwun* must be buried with such a cloth. It is omitted in all other cases. If this red cloth is not used, then within a very few months someone else in the village will die a bad death. At the stage of the funeral when the corpse is given the second and last change of clothing (*kéu-léu*), a priest (*molan-maran*) will take this piece of red cloth and place it on the chest of the corpse. It appears that prior to the funeral he will have held a ceremony (*poan-kémir*), to take up the badness from the village which is associated with this death, and the badness would seem to be taken into the red cloth at that time.[9] It is then buried with the corpse.

When it is placed on the chest of the corpse, the priest will make, as I was told, the following chant of farewell:

Oi toher,	Farewell,
Belé baraq.	Release your burdens [illnesses and sins].
Moo reqé diqén,	Your goodness,
Moo reqé datén,	Your badness,
Reqé léwun,	Faults and
Uda lau,	Illness,
Oi belé,	Farewell,
bai dopé.	Depart.
Moré lojo kolé,	Travel with the turning sun,
Ula heléng.	The setting moon.
Opa moi,	Your contents [i.e. life], [return to]
Peti ai,	The wooden chest,
Muing moi,	Your container,
Walang laléng.	The inside of a bamboo.
Puli nobol,	Store your alliance relationships,
Hering téqa;	Put up your bridewealth.
Aréq pai,	Your wife redeemed [i.e. her bridewealth paid];
Binin belé.	Your sister released [for the same reason].
Ori rupaq,	Cancel appointments,
Tada kawé.	Sail from acquaintances.
Kara kuq seraq,	Do not take and give,
Kara meq papang.	Do not take and return.
Kara bun nuté,	Do not exchange words [any longer],
Kara dahang tojéq.	Do not ask [more] questions.
Kara pan kolo,	Do not come back,
Kara beq balé.	Do not return.
Pan moré nébol wata palan,	Go and anchor at another coast,
Dau léu mijéq.	Climb to another village.

[9] 'The "impure cloud" which, according to the Olo Ngaju, surrounds the deceased, pollutes everything it touches . . .' (Hertz 1960: 38). Only a *reqé-léwun* is contagious in this sense.

Kara tobol nuté,	Do not cling [to us with] words,
Kara ewé tojéq.	Do not grasp [with] conversation.
Oi-bai bahé,	The greetings are over,
Tanang-tonong di bahé.	The farewells are finished.

Following this short ceremony, the face will be washed in the same symbolic way already described for an ordinary death. In this case, however, the banana trunk will be taken from a banana tree of the type *muqu hiuq*. The stalk of bananas from this tree will have already been used in the ceremony before the burial. In this case they will have to use a stalk on which all of the bananas have emerged, leaving a bit of blossom (*imiq*) at the very tip. If this blossom has already been removed, these bananas may not be used. This indeed provides the only clue I have as to why this type of banana is chosen. It would appear that an especial characteristic of people who die in this way is that they have had their lives cut off short. Their souls are commonly thought to be barred from the normal advancement to the land of the dead. We might suppose in this case that ceremonial associated with the burial of such a person would be concerned with bridging in some way this incompletion. On this assumption, I will make the following interpretation. It is unfortunate, however, that it cannot be said to be more than speculation. I was told that *muqu hiuq* differs from the type ordinarily used (*muqu erun*) in its property of fruiting all the way to the end of the branch. The other type characteristically leaves a few undeveloped fruit towards the end. It would seem that this completeness of the branch might enable it to compensate in some way for the incompleteness of the dead person's life.

After the preliminary stages of the funeral are completed, the corpse is taken outside the village to be buried. This will be in a canyon; thus, drawing a parallel to other things (such as a *balai* on which a corpse has rested) which are thrown away in the canyon to be taken to sea. The corpse, however, is, in this case, actually buried, not put in a tree. Beckering (p. 199) says in fact in 1911 that placing corpses in trees seemed already to have disappeared in Kédang. According to him in all the coastal villages, everyone was buried. However, I was told that during a great plague (evidently the influenza epidemic) around 1918, when a large number of people died, many people were placed in trees; and there seem to have been individual instances in Kédang more recently. According to some people, tree-burial would only be employed in the case of a death in war, and then only if there is difficulty getting the corpse back to the village. Whatever institutions were associated with the practice have so faded from memory that it seems not to be possible to get a coherent report of its occasion. All of the deceased's goods must be taken with him and thrown away in the canyon.

On returning from the burial, the participants encircle a tree in order to confuse the soul of the deceased, so that he cannot follow. Then, when they return home, they will put up a sign to prevent the dead soul from entering the home. This sign would consist of branches of *ai nona*, placed on the ground in front of the door, upon which is sprinkled ashes. In addition, the leaves of *sirih-kaja*, or those of a plant called *mular*, are hung at the four corners of the roof. This manner of sealing a house to prevent the dead soul from entering occurs on other occasions, such as when a woman dies leaving an infant, or after a ceremony to renew the navel cords. The procedures are similar or identical in each case. It also resembles the practice of laying branches around the borders of the fields. This is done every year after planting and is intended to keep the wild pigs out. The tips, however, must all point in the same direction according to the principle of travelling to the right (*wana pan*), otherwise the pigs can get in.

The place where deaths of this type are buried would be called *rauq-roan*. The location of the market at Léuwajang is called *rauq utuq* because (as the name indicates) it is a tip of land jutting into the sea at the mouth of a canyon commonly used for such purposes. In this regard it is worth mentioning that there are at least two markets in Kédang which are located at places associated with death. The second of these, near the village Atanila, will be described shortly. I do not have the information for other markets in Kédang to be able to pursue this; but it would be an interesting comparative question to see if there may be a significant association between markets and death in Indonesia.

There is no rule that a feast should not be held following a burial of this type. This depends simply on the desire of the clan. However, it was pointed out that one of their considerations would be that few people would come to the funeral of such a death from fear of its badness. Most of the special procedures for such a burial seem to rest on just this fear of contagion and to have the intention of freeing the village of the contamination associated with the death. The souls (*melo maing*) of people who have died from *reqé-léwun* are supposed to become sea cows (*djurun*). This is supposedly because they sometimes observe sea cows coming up in the sea with coconut leaves, which suggest the shroud used in this type of funeral.

5. BURIAL IN 'LÉU TUAN' AND CREMATION

It has been mentioned that there may be no burial within the old village (*léu tuan*) for fear that it would cause an unending series of deaths. Burial must be made just outside the village (*léu obi*). Formerly, this was done only in the nearby hamlets Uru and Napoq Wala and in the near vicinity of *léu tuan*. Only in recent decades have they started burying in more distant hamlets and at the beach.

Unlike many other Indonesian societies, this one does not allow cremation. It is, in fact, regarded with a certain amount of terror. It is feared that if a corpse were to be burned, the wind would come to the village and bring a great plague. Related to this conception is the prohibition of burning bandages, or the *balai* upon which a corpse has lain or a woman sat during the restriction after birth when she is still discharging blood. In my opinion, this is not because cremation has a different symbolic significance in Kédang than in those societies which practise it. I think in both cases it is a form of bringing about the translation of the body to another realm. However, much of the funeral ceremony in Kédang seems to me concerned with effecting the separation between the soul and the body. Hertz (1960: 48) remarks that 'death is not completed in one instantaneous act', and further, 'death is not a mere destruction but a transition'. I will later attempt to show how each stage from physical death until the funeral feast is a part of the progressive separation of the soul from its body and its advance to the new realm of the dead. I will also argue that the orientation of certain stages symbolize the idea that the body is in some ways expected to go in a different direction from the soul. Were it to be cremated, then quite possibly this would mean that it would accompany the soul. This would be a double, simultaneous transition of the sort for which in other instances they show a marked dislike. It falls, I think, into the same category as the birth of twins,[10] the birth of two children of different mothers on the same day, and double or simultaneous deaths. It poses a kind of categorical confusion.

6. SOULS OF THE DEAD: DEAD AND DREAMS

The soul of the dead while it is still around awaiting burial and the feast so that it can enter the land of the dead is called *tuberéuq*. The first word means 'soul', the second 'voice'. When it is heard, it is a sign that someone will die within a day or two. The souls of the longer dead and the ancestors are the *tuan-woq*. Vatter (1932: 214) suggests an etymological connection with the Lamaholot word *kewokot*, which means 'the souls of the dead'. Although this may be correct, it is not certain and is somewhat unusual. *Woq* by itself means 'joint' or 'node'; and I think it is applied to the ancestors and the dead souls because these are set apart as having already gone through a critical transition. *Tuan* derives from *tua*, meaning 'old'. In Indonesian, *tuan* is an honorific term meaning 'master'. It is characteristic that it would be applied to the ancestors, who must be honoured and who are regarded as extended beyond age. That is, there is an unbroken line of increasing dignity through the elderly living to the ancestors.

I was told that they feel great anguish at a burial because of their many memories of the dead person. For some time he is likely to return to them in their dreams. When they dream of the dead, they see them, so I was told, as though real, and they meet with them, sitting and talking, or eating just as normally. During illness one's soul is thought to go to the land of the dead; and someone in the last stages before death who talks in delirium is considered to be talking to the dead. In addition, on several occasions my acquaintances have dreamed that they were being fed. This is invariably interpreted as meaning that they have been fed by the dead ancestors, who are trying to entice them to follow. They always have a ceremony then to return the food to the ancestors so they will not be endangered. All these instances show that they do not consider the border between the realm of the living and that of the dead to be impenetrable, and it is especially easy to bridge it when dreaming.

[10] 'If twins are born—then, according to the illuminating expression of the Ba-Ronga, "this birth is death"' (Hertz 1960: 85).

7. DESTINATION OF THE DEAD

In the chant quoted above, which is used in the funeral following a bad death, there is a line telling the deceased to follow the path of the turning sun and the setting moon. This shows that this conception, so common elsewhere, that the dead go to the west where the sun sets, is known in Kédang. This is, however, the only evidence I ever found of it.

Another point which remained obscure for me for a very long time was whether the soul of the recently dead returned to *léu rian* at the top of the mountain. Many people affirmed that this was the tradition when I asked, but it was difficult to elicit a reply in such a way that I could be sure that I was not imposing the idea with my own question. I finally got a detailed and spontaneous report showing beyond doubt that this feature is indeed a part of the indigenous tradition from a school-teacher from the village Léunoda. The tradition is important to the interpretation of the funeral. It may be that not everyone subscribes to it just as there are conflicting views about the construction of the building and platform used in connection with funerary procedures; but it seems to result in a systematic way from Kédangese ideas about space, birth, and death.

There is no question though that the destination of the souls of the dead is ultimately the small island Pulau Rusa in the straits south of Kédang.

The fullest form of Kédangese tradition on this point is then this. The soul after death first goes up to the original village, *léu rian, léu éhoq*. It will be remembered that there is a vent in *léu éhoq* which is thought to run through the mountain and emerge in the sea at a place called *wowon* near Atanila. The teacher from Léunoda said that the dead soul descends from the top of the mountain to a small island near the southern peninsula (Tandjung Leur) called *pahang waq, belu téban*. This tradition is not known in Léuwajang and he could not translate this name. My own knowledge of the language is not sufficient to give a complete translation. At any event, the soul goes from there to a place named *tuan léu* ('the dead's village) near Atanila. This is again in accord with the traditions of Léuwajang, where it is said that the soul descends from *léu rian* to *wowon* which is located at the base of a large cliff near Atanila (*waq rian puén*). This cliff drops directly into the sea, and when people hear great booming sounds there in the night, it is a sign that someone has died. The name *wowon* derives from *wowo* which means 'voice'. It is believed that if someone passes there when there has been a death in his own village, he will hear the voice of that dead person shouting to him. If the dead person is a woman, he will also hear the sounds of crushing maize; if a man, he will hear the sounds of the dead person singing while tapping palm wine. Because this area is associated with the dead, it is forbidden to take coconuts or lontar fruit to the market at Aran Hading near Atanila. This is because they think that the souls of the dead also go to market there (which is, supposedly, held at night). If one were to take one of these fruit, it would be like taking one's head to the land of the dead.

The soul of the dead then goes across the sea to the island Rusa. There they must stay at the beach until the feast is given for them in Kédang. If they are good people, the dead on the top of the hill on that island descend to the beach to receive them, and take them up to their village. If they are bad or wicked, however, they are not taken up, but become fish and shellfish of all kinds.

Pulau Rusa is described in the Sailing Directions (U.S. Navy H.O. 1962: 262) as 1,119 feet high and overgrown with alang alang (a tall grass). 'The coast is mostly steep and rocky; a plateau, with gradually increasing depths, extends from the west and south sides . . . Watu Balu, a wooded rock 92 feet high, lies on the above plateau.' Its name in Kédangese and Lamaholot is *Nuha Kakan*, *Waq (Watu) Balu*, 'Great Island, Round Rock'. Vatter (1932: 214) identifies the land of the dead with both Pulau Rusa and Pulau Kambing; this is plausible, but evidently Pulau Rusa has superior claim to the distinction. It is interesting that the villagers of Lamalerap, on the southwest coast in the Lamaholot section of the island, also believe that their dead go here. The island is uninhabited, but Bouman, who has been there, says that there are several antiquities found on the island which are greatly venerated by the inhabitants of nearby islands (i.e. Pantar and Marisa; 1943: 498). Among them are 'an object of singular form, which lies in a great shell near the beach, further a small bronze Hindu-figure, which stands on a small knoll, and a monolith erected near the beach of such peculiar regularity that it gives the impression of having been worked by human hand'.

These antiquities as well as the many scattered potsherds and venerated bronze rings derive according to the population from the old inhabitants of the island Bawa, which is supposed to have broken up sixteen generations ago through a volcanic eruption into three islands, among them Rusa, and otherwise sank into the sea.

The dead stop there only for a time, for they are eventually reborn as humans on the level below (*ahera* or *auq ubéng*, 'under the earth'). The universe is constructed of levels, as has been explained, each level a world like this. The inhabitants of this world have already gone through seven levels above. They will go through five more lives as they descend through the five levels below. When the fifth is finally completed, the body becomes a fish and the soul goes up to God where it may start the cycle again.

Concerning the *melo maing*, the souls of those who have died a violent or bad death (*reqé léwun*), they go, according to Vatter, to Waq Balu, which he places in the sea near Pulau Rusa. This report is probably incorrect. Some told me, indeed, that they went to Pulau Rusa, but there they were separated from the other dead, being left at the beach and then distributed to various other places. At any rate they are not reborn on a lower level, but stay on this. One of the supposed abodes is *eléng puén* ('the trunk of the sky', i.e. the horizon). They do not stay there, however, but, as Vatter also mentions, come back on the wind to cause misfortune. A month or two after their death they may return; however, they can only come when the moon returns to the sea (as viewed from Léuwajang), that is, the beginning of the waxing moon. During the full moon they are not around. They may appear (perhaps in front of the door) to trick people. They are evil spirits with Satanic bodies; that is, they may look human but will be very large and very black. Alternatively they may have no heads at all or only small ones. It is said that if a Kédangese is killed in a war on another island, his soul will return to Kédang; however, no *melo maing* of another region will come to Kédang. The soul of a woman who dies in childbirth will become a fish.

8. INTERPRETATION

Van Gennep (1960: 146) remarks of funerals that 'a study of the data . . . reveals that the rites of separation are few in number and very simple, while the transition rites have a duration and complexity sometimes so great that they must be granted a sort of autonomy'.

In my interpretation most of the stages of the funeral directly associated with the corpse are simultaneously rites of separation, transition and incorporation. Death, as Hertz remarks, 'is an initiation'; but death 'should not be compared only with initiation. The close relation that exists between funeral rites and rites of birth or marriage has often been noticed' (1960: 80).

The impression one takes from a close study of Kédangese funerary customs is that Hertz must certainly be right that death is not an instantaneous act and that it is a transition rather than a mere destruction. Were the corpse dead when the pulse ceases[11] and breathing stops, then we would expect little more than the immediate expression of sorrow and the quickest disposal of the corpse. That things are different is seen first in the fact that the corpse must be guarded during the night before burial. This night of guarding is frequently associated with coming into being of life: in Léuwajang with the erection of a house without posts, in East Flores with planting rice, and in Lamalerap with first launching the whaling boats. It is associated the world over with such a variety of ceremonials and passage rites that the only common element to be found among them is that they are cases of the transition of life. Further reduction than this does not seem possible. Next we may notice the frequency with which the number four and its equivalents (two and two, eight) occur. Were it not for government order, burial could not occur until four days after death; the clothing at the stage before removing the corpse from the house must be counted four times in succession; the banana stem which takes up the badness must circle the body four times before it is thrown away; the bindings must be twisted four times in each direction; the corpse of a very prominent person may be danced around the house (or platform) four times; the grave is swept four times around; the feast should be four or eight days after burial; the period of restriction (*iréng*) following burial lasts four days, eight days, or two days and two nights.

Each of these occasions marks the completion of a stage in the gradual process of death. First of all, we may view physical death to be a process lasting from the ceasing of the pulse until the end of the four days of waiting, when the relations gather for the

[11] They observe the stopping of the pulse and heart beat as signs of death

ceremony. Then, with the first changing of clothing and his last meal, the deceased takes departure from his clan (symbolized by tearing the black cloth an uneven number of times for the still living), his alliance relations, his household, and his possessions. To this point, the ceremony seems to consist almost entirely in rites of separation. There is perhaps little more of incorporation at this point than when a European puts on his suit in preparation for going to church.

Once at the platform set up outside the house, the ceremonial becomes more expressly concerned with incorporation, though it has not ceased to be concerned with separation. The corpse is given the change of clothing which is called the *kéu léu*, 'to enter the village' (i.e. the new village). And this clothing includes the pieces which, as their name indicates, are intended to show him the way, to lead him securely on his path. The separation between the spirit and the material, which has begun with the last meal, is advanced here. He could not ingest the food, so its consumption had to be indicated by breaking the pots and pouring the food on the ground for the dogs to eat (a universal means by which gods and spirits consume offerings in Indonesia). Only the spirit of the food could be consumed in this case (I have reason to believe that this distinction is explicitly understood in Kédang). So too, the deceased takes only the spirit of the clothing given him to the land of the dead. For this reason, the corpse may be plundered of its valuables. Whether these things are left with the body may depend to some extent on the dignity of the person buried. In most cases I witnessed, the corpse was buried in clothing which, although new, was not of extraordinary value. (When plundered, the corpse is never left naked or in disarray.) Only in one case, where the deceased was very prominent, was anything of especial value (a golden ear-ring) confined to the grave.

From this point until the grave is completed, the ceremonial is largely concerned with the separation of the body and the spirit, not just of the deceased, but also of the things which accompany him. Thus, once the grave is finished (or at the earliest after the corpse is taken to the grave) his possessions which were hung at the head of the platform may be broken and thrown seaward, and the provisions sent with him for the ancestors may also be thrown seaward.

After burial, there is only a question of spiritual transition until the soul of the dead has entered the village of the dead, and separation of soul and body are no longer a problem.

Now it seems that though there are traces of separation and incorporation throughout and the whole is concerned with transition, the whole ceremony can be divided into stages in which the primary concern does correspond to van Gennep's terms. In this way I would regard the period from physical death until the removal to the platform (*nekaq-madaq*) as primarily concerned with separation. In the second stage, lasting from the placing of the body on this platform until the final sweeping of the grave, it is not possible to say that separation or incorporation is predominant, and one may employ only van Gennep's more neutral term transition. Finally, the last stage, during the period of restriction and ended by the feast, is primarily a matter of incorporation for the dead soul into his new home, and perhaps also, as Hertz and van Gennep interpret it, a reincorporation for the still living into the community.

On the basis of this interpretation of the funeral ceremony, I should like to turn to the analysis of the orientation displayed in it. It will be recalled that throughout the ceremony the corpse lies with his head to the right in relation to the slope (*oté*), and the only oriented motion, from the platform to the grave, is from the right to the left. This might possibly be directly interpreted as travelling to the left. This is certainly an idea found in other Indonesian societies, and is in many ways a symbolically satisfactory procedure. However, this interpretation was never put forward, and all reports said that this motion should be considered an instance of travelling to the right. Furthermore, it has been shown that orientation is not such a simple matter in Kédang, and I find that an interpretation of travelling to the left does not reflect the full importance of the path of the corpse. Two other possibilities must be disposed of before this can be shown.

In some neighbouring societies, it is thought that the corpse travels with the sun (i.e. towards the west). Evidence for this has been shown in Kédang; but I do not think it is represented in the funerary procedures themselves. This interpretation might appear valid in Léuwajang because the corpse happens to lie with his head to the east, so that he travels to the west. That this is only coincidental was proven by inquiries on the south side of the mountain, where the corpse in fact lies with the head to the west and travels to the east. Thus, the orientation can only be understood in relation to the Kédangese quadrant, and not in relation to the sun and east and west.

Secondly, it might be thought that the dead descends to the sea, as is the case so often elsewhere. Surprisingly, this is in fact true. The imagery of sailing is present both in a cloth given him (*tené uring*, 'steering the boat') and in the chant given above. This is also made quite explicit in casual conversation; and the dead soul after all does eventually go to Pulau Rusa. However, it is not this idea which determines the immediate orientation of the funeral, for the corpse never travels towards the sea (that is, down the mountain). This idea must belong to the period after the funeral and not to the funeral procedures themselves.

I will put forward here the following interpretation, which is the only one I can find which makes sense of the funeral.

In my opinion, the orientation of the grave can only be understood if we compare it with other explicitly oriented features of Kédangese culture. Particularly, the orientation during the period of restriction after birth and the orientation of the house must be referred to. It is the latter which provides the explanation for the other two. The structure of the house may be reduced to a rectangle; motion around this rectangle, it will be remembered, is counter-clockwise. In the upper right-hand corner (in Kédangese or heraldic terms) is to be found the *lili wana*, the right house post—a point of controlled access to the souls of the dead. If we compare the orientation after birth to this, we find that the woman must face down or to the right; her hearth must be above and to the left. Thus her hearth corresponds to the upper left-hand corner. This suggests, then, a correspondence between the upper side of the rectangle and the period of restriction following birth. In a sense this side lies between the hearth (*lia maten*) and the *lili wana*. The hearth then must correspond to the womb.

There are a number of indications that life is associated with descent. The village, in a sense, looks down. The ancestors descended from the top of the mountain. Life is also said to be associated with the right. Therefore, man's life in Kédangese terms plays itself out on the right side of this rectangle. The ancestors, in their controlled and benevolent aspect, are situated behind and above.

Where, then, is death? Physical death in such a scheme should lie diagonally opposite physical birth, hence in the lower right-hand corner. As it happens the bottom two corners are situated in the same way as the burial platform and the grave. The only way in which the motion at this stage of the funeral could be interpreted as travelling to the right is to assume that this motion lies at the bottom side of the rectangle. The *nekaq-madaq* is oriented in such a way as to fall in the bottom right-hand corner of the rectangle, the grave itself in the bottom left.

If the reader will examine Figure 7 closely, he will see that this image of the rectangle allows the systematic ordering of a series of important oppositions associated with life and death under a single law: *wana pan*, 'travel to the right'. It accounts for all major

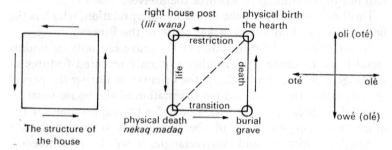

FIG. 7. Representation of Kédangese ideas of life and death.

instances of prescribed orientation in Kédangese culture (following birth, the funeral and the construction of buildings) in terms of Kédangese concepts of space. The transition from physical death to social death is represented by the movement from the *nekaq-madaq* to the grave and corresponds to the bottom side of the rectangle. Social death itself falls between the grave and birth on the left side of the rectangle. It stands under an inverse sign to life, but under the same law.

At this point it may legitimately be objected that this does not account for all stages in the cycle of life and death. Where for instance lies the period of restriction following burial, or the period from physical death until the corpse is placed on the platform? Where is the period from conception to parturition? The only answer which can be put forward is this: the interpretation only attempts to account for what is actually ordered in Kédangese representations, not to introduce a new metaphysic based on them, and it is only these two occasions which are explicitly oriented by the Kédangese themselves. Given that it is only these two stages (restriction after birth and movement from the platform to the grave) which require, on the basis of the facts themselves, an interpretation, then the one put forward here seems adequate.

The question which remains is whether anything in the Kédangese representation of death corresponds to the left side of the rectangle.

There are two ideas which could be viewed as corresponding to this pattern, and they are fittingly close to the ceremonial of burial. It has been remarked that after the corpse is buried, various possessions and food situated actually behind the deceased, that is to the right (*oté*) from the platform, are thrown towards the sea. The spirits of these things are intended to follow the deceased to the land of the dead; yet they are not thrown in the direction in which he travels. It is possible to say that once buried he turns towards the sea. Another interpretation is that he turns up towards the top of the mountain. It is clear that one or the other of these views must be adopted. It seems to me to make the most symbolic sense to assume that he goes up. If this is correct, then the throwing away of the things serves the same symbolic purpose as the breaking of the pot in his last meal or the plundering of the corpse. It effects a separation of spirit and substance. The sea removes debris and impurities. Thus the merely material is separated from its spirit by being thrown in the opposite direction; the spirits of these things follow the dead soul up the mountain. There would be little reason to think this were the case, had I not been able to establish beyond doubt that there is in fact a tradition that the deceased goes to the top of the mountain immediately following burial. That he does so is just another of the many familiar instances in which death and birth are associated. Beyond this point, quite naturally, the orientation exhibited in Figure 7 ceases to have any effect on the course of the dead soul, which descends the mountain again to *wowon*.

XI

WITCHES, SPIRITS, AND MAGIC

THERE is a distinction in the culture of Kédang between what I choose to call a witch and a spirit. The former of these is called a *maq-molan*, and in his outer form is a human being, possibly a member of the community. The latter, for which there are a variety of names but all apparently considered to refer to the same kind of being, is associated with what we would regard as inanimate objects such as boulders and cliffs, with trees and with animals, but not primarily with human beings—though it may manifest itself in this form as well. The latter category is in the realm of the usually malevolent, unstable, and only half-embodied spirit.

1. WITCHES

The full name for the witch is *maq-molan, odo korong*. The word *maq* means either 'to be a witch' or 'to steal' (the latter sense is made explicit in the form *maqo*). This does not mean that thieves are necessarily witches; but it does show that the two categories are close. *Molan* otherwise only appears in the name for a priest. Presumably this points to the spiritual powers of the witch. Concerning *odo korong*, it was explained to me in this way: the term is used when one defecates and only a small amount of excrement emerges and then only part way. The reason the phrase is applied to the witch is this. The soul or spirit which dwells in a witch and is the source of his evil powers—called his *éqong* (cf. Lamaholot *eo*)—enters and leaves by way of his anus. This conception is, of course, the inverse of that for a normal human, whose soul enters and leaves primarily by means of his mouth. It underlines how the witch stands in opposition to normal humans, not only socially, but in his make-up. When a witch sleeps his *éqong* emerges and goes off elsewhere, leaving only his corpse. One may kill a *maq-molan* by reversing the position in which he lies while the *éqong* has gone away. When it returns, it cannot find the entrance (cf. Arndt 1951: 190; Vroklage 1952: 2: 20). I asked if the returning *éqong* may take the form of a mouse as

Vroklage reports, and was told that this had been heard of, but the most frequent form is that of a snake. They say of a witch if he is still sleeping after the sun has risen that his soul is not complete (*éqong ohaq nau anaq*), meaning that his *éqong* has not yet returned. While the *éqong* is away, the body is incapable of moving and shows no reaction if shaken.

In general the *éqong* of a witch may take the form of a crow (*béang*) or a *tuaq wolo* (owl?) or of rats or snakes. They take the form of the two birds to disguise themselves while travelling. They may then leave the form sitting in a tree and travel invisibly on the ground. If one hears the call of the crow at night, it is a sign of an impending death. Should they hear the call of the *tuaq wolo*, they will turn a sleeping infant on its side to protect him from harm (which side does not seem to matter). Regarding this latter bird, I was never able to get an identification.[1] Some said they had never seen it, and one man said that it had feathers only on its wings.

One says of a *maq-molan* that he is *obi-laléng*, literally, 'outside-in', because he speaks well, but has evil intentions. It is common for witches to sit at the side of a road at night or under a tree. They are not particularly associated with cross-roads. They have also been seen at midday sitting under a tree picking lice from their hair after having removed the whole head to get a better view of it. This means that they pull the skin off the head as though it were unconnected to the skull. Their hair is tangled (*riwong-rawong*); their clothes are disordered, and the face is the colour of earth (*ning-mato auq-auq*, i.e. dirty).

One of my friends who has experienced being possessed by an *éqong* of a witch, described it as follows. One feels it coming over one when dropping off to sleep. It possesses one so that one cannot move. Only when it leaves again is it possible to move. It is impossible to identify the witch taking one over; and one is not afraid while it is happening. Only afterwards is one afraid. The *éqong* enters the house through the door or through the ridge of the roof (*wolar-bala*). A victim possessed by an *éqong* is like a corpse.

A witch may kill a person in many ways: by poison, or by causing him to fall from a tree or from the trail. They may also

---

[1] The owl is often considered an ominous bird in Indonesia and is a possible identification for the *tuaq wolo*, which seems to be a night bird (cf. Verheijen 1950: 67).

eat the soul. I was given the example of three witches, each had singled out a person against whom he had a grudge and whom he wished to harm. After conferring, they decided on the first victim. They then took his soul and transformed it into an animal, such as a goat or a pig, which could then be cut up and eaten. It seems, however, uncommon for them to use poison, and they do not necessarily kill. Usually they confine themselves to lesser injuries, such as causing wounds on the feet (a perennial complaint of anyone living in Kédang). Their ill will may be elicited in the first place by refusing a request for something or by not giving them sirih-pinang when they visit the house.

Descendants of a witch may become witches. On the other hand, it seems that a witch's victims are not thought to become witches themselves. I was told that the witch may call a spirit (*sehar-metung*) to enter his body so that he may acquire the powers of a witch. However, it seems to be more commonly thought that the process is involuntary. He would then become a witch through possession by a spirit, involving the gradual dissociation of the victim's soul and its replacement by the *éqong*. Such might happen for instance in a case where someone thirsty from work in the fields were to drink from a puddle of rainwater located near a rock or tree. The spirit would then enter his body, after which he would gradually lose control of himself, becoming insane (*kamunger*) and finally a witch.

One calls upon a priest (*molan-maran*) to find out who the witch is who has possessed one. He can see if an illness were caused by a witch or not because his eyes are sharp (*mato déjéq*). He may treat the person so possessed by putting chalk around the sides of the balai and then sprinkling it on the victim's body so that the *éqong* could not come back. If he saw that the witch were still in the patient's body, he would grab the patient's big toe. Then the witch would, through the patient, utter his name. The *molan-maran* would then ask if he would give up or not. If the witch gave in and would leave the patient, the *molan-maran* would release the toe and he could go home. If not, he would tie him by some medicine sewed in a cloth put around the patient's waist. In this case the *éqong* could not return home and would die. The next day, they would find his corpse. Alternatively, they may find out who the witch is by having a priest employ his bamboo stick augury.

A person may attract suspicion if he had been to the house and there had been an argument or fight, and if, after he had left, the owner had fallen ill. In this case the witch did not hurt the body but ate the soul. They do not now kill witches. This is of course now illegal and disapproved of by Christians. They seem never to have indulged in it quite so much as is done on Adonara. Nevertheless, I recorded one case in which a man accused of witchcraft was killed by men still living. In that case, after having determined by augury who was guilty, they entered into a plot with the intended victim to steal a goat. The incident occurred with the complicity of the then head of the village government, and, after the fact, that of the then *kapitan* of Kédang. Having stolen their goat, they gave it to him to carry. While he was carrying it, they killed him. They did not simply sever his head because a witch is capable of putting his head back on. Instead, they cut off his nose and ears as well. When the case came to trial, it was officially declared that the goat which he was carrying had stabbed him to death with its horns.

If someone is known as a witch, they are afraid of speaking his name because he will then cause illness. Only after his death will people feel free to refer to him; however, I have observed that decades after his death they will remain very reluctant to do so. If someone looks at his own shadow, it may be taken as a sign that he is a witch. Furthermore, one should avoid stepping on another person's shadow (*kihaq onin*) and avoid letting him step on one's own. He may be a witch, and if so might then bewitch one. It is clear from this formulation that the restriction applies only to strangers or to someone who is suspected of witchcraft. An intimate whom one knows not to be a witch could hardly pose a threat in this regard. I will also note that this rule, by my observations, is as good as completely ignored. I have never known an occasion when anyone paid the least attention to what his shadow was doing. No one could explain why the danger existed, and they were unfamiliar with the idea that the shadow may be a soul.

It has already been mentioned that a pregnant woman must avoid going outside at night or sleeping alone in the house for fear that the sweet smell from her vagina may attract a witch. There seems to be no tradition of the evil eye. There also seems no tradition that the eyes of a witch are red, as is reported from Lamaholot (Arndt 1951: 133).

2. SPIRITS

It was mentioned in the first chapter that *neda*, the interior of the earth, in the phrase *neda bua, hari belé*, concerning the original creation by the earth and the sea, was compared to the waters which come from below the earth. It was also compared to the *sehar-metung*, the spirits, which likewise came out from the earth. There are a number of names for these spirits, all seemingly more or less synonymous and all nearly impossible to translate.

I could never get a list of traits peculiar to each name, and I observed that they were used interchangeably in the same contexts; so I eventually was forced to conclude that they are all more or less the same. The most frequently used term is *sehar-metung*. *Metung* means 'empty'; *sehar* is otherwise used for black magic. Why the word empty is attached to it is an enticing problem, but one which proved impossible to solve. Comparison in any event must be made to the name of the altar (boulder) which protects a person's fields, *éwaq-metung*, which shows the same feature. Other names are *niting-natan* (*natan* means 'each' or 'individually', *niting* is untranslatable); *ruha-kuba* (*ruha* is a 'deer', *kuba* is unknown); *rungan datén* (*rungan* is unknown, *datén* is 'bad'), and *murin-beriwong* (both words untranslatable). These spirits are thought to inhabit large stones, rock walls, and trees, especially banyans. A stone inhabited by a spirit can be recognized by its red or yellow colour.

Normally they do not bother people but if one is not careful around their place of habitation, one may become possessed. I have encountered a number of different instances in which such possession was thought to occur. One case has already been described. A friend once included among the possible causes of his illness that he had hunted pig near a large cliff, and thus angered the spirit which lived there. A woman in the village was insane, and her case was explained as possession. She had made her field near a spot inhabited by a spirit, though she had been warned not to. As a consequence, the spirit married her without anyone knowing it and in a few years she became insane. This recalls the fact that a woman who washes her hair at the spring may be married by the guardian spirit of the spring and driven insane. There is clearly not much difference between guardian spirits and spirits of this kind. The former, however, are linked to places or constructions vital to human well-being and are usually benevolent. The latter are more indifferent. A friend of mine had his field altar near a large rock wall, and we had to eat the offering on the spot because the spirit of the rock wall might accompany us home and possess us if we ate the food in the house. This was not a problem for altars in more isolated locations; and there was no danger of possession as long as we stayed on the spot, providing that we treated it respectfully.

Another example was a lava flow below our hamlet called *nubaq pulin*, meaning the place where an ear-ring (*nubaq*) had been stored (*puli*). The name results from a tradition that someone had once lost an ear-ring there. People passing did not take it, it seems, because they considered it to belong to the spirit living in that place.

These spirits have been described for me, in their manifest form, in a number of ways. They seem often to be very furry. The *murin-beriwong* was said to be large like a buffalo, or smaller like a deer. They can also take human form. They may appear with buffalo horns and covered with long fur like human hair, and they may make sounds like a deer (loud barking sounds) in order to scare off the people guarding their fields at night from wild pigs. They live in the forest; and they may have four, three, or two feet. Spirits are sometimes described as having arms and legs on only one side. It is clear though that the spirit is free to adopt a monstrous shape of any kind and after its own choosing.

There is another creature called *murin datén* ('bad *murin*') or *ka deruq* ('eat excrement', a common curse, especially among children). If one is bitten by this creature, then the only medicine is human excrement. The people who told me about it had never seen it, but said that there were two forms: one is black and like a snake but smaller, the other black and shaped like a pebble. Though this was not said, it seems a plausible guess that this terrible creature is itself excrement.

They have a prohibition on mocking or speaking to animals (*kara tutuq*, or *tawé*, 'laugh at', *éwang-nawang*). The reason for this is that spirits are capable of taking the form of animals. If one does this to an ordinary animal, nothing will happen, but if one happens to do so to one which has been possessed by a spirit, it may answer back, just like the dog Iku Bojang during the festival at the original village. If it does, the person who spoke to it will be stricken dumb (*bukéq-bekéq*). I should report that I was very far from being the only person in Kédang who consistently violated this prohibition.

This idea is reminiscent of their fear of pointing at Ursa Major. It is also related to their fear of pointing at a *nado-tado*, that is a rainbow or any other rising effulgence of a spirit. If one does point, one runs the risk that one's finger will be permanently bent. In the same way, one must not point at a young, still small pumpkin. If one does, the fruit will die. This is not the place to undertake an explanation of the various prohibitions on pointing, but it is clear that these are related to the highly developed prohibition in western Indonesia of pointing at a person. It is also of use to note that this particular prohibition does not exist in Kédang.

3. MAGIC

I found very little reference to black magic. Only in one case, in which an infant died, did it become a topic of conversation. It seems that it is called *sehar* (perhaps the same as Ind., *sihir*). The methods seem to be individual and secret, known only to those who have the skill. There is a *sehar* of fire, of wind, of wire, of a fishhook, and so on; but what their techniques were could not be described for me. I was told that there are people in Kédang who know how, but it is the traders from Alor and Bernusa (Pantar) who are particularly known or feared for it. It is especially frequent among merchants. It may be sent across great distances. One will be made the victim in the event that one has refused the person with this knowledge a favour, such as loaning him money. The person who does black magic is not a witch (*maq-molan*); and a priest (*molan-maran*) is of little help. A guardian spirit ceremony is of little use. If one is made a victim, there is little recourse except to get help from someone who knows how to make this medicine. The best thing to do is to get the person who has done it to take it back. The means to do this is a payment of money.

Another technique of harming another person, available to those who do not have the powers of black magic, is to have a priest perform a ceremony called *nuba-lapaq*. The name itself reveals little; it just refers to the little altar stones used in any ceremony (*lapaq* in Kédangese, *nuba* in Lamaholot). The ceremony involves an offering of an egg or perhaps a chicken with one piece of red cloth and one of black. It must be done secretly. After the ceremony, the cloth and stone are put near a path where the victim should pass. If he goes by, he will be killed. Otherwise it may be hidden in some rocks, where it will cause the wind (*nukun-angin*) to come during the rainy season and do the required damage.

The priest in such a case does not carry any responsibility; this lies only with the man who hires him. However, the priest must be paid to keep it secret. Should it later be discovered (by inspecting water or some such technique), there is no legal or formal case against the guilty party. The only retaliation is to conduct a ceremony to send his magic back against him. If someone dreams of a snake, this may be taken as a sign that someone in the clan has held such a ceremony against his own clan. If this action were detected in this manner, then someone with the powers to see causes (*wangun-léan*) and interpret signs would be called upon to find out who was guilty. This he might do by looking into a bowl of water. Then they would have a ceremony to clean away the faults. A chicken would be offered and a goat would have its throat cut, so that the blood would fall into a hole dug in the ground. This is actually an offering to the wind to get it to remove the illness or what-not. Then the hole is covered with a stone and dirt put over it. The original stone would have to be found for this ceremony. One man who had the power to do this and who in fact did collect a lot of stones which he found, through dreaming, had been left by people, usually dead, would go round with a bowl of water. While he looked in this, his spirit would rise up (*nado*) and go around until it found the stone. He would then point in the direction, and the people accompanying him would go and get the stone. It was said that they invariably find it where he says it is.

I found only very little concerning love medicine. Those I asked claimed not to know themselves, but described the use of such things as water or grass. One might prepare a potion and give it to a third person to hand the person it is intended for; alternatively one may sprinkle the water at the door of his (or her) house or around the house, or blow it on a rock and speak into the rock and then throw it over the roof. Another technique is to put one's own name, together with the name of the desired person, on a piece of paper.

XII

THE MAIZE HARVEST OFFERING

THERE is, unfortunately, no room to undertake a thorough description of all ceremonies in Kédang. I have chosen instead to outline the offerings made at the field altar each year before picking the maize. This ceremony is both representative and at the same time simpler than many others. In describing it, it is possible to introduce the basic paraphernalia and techniques which are also employed in almost all other ceremonial offerings.

1. DESCRIPTION

The field altar is a large boulder called an *éwaq-metung*. These are characteristically held by brothers and are inherited patrilineally, but my evidence shows that they may sometimes be transferred to adjacent lineages within the same clan, if for some reason the owner moves away or otherwise abandons it. Not everyone has such an altar for his fields; and some, while retaining the traditional religion, seem sometimes to lose interest and allow them to lapse. I observed in one such case, however, that abandoning the ceremony at the *éwaq-metung* is very likely to be considered the cause if later some misfortune occurs; and the altar and its ceremonies will again be taken up. Those who do not have such an altar may still have a ceremony when their maize is gathered together and put in the granary. In this case, the priest will conduct the ceremony at the granary itself. In some cases, a person without an altar may learn by dreaming that he must acquire one, and then the priest will prepare him one (*heriq éwaq*) or he may renew a long abandoned one. If the renewed altar is located in a different place, he may take the soul string (*tuber-nawaq*) and 'drag' the *éwaq* from the old location to the new. In this case he simply drags the string along the ground from the old boulder to the new one.

Interpreting the meaning of the name is almost impossible. The word *éwaq* could reasonably be related to the Sanskrit *dewa*, meaning god or demon. The latter word is commonly found in eastern Indonesian languages, and is known in Indonesian as well. There is also a similarity of meaning. Nevertheless, the word if related has undergone such a transformation that it is not possible to prove the connection. The mystery is increased by the fact that the second term (*metung*) means 'empty'. No one was able to explain why this term is used. I once asked a young man (a Catholic) about it, and he decided that the name of the altar must mean, in Indonesian, *dewa kosong*, that is, 'empty god'. By this interpretation, the earth-bound and rather inferior manifestation of divinity in the altar is contrasted to God who is *dewa penuh* or a 'full god'. This seemed an enticing explanation at the time, but I later never found any sign that the proposed distinction corresponds to Kédangese idiom. An alternative is that the word is applied to the altar because the ceremony is conducted there at the time when the granary is empty, but this is by no means certain. It must be recalled that there is a parallel (*sehar-metung*, 'spirit'), which this theory would leave unexplained. I can offer instead only the rather weak explanation that the word empty is applied to these spirits because they lack substance, the stone or tree which they inhabit in either case being not their form but only their residence.

In any case, the *éwaq-metung* is thought to be inhabited by a spirit which guards one's crops, one's livestock and one's own valuables (such as gongs and tusks). If one fails to make the yearly offering then one runs the risk that the spirit of the altar may take the form of a snake and kill one's animals or that one's crops, no matter how plentiful they may appear when stored in the granary, will be rapidly exhausted. If on the other hand one has properly carried out the offering, then the same fate will be met with by anyone who steals from one's fields. The snake in this case was graphically described to me as coming and rising up, opening his mouth while twitching his tongue in and out. This twitching of his tongue he may direct at a goat, pig or chicken or even at a human being, causing thereby his or its death.

I was told that when harvesting rice, one may not bathe or wash one's clothing or hair until the harvest is finished. One may not, also, eat from the rice until it has all been harvested and husked. When someone is working in a rice field, it is forbidden for a passer-by to call to him; should he do so he must pay a chicken and stalk of bananas of the type *muqu erun*. None of these prohibitions apply to maize. On the other hand there is no ceremonial particularly associated with rice. Since maize is the staple, the field ceremonial is primarily associated with it. Nevertheless, this ceremonial is intended to ensure not just the maize crop alone, but all of the crops and livestock. One cannot begin to eat any of the maize until the ceremony at the *éwaq metung* is performed, but this restriction applies only to those fields in or near the old village (*léu tuan*). Fields farther away from the village require no ceremony at all.

Supposedly one should have a priest conduct a ceremony using only an egg at the time of planting, but this seems almost always to be disregarded. However, when they have not had this ceremony conducted at planting, they do include the egg in the ceremony preceding harvesting.

The site of such an altar is not very imposing. It is just a large boulder, of which the terrain is full. On the sea or down-slope side of this boulder will be a ring of damar or similar small bushes or trees which provide a sort of protective hedge enclosing the area (of perhaps a square metre or less) where the ceremony is conducted. This hedge is not always present and the site is often so overgrown that it is hardly recognizable. The ceremony is never conducted with pomposity or exaggerated piety, and the site itself is treated rather matter-of-factly. Commonly they hack the hedge back to make room for themselves, without showing any concern that it remain orderly. One could easily be misled into thinking that the site was in no way set apart from the surrounding terrain; however, this would be mistaken. Once, while they were conducting such a ceremony, some children were playing on the altar, which is not itself a matter of concern. However, one of them began to spit on it, and this caused the first and only signs of anger I ever witnessed in such a context. The old men ordered the children to go away (and quite uncharacteristically they obeyed); and they explained to me that it is forbidden to defile the stone with spit, urine, or excrement. Likewise, the priests were never concerned about interrupting the ceremony. They would often laugh and talk with other people in the midst of it and would frequently stop to try to explain to me what was going on (never very coherently, unfortunately); yet every once in a while I was told to be quiet and wait until a certain part was over with.

The priest conducts the entire ceremony by himself, but the bystanders often help him by preparing some of the equipment (such as the cotton pellets) or handing it to him, or even by helping drip the blood from the offered chicken round when this is required. There is no role of assistant, however, and no special requirements or training for those who do help.

Before beginning, he must set up the site. Four small, flat offering stones (*lapaq*) are required. These are usually still lying there from last year's ceremony, but if any are missing, then a replacement is easily found in the vicinity. These four stones were explained to me as representing *éwaq* and *metung* and *éwaq*'s

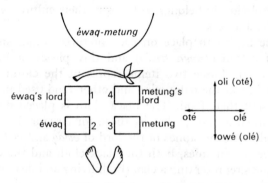

FIG. 8. The orientation of a *poan éwaq*.

lord or owner (*éwaq né tuan*) and *metung*'s lord (*metung né tuan*). It seems that *éwaq* and *metung* must be considered in this case as synonymous; the splitting would then be reduplication rather than opposition. On the other hand, the other splitting between *éwaq* and *metung* and their lord seems to draw an opposition between the site or altar itself and the spirit which inhabits it. These four stones are placed below the boulder itself, as in Figure 8. Above them is placed the stalk of bananas of the type *muqu erun*. From this all but the last two or three bananas have been cut and will later be roasted and eaten. The orientation is invariable; the end of the stalk with the remaining bananas lies to the left (*olé*). The priest squats below the four stones facing the boulder. The flat stones and the banana stalk appear not to be oriented in relation to his own body, but to the slope on which the ceremony is conducted. In understanding the way in which the stalk of bananas lies, it is important to know that they do not take into consideration the direction in which the stalk grows out from the trunk. Instead they observe that the stalk hangs down, so that the end connected to the tree is 'up', while the tip is 'down'. Thus, it lies in the setting with its 'upper' end pointing in the same direction as would the bamboo parts on the up-slope side of the house.

The priest begins by pouring palm wine on each of the stones. This is by prescription coconut palm wine. I have never seen a case, however, in which they used coconut palm wine, even when they had it. They always used their own, local lontar palm wine. This rule obviously belongs to those in their culture which have become dead letters.

Next he begins to place on each of these stones small rolled pellets of cotton (*panga lewéq*) and tiny pieces of black cloth (*nutaq miténg*). These two items represent the clothing for the ancestors, just as the palm wine and other food used in the offering represent their food. The black cloth is placed only on the stones marked 2 and 3, that is, those for *éwaq* and *metung*; the cotton pellets on the stones of the lord of *éwaq* and *metung* (1 and 4). In other ceremonies, both the black cloth and the cotton are put on stones representing a clan (both living and dead members), but just the cotton on stones representing the wind or God (as Tuhan Allah or Ula-Lojo). The black cloth, I have been told, always represents the ancestors. One gains the over-all impression, then, that the cotton (which is white) stands often for the spirit as opposed to body, represented by the black cloth; in other cases the cotton seems to stand for pure spirit (the wind, God) as opposed to spirit which has undergone the transformations connected with embodiment (the living and the ancestors together).

First the priest puts tiny pieces of black cloth, which he has cut off by a short strip, on the stone for *éwaq*. This he does by taking three pieces in a bunch and putting them down and then repeating this seven times. Following this he puts cotton pellets on the stone for the lord of *éwaq*; this also is done in groups of three, seven times. The same process is repeated in putting black cloth on *metung* and cotton on the stone for its lord. Then the whole series is repeated, only putting one pellet or piece of cloth down each time, but nevertheless doing so seven times on each stone.

While doing this he chants calling the spirit of the altar to come. I give here a representative fragment of this chant:

Tuan éwaq-metung,	Lord *éwaq-metung,*
Éwaq né tuan,	*Éwaq's* lord,
Tebéq ajaq,	Sit in the centre,
Mader tuan.	Stand lord.
Mahing malaq,	Give much,
Mirang ratang.	Always something.
Hojoq leran,	Succour the village,
Libur behiq.	Protect the community.
Tawan méan,	Wealth of the fields,
Koaq boléng.	Enter the granary.

When this is finished, a few seeds of unhusked rice are broken open and placed on the cotton together with a little fish and sirih-pinang; and palm wine is again poured on the stones. Following this an egg is offered, accompanied by a very similar chant, and its contents placed on the stone (no. 3) for *metung.*

Next comes the most spectacular part of the ceremony. A chicken is brought out (for this ceremony it must be male), which the priest grabs in one hand (neither the right nor left is prescribed) by the neck, pressing its throat shut with his thumb. This he holds towards the altar, and then he spits on its chest. The chicken is then throttled in this manner, while the priest repeats the following chant or one similar to it.

Mamaq rutaq, mamaq rutaq.	Gather the bird [i.e. spirit]
[i.e. *mahu manuq rutaq.*]	which husbands [us].
Manuq ula,	Bird of the moon,
Manuq lojo,	Bird of the sun,
Manuq tiju,	Bird of the stream,
Manuq tongo,	Bird of the puddle,
Manuq eléng,	Bird of the sky,
Manuq wang,	Bird of the heavens,
Ko tiong,	Crow and shy away,
Lering barang;	Travel and visit with companions;
Lédo wehéq,	Travel low,
Pan auq.	Walk on the ground.
Naja moo, hara ria;	Your name, very great;
Oli moo, hara baraq.	Add to your name, very important.

K—I

Bungan oté ula-lojo;	Visit above in the heavens;
Barang olé ero-auq.	Sit with companions below on earth.
Tutuq uli,	Tell of the creation,
Pau koda;	Recite the history;
Pilir milir,	Comb smooth,
Péir méir.	Thresh clean.
É bukaq nuté,	We open the words,
Loing tojéq;	Call the words;
Tojéq nuté,	Words, words [dreams of],
Wangun-léan,	Causes,
Hapang awil,	Finished and ready,
Ehe lakan.	Throw out the offering.
Biti wana naiq,	Raise the right high,
Belé weri wehéq.	Drop the left low.
Éaq awaq,	Throw out the fishing line,
Polo paka.	Throw away the wire.
Moho wéi,	Release the rotan,
Batal uléq.	Take out the peg.
Ko onga,	Drop from the shoulders,
Lahaq leké.	Throw away.
Tutuq-nanang,	Speech and
Loing lering,	Conversation,
Tojéq maté,	The words are dead,
Nuté pilang.	The words are finished.
Bunung nuté,	The words are exhausted,
Loter mahu.	Over and done.
Peq kuhi,	Invert the bowl,
Req tajong.	Put up the basin.
Lepé nuté,	Do not repeat the words,
Peling tojéq.	Finish them.
Witing maté,	Goat dead,
Tuaq luru.	Palm wine finished.

The chant only ends when all signs of life are gone from the chicken. It can be prolonged indefinitely by repetition or by adding more lines from the common stock of ritual language. Other than the standard opening (cf. Vatter 1932: 213) it is safe to say of this chant, as of all others, that there is no fixed order of lines, nor even any regularity of what lines will be used. Most of the lines quoted here will appear just as well in ceremonies of a very different nature.

The chicken is supposed to represent a huge goat or pig. Eggs used in these ceremonies are commonly thought to substitute for, at least, a chicken. The point of throttling the chicken is to call the guardian spirit and to see whether or not the ceremony has gone favourably. Special attention is given to how the feet of the chicken lie after it is dead. Vatter (1932: 213) reports that it is taken as a good sign if the chicken sticks both out in front of it or if it raises the right leg high. The name of this stage is in fact *hala boté wana*, which means to put up the right. It was explained to me in Léuwajang by a layman that if the right leg lay over the left it was a good sign, if the reverse a bad. However, the old priest who usually conducted the ceremonies I witnessed always insisted that either left or right was a good sign. I think, though, that this attitude was conditioned by the desire always to have a good result. If the sign is interpreted as bad, a new chicken must be offered; I only witnessed one occasion, in a very different sort of ceremony, where they actually decided to use another chicken. Although they always accepted a left leg as a satisfactory result in the ceremonies I attended, they were always visibly pleased when it came up right.

When the chicken is dead, the priest spits some sirih-pinang on it and then its mouth is slit open. Blood is then allowed to drip on the stone (no. 1) for *éwaq*'s lord, the banana stalk, and the boulder. I once thought that the order in which this was done was prescribed, but continuous observation of these ceremonies convinced me that they do not take any care in this regard. Feathers are then ripped from the bird and put on all the blood spots. The long feathers of the wings are carefully pulled out and collected and then placed above the banana stalk.

While the priest was conducting this part of the ceremony, the others built a fire to roast the bananas and chicken. This fire must be built outside, and it must be built on top of stones. It does not matter what wood is used, but the fire may not be started with fire from a hearth. It can only be started with fire sticks, flint and stone, or matches. It must, that is, be completely independent. I finally convinced myself that it does not matter where the fire is built in relation to the altar, but in fact it is usually above the site of the ceremony, perhaps simply to keep the smoke from bothering the priest. After the feathers are removed, the chicken is roasted in the fire. Then some banana and meat are put on the stones representing *éwaq* and *metung* and palm wine is poured on them. Following this, the meal may be eaten. This is usually done outside, near the site of the ceremony itself. However, this was not always so, and there seemed no especial reason to do so except when the *éwaq-metung* itself was located near a large rock face which might harbour a spirit who could, if mistreated, possess the partakers. Women are absolutely forbidden to eat anything used in this particular ceremony. This may well be due to the relation between the guardian spirit of the *éwaq* and that of the village. They are likewise forbidden to eat anything used in the ceremony at the village temple.

When the food is finished, then all the bones and banana skins and other debris are gathered together and placed near the altar. The priest takes back to the altar the parts of the chicken which constitute the *hui mapur*, which includes the lower beak, tips of the wings and toes and pieces of intestine. This is put on the stone (no. 1) for the lord of the *éwaq*. More palm wine is put on the stones and then the twisted string called the *tuber-nawaq*—which throughout the ceremony has lain on stone no. 1—is taken up. This string is actually taken from the ravellings of old sarongs. It is supposed to consist of five strands, twisted seven times. Some of these strands are white and some black. This is used in all ceremonies and it stands for soul, in most instances the soul of the person for whom the offering is made. In this ceremony, it stands for the soul of the maize. This thread is then whirled around (*wating*), while held from above, over the stones on the right, and then over those on the left, while a chant is spoken, of which the following is representative:

Loq tuber,	Drop the soul,
Belé nawaq.	Release the soul.
Tuber belé,	Release the soul,
Léi belé.	Release the feet.
Hikun belé,	Release the left,
Wana belé.	Release the right.
Belé tuber,	Release the soul,
Belé tuber.	Release the soul.

For a considerable time I tried to convince myself that this thread should be whirled in a counter-clockwise direction. I now think that, if anything, it should be in the opposite direction. The first conception, at least, did not fit what was done. But the difficulty of observation was increased by the fact that it was always done rather carelessly and the priest frequently changes his hand. I once tried to clarify the point with him, and he objected to my interpretation that it must be twirled counter-clockwise, and said that in fact it should be in the opposite direction, but from there the conversation fell into confusion. I can report though that when twirled, it should be twirled four times. This process marks the end of the ceremony.

A strand from this string is taken out and tied around one of the stalks of maize. This stalk then becomes the soul of the maize (*watar tuber*) and is the first cut when the maize is harvested. They do not free the ear from the stalk in this case as is usually done; instead, they cut off a section of stalk on either side of about two feet or so in length. This is eventually stored in the floor (underneath) of the granary near the right post (*lili wana*). Next year, when planting starts again, a few grains are taken from these ears and are the first planted. The remaining strands are given to the owners of the altar, and these they may tie on a pig pen, near the chicken nest, or put near the right post of their house.

2. INTERPRETATION

Some comment should be made concerning the orientation in this ceremony. In almost all ceremonies, the priest faces the direction which is up the slope. Only in certain very specific ceremonies in which he calls the wind to enter the village does he reverse this position. Ceremonies at the *éwaq-metung* are invariably as in Figure 8. It is very regular, and it appears to correspond, for example, to the orientation of a building. In this case, this is very probably so. One might then suppose that all motion in the ceremony is regularly counter-clockwise through the series of stones. This, however, is not so, even in this case. In other ceremonies where the number of stones used becomes much greater and their arrangement loses all appearance of correspondence to the house, the movement is likewise completely irregular. There is no hope, then, of finding a regular, prescribed orientation when one looks into the detail of the arrangement and motion of these ceremonies. This can be found only in the grosser features.

Why the priest faces as he does is not hard to guess. The altar, like the mountain, the village, the clan temple, and so on, is inhabited by a spirit. These spirits stand at an origin, as do the ancestors when they appear in a controlled manner. These points of origin seem to be associated with the right and above, or with the head, when not with the centre. Therefore, in the same way that the altar of the church is in the symbolic east, the normal altar in Kédang is above, nearest the origin.

It should be clear from the arguments already put forward in earlier parts of this book, why the uneven numbers appear as they do in the ceremony, and why the string is whirled four times. The cotton and cloth are put down in uneven bunches an uneven number of times because in this case the priest is just preparing the offering for the spirit of the altar; this does not represent a transition in any sense. However, when the string is whirled four times, this is a transition. Presumably the soul from the guardian spirit comes into the string at this time. At any rate as the primary result of the ceremony the string may now be tied to the stalk (or stalks) of maize which is to preserve the soul of the maize until the next year. It is no longer, as it was before the ceremony, just a piece of ravelling. The Kédangese provided no deeper exegesis than that related.

The occasion of the ceremony certainly is a transition, not primarily a human one, but nevertheless one for the field products, which are also living things. The funeral was interpreted as primarily concerned with transition, but it was shown that it also contained offerings. The harvest ceremony contains elements of transition, but it seems primarily concerned with an offering, and with the receiving in return of the prestation of life in the form of the protection of the crops and livestock. While the first stage of the funeral was concerned, above all, with separation; the first stage of the harvest ceremony, leading up to throttling the chicken, was concerned with preparing the offering to be received by the spirit and calling him to partake, thus a sort of incorporation. The throttling of the chicken marks the actual coming of the spirit, coincident with the passing out of the living spirit of the cock. This may be regarded as a transition. In the following stage both the spirit and the men partake of the meal. This stage of the ceremony is marked by the taking up of the soul string, and this seems formally to be a separation from the spirit.

XIII

MATAN AND PUÉN

IN this chapter, I wish to turn attention to two words which seem fundamental to the proper understanding of the culture of Kédang. The first of these is the word *matan*, which occurs in a seemingly bewildering variety of contexts. It is related to the word *mato* meaning 'eye'; it can be used to mean 'bud', 'lid', 'source', and quite a number of other things. In ritual language it is commonly paired with the word *puén*, meaning 'trunk', 'base', 'origin', or 'source'. Examples of these usages will be given below, but it might be useful to remark first that these terms do not pose a problem in Kédang alone; they are characteristic for Indonesian languages and therefore provide both a comparative problem and a means for undertaking comparison.

I. 'MATAN'

I wish to introduce here in a very cursory form some of the issues involved in the interpretation of the word *matan* and its cognates. The original form, according to Dempwolf (1938), is *mata*. This word in Bahasa Indonesia has the primary meaning of 'eye' and of 'centre', 'core', 'nucleus' (Echols and Shadily). From there the dictionary entry continues until it is quite sizable. In the Table 3, I present the terms for 'sun', 'eye', and 'spring' in Bahasa Indonesia, the languages of the two central Flores peoples of Lio and Ngada, in Lamaholot and in the language of Kédang. I have remarked that it is very common for a word meaning sun to be

TABLE 3

Comparative sketch of the use of *mata(n)* in five Indonesian languages

	Bahasa Indonesia	Lio	Ngada	Lamaholot	Kédang
Sun	*Matahari*	*Mata ledza*	*Mata leza*	*Lera matan*	*(Lojo matan)*
Eye	*Mata*	*Mata*	*Mata*	*Mata*	*Mato*
Spring	*Mata air*	?	*Mata vace*	*Wai matan*	*Wei matan*

combined with *mata* or a variant; and this usually means 'sun'. In Kédang, it means 'the dry season'. The word is also very commonly combined with a word meaning 'water' to form a phrase meaning 'the source of a spring'.

Additional uses in Kédang include the following:

deséq matan	lid of a tobacco basket.
wajaq matan	Lid of a sirih-pinang basket.
kong matan	the rounded bulge in the centre of a gong.
maqur matan	the yard in front of the door.
wéloq matan	the door to the old village, *léu tuan*.
ai matan	a knot or hole left at the base of a branch, or else the depression in the earth below the trunk of a tree.
taq matan	the base of a coconut where it was attached to the tree and from which the shoot will emerge.
u matan	a boil (*matan* is the ring around it from which the pus emerges).
pédaq matan	a strong field-knife.
lia matan	the hearth.[1]

In addition, the tip of a seed from which the sprout emerges is called *matan*. Each year when planting, they check the *matan* of the maize seed to see if it is 'white' (i.e. semi-transparent). If so, it will germinate, if black, it will not. (This provides an opposed case to that in which water is called 'black' rather than 'white' because it is clear, showing that it is the relation of opposition rather than absolute colour or light intensity which matters.) It is interesting in this regard that the pupil of the eye is *mato uluq*, or 'seed of the eye'. *Mata* in the other languages consulted would mean the cutting edge of a knife; in Kédang there are other words for this and the meaning of *matan* in this case is 'very strong' (as I was told, the blade would not break if it hit a knot, *ai matan*). The idea of strength may very well be part of the meaning in other cases as well, for example, for the spring or the door of the old village. But this idea of strength is probably close to the sense of 'potential'. For the knife, it is clear what this means. For the spring or the door of the village, it is the potential of bringing into being and is connected with spirit. That fear may be associated with this potency is neither implied nor necessarily barred. In most cases it is clearly not present.

[1] On Seran and Ambon, *Liamatan*, and related forms, is the name for the sun (cf. Maass 1920/21: 60).

2. 'PUÉN'

The second word, *puén*, is also widespread in its various forms in Indonesia. Cognates occurring in other languages include *puken* in Lamaholot, *pukong* in Coastal Alorese, *hu* in Rotinese. It is interesting that this word is characteristically paired in ritual language with *matan* and that it has very similar meanings of 'source' and 'origin', but that the two words effect a division within their common meaning. To understand the relation, it is best to refer to an example such as the parts of bamboo as represented in Figure 9.

This figure shows a branch (*limaq*) emerging from a node (*woq*). It will be recalled that a piece of bamboo consists of sections called

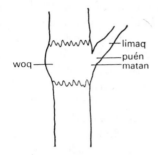

FIG. 9 The node of bamboo.

laru, interrupted by nodes called *woq*, and that these words have other significances of interest. At each node of a bamboo there is an eye from which a branch may bud, and this is called *matan*, both before the branch has emerged, afterwards, and even after the branch may have been cut off. The thickened base of this branch adjacent the *matan* may be called *puén*—just as the trunk of the whole bamboo is *puén*, and the place in the earth from which it emerges is *matan*. From this figure it is easy to understand then why the two words may share the meanings of source and origin. At the same time, it is possible to see that *matan* really means no more than a point of emergence or transition. It thus has something in common with *woq*.[2] *Puén* may be associated with ideas of substance, solidity, and durability.

[2] Schuster (1951) shows that this association, joint-eyes as he calls them, is found all over the world.

3. IMPLICATIONS FOR THE CULTURE OF KÉDANG

Both *puén* and *matan* show by the terminal *n* that they are not
the root forms of the words. In fact, there happens to be a phrase
pué-mata, which preserves both the root forms and the root meanings of both words. This phrase was translated for me as meaning
in Indonesian *masing-masing* or 'each', 'respectively'. It is an
individualizing phrase: when two things are *pué-mata* they are
of two different kinds, unrelated, separate. The implied image—
and simultaneously the explanation for the usage—is that they
each have a separate origin and source. This is the closest, by the
way, that we can come to finding a Kédangese equivalent to the
English word 'individual'.

A little reflection on what has so far been said about origins
and sources and particularly about the construction of the house,
will show why it is necessary to understand these words and to be
familiar with their uses. In a house it is important to preserve the
original orientation of the trees and bamboos used in it, and this
means keeping, above all, one's trunks and sources together. It
has been shown, furthermore, that it is not just a question of plant
symbolism. It happens that plants are under the same rules of life
and death as men and buildings, and the same orientation must
be preserved in all cases. For all things, the most immediate
source of life is under the ground.

The usages of *matan* quoted above, in all their diversity, are
concerned with transitions of one sort or another (primarily potential ones). We are familiar with ideas such as that the eyes are
doors to the soul, but we might be sceptical that eyes are thought
of in a similar way in Indonesia if we had not already encountered
the story recorded in an earlier chapter in which the eyes of the
civet cat are planted and sprout into the tree of wealth.

It seems that all objects which have being are subject to representation in Kédang according to the same principles. This being
need not imply substance, but may be purely conceptual, as in
the case of time. In so far as there is motion, it is oriented in a
single direction and stands under the law of travelling to the right.
In so far as being has structure, this structure is segmentary, consisting of inter-nodes and points of transition. Motion itself is
subject to this same principle of structure. The orientation of
being and motion is determined by the point of origin, and the

frequency of the terms *matan* and *puén* point out how concerned the Kédangese are with these origins. These considerations show how inadequate it would be to assume that the collective thought of the people of Kédang is ruled by any one metaphor of being—such as anthropomorphism or plant symbolism. Where all being is represented according to the same principles, how is it possible to single out any one version of being and say that this determines the rest?

In the following chapters there will be occasion to show how the ideas reviewed above have an important role in the social order.

XIV

SOCIAL RELATIONS: THE CLAN

DESCENT is patrilineal in Kédang. Based on this principle of tracing descent through males, is a segmentary social order of villages and clans. Appendix II, which shows a version of the descent lines of the indigenous clans of Léuwajang traced back to God, demonstrates several features of this segmentary system. Not only does it establish agnatic relations among ten of the clans of the village, but it purports to show relations of the same sort between these clans as a village and other villages and even with quite distant regions such as Gunung Api (Lewotolo) to the west or Witi Hama on Adonara. Ideologically, agnatic relations of this sort could be traced with all villages of Kédang and with all clans, excepting only those with an express tradition of having immigrated into Kédang. To do so with more than a few villages would be beyond the capacities of most people, and would, in any case, probably require a certain amount of invention. To take only adjacent villages, agnatic ties are claimed with Léuhoéq and Léudanung, but Maramamuq is, if at all, far more distantly related and Atarodang Édang is not related at all. The latter descends from a group which moved to the present location from Atarodang Wua Wutuq.

Single clan villages probably do not exist, but the village is in principle different from the clan only in being at a higher structural level. In fact, it usually consists of a set of related clans which hold traditional rights to govern and in many cases one or more additional client clans whose ancestors usually have fled from another village and requested the right to live and open fields in their present village.

In Léuwajang the clans are actually represented as consisting of three groups. The first of these, comprising the clans Hiang Leraq, Buang Leraq, and Boli Leraq is called *Laba Waq* ('to chisel a rock'). The name derives from a story, which I cannot give here, in which men of the village acquired wives by chiselling open a large boulder, still to be seen above the old village, now called *waq laba*. The second group is called Léuwajang and consists of the clans Apé Utung (the lord of the land), Apé Labi (head of the village), Apé Worén, Apé Liling,[1] Apé Nobé, Apé Tatu, and Amun Toda. Both groups are agnatically related, and the distinction between them is not now of any practical significance. However, once for a short period early in this century the two split and had separate village governments. The full details have escaped me, and this is not the place to reconstruct what I know. It did not last long, and I would assume that the members of both sets of clans lived interspersed in the village site as they do now. Both share the same old village, as they always have.

The third group comprises three client clans (*tudéq erun*, 'late arrivals'): Laong Hodiq, Hoqaratan, and Toul Wala.[2] The names of the latter two indicate their villages of origin. Laong Hodiq comes from the village Léutubung and it still maintains close (informal) relations with the clan Léutubung in the neighbouring village Atarodang Édang. This latter clan descends from the same ancestor who left Léutubung and moved to Léuwajang. These client clans have no traditional rights in the village government; however, the *aqé-amé* of each has equal status in village affairs as those of the other clans, and one of the four new offices of *pamong* (assistant) is held by a man from Toul Wala. Other than the traditional restriction that they may not build their clan houses inside the old village and that they receive no prescribed part of the animal at a village ceremony, they do not suffer any discrimination.

There are no animal totems for the clans (as there are in Lamaholot); and the clans do not have individual food restrictions. I cannot of course vouch for the fact that this holds true for every clan in Kédang, but I have never encountered a case where it was not true. The only word for clan recognized in Léuwajang is the common Malay *suku*. This would, of course, apply to any structural level below the village, but I know of no usage above that

[1] Apé Liling now has only one living male, who has no children; and it is expected that the clan will die out with him. He actually lives a few hundred yards away from Léuwajang in the village Atarodang Édang; so this clan is not actually represented in the village any longer. Formally the clan remains a constituent part of the village. It has always consisted of a single lineage, and because of its numerical weakness is closely bound to the agnatically related clan Apé Worén. It may turn to Apé Worén for assistance in bridewealth matters.

[2] A segment of the clan Tuaq Henéq of Léudanung lives in Léuwajang as dependents of the clan Boli Leraq.

level. It does not retain its other western Indonesian meanings: 'leg', 'ethnic group', or 'quarter'. The word *lélang*, which is used to mean clan in Lamaholot and on Alor and Pantar, occurs in clan names in the eastern part of Kédang. It derives from *léla*, 'long' (of time). In some villages, the word *huna* ('house') is employed.

There is a wide variety in the means employed to name individual clans. Some of these are displayed in Léuwajang. The three clans of Laba Waq are named for the sons of Leraq Beni from whom they descend. Amun Toda is also named after an ancestor. Five of the clans of the section Léuwajang descend from a man named Maing Wehéq. Their clan names contain the given name of the son from whom each descends, but the name Maing drops out. Instead the word *apé* is placed in front. This word means 'cotton' or 'thread', and it seems that it may have been chosen to represent the tie which unites the members. Other means are shown in different villages. In Léunoda, two clans are called Lili Wana ('the right house post') and Lili Weri ('the left house post'). In Léunapoq, clans are designated *tubar* ('head'), *léin* ('feet'), and *oroq* ('chest'); this also occurs elsewhere. These designations probably originally were associated with ritual obligations and the ceremonial division of the animal. In the villages mentioned, this seems, however, to have disappeared. The point of giving these facts is to demonstrate that the people of Kédang have available a variety of logically coherent means of arriving at clan names. They do not rely on any one way which can be taken as primitive. Kédang does not represent a stage of the decay of an original totemism; and any one means is logically sufficient and intact, despite the fact that it is not universally employed.

The clans of Léuwajang range in size from 2 members to 169. Each is an exogamous corporate group with a recognized elder (*aqé-amé*) responsible for bridewealth and other traditional matters and now a clerk (*pegawai*), a young man responsible for transmitting government orders and assisting in keeping records. In some ways they are more administrative segments than political groups. At least, that is often the way they are used by the modern village government. Labour on village projects and other tasks for the district government is often assigned by clan. Now that warfare is ended, they never form the basis for power moves based on war, and they do not take on the character of political parties or agitation groups. There is no hierarchy or ranking of clans, and thus no striving to increase the clan status. There are no social classes within the indigenous population, other than the distinction between the ruling village Kalikur and the rest of the population. Since that village has been removed from power, this distinction has become largely inconsequential.

One does not find in Kédang, as is so common in some areas of Lamaholot, large clans spread over several villages. In most cases the clan is identified with a single village and most of its members are resident there. When parts of a clan move away permanently, this usually results in severing relations and acquiring the status of a new clan. There are some interesting variations which make summary characterization difficult however. If there has been a major fight, then usually all relations are dropped and forgotten. However, even in such cases, later descendants may remember the connection and consider themselves members of the same clan, while keeping corporate affairs separate. Thus, there is a section of Apé Utung in Léuhoéq. The members of both clans remain friends and are recognized as being of the same clan, but bridewealth transactions are separate and they are each fully integrated in their own village. In another clan, a segment split off and moved away several generations ago and almost completely broke all ties. Curiously enough, in my last year they had decided that the original fight was sufficiently forgotten and they requested to return to Léuwajang. The preparations for the ceremonies necessary for their reincorporation into the village and the clan were being made as I left.

In Léuwajang, many have their fields several kilometres away near the village Léubatan on the southeast side of the mountain. In many cases they live more or less permanently there during the agricultural season. Some people live even more permanently at their fields. This does not matter, so long as they maintain ties with the village. For all governmental and practical purposes they are considered to remain village and clan members of Léuwajang. However, even when a line may move permanently away from the village and stay for several generations, this does not necessarily mean that they lose their status in their original clan and village and take up new ones. In fact the *aqé-amé* of one of the most important clans in Léuwajang lives permanently in

Léubatan, as had his father. In this case the position was shared with another man living in Léuwajang to make the arrangement of bridewealth affairs within the village more convenient, but he nevertheless was senior. Separation from the clan and village, then, is a matter of individual decision or of expulsion, but it is not a question of residence. The means whereby a person or group may be incorporated into a new clan will be described below, for it really belongs to the topic of marriage.

In Kédang there are no named lineages within clans, so the corporate structure does not extend below the clan level. This has consequences for the relations between clans, as will be shown below. In certain practical ways, more restricted groups do come into play, so the segmentary potential of the descent rule is not completely ignored, but since these groups are not named and lack corporate organization, they have no lasting significance for the society.

In this chapter, I have tried to provide information of a very general nature about the clan to aid in understanding what will follow. Since the clan acquires most of its meaning and even organization through its external relations with other clans, there is not much more to be gained by this essentially internal approach. If the clan were to be defined by its chief activity, then the clan in Kédang would have to be called a bridewealth exchanging group. It follows from this that there is more to learn about the clan by studying marriage, than there is in concentrating upon it in isolation. I have said very little about the meaning of descent here because it too can best be approached in connection with a discussion of relations acquired through marriage.

XV

SOCIAL RELATIONS: ALLIANCE

THE people of Kédang have a social order based on asymmetric prescriptive alliance, or what the Dutch have called circulating connubium. In some ways it is an almost ideal example of this form. However, a rigorous empiricist might deny that they belong to this type of society at all.

It is not my aim to secure a categorization for them, but to set the facts out in the clearest way possible so that they may be apprehended correctly irrespective of the reader's individual terminological predilections. This means that the way the Kédangese represent their social order has to be set out in all detail first. Only then can the question whether social action accords with it have meaning. Then if one person chooses to say that they have prescriptive alliance and another to say they do not, we will know that the first refers to rules and relationship terms in applying his own categories, and the second, being a realist, insists on referring to relations between groups (cf. Needham 1966: 67). The facts will then not fall into doubt, and disagreement can be seen to lie in personal philosophies.

I. THE MARRIAGE RULE

Fischer (1935: 278–88) says, in societies of this sort it is not the individual who 'acquires relatives through his marriage, but his agnatic group which is allied to that of the spouse'.[1]

With such important consequences resting on the marriage, it is of first importance to ask how the spouse is picked. In Kédang, this means that one must ask separately what is the marriage rule? what is the marriage preference? and what is the marriage practice?

Marriage in Kédang is prescribed with a woman of the relationship category *mahan*. The rule is expressed in this phrase, *pau mahan, déi nopin; kihaq léi dero, beq wéla léin*.

---

[1] Kédang happens to have a principle of patrilineal descent, as do (or as appeared at that time) the societies Fischer was considering. Agnation is not of course a necessary concomitant of asymmetric alliance, nor are actual descent groups required (Needham 1964a: 237).

Pau seems to mean 'to speak to' or 'address'. To narrate history is *pau koda*; and a sort of insolent way to answer a person (which often occurs in myths) is to say *pau oté wau*, as much as to say 'address my forehead'. *Nopin* seems untranslatable in Kédang, but it is used in this case as though it were synonymous with *mahan*, the name for the prescribed category of women (for a man) or men (for a woman). The full name for the category is then *mahan-nopin*. My notes from Wailolong, East Flores show that the prescribed marriage category there may be called (among other things) *maha-nopi*, which is especially used for a man or woman with whom a future marriage has already been arranged. Father Jan Krol kindly loaned me his unpublished Lamaholot dictionary (Krol, n.d.). He gives for *maha*, 'betrothed, affianced', and relates it to *paha*, 'to propose marriage'. *Nopi* he translates as 'like', 'thus', 'such as this . . .'

Thus the first two phrases of the line given above expressing the marriage rule mean 'to address the *mahan*, to follow thus' (i.e. this category). The second group means 'to step on the heel, tug at the hem of the sarong'. This indicates that a woman follows previous generations of women in the clan, in the same way that (perhaps) a young child might follow her older sister. Value is placed then on the idea that a marriage follow the path established by previous marriages. In ordinary conversation, they express a great liking for this type of marriage.

Theirs is a prescriptive terminology, and marriage is prohibited with all other categories of women. In those cases where a woman is removed from the category *mahan* to another category (e.g. BW, SW, etc.), this transference means a removal to a prohibited category. There is a strict prohibition on marrying a woman within the clan; this includes genealogical mother and other wives of men called *amé*. There is a formal prohibition on marrying a woman in a line regarded as consisting of siblings. The means of tracing such a relation and the consequences, mostly ceremonial, of breaking this prohibition will be described below. Marriage with women from a line which takes its wives from one's own is also strongly prohibited.

The marriage preference is for a man to marry the daughter of his genealogical mother's brother; conversely, a woman should preferably marry her father's sister's son. Both individuals may be designated *mahan até nimun*, 'the true *mahan*'. True *mahan* are the closest members of the category; it includes the genealogical MBD (for the woman, the FZS). Most distant *mahan* are *mahan néheq* ('distant'). I do not think that there is a precise genealogical definition for the 'true *mahan*', nor a predetermined boundary between the two types. My impression is that 'true *mahan*' are members of mother's clan with whom there are close ties, above all MBD, while 'distant *mahan*' will be members of her clan with whom there are no immediate ties and above all *mahan* not in mother's original clan. In line with the marriage preference is a contingent payment of bridewealth, called *hudé hén*, which must eventually be paid the mother's brother's clan, should marriage be with a woman not in this clan.

The genealogical FZD (and perhaps other genealogically close members of the category) is the *iné utun até nimun*, 'true *iné utun*'; she is strictly forbidden. *Iné utun néheq*, 'distant *iné utun*', while not according with the rule of marriage, may be married without incurring the consequences of marriage with the 'true *iné utun*'.

It is not forbidden in Kédang, as it is in some other societies, for two brothers to marry two sisters.

Concerning the marriage practice, my records show that there are some 31 per cent of marriages in which there is no previous traceable relation. Of those marriages though in which a previous relation does exist, 87 to 90 per cent are with women who are in one degree or another in the prescribed category (i.e. *mahan*) and only 10 to 13 per cent with women in a prohibited category. However, of the marriages I recorded in which comparison could be made to the man's father's marriage, only 17 per cent were with women of the mother's brother's clan, and of these, only 26 per cent married a genealogical mother's brother's daughter. Contrarily, there were two cases of marriage within the clan, no marriages with the genealogical father's sister's daughter, but two cases of direct exchange between sets of siblings. In addition it can be shown that the marriage relations between most of the clans of Léuwajang show reciprocal exchange of women. These matters are fully dealt with in Chapter XIX.

Arranged marriages and forced marriages—if they occur at all— are rare. So far from there being an insistence on children carrying out marriages arranged by their parents, the parents, as I was told, must acquiesce to the desires of their children. They even went so far as to say that it is the customary law that if the parents oppose a marriage, they must nevertheless reconcile themselves to it, if their child is set on it. I know of one case in which a very strong-minded woman prevented her daughter from marrying a man whom she, the mother, did not like. But, despite exceptions of this sort, generally the young people are left to themselves to pick their mate. The bridewealth is always provided by the clan for any marriage, barring a violation of clan exogamy. If we had statistics on the number of cases of coercion by the parents in marriage, they would probably be close to those of a western society.

2. THE ALLIANCE RELATIONSHIP

Marriage is regarded as establishing an alliance relationship between the clans of the two spouses. This is a dyadic relationship between the superior, wife-giving clan, *epu-bapa*, and the inferior, wife-taking clan, *maqing-anaq*.

The first marriage contracted between two clans is called the *bunga karé*. It is not clear if *bunga* is related to Indonesian *bunga*, meaning 'blossom'; it means however 'to visit' (as in *bungan-barang*). *Karé* means 'to make known'. Should the two clans in question belong to different villages, then in the first instance, this would be regarded as initiating an alliance between villages; and the heads of the villages would have to share in the prestations given under this name. A marriage of this type which initiates a relationship would have to be accompanied by a special initial gift. The wife-takers would give an ear-ring, goat, or tusk; the counter-prestation would be a *lipaq* (man's sarong).

Subsequent marriages between those two clans would be called *nobol tuan*, 'old *nobol*'. This refers to the only expression which we could use to translate the word 'alliance'. There is no term made up from the names of these two groups (as for example *epu-maqing*) to represent the relationship and parallel to similar expressions (*mayu-dama*, Kachin; *yera-ana kavine*, Sumba; *hula-hula-boru*, Batak) in other asymmetric systems.[2] This does not mean that the relationship is not dyadic (rather than triadic) in nature. The alliance relationship is called *nobol-téqa* or, in a longer form, *nobol-atar*, *téqa-baraq*. *Nobol* are large studs in the

---

[2] The only similar term is *binin-maqing*, made up of the terms 'sister' and 'wife-taker'. This occurs in the expression *pan tutuq binin-maqing*, which means 'to go to discuss bridewealth matters'. It seems, in this the only usage I know, to refer to the negotiations which are a consequence of the relation rather than to the relationship itself.

floor of the granary; *téqa* seems to have no independent meaning. *Atar* are the split bamboo mats which cover a platform (*balai*); *baraq* are the large bamboos which make the horizontal frame of such a platform. These terms suggest that the relationship between two such clans is of the same interlocking nature as is to be found in the structure of a granary or *balai*. There is a ritual admonition based on the name: *nobol kara kodol*, 'do not throw away the *nobol'*, *téqa kara léngan*, 'do not knock over the *téqa'*—i.e. do not disrupt the alliance.

Alliance relationships are not exploited for political purposes as they sometimes are in other societies, though the Radja of Adonara did employ the form when establishing his power in Kédang under Dutch protection. This potential of employing the alliance idiom[3] for political relations does exist, but at the village level and lower seems never to be used. The implications of such an alliance for the clan are confined primarily to the bridewealth obligations which accompany them and the necessity to appear at certain feasts and ceremonies in the relation defined by a given marriage. This means in many cases, since the relations between two clans are actually often reciprocal, that a clan may on one occasion take the role of wife-giver in relation to another, on another occasion the role of wife-*taker* to the same clan. As I have witnessed, this shifting of roles may take place within a few moments.

From a formal point of view, relations can always be traced to lines with which one's own clan has no immediate tie (though practically this may in some cases be difficult or impossible). Members of one's own clan are regarded collectively as *kakang-aring* (or *kangaring*; compare Ind. *kakak-adik*; reference should be made to the terms *aqé* and *ariq* which include siblings). This category may be split into more distant members called *meker-éhoq* and closer ones called *eruq-anaq*. There is no definition to indicate

---

[3] Where it is employed, it is not separated from descent idiom. The Radja of Adonara gave a wife to the *kapitan* of Kédang, so that he would stand in the inferior position of wife-taker. The ruling clan of Kalikur regards Léuwajang also as wife-giver. On this basis, the Radja of Adonara chose to regard Léu-wajang as a form of siblings (*meker-éhoq*). When he came to Kédang he did not go directly to Kalikur but stopped in Léuwajang (or Léuhoéq where the same relation existed). Then someone from Léuwajang was sent as envoy to Kalikur to announce his arrival. These relationships depended greatly on whether the Radja chose to recognize them or not. He spoke Lamaholot not Kédangese, but the same system exists there.

where the split occurs. Genealogically very close members obviously fall in the second category. Otherwise the term is applied, as I was told, on the basis of feeling, i.e. friendship. The term for the more distant members, *meker-éhoq* (i.e. 'eldest and younger'), can be applied to any line which has taken women from one's own wife-givers. It has been mentioned that such a relationship may be validated by bringing a black cloth and baskets of maize for use in a funeral. Marriage with such a line is formally incestuous. These relationships are actually valued; they are not simply curious logical extensions, and they should not be considered structurally irrelevant parts of the social order.

Wife-givers of wife-givers are termed *epu-bapa*, i.e. 'wife-givers'. Wife-takers of wife-takers are *also* termed *epu-bapa*, 'wife-givers'.[4] Thus there is a formally closed cycle (also reflected, as we shall see, in the relationship terminology). Any line may fall into one of three relations with one's own: (1) superiority, wife-givers; (2) equality, siblings; or (3) inferiority, wife-takers. In this system, one may not take women from a wife-taking line (*maqing*), but it is quite possible that one's own wife-givers (*epu*) will; therefore, one must regard this wife-taking line at second remove as being—as they in fact are—potential wife-givers. By the same logic, wife-givers of wife-givers may be one's own wife-takers. Why then are they not called wife-takers?

The answer is two-fold. The most general is that of two possible designations the Kédangese always employ the more respectful. Their system of relationship terms is hierarchically ordered so that a superior of a superior must be referred to by a term of at least equal respect. Ample evidence will be given soon. Secondly the wife-givers of one's own wife-givers may be considered to transmit, indirectly, to oneself whatever they transmit to one's wife-giver. This means in one case the spiritual well-being for which, as will be shown, one is dependent on one's mother's brother's line, depends also on *his* mother's brother's line.[5]

Additionally, the obligations, particularly those of bridewealth,

[4] These are terminological issues; they do not define a section-system. There is no rule against taking wives from wife-givers of wife-givers or giving them to wife-takers of wife-takers. There are plenty of instances of both. Alliance status remains relative (cf. Needham 1961: 108).

[5] Concerning these, as Fischer calls them, bride-givers to the second power, he says, 'The group of bride-givers is a well of life-force for the bride-takers, the bride-givers of bride-givers are then this [too] *a fortiori*' (1935: 374).

one's wife-givers acquire by marriage become in some sense one's own. Thus one says of people who marry the daughter of a sister, *anaq todéq, baré né iné*, 'the child follows and carries her mother'. This means, if the sister's husband does not have the bridewealth, then we go to *his maqing-anaq*—who have taken his daughter—for payment because we are invested in a right to the bridewealth received for her.

This cyclical series of relationships may be represented as in Figure 10. The 'peg' represents a terminological line.

This shows how dyadic relations, irreversible and hierarchic in character, come to form a cyclic structure. That it is triadic in this case simply indicates that the Kédangese collective representations are restricted to the logically minimal (hence most efficient)

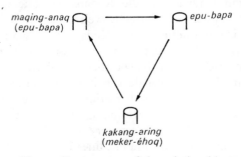

FIG. 10. The cyclic structure of the relationship system

number of lines. We have already seen how these logical features have produced cyclic systems in other areas of Kédangese collective representations.

This is a discussion of categories and ideal relations. It does not mean that actual lineages are ordered in a series of ranked statuses. This should be clear from the fact that a given line traced through one's own wife-takers are categorically wife-*givers*, even though one may make demand on them for payment of bridewealth. The Kachin are a society with both asymmetric prescriptive alliance and a class system, and this combination seems to have caused Leach difficulty in seeing the important distinction to be made between the relation of superiority and inferiority in a complementary pair of categories on the one hand and on the other the status inequalities of social groups (Leach 1961: 71, 85; 1954: 78). In a recent encounter with Lévi-Strauss, he even appears to take the position that a ranking of a series of relationship terms is in conflict with an ideology of circulating connubium (Leach 1969: 278). I cannot agree with him, and I think the material from Kédang shows conclusively that he is wrong. He might have missed some confusion if he did not have a weakness for translating the Jinghpaw term *ji* as 'grandfather' (Leach 1961: 40; 1954: 84). Though applied in part to a different set of relations, *ji* presents the same formal problem as the Kédangese term *epu* (refer to Chapter XVII). Where would we be if we insisted on viewing wife-giving affines as being primarily grandparents?

It must be emphasized then that in Kédang, the cycle is not a fiction produced by the theorist's model. Nothing in Figure 10 has been invented. It simply represents what is to be found in the statements and language of the Kédangese. The cyclic consequences of the system are perfectly well known to them. In what sense it is or is not a fiction of the Kédangese's own making is an issue to be explored later. As this investigation is primarily directed to the thought rather than the social action of Kédang, it is clear the cycle cannot be pushed aside as being irrelevant, inconsequent, made up, fictional, or even as distorting reality. It is real.

It is a consequence of the terminological system that one's own wife-givers fall into the same category as one's father's, whether or not these belong to two different lines or clans. This is related to the fact that it is expected that the affinal ties will be inherited and renewed. It is also related to the fact that superior statuses of sometimes diverse kinds are frequently indicated by the same term from a hierarchically ordered series of terms. This means that the terms themselves must be treated as forming an ordered system, independent of the relations which come to be labelled by them. To show this, I will give two examples from a quite different realm, which I think exhibit the same feature. The term *radja* is usually applied to a king or prince. The people of Kédang were under the Radja of Adonara. The *kapitan* of Kédang was not a *radja*, but he was sometimes loosely referred to by that term. When in a boat in a rough sea, they may address a wave as *radja*. This would be senseless were they to feel restricted by the kinds of limitations about substance that we might think relevant. There is no confusion here. Their language just allows them to employ this highly respectful term in contexts where we would not. A second instance is the name of the crocodile, *bapa*. This happens to be the term of address for the category *epu*. Comparatively, the word is employed in such a variety of ways in adjacent languages that we cannot say what its real meaning is. We can say though that it is always a term of respect.

A man's relations to his own wife-givers (if they are different from his father's) is marked by reserve and respect. For a young man, newly married, it is obligatory that he visit his wife's family and assist them whenever occasion requires. This is not, however, a formal institution of paying bridewealth obligations by service. Ceremonial obligations, such as those entailed by a funeral, also are acquired with marriage. Anyone who is distant and unfriendly to his wife-givers would be thought to be in conflict with normal standards of good behaviour; and, in fact, such relations may be cultivated into ones of mutual friendship and assistance. This assistance is not necessarily one-sided, but the primary obligation lies with the wife-taker. Wife-givers are not generally feared or regarded as excessively exploitative in Kédang.

A man's relations with his father's wife-givers are likely to be more intense. The bridewealth obligations and the expectation to take one's own wife from them is inherited; but in addition one's personal well-being is felt to be in their hands in a way that it is not in the hands of the wife's line. Within the relation between *epu-bapa* and *maqing-anaq* is a more specific relationship between the *epu puén* ('trunk *epu*') and the *anaq maqing* (child on the *maqing* side). This is a relationship in the first instance between the genealogical mother's brother and the genealogical sister's child (the primary concern is the sister's son, *anaq maqing*, rather than the sister's daughter, *iné utun*). Should the mother's brother die, then the position passes to his son, and eventually to his son's son. Should there be factors which inhibit determination of the role in this way, then some other member of the mother's brother's clan closely related genealogically will be designated. So far as I know there is no competition for it, nor does so much rest upon it as seems to be the case for the corresponding position, *tob-huk*, on Roti. Certainly there are not such complicated and public procedures for its determination as Fox describes (1971b: 228–33).

Van Ossenbruggen (1935) has devoted extensive attention to the role of the *hulahula* (wife-givers) among the asymmetric Toba Batak as the source of life and prosperity. This is a common idea in

Indonesia, and is not confined to societies with asymmetric pre-scriptive alliance. For the Toba Batak this influence is called *sahala*, a term for which the Kédangese have no equivalent. Should the wife-takers be childless, suffer long illness, deaths in the family, or fires, they may turn to their *hulahula* for help from its *sahala* (Vergouwen 1964: 55; Fischer 1935: 291). Among the Belu of Timor the *uma mane* emit a kind of power which may cause illness and death for men, livestock, or the crops, and it may also cause fires (Vroklage 1952: 1: 252). For the Batak, the *hulahula* is a sort of stand-in for God to his daughter's children. I was told the same in East Flores concerning the *opu puken*, the mother's brother or equivalent.

In Kédang, this person apparently cannot destroy crops or cause fires. However, health rests in his hands. The full title for this person is *epu-puén, bapa-matan*, 'the trunk *epu*, the source *bapa*'. The fact that one would not exist (would not be born) without the line of the mother's brother is important to them. The name indicates the fact that they are the origin and source of life in this sense. The reason for this is quite clear: they provided the mother; had they not given her there would be no children. This adequately states the social situation, but there is more to it than this. They provide the blood, which, as can be seen from the ritual language, is regarded as a form of life fluid (*werén-lalan*). I have mentioned that what lies behind patrilineal descent is the common tie to some woman, and this tie is represented as attachment to the womb. It seems then that agnatic ties are based on shared blood originally acquired from another group.

This is brought out clearly by the highly valued form of marriage with the *mahan* who is simultaneously the daughter of a daughter of a clan sister (i.e. a clan sister of Ego's FF). Thus, this means a completion of an alliance cycle. This form of marriage, which is relatively rare, is called *pau wéiq balé* or 'to return the blood'. This can best be understood by comparison to marriage of the daughter of a clan sister (*iné utun*), which is strictly prohibited on the grounds that she is of the same blood. What is curious is that in the second instance, identical blood is the cause for a prohibi-tion, in the first it is a cause for what is the most ideal marriage one can make. One man even equated *pau wéiq balé* with *pau mahan* (to marry into the prescribed category). To understand this, it is probably easier if we refer to a kind of image we often find in

Kédang. On Roti, the mother's brother is said to plant the child (Fox 1971b). This is not actually said in Kédang; but the mother's brother is called the trunk *epu*. This suggests the image of a tree. If he is the trunk, the sister's child must be the upper part.[6] Should this relation be reversed by direct marriage exchange, the imagery would suggest that such a marriage would be very much like putting a house post in the ground in the reversed position. However, it is possible to leave this 'tree' growing properly and yet tap its life fluids, if only one's wife-givers intervene and provide a link.

It seems that the hair also represents this essentially spiritual gift from the wife-givers. For this reason the *epu-puén* may demand payment for the hair (*otéq-noloq*) upon the death of the *anaq maqing*.

It is said that the *epu* grabs (*pené*), i.e. supports, his *anaq maqing*. This means that he takes his interests into his own hands and cares for his health. It is required that the *anaq maqing* continually visit his *epu-puén*. If he is ill, he must inform his mother's brother. Should he die without having done so, then the mother's brother may demand a fine in the form of an elephant tusk or ear-ring.[7] In most cases of illness, the *anaq maqing* will enter his mother's brother's house (*udu-loko*) in order to be cured. Formerly, a tusk called *bun-lewéq*, could be demanded of him on this occasion. The name means to roll the small cotton pellets (*panga lewéq*) used in a ceremony, and presumably the intention is that the *epu* acts in a manner similar to that of a person who prepares the cotton in a ceremony occasioned by ill health. When the mother's brother takes this role, it is said that he is *tuan ula-lojo mier*, which might be translated 'the protecting God'. A woman having a difficult childbirth should go to her mother's house or to that of her own *epu-puén*.

In the case where the *anaq maqing* does not frequent his *epu-puén*'s house, does not pay bridewealth or otherwise opposes him and fails to respect his authority, the *epu* may curse him by performing privately a ceremony called *ka, luruq nobol-téqa, Ka* means 'to eat', *luruq* 'to pour', but the whole phrase means to feed

---

[6] This pervasive metaphor of planting and growing dominates the Rotinese conceptions of affinity. 'Their relationship terminology . . . divides all individuals into "those planting" and "those growing" ' (Fox 1968: 291).

[7] Compare Roti where a man must give a payment to his mother's brother if he injures his own body. This is called 'to give [a payment for] the blood' (Fox 1971b: 236–40).

nobol-téqa i.e. the guardian spirit of the alliance. In this ceremony, the *epu* pours a little palm wine and places a little food at a corner of the *balai* where the two *nobol* or *baraq* (large bamboo frame pieces) come together. This may be done at any of the four corners, and it is done at only one of them. The intention of this is to make the *anaq maqing* sick. The ceremony does not require a priest (*molan-maran*) and has no set words. However, I was given a set of expressions made up to the occasion as an example of what he would say. They are revealing enough, I think, to repeat here.

O beté eléng doq, ko?	Did you just descend from the sky?
O belé auq kéu?	Did you just arise from the earth?
Mé, o ohaq ebéng éqi, o.	If so, then do not heed me.
O nobé, éi-ko binin [name] *neti buaq o;*	You there, my sister [name] gave birth to you;
Ména o ko balé haba éqi ramaq.	Therefore, you come back and seek me out again.

This curse would then make the *anaq maqing* ill. If he did not relent, his *epu* would not help him and he might die. If he gave in, then they could call a priest and have him perform a ceremony called *hitaq nutaq*, 'grab the [black] cloth', *bela tuan-naban*, 'grab the *epu*'. This would bring an end to the disaffection; the *anaq maqing* would signal his submission, and the *epu-puén* would again take up his protective role.

To this point, I have only used the expression *epu-bapa* in discussing the wife-giving role. This is indeed the correct term, but the Kédangese more frequently use the synonymous expression *iné-amé*. This is made from the term *iné*, which otherwise includes the mother, and *amé* which includes the father. There are actually two phrases *iné-amé* distinguished in pronunciation by the relaxing and tightening of the throat. The elder generations of one's own clan are called *iné-amé* (where the throat is tight and the pronunciation more distinct); the *epu-bapa* are *iné-amé* (where the throat is relaxed and the pronunciation less distinct). There is no question that these two phrases have an identical etymology, but the distinction in pronunciation is an invariable one and the Kédangese are never confused about the intention. Parallels are common in other societies. The wife-giving group among the Belu may be called *ina-ama* (Vroklage 1952: 1: 255); and I found that the same group in East Flores is also called *ina-ama*.

3. SUMMARY CONSIDERATIONS ON ALLIANCE AND DESCENT

This use of the term *iné-amé* may appear to us as highly confusing. In my view though, it is a question of authority.[8] It is true that this authority is based on, in the one instance, one's own dependence on this group for life, in the second, on one's children's dependence. But we must avoid thinking that this has something to do with corporate organization. Before we apply terms like descent or filiation, perhaps it would be best to go back to what must be for the Kédangese first principles. The wife-giving group is a source of life; even the terms applied to them draw a comparison to other sources of life like the spring, the house post and so on. We have seen time and time again that they distinguish between such sources of life or points of access to spiritual influence and the intervening, often solid, areas and sections. The one seems to articulate the world, the other to give it substance, duration and so on. A very similar division was found in the structure of authority in the village government. One clan has the lord of the land, with ultimate authority and responsibility; and one clan has the village head who executes his requirements. The distinction in this case actually becomes one between authority (primarily spiritual) and power (primarily temporal)—see Leach's important arguments (1961: 19, 21). This is a form of diarchy which Dumézil (1948), Coomaraswamy (1942), and Needham (1960) have discussed in other contexts.

Now the authority of the *epu* is essentially spiritual. He demands respect and obedience; but there are definite limits to his powers. Other than demanding that bridewealth be paid, he has no say concerning the bridewealth valuables within the clan of his wife-takers. He has no say how they govern their affairs. Within the household of his sister's husband or his sister's son, he is an honoured guest, but he is not owner, ruler or head. We have seen that he is the source of spiritual well-being (which Leach calls uncontrolled mystical influence) and that he may curse (which Leach calls controlled supernatural attack). Leach has argued that where these two are found together, 'that source is in a position

---

[8] Concerning the Atoni of Timor, Cunningham (1967a: 58–9) says, 'allied groups are called "one stem" (*uf mese*), and the title *uf* is also used for the founders of a descent group . . . The use of the term *uf* in this affinal context (i.e. *uf mese*) is consistent with other Atoni usages in which affinal alliance is expressed in an agnatic idiom to denote an authoritarian relationship . . .'

of political authority vis-à-vis Ego' (1961: 25). This then is precisely the issue. His authority is not political in the usual sense. He does not direct, issue regulations, tell his sister's son what to do and what not to do.

In contrast, the elder members of one's own clan have an effective temporal power. Their decisions bind the younger members. If they contract debts, these are passed down. One's father's word must be obeyed. The clan is a corporate group. Likewise, descent through males is remembered for generations, but one does not know much about the descent line of one's mother's brother or wife's father, and nothing at all about the descent line of their wife-givers. Descent, then, if recognized at all through females, is exceedingly truncated, not going farther than one remove and having no implications of corporate membership whatever.

It would seem that what we call descent and alliance in Kédang have no definition independently, yet are very much opposed. They stand in the relation then of complementary opposition. This suggests that they should be regarded as the two opposed aspects of the same thing, but that this thing should take its definition from either one of the halves seems to me very unlikely. According to one theory, they might be regarded as two aspects of descent. This suggests the opposite, that they may be regarded as two aspects of affinity. Thus, we might call the descent system of Kédang an example of 'complementary affinity' or 'imaginary submerged alliance' (see the remarks by Dumont 1961: 78). This is outlandish and unhelpful of course, but it may have its uses as a corrective. I think the term we are looking for might be governance (Needham 1967b: 425; 1968: xii). Governance in Kédang consists of two aspects, characteristically kept separate: the spiritual, concerned with life forces and general well-being, but not in itself active; and the temporal, concerned with corporate responsibilities, power and its execution. We have seen that these two aspects are hereditary in the village structure. They are also hereditary when we step down to the structural level of the clans. Stability and permanence are to be found in the corporate structure of the village and the continued care of the village head. They are also exhibited in the corporate structure of the clan and in the continued care of its elders. Taken strictly internally, the two aspects of governance show a tendency (at least conceptually) of being merged into one office (the *aqé-amé*, who care for *talu* and the clan temple as well as bridewealth). If the clan is not considered in isolation, as it cannot be in the question of marriage, they are separate. Continued life depends, for the village, on the spiritual authority of the lord of the land. Continued life depends for the clan on marriage, and hence on the wife-givers. In all cases we find that structure depends upon articulation.

XVI

MARRIAGE

I. GENERAL

NOWADAYS, most marriages involve at least one person who is Catholic or Muslim; in these cases, the formal marriage ceremony of that religion is followed. The traditional customs are also observed so that there has come to be an amalgam.

Formerly (and in rare instances still today), there was no marriage ceremony. Usually a couple came (as now) to a decision themselves whether they wished to marry. The Kédangese usually show a good amount of circumspection in these affairs, and lovers usually meet only away from the home: at market, dances, and similar affairs. If the decision to marry has been made, then the proper procedure is for the man to inform his father, who then notifies the *aqé-amé* of the clan what is under way. These three then must give attention to the availability of bridewealth and so on. Responsibility lies in the first instance with the man and his father, but eventually it is the whole clan which will make good the obligations. Then a spokesman is chosen, commonly a friend of the man or his father. This spokesman is called the *marang wala*, the person charged with speaking. He must then go to the woman's parents and approach them on the question. I was given no instances of the highly oblique language which is commonly employed in other Indonesian societies on such occasions; and I think in Kédang this circumlocution is confined to spending a lot of time not getting to the point. Should, however, the *marang wala* get a favourable reaction from the woman's parents, it is time for the man himself to go to them.

In this case he prepares a preliminary prestation of sirih-pinang, some cooked rice, some fish and *kaléso*, a rice and coconut mixture wrapped and cooked in a small coconut-leaf package. This he takes to the home of the parents of the woman. If they accept it, then this is a sign that they agree to the marriage. They then distribute the food among members of their own clan and the village head and perhaps other village government officers. The redistribution is a means of making known to the clan and the village head (who must always know about these things) that the marriage and attendant relationships are going to be taken up. The woman's parents then make a similar prestation of food, excluding the sirih-pinang, to the man's parents, who will likewise distribute it among the members of their clan and to the same government officials. Before the introduction of outside religions, this was all that was required to initiate the marriage. The couple could then begin sleeping together; and the man would move immediately into the house of his new wife's parents. Today, however, the Catholics must wait until they are married in church. According to the present regulations of the village government, an engagement initiated in this manner can last at the longest two years. Within this time marriage must occur. Breaking an engagement by either party entails a fine of an elephant tusk.

The men do not always follow the correct procedures, but some-times just elope with the girl. This is always considered insulting by the wife's parents and requires the payment of a fine.

By tradition, sexual intercourse was not allowed before the prestation of sirih-pinang. If an unmarried couple were caught having sexual intercourse (at a dance or market, perhaps), they could be forced to marry, or the man forced to pay a fine. How-ever, the genealogical records show a rather large number of un-married mothers; so it is clear that the rule does not hold absolute sway over behaviour. I am not absolutely sure that the idea of the fine is not a recent introduction of the Christians. There is not much attention given to virginity, and there is no such institution of demanding payment of a fine when it is lost as occurs among the Belu (Vroklage 1952: 1: 223).

To marry is *ku weq*, 'to take each other'. *Weq* means 'body'; this might lead to misunderstanding. In the above expression it is a reciprocal and does not mean 'body'. It is the typical particle for reciprocal action; thus: *tanang-tonong weq*, 'to say goodbye (hello) to each other'; *awé weq*, 'to fight'; *miqi weq*, 'to have sexual inter-course'; *bungan-barang weq*, 'to visit each other'. Compare in this regard Lamaholot *weki*, 'body', 'self', 'own' (Arndt 1937: 57) and *weki-wolor*, 'body' and *wekik*, 'self', 'each other' (Krol n.d.). A woman *ku até-rian*, 'takes a husband'. A man *ku weq-rian*, 'takes a wife'.

It is expected that a newly married couple will live with the wife's parents for a period of time. Its duration ranged, in different reports, from a few months to a year. I never encountered a case where a couple were living with the wife's parents, but this may have simply been because there happened to be very few around. In the two cases of new couples in the hamlet in which I lived, both had already established independent households before the birth of the first child (and before we arrived), therefore, as I would estimate, well before the lapse of a year. Building one's own house does not require much work; and couples always prefer to have a house of their own. At any event, this initial period of matrilocality is in itself of very short duration. It sometimes happens that a couple will then build a house of their own next to the wife's father's house or (where there is a difference) in his village. This is not a very frequent procedure. In general, despite these occasions, we can definitely say that the rule of post-marital residence should *not* be characterized as matrilocal.

Whether there is any real sense to saying that they exhibit a type of locality at all is another matter. For one thing, a couple will tend to live in several different places within a life-time, both within and outside the village. The population of any given hamlet is not particularly stable. Married sons do not characteristically live near their fathers, though they sometimes live in the same hamlet. As long as a marriage occurs within the village, then (after the initial period of matrilocality) it is often difficult or impossible to find criteria to determine whether a couple live matrilocally or patrilocally. Usually all one can say is that they are living in the same village as the parents on both sides. When the couple come from different villages, however, then in the long run the pattern tends predominantly to be patrilocal. This follows from the corporate nature of the patrilineal clan. In so far as locality is an issue then, we must say that Kédang is patrilocal, but this is not obligatory.

There is no ceremony particularly associated with moving from the wife's parent's home into a home of their own. The only ceremony which could occur about this period would be the guardian spirit ceremony associated with pregnancy or the birth of a child. There is also no ceremony incorporating the woman into her husband's clan, unless the ceremony following the completion of bridewealth payments is considered such (this is clearly the case for some Atoni; cf. Schulte Nordholt 1971: 116), but this might occur after her death (this ceremony might well be regarded as the formal marriage ceremony, given that one absolutely insists on finding an equivalent). She is, however, considered to become a member of the husband's clan. This means a simple shift of corporate allegiance. So far as I could see this shift did not cause any structural problems; but the question of corporate membership really is of very little concern to the woman herself. She does not, of course, sever her personal ties to her own family, but there is no occasion for her to demonstrate that her membership remains with their clan as seems to occur among the Gauri of Burma (Leach 1961:118).

2. POLYGAMY

Polygyny is permitted. It has a small incidence but it occurs regularly. The genealogical records from Léuwajang show that ten per cent of men had more than one wife; fewer than one per cent had more than two wives. Of polygynous marriages, twenty per cent were with sisters.

A second marriage is subject to the same restrictions as a first marriage. That is, it should be with a woman in the category *mahan*. It entails the same bridewealth obligations. A marriage outside this category brings the same consequences as in the case of the first marriage. The most suitable, and indeed a frequent, form is marriage with the wife's sister. It may occur as well with MBSD, WBD; but BW, SW, BSW, and SWZ are not permitted. The occasion for taking a second or third wife is usually childlessness. There are in fact more causes for this than just sterility (infant mortality is high); and it need not be absolute childlessness.

The woman, here, has always had the right to withhold permission for her husband to take a second wife. If she agrees to it, the second wife works in the kitchen and with her husband in the fields. The first wife lives, on the other hand, in relative (not absolute) comfort and freedom from such tasks.

Polyandry is forbidden. Thus, a woman may not marry her husband's brother while her husband is still alive. Nevertheless, my investigations uncovered a case in recent history (middle-aged men had seen the parties in their youth) where a woman from Léuwajang married two brothers from another village. She was reputed to have been absolute master in the house. She received visitors while her husbands had to stay back and prepare the meal (the normal role of the wife). She took over their role in discussing bridewealth matters within their clan. It is even said that if her husbands did not have the food prepared by the time that such a discussion was over, she would beat them. The case is a historical one, and it is flagrant violation of Kédangese standards. It is an interesting coincidence that this woman's mother was named Tana Ekan, the Lamaholot name for the earth-goddess, known for drinking human blood.

A woman may marry another man in her husband's clan if her husband dies, but she is not free to marry outside this clan. In the few cases I have on record, the woman did not always marry the husband's brother nor even a genealogically very close member of the clan. There is no requirement that she should do so though. If she marries a man from another clan, her new husband is obliged to pay bridewealth (as a fine) to the first husband's clan, even if he has not himself yet given bridewealth. I had no opportunity to trace an actual case to see how this really works. She is not obliged to remarry; and these issues are independent of those of divorce.

3. DIVORCE

Divorce occurs with a certain amount of regularity. It could not be said to be made extremely difficult, nor is it made especially easy. Either party may make the decision. If bridewealth has been paid, then a woman's later children, after a divorce, belong to her first husband. She is, however, free to divorce and marry again if she wishes. If bridewealth has not been paid, the children belong to the woman's original clan, where they remain in a rather embarrassing legal position until an eventual remarriage (actual or fictional, i.e. merely ceremonially effected) and payment of bridewealth by a member of another clan, which makes them members of this new clan. Divorce in all cases requires the payment of a fine. This is demanded in the first instance from the person who has caused the divorce, either the man or the woman.

I witnessed a discussion of one such case, and the head of the village (who is, by the way, an expressed feminist) declared that the search for responsibility must go farther than just the inquiry as to who left first. His opinion, which met general assent, was that they must find the reason for the separation. In the case under discussion, he said there had been repeated fights, and both accused the other of not doing his or her share, so both were equally at fault. He thought, however, that the man's responsibility is generally greater than the woman's, for he must be 'political' and hold the family together. Furthermore, there had to be a penalty. The clans of the village could not just let their women be divorced without any consequences. In this case the village (that is, the conference of clan elders of the village) alloted a fine to both parties, that of the man being twice as high. This of course was paid by the clans and not the individuals. It was also not paid immediately, but added to the list of outstanding obligations. Since each clan was recipient of the payment by the other, this amounted to a one-way transference of half of the fine assigned to the man.

How much of the above is to be attributed to modern influences and how much is traditional is difficult to say. It represents fairly, however, how these matters are approached at present. I think, although this can only be a matter of opinion, that it is not too different from the solutions which they would have tried to work out in previous decades. It is in keeping with general principles of Kédangese culture that the responsibility of the wife-taker be greater than that of the wife-giver, and that his payment be approximately twice that of the wife-giver.[1] This is always the case in any delict between wife-giver and wife-taker. Should a wife-taker hit a wife-giver, for instance, he would have to give in payment a rather large tusk. If the reverse were the case, the penalty would be confined to a less expensive payment of clothing.

Formerly divorce would require a ceremony, *baké-belé* (also used in cases of incest) primarily devoted to separating the life-fluids of the two parties. This does not seem to be frequently resorted to at present.

4. ADULTERY

Adultery may lead to a fight between the two men; possibly also to a beating for the woman. There seems to be no formal penalty for the woman, however. The present regulation in Léuwajang is that a payment in bridewealth of ten units (*lemén sué*) be given the husband. In the case of molestation of an unmarried girl, a payment of two units (*suén udéq*) is required. The

---

[1] Cunningham reports the same two-for-one ratio in favour of the wife-givers among the Atoni of Timor (1967a: 68).

regulations under the *sajin-bajan* agreement, now a dead letter, were discussed earlier.

5. INCEST

Formally speaking marriage or sexual intercourse with any woman not in the category *mahan* is prohibited, and this rule would have to define incest in Kédang. They never expressed a great deal of horror at the thought of incest, but they were neither very co-operative in discussing the relative shadings of different types. Thus, I could not find out whether sexual relations between mother and son were regarded as worse than those between daughter and father. The most that I could get was that these relations were not allowed; sexual relations between brother and sister or parent and child lead to expulsion from the village unless, apparently, they submit to a ceremony separating them. This, however, holds for all such relations within the clan.

Relations of this sort between lines which are related as siblings (*meker-éhoq*) is likewise a form of incest. It is spoken of as *huna-huna, wéloq-wéloq* ('house-house, door-door'). The meaning is that the two fathers are (figuratively) of the same house, the two children however have entered into marriage establishing a relationship of wife-giver/wife-taker, like two houses standing with their doors opposite to each other. Thus the house has been split. It is also called *hunéq-koloq*, 'to turn upside-down' (as also to turn a house post upside-down). A marriage of this sort would require a ceremony called *koloq nutaq, balé tawan*. This means to return the black cloth and food which is brought to a funeral by the deceased's clan or lines regarded as agnates. It has been mentioned that this is a means of validating a sibling relationship between two different clans. This means that it is optional whether the relationship is taken up; and hence the possibility of marriage between two such lines becoming incest depends on whether the relationship of *meker-éhoq* has been formally recognized.

The two expressions given above appear to be general terms for incest. They are used most appropriately in the above case because they are rather mild. A much more coarse expression (because so extreme) is *ula-lojo*, which means in this case, as I was told, 'feet to the sky'. This would be used particularly for relations within the clan. I witnessed a ceremony in which a friend who had recovered from a very long illness was trying to do away with the

causes (*wangun-léan*) of his sickness. One of these was an incestuous relation he had had with a woman of his clan when he was a
young man. The ceremony accordingly included a version of the
ceremony to do away with the consequences of incest. The
woman was not present, so the ceremony was not complete. It
included a stone (*lapaq*) for *ula-lojo* and a piece of aerial root of a
banyan which stood for the banyan named *ula-lojo* (it must be
recalled that this is on the moon, but that there is a banyan of
identical name at the top of the old village). Incest is like confusing
the sky and the earth, and therefore the sky must be ceremonially
brought down so that it may then go back up and effect the division which is necessary to return everything to order. A chicken
and an egg are required, one representing a large goat (with horns
the length of the forearm) and the other a pig (with tusks of about
six inches). The goat stands for the man, the pig for the woman.
They are also associated symbolically with the above and the
below respectively. The chicken which represents the goat must be
killed by beating it on the head. Thus, in this ceremony, the priest
killed it by hitting it with the butt of his knife while at the same
time he made squealing sounds. This chicken may not be eaten
by the members of the clan in question.

The full ceremony for separating an incestuous pair would involve the use of two strings of red and white strands. According
to the description, these strings represented the fecundating fluids
of the man and the woman, but seemingly not, as I would have
expected, that the red was associated with the woman's blood and
the white with semen. Supposedly no such differentiation is made,
but I never got to see such a ceremony, so I could not check. This
ceremony is called *baké-belé* ('to separate') and *koloq mijé-tén,
belé werén-lalan* ('to return the fecundating fluids'). When it is
over, the woman takes one string and puts it inside her clothing
near the genitals, and the man does the same with the other string.
This effects the separation and the returning of the fluids of each.
There is *no* custom of cutting a string held at either end by the
man and the woman.

I was told that the same incest ceremony would be required in
the case of sexual intercourse with women in the category *iné utun*
(FZD, etc.). This would seem though, if at all, to be used only
where the genealogical relation is very close. At present an appreciable absolute number of marriages are with women who, in one

degree or another, fall into this category. In the case of marriage into this category, or of direct exchange, a fine called *poroq-tobuq* would be owed by the man who reversed the relationship to be paid the original wife-takers. The full expression is *poroq mawang*, 'to slip off the bracelets', *tobuq wéla*, 'take off the sarong'. This means that the wife-giver removes the bracelets (figuratively) which he has received as bridewealth and the wife-taker removes the sarong (figuratively) which he has received as counter-prestation. Instances of various kinds of improper marriages will be given in a later chapter.

6. INCORPORATION

Adoption is unknown in Kédang. What is meant by this is, if the parents of a child die, he will find a home with agnatic relatives, who in any case stand in the same relationship to him as his parents. Thus, there is no need in such a case of an institutionalized form of adoption. In Kédang there is a strict coincidence of patrilineal descent and clan membership. They differ therefore from such societies as the Atoni of Timor, who have an ideology of patrilineal descent, but for whom 'persons may be attached to a descent group through either parent (or sometimes other relatives)' (Cunningham 1967b: 1). There is no possibility, for example, that the mother's parents would request a child. Nor is there a custom of borrowing children within the clan. Children stay in their father's household.

In contrast, children of unwed mothers pose a problem. Since bridewealth has not been paid for them, they remain in the mother's clan, and as such represent an exception to the rule of patrilineal descent. It is also felt that they confuse the bridewealth, i.e. their birth is not connected with an exchange. It happens then that these children are often incorporated into other clans. There happens to be a coincidence of needs; for the children need a father and a proper clan membership, and the clan which requests them wants children for a member, whether living or dead, who has produced no children (or at least no sons). The transfer of membership is first arranged by consultations between the two clans. The approval of the children, particularly if they are grown, is always sought. This is based on common sense. If the children do not agree, they will not enact the role expected of them and all will be lost. One man went into great lengths about the dangers of such a procedure, because, he thought, if they do not get along, they will go back and search out their *amé nulon*, 'former father', i.e. genitor. Ties of sentiment, in this case, are apt to run counter to legal ties.

The transfer, if it is agreed to, is effected by the payment of bridewealth in the full amount to the woman's clan. Incorporation itself is effected ceremonially. I have not seen this, but I have some circumstantial detail concerning the case of one of my neighbours. His father was the child of an unwed mother, and this father was known as Bala Peni. That is, his second name, instead of being the given name of his own father, was the given name of his mother. The clan Boli Leraq invited him to become a member; one of its lines had died out (leaving, that is, no sons). The last male, Léaq Beli, of that line had died before marrying, and only his sisters were still living. Bala Peni was invited to come and take up the house and social responsibilities of this line, and to become the son of Léaq Beli. This was achieved by marrying Bala's mother Peni to Léaq. This required a ceremony (*baké-belé*) to separate her fecund fluids from those of the genitor of her children and a ceremonial uniting (I do not know how this was done) with Léaq. It also required that she be dug up in her original village and be reburied in Léuwajang. In this case marriage was contracted between two people already dead. It was fully as binding and had the same corporate consequences as a marriage between two living people. Bala became Bala Léaq instead of Bala Peni. The clan continues in full vigour, thanks as always to life given it by another.

This particular clan, which is a small one, shows a rather large number of such instances; but though in this case it is clearly a resort to avoid extinction, instances are not uncommon in large clans. Where a still living individual searches out such children and arranges that they enter the clan as his own children, we can easily ascribe this to a personal desire to see himself perpetuated. But when the clan arranges it for a member long dead, it is clear that it is not an individual matter at all, but a corporate one. There is clearly no one person in that case who will benefit from the rather large bridewealth expense which incorporation requires; yet it remains a popular procedure. This would seem only to be understandable as based on a sense of community (solidarity) within the clan, and one, at that, which is not restricted to the presently living members but which includes the dead as well. It provides another instance that social death does not bring an end to social personality.

XVII
THE RELATIONSHIP TERMINOLOGY

I. THE EVIDENCE

IN Kédang it is necessary to distinguish between the relationship terms used for reference and those used for address. It is also important that the terms used by a man be recorded separately from those used by a woman. Even where anthropologists collect the terms for a male and a female ego independently, which is rare enough, it seems that they always publish them in the same list. I have found that there is something to be learned by keeping them separate; so I will give here four lists keeping the terms of address separate from the terms of reference and keeping the terms used by a woman separate from those used by a man.

The definitions of the terms are different from the genealogical specifications which the anthropologist may collect as examples of their use. Properly speaking, the former are the object of our study, but the latter are a means of arriving at the definitions. It is not adequate to rely on them alone, but they are, after all, the means by which the ethnographer orients himself; and they provide the reader with a way of checking later definitions and analytical assertions. Therefore, before entering upon the analysis, I present a fairly full list of characteristic genealogical specifications for each of the terms. The lists cannot be made complete; and as they stand they include some specifications which might be considered of very little practical significance; but even so they show how the categories may be applied in a variety of instances.

There are a number of subsidiary terminological usages which should be described here. The ancestors may be referred to with, besides *tuan-woq*, the expression *inan-aman*. A fuller form is *inan-aman meté kéu*, or 'the ancestors up above', and it probably contains the implication 'the ancestors behind us up the mountain'. The second ascending generation in one's own line may be called *amé-epu* or *epu amé*. The first I think is a formation parallel to *aqé-amé*; if this is correct it should include by implication relatives designated *amé*, but with the primary emphasis on the senior of the two categories. The second expression, according to the grammar of the language, should just mean 'father's' *epu*, that is, those traced through *amé*. It is a way of specifying within the category. There is very little actual occasion for using either expression. When referring to those who have authority within the clan through seniority, *aqé-amé* is most often used; and this expression by no means implies the exclusion of the males of the second ascending genealogical level.

TABLE 4
Relationship terminology (terms of Reference, male ego)

1. *epu*	FF, FFB, FFZ, FFZH, FFZHZ, FM, MF, WFF, MM, WFM, MB, WF, MBW, WM, MBS, WB, MBSW, WBW, MBSS, WBS, MBSSW, WBSW, FZDH, ZHZH, FZSDH, ZDH, SWB, SWBW
epu anaq-abé	all male *epu*
epu aréq-rian	all female *epu*
2. *amé*	F, FB, MZH, FZHF
3. *iné*	M, MZ, FBW, WFZ, FZHFZ
4. *maqing*	FZH, ZHF, FZS, ZH
5. *aqé*	eB, FBSe, MZSe, eZ, FBDe, MZDe, FZ, ZHM, FZHZ, eBW, WZHe, FZHZH
6. *ariq*	yB, FBSy, MZSy, yZ, FBDy, MZDy, yBW, WZHy, SW, BSW
7. *binin*	Z, FBD, MZD
8. *mahan*	MBD, MBSD, WBD, WZ, BW (before her marriage), BWZ
9. *weq-rian*	W
10. *iné utun* (or *iné éhoq*)	FZD, ZHZ, FZSD, ZD
11. *anaq*	C, BC, FBSC, MZSC, WZC, FZSSW, ZSW, DHB, DHZ, SW, BSW, SWZ
lamin	own son
anaq meker	eldest child
12. *anaq maqing*	FZSS, ZS, DH, BDH

TABLE 5
Relationship terminology (terms of address, male ego)

1. *bapa*	FF, FFB, FFZ, FFZH, FFZHZ, FM, MF, WFF, MM, WFM, MB, WF, MBW, WM, MBS, WB, MBSW, WBW, FZDH, ZHZH, (for ceremonial occasions): MBSS, WBS, SWB, FZSDH, ZDH
2. *amo*	F, FB, MZH, FZHF, FZH, ZHF
3. *ino, inaq*	M, MZ, FBW, WFZ, FZHFZ
4. *tata*	eB, FBSe, MZSe, eZ, FBDe, MZDe, FZ, ZHM, FZHZ, eBW, WZHe, FZS, ZH, FZHZH

N.B.: the use of *tata* for FZS, ZH is a matter of courtesy but is not a regular practice.

There is an expression *epu rian* or 'great *epu*'. One younger man thought that this was part of a distinction within the category *epu*: *epu rian*, those older than ego, and *epu utun*, 'little *epu*', those younger than ego. This interpretation seems to have been wrong;

TABLE 6

Relationship terminology (terms of reference, female ego)

1. *epu*	FF, FFB, FFZ, FFZH, FFZHZ, FM, MF, BWFF, MM, BWFM, MB, BWF, MBW, BWFW, MBS, BWB, MBSW, BWBW, MBSS, HFF, HFM, HMF, HMM
epu anaq-abé	all male *epu*
epu aréq-rian	all female *epu*
2. *amé*	F, FB, MZH, HMB, HFZH
3. *iné*	M, MZ, FBW, HMBW, HMZ
4. *aqé-amé*	HF, HFB, ZHF, HM, HMZ, ZHM, HFF, HFM, HMF, HMM
5. *aqé*	eB, FBSe, MZSe, eZ, FBDe, MZDe, FZ, MBDe, MBSDe, BWBDe, FZH, HeZ, HeZH, HFZ, HFZH, HMBSWe, HZH, HZHZ, eZH, ZHZe, HMBDe, HMBSe, eBW, FZHB, FZHZ, eBWZ
6. *ariq*	yB, FBSy, MZSy, yZ, FBDy, MZDy, BC, MBDy, MBSDy, HyZ, HyZH, HZC, yZH, ZHZy, HMBSWy, HMBDy, DHZ, HMBSy, SW, SWB, SWZ, DH, DHB, HMBSD, FZD, yBW, BWBS, BWBSW, yBWZ, BWBDy, BSW
7. *narin*	B, FBS, MZS
8. *binin anaq*	HZ
9. *mahan*	FZS, HB (not marriageable until husband dies)
10. *até-rian*	H
11. *anaq*	C, ZC, HBC, BDH, BDHZ, DH, DHB, DHZ, SW, SWB, SWZ, FBSC, MZSC
12. *maqing*	DH

TABLE 7

Relationship terminology (terms of address, female ego)

1. *bapa*	FF, FFB, FFZ, FFZH, FFZHZ, FM, MF, BWFF, MM, BWFM, MB, BWF, MBW, BWFW, BWB, BWBW, HFF, HFM, HMF, HMM
2. *amo*	F, FB, MZH, HMB, HF, HFB, ZHF, HFZH
3. *ino, inaq*	M, MZ, FBW, HMBW, HM, HMZ, ZHM, HFZ, BW, BWZ, HMBSW, BSW
4. *tata*	eB, FBSe, MZSe, HMBSe, eZ, FBDe, MZDe, HMBDe, MBSe, MBDe, BWBDe, HM, HMZ, ZHM, FZ, FZH, HeB, eZH, FZHZ, HeZ, ZHZe, HeZH, HZHZ

older men denied it. Instead, in their view, *epu rian* is an honorific to be applied to an *epu* who, for whatever reason, is socially prominent, to an *epu* one wishes to flatter or to an *epu* (probably already dead) of preceding and rather distant genealogical level. Thus, one might use it to flatter one's MB; alternatively one might use it to distinguish between one's own MB and one's father's or father's father's MB, in which case the term would be used for one of the latter. If perhaps the *kapitan* or other politically important person could be regarded (however distantly) as *epu*, he would be *epu rian*. Usages such as in the first interpretation are known in other terminologies, but in my experience the latter is more characteristic of Kédang. There is a phrase *epu utun, anaq maqing*, which is applied by the latter interpretation to the FZSS, ZS, etc. This means that *epu utun* is synonymous with *anaq maqing*. This meaning is understandable as a parallel to *iné utun*. *Iné* and *epu* are sister and brother, so too are *iné utun* and *epu utun*.

Some young men said there was a distinction *rian* ('great')/*utun* ('small') within the category *amé* as well. This is very common in Indonesian terminologies and corresponds to the *bapak besar* (FeB)/*bapak ketjil* (FyB) of Bahasa Indonesia. Nevertheless, older men said that this was not an original Kédangese usage and had been introduced, in so far as the usage is recognized at all, recently on the model of Bahasa Indonesia. In the present historical context, I find this view quite convincing.[1]

A third, parallel issue is the term *binin tuan* or *binin rian*. Everyone had difficulty giving me a genealogical specification for this term; but at first it was suggested that it was comparable to *amé rian* or *epu rian*. It later emerged (with less question than in the above instances) that this is usually employed for women of the clan (clan sisters) of previous generations and by now probably dead. I had ample opportunity to confirm this usage when I began to collect the remote parts of the clan genealogies and came across half-forgotten former clan sisters. When reminded of these women, they often uttered the expression, 'Ah, *binin tuan!*' A *maqing rian* or *maqing tuan* would be the husband of such a *binin tuan*. *Maqing werun* ('new' *maqing*) would, correspondingly, be those closer to one's own generation or younger.

---

[1] A distinction between MeZ and MyZ, which is also found elsewhere, is ruled out in Kédang, as the essential expression for MyZ, *iné utun* (or *éhoq*), has been pre-empted by another category of women, FZD, ZD, etc.

All women born to the clan are *binin*. More specifically they are *binin-auq* or *binin-otéq*, *auq-taq*. The first phrase means as much as they are sisters of our land. Expanded into the second phrase, they become included in the valuable possessions of the clan, divided into the low: the sisters (*binin*) and the land (*auq*), and the high: the hair (*otéq*) and the coconut palms (*taq*). The *otéq-noloq*, the hair, seems to be among those things the clan gives its sisters' children. *Binin-anaq* are the same as *binin-auq*. There is an expression *binin-anaq, tuan-wénaq* referring to the clan's sisters, children, and the sisters of male ancestors (*binin-tuan*). *Binin-naré* are the same generation male and female clan mates. *Binin-lamin* are children (see below).

Concerning the etymologies of the relationship terms, *amé*, *iné*, *aqé*, *ariq*, *binin*, *narin*, and *anaq* are very common in Indonesian languages, and some of them even occur in more distantly related languages. *Epu* requires an etymological study of its own. For the moment, it should be referred to Lamaholot *opu, opo, opung* used in different areas by itself or with qualifier for either wife-giver or wife-taker or both (with a distinction of qualifier) and used in the Coastal Alor language as an undifferentiated term for affines who are both wife-giver and wife-taker (cf. Needham 1956; Barnes 1973). Whether or not it is related to Lamaholot *ĕpu*, a special place where palm wine is drunk (Arndt 1951: 213), is not certain. The term *maqing* is used in the form *making* or *maki* in Lamaholot dialects on Lembata to mean wife-takers (in the dialect of Ledo-belolong, which is close to Kédangese, wife-takers are *opu-maqing*). The word *making* occurs in the names of lineages in East Flores, where I was told it means 'to descend' or 'descendants'. That it might be related to Indonesian *maki* ('to abuse', 'to curse') might be very hard to demonstrate.

The word for wife means literally 'great body', that for husband 'great person'. Both terms are by implication honorifics. *Weq*, 'body', is also a reflexive; and the term is suggestive of the sense that of the two bodies of a married couple, that of the woman is the most important; while of the two personalities, that of the man is the more important. In any case, these statements are certainly true in Kédang.

Lamin is an unusual term, as it refers to one's own, genealogical son as opposed to all other sons, including brother's son. There is no equivalent for own daughter, although one might use *lamin* loosely on some occasions to refer to all one's children, both sons and daughters. Children are *binin-lamin*. *Aman-lamin* are the genealogical father and son taken together. There is no equivalent for mother and daughter.

Finally there are no terms for the second descending genealogical level. I found that this was commonly true in Lamaholot too. The word *anaq* which can be used with the same breadth of application as our 'child', would be employed for anyone of this level.

2. ANALYSIS OF TERMS USED BY A MALE EGO

The relationship terms accord with the rule of patrilineal descent and the prescribed matrilateral marriage. The following equations and distinctions may be selected from among many more which confirm the lineal character of the terminology.

$$
\begin{array}{ll}
F = FB & FB \neq MB \\
M = MZ & FZ \neq MZ \\
B = FBS & B \;\neq MBS \\
Z = FBD & B \;\neq FZS \\
S = BS = FBSS & Z \;\neq MBD \\
D = BD = FBSD & Z \;\neq FZD \\
& S \;\neq WBS \\
& S \;\neq ZS
\end{array}
$$

That the terminology conforms to patrilineal descent is shown by the following relevant equations:

$$
\begin{array}{l}
MB \;= MBS = MBSS \\
FZH = FZS \\
FZD = FZSD
\end{array}
$$

The matrilateral prescription is demonstrated in the following:

$$
\begin{array}{ll}
FB \;\; = MZH & MB \;\;\neq FZH \\
MZ \;= FBW & FZH \neq WF \\
MB \;= WF & FZ \;\;\neq MBW \\
FZ \;\;= ZHM & MBS \neq FZS \\
MBS = WB & WB \;\;\neq ZH \\
MBD = BW & MBD \neq FZD \\
B \;\;\;\; = MZS, WZH & WBW \neq Z \\
FZS \;= ZH & WBS \neq ZS \\
ZS \;\;\; = DH & SW \;\;\neq ZD \\
S \;\;\;\; = WZS
\end{array}
$$

The specifications ZHZH, FZSDH, ZDH for the term *epu* demonstrate the closed, cyclical form of the terminology.

The terms of reference for a male ego may be ordered as in Table 8.

From Table 8 may be extracted the terms concerned only with

TABLE 8

Categories of descent and alliance (terms of reference, male ego)

(m)——(f)		(m)——(f)		(m)——(f)		(m)——(f)		(m)
	epu iné (FZHFZ)	epu amé (FZHF)	epu	epu	epu	epu	epu	[epu]
	aqé	maqing	aqé	amé	iné	epu	epu	[epu]
epu	iné utun	maqing	binin aqé ariq	aqé ariq [Ego]	mahan weqrian aqé/ariq (BW)	epu	epu	[epu]
epu	iné utun	anaq maqing	anaq	anaq lamin	mahan ariq/anaq (SW, BSW)	epu	epu	[epu]

TABLE 9

Categories of descent and alliance (terms of address, male ego)

(m)——(f)		(m)——(f)		(m)——(f)		(m)——(f)	
	bapa ino	bapa amo	bapa	bapa	bapa	bapa	bapa
tata	tata	amo	tata	amo	ino, inaq	bapa	bapa
bapa		tata	tata	tata [Ego]	tata	bapa	bapa
(bapa)						(bapa)	

alliance. Table 12, which is modelled on Figure 10 in Needham (1966: 25), demonstrates categories of alliance for a male ego. Terms within ego's patriline may be extracted and represented as in Table 13.

From Tables 12 and 13 it is possible to extract the following rank order series: (1) *epu* > *maqing* > *anaq maqing*; (2) *epu* > *amé*

TABLE 10

Categories of descent and alliance (terms of reference, female ego)

(f)	(m)◄——(f)		(m)◄——(f)		(m)◄——(f)		(m)
		epu	epu	epu	epu	epu	epu
	aqé	aqé	aqé - amé aqé	aqé - amé aqé	amé	iné	epu
aqé	aqé ariq	aqé ariq	mahan até rian aqé ariq	aqé ariq [Ego]	narin aqé ariq	aqé ariq	epu
ariq anaq	ariq anaq maqing	anaq	anaq	ariq anaq	ariq anaq	aqé ariq	epu ariq

TABLE 11

Categories of descent and alliance (terms of address, female ego)

(m)——(f)		(m)◄——(f)		(m)◄——(f)		(m)
	bapa	bapa	bapa	bapa	bapa	bapa
amo	tata	amo tata	ino tata	amo	ino	bapa
tata	tata	tata	tata	tata	tata ——ino——bapa	tata
			[Ego]			
					tata ——ino	

> *aqé* > *ariq* > *anaq*. In the first series, I have excluded terms for women. They present certain problems which make them hard to fit into such a series. It is my intention here to unfold these problems gradually and to give the reasons; but first we should note that while in Table 12 it is easy to see that *iné* is superior to

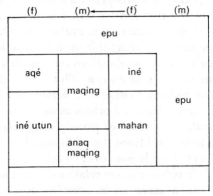

TABLE 12

Categories of alliance (male ego)

TABLE 13

Categories within ego's patriline (male ego)

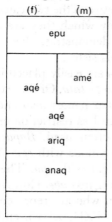

aqé; there are difficulties relating *aqé* to *maqing*. If we revert to the original table and attempt to construct a rank order of terms applied to women alone we again discover difficulties. Excluding *mahan* and *iné utun* we can do well enough: *epu* > *iné* > *aqé* > *ariq* > *anaq*. But where in the series do we put the first two terms? *Mahan* is, in a sense, a term of equality, and as such it might fall between *aqé* and *ariq*; but this tells us nothing about its meaning. Furthermore, it is not clear how it related to *iné utun*. If the women have the same status as their descent lines, the *mahan* is the superior of the two terms; but it is not possible to point to anything which corroborates this evaluation. There is also the peculiarity of the name *iné utun*; this means 'small *iné*', suggesting a sort of superiority. The specifications for *epu* show us the reason for this. *Iné utun* is a wife of an *epu*. This means that potentially she is also an *epu* and the mother of a *mahan* to boot.

These analytic difficulties and others as well derive from the fact that there are really a number of principles governing the use of the relationship terms and from the additional fact that while men are rather fixed in their relations to each other, women are a moving element and therefore change relationships; a *mahan* becomes a *weq-rian*, *aqé*, *ariq* or *anaq*, an *iné utun* becomes an *epu*.

One of the problems mentioned above can be solved by referring to the terms of address for a male ego (ordered in Table 9). The FZH falls in the category *maqing*, which expresses only an inferior relation. His sister is *aqé*, a form of superiority based on age. The relationship between the two categories is not clear unless we refer to the terms by which they are addressed, i.e. *amo* and *tata*. These two terms demonstrate that, on the basis of sex, the *maqing* is superior to his sister.

The terms of address are easily placed in a rank order series as follows: *bapa* > *amo/ino* > *tata*. Of these terms, *bapa* is frequently used instead of the given name; *amo* and *ino/inaq* are also frequently so used but with less restriction on substituting the given name, and *tata* is not often used. *Bapa* is also often used as a term of reference synonymous with *epu*. As a term of address its range is almost coincident with *epu*. The same is true of *ino* in regards *iné* and *tata* as regards *aqé*. However, *amo* is extended as a term of respect for men who are represented only as inferiors in the terms of reference (FZH, ZHF), and the same tendency is shown by *tata*. The term *bapa(k)* is a very common respectful term of address for strange or unrelated men in eastern Indonesia (also in Lamaholot). This is not possible in Kédang. Here it may be used for very old men or women, for whom no relation is known. *Amo*, however, can be applied to any male, *ino* to any female, regardless of age, providing some specific relation does not supersede it. Infants are often addressed *amo* or *ino* by their parents. Where terms of address are not employed, the given name is used. The given name may be freely substituted for the term of address in all cases. This is least often done in the case of *bapa*, most often in the case of *tata*.

In the upper left-hand (in heraldic terms, upper right-hand) of Tables 8 and 9, there is a sort of shadow formed by the terms *amé, iné, aqé* and *amo, ino, tata*. This is because these genealogical relations are regarded as neither standing in a relation of alliance (unless, in fact, such an alliance was contracted at that level, then other terms are used) nor are they traced through relatives of the second ascending level (as are FFZH, FFZHZ). As they are then only genealogical relations of wife-takers, they merit somewhat less respect, their only claim being that of age. Both tables show the diagonal skew which Needham (1964a: 233) has elsewhere mentioned as characteristic of the diagrams of asymmetric terminologies. In conformity with patrilineal descent the skew runs in this case from the heraldic left down to the heraldic right. As the 'shadow' results systematically from the principles governing the use of the terms, it appears here as part of the diagrammatic skew. It might be mentioned too that these tables have been designed to conform to present conventions (see Leach 1961: 40; Needham 1962: 76). Were I to have designed them (and Figure 10 as well) solely with the view of consistency with other aspects of the culture of Kédang, I would have reversed the lateral orientation so that, for instance, the structural concordance between *epu* and *oté* would be clearly visible.

3. INTERPRETATION OF TERMS USED BY A MALE EGO

It is of use now to draw together the principles which lie behind the distribution of the terms. We know from previous chapters that wife-givers are superior to wife-takers, greater age is superior to lesser, and men are superior to women. Authority is associated with superiority of status. Of the two types of authority, spiritual and temporal, the former is superior to the latter. Thus, it seems that wife-givers are spiritual authorities, while elder members of one's own clan have temporal authority. Within the clan it is the men called *amé* or *aqé* who have the temporal authority, while the authority of men and women of the second ascending level again appears to become spiritual. Thus, in both instances *epu* is associated with spiritual authority and opposed to *amé* and *aqé* who have temporal authority. Women, though not usually in positions of authority over men of the same level, are nevertheless associated with spiritual influence in ways which men are not. This is even represented in the fact that there are certain realms where they have an authority which men do not have (e.g. the granary). This suggests again that women are associated with a sort of spiritual influence as opposed to the temporal authority of the men. By the time men and women are in the category *epu*, the distinction begins to disappear, mostly because the temporal aspects of authority recede. Here, then, is a series of reasons why the term *epu* leads all the rank order lists. It is exclusively associated with spiritual authority. Here is the greatest unity between status and category. Moving away from this is a movement towards differentiation, which means there is not always a perfect accord among the various principles. As the categories still seem to be systematic (i.e. there are few cases of alternative terms for a given genealogical relation, and then only in the form of moving from one category to another), there must then be a ranking among the principles.

I suggest this ranking is as follows:

(1) wife-givers are superior to wife-takers.[2]
(2) elder is superior to younger.
(3) men are superior to women.

Terminologically there are no exceptions to the first rule. This means that this is the most important. Exceptions to rule (2) occur only when it comes into conflict with rule (1). Exceptions to rule (3) are numerous and they are brought about by conflicts with (1) and (2).

Now surprisingly, if Kédang is compared with other Indonesian societies, it is not rule (1) which holds common sway over all the relationship systems,[3] but rules (2) and (3). This means that the

---

[2] The rules of patrilineal descent and matrilateral marriage are taken as given.

[3] Wife-givers are commonly superior to wife-takers in Indonesian societies

rule which is most important to the relationship terminology of Kédang is also the one which is most characteristic of Kédang.

Rule (3) is certainly the most ambiguous, and it is also the one which finds the least expression in the relationship terms (in the reciprocal terms *narin/binin* and in the term *lamin* which has no pair). It seems to me that it is the ambiguous and ineluctable quality of the opposition which marks it as the most fundamental to the culture, and indeed not in a way which sets this culture apart from others, but in a way common to all. Perhaps the whole of the social order of Kédang can be seen as attempting to cope with the consequences or possibilities of this distinction within the context provided by the also ineluctable fact of ageing and the need to meet physical requirements within the given environment. If the opposition is so fundamental, then it is not surprising that this study makes no attempt to explain it, but is solely concerned with describing it.

4. ANALYSIS OF TERMS USED BY A FEMALE EGO

For the female ego, categories of descent and alliance are of a very reduced significance, and the terminology shows in this case an increased reliance on relative age. Nevertheless, the equations and distinctions which were listed as confirming the lineal character of the terminology used by a male ego also hold in that for the female ego with the following exceptions: $S \neq BS$; $D \neq BD$; $Z = MBD = FZD$; $S = ZS$ ($S \neq WBS$ could not apply). That $S = ZS$ for the woman is a systematic feature of lineal terminologies of the same nature as $S = BS$ for a male; the same is true for $S \neq BS$, $D \neq BD$ for the female ego which is the necessary converse of $S \neq ZD$, $D \neq ZD$ for the male.

The patrilineal rule is demonstrated by the equations $MB = MBS = MBSS$, but the equations $FZH = FZS$; $FZD = FZSD$ do not hold.

The matrilateral prescription is demonstrated in the following equations and distinctions:

FB	= MZH	MB	$\neq$ FZH
F	= HMB	FZH	$\neq$ BWF
MZ	= FBW	FZ	$\neq$ BWM

even when they do not have terminologies of asymmetric prescriptive alliance, but in those cases the categories are not systematically governed by the rule of superiority of wife-givers.

M	= HMBW	MBS	≠ FZS
MB	= BWF	BWB	≠ ZH
MBS	= BWB	BWBW	≠ Z
MBD	= BW	BWBS	≠ S
B	= MZS	BSW	≠ D
FZS	= HB		
Z	= HMBD		
S, ZS	= BDH		
BD	= SWZ		

We can confidently conclude then that this is a terminology of asymmetric alliance and patrilineal descent. Ordered as in Table 10 it demonstrates the same diagonal skew as the terms for a male ego. What is immediately striking, however, is the nearly total absence of the terms designating the inferior position of the wife-takers. In no case has a category of persons superior to a male ego been relegated to an inferior position to that of the female ego. On the other hand, many categories which were inferior to the male are now designated by terms of relative age: *aqé, ariq, anaq.* Nowhere is *aqé* applied to a younger person or *ariq* to an older, except possibly a HZH or HZHZ, where the status is evidently taken from the husband, but even here the possibility of distinguishing according to age relative to ego is shown. Another feature of the terminology is the number of instances in which alternative terms may be applied to a genealogical position. More striking yet is the tendency, when compared to the terminologies for the male ego, becoming especially apparent in the heraldic right side of the table, to fragment the categories so that a number of terms are applied for different genealogical specifications which would otherwise be equated under one term. Thus, for example, it is surprising not to find the equations FZ = HM, FZDe = HeZ.

Two categories need especially to be discussed. *Mahan* is the prescribed category and is applied to FZS. It is therefore not available for MBD, etc. *Aqé* and *ariq* are used for the latter, demonstrating what has been shown before, the tendency for *mahan* to be replaced by these latter terms. In this case it causes no confusion of the prescription; but it may be of use if compared to instances such as that of the Purum where the MBD is included in a category also applied to siblings (Needham 1962: 76–7). The term *aqé-amé* is applied to HF, HM, etc. I was once told that a distinction of pronunciation similar to that between the two forms of *iné-amé* is used to keep the males separate from the females; but that is of small analytic concern. Like the category *epu*, that of *aqé-amé* can include men and women (a usage unknown for the male ego). This fact provides no problems I think, but it should be noted that the term has much the same connotation here as for a male: it designates the category of persons who have jural authority over ego.

When the terms of address are ordered as in Table 11, they show similar features to those for a male ego. There is an exception in that more honorific terms are employed in the same and the first descending genealogical level for BW, BWB, BSW than for MBD, MBS, and BWBD. This suggests a loss of involvement with the alliance relation traced through MB and BWB after the passage of a generation, while she is in some ways concerned with newly established ones. This effects a terminological distinction between two types of wife-givers otherwise not recognized; but it occurs in this case because of ego's lack of direct involvement. The use of *tata* for BWBD and in the reference terms *aqé* for MBSD, BWBD depends on the small chance that these people are older than ego. The term *bapa* is probably applied to BSWB, but I failed to ask.

5. INTERPRETATION OF TERMS USED BY A FEMALE EGO

What then can be concluded about the form of this terminology? It conforms to asymmetric alliance and patrilineal descent, and is modified in accordance with the systematic feature that the woman is the moving element in such societies and changes clan membership. The terms used by a woman are in a number of instances no longer directly determined by rule (1) that wife-givers are superior. Her father's wife-takers acquire jural authority over her, so she must employ terms which reflect this fact, in most cases those whose use is ruled by relative age. Furthermore, she does not employ (with the exception of DH) the same terms for the wife-takers of her husband's line that her husband does. Again she uses terms based on relative age. It would be incorrect to say that the terminology breaks down; it becomes somewhat less systematically ordered, but in a measured way resulting from a necessary feature of the system in operation. Nevertheless, it shows in this some of the tendencies to be found in the actual breaking down of systems of descent and alliance; that is, terms of which the definitions are determined by the rules of descent and alliance are replaced by terms of which the definitions are determined by the criterion of relative age.

6. SUMMARY REMARKS ON AFFECT AND SOCIAL
   RELATIONSHIPS

I had no success in eliciting normative descriptions concerning the emotional tone among various relations. When I asked, for example, should one show more respect to the MB or to the father, I was told one should respect both; and I soon found that they were prepared to give this answer to any relation I might name, even the child. When I reflect upon my own observations, I find it impossible to confidently set up a scheme applying pluses and minuses even to the four relations which Lévi-Strauss (1963: 42) says are basic to the avunculate. There are no avoidance relations, for instance, and no pronounced joking relations.

Most clear, from observation, is that the relation to a MB, FMBS or equivalent may well be marked with intimacy and affection on the part of either a boy (*anaq maqing*) or girl (*iné utun*) and these feelings are reciprocated. But the structural properties of the relation between *epu-puén* and *anaq maqing* would have to be assigned both a plus and a minus, for the *epu-puén* presumably will not tolerate refractory and inattentive behaviour from his sister's child, and may even resort to punishment by spiritual means. That both a negative and positive sign belong to this relationship should be clear from descriptions of the equivalent relation in other Indonesian societies (Vergouwen 1964: 54–6). The son should be respectful to his father, and I know a number of instances of cool or distant relations of this sort, but I would not say this was the typical quality of the relation because father and son are often on a basis of easy intimacy. There is no reason why, for example, the son should not ask his father a direct question and there is no restraint on laughter in his presence (Cunningham 1967a: 59–60). There is even a special term for the relation between a man and his own son; and an instance has been given where a man was of the opinion that the ties of sentiment between an actual father and son might be stronger than a mere jural relation of the same sort. Mother and child are, I think, usually affectionate, but the relation is punctuated by the normal family spats. The mother and daughter are perhaps closer than the mother and son. Brother and sister tend to stay apart, but the relation is not otherwise negative. Brothers stay together and always assist each other. The elder has a degree of jural authority over the younger. I would not say, however, that there is marked jealousy or hostility between them as appears to be true for the Atoni (Cunningham 1967a: 62). There is a term, *eruq-anaq*, for the presumably affectionate ties between genealogically close 'brothers'. Wife and husband may often quarrel and the relation may well be cool; but the woman is not unusually repressed and she bears no unequal burden of labour. The man has jural authority, but even so the relation is often easy.

When one goes farther afield than this, the relations are usually even more difficult to typify. The FZ as the terminology indicates is like an elder sister. The ZH or FZH are structurally inferior and may be expected to lend assistance and show respect. On the other hand if they are older this provides them with a claim on respect. The terminology does not even indicate the relationship between grandparents and grandchildren; but it will be marked by respect and affection.

I conclude then that Kédang is marked by a reluctance to emphasize distance or to draw out typically negative aspects of relationships, without which one cannot have the contrasts necessary to set up a scheme on Lévi-Strauss's model. This in fact accords very well with my general impression both of daily affairs and the culture. They generally suppress signs of hostility, are quite frightened in fact to show them, and their institutions are marked by the general avoidance of emphasis of the inferiority of certain categories of persons.

XVIII
BRIDEWEALTH

IN his examination of the gift, Mauss refers to *total prestations*, obligatory gifts between two groups, which deserve description as *total* because they cover such a wide range of goods and services, going well beyond the sphere of merely economic use and value. These presentations link groups in the obligation to give, to receive and to return. It is in a society such as Kédang where the idea of total prestations is best exemplified, particularly in those obligatory exchanges which are initiated at marriage and which pass between the wife-giving and the wife-taking groups. Van Ossenbruggen (1930: 221) remarks that most terms used for such goods in Indonesia mean not 'price' but 'bridewealth', and Fischer (1932) usefully summarizes the arguments against applying the term 'brideprice' generally to these reciprocal gifts.

1. DESCRIPTION OF BRIDEWEALTH VALUABLES

In Kédang the major parts of these exchanges are not usable goods at all but are very expensive objects which have no other, or hardly any other, use than to be given and received in exchanges between groups allied through marriages. These make up the prescribed core of prestations between these groups, which expand into a larger list of occasional and sometimes less obligatory and often consumable goods and services. Among these, the ritual services and gifts expected from the mother's brother at various times, especially at a funeral, and the food and assistance expected from the wife-takers on similar occasions, have already been mentioned. Here, we are concerned with the more restricted list of objects which are called *panga-liar*, and whose settlement is the occasion of lengthy formal negotiation, and final ceremony and communal meal.

Kédang is like Kodi on Sumba in not regarding the two opposed forms of marriage prestations between the two groups as being of masculine and feminine types (cf. van Wouden 1956: 238). Nevertheless the actual goods used, and their division, are similar to those in societies which employ these designations, and they allow us to see that there are similar ideas at work. The first bride-wealth in Kédang seems to have consisted of all the decorations which a woman might use for ornament: bracelets, rings for the ankles, ear-rings, and an ornament which is no longer to be found in Kédang—but of which Drabbe (1940: Pl. XXV, Afb. 57) has a photograph—silver clips worn around the helix of the outer ear. Later, bronze gongs were introduced, and then elephant tusks. Today, bridewealth given by the wife-takers consists primarily in gongs or tusks, which are interchangeable, and for lesser values silver ear-rings and ivory bracelets. The return gifts are usually expensive hand-woven and dyed sarongs, decorated by the *ikat* process in which the pattern is produced by tying bands in the appropriate places around the woof strings before dyeing. In addition may be used the cheap cotton Makasarese *lipaq*, or men's sarongs, or other items of apparel, but sometimes the return may consist in part of items of the type usually received from the wife-takers. In general the goods given by the wife-givers are more readily regarded as consumer goods than are those given by the wife-takers.

The sarongs deserve brief discussion. Traditionally, it was pro-hibited to make cloth in Kédang. Thus, the interpretation which one finds in East Flores that this part of the exchange represents what is made by the woman is here somewhat out of place. Very possibly the use of sarongs as prestations from wife-givers was adopted in Kédang simply by copying the Lamaholot model. Until very recently—and to a great extent still—the Kédangese depended on the weavers of Gunung Api (Lewotolo), or those which the *kapitan* imported from Adonara to Kalikur to supply these cloths. However, in Lamaholot the fine sarong is generally red. Red sarongs may not be used in Kédang; it would be considered an insult if the wife's clan were to give a red cloth to her husband. Therefore, black sarongs must be made for sale in Kédang. There are actually several different types of sarong of different values. For the purpose of bridewealth exchange the most commonly used consist of three sections, the two outer ones decorated with coloured thread (yellow or even red may be used here) and *ikat*, while the central one is entirely black (actually dark blue from indigo). For the mountain people this is usually a fairly coarse piece decorated with ordinary cotton thread, but before the last war, the villagers of Kalikur and a few rich men elsewhere could afford finer pieces in which most of the thread, while locally manufactured, was more finely spun, and thread of Chinese silk was used for decoration.

2. ESTIMATION OF VALUES

The goods, of all types, used in these exchanges may be valued in terms of a common standard. This is the *munaq*, which means 'complete', but which can be exactly translated in this case by the word 'unit'.[1] A sarong such as that just described would be three *munaq*, a silver ear-ring one. Such a *munaq* has a currency value of about Rp 2000 or $5.30. This can be taken as a rather exact equivalent at present, but if anyone were to buy a gong or tusk he would probably pay in kind—maize, rice, a goat, or a pig—and would use a mixed assortment of goods to meet the total cost. This means that the cost would be subject to the seasonal fluctuations which crops and animals always undergo. An ear of corn buys more in the hunger season than at the end of harvest. Furthermore, the actual price is regularly considered to fluctuate according to whether it is the buyer or the seller who is in the position of need. This is considered to be expressed by a factor of two to one. Someone who is hunting for a tusk must pay twice its value. Someone who needs money and wishes to sell a tusk may expect to get half its value. This of course represents the initial bargaining position; for the actual price is always the outcome of long dickering and may not correspond to this two-to-one formula.

The value of a tusk is estimated according to its length and circumference; that is, a solid measure is employed. Thus a *munaq éhaq* ('just a unit') is a tusk stretching from the tips of the fingers to about the lower side of the upper-arm, with a circumference which can be spanned with the thumb and forefinger leaving a gap between their tips of the width of one finger. A *telun* or *munaq telu* ('three units') stretches from the tips of the fingers to the shoulder of the same arm, with a circumference so large that there is a gap between the fingertips of three finger widths or a tusk with a length from the finger-tips to the breast on the same side and a gap of two finger widths. The tusk sizes move progressively across

[1] There are other words for multiples of this unit; thus two *munaq* are *suén* (from *sué*, 'two'); three, *telun* (from *telu*, 'three'); five, *lemén* (from *lemé*, 'five'). Ten are two *lemén* or one *unan*. This latter word means 'slave', and no doubt it indicated one of the means with which these tusks and gongs were once bought from traders.

the body in this manner.[2] Naturally, because some people are larger than others, the corresponding stages on the body are not the same for everyone. But the measuring of tusks is a matter of continual concern, many tusks are in the village possession for years and are used again and again in these transactions, so there is ample opportunity for an individual to learn how pieces of commonly accepted value correspond to the size of his own body.

Uncertainty exists to some extent when a new piece is introduced to the village, and in particular one piece may not have exactly the same agreed value that it would be given in another village. Disagreements are resolved in consultations which make up an integral part of the bargaining at bridewealth discussions. This is a greater problem between two different villages. Within the village, the piece is assigned a value in discussions which must always include the elders of all the clans and the head of the village. Private bridewealth transactions are not allowed. The value is assigned and agreed to by the village elders as a whole, and from then on it must be given and received as being this value in any subsequent transaction within the village. This greatly reduces the room for haggling.

Between two villages such communally binding standards of value do not exist, and therefore the value of the goods themselves becomes the object of bargaining. Nevertheless, once a piece has been exchanged between two villages, it acquires a history, and they try to ensure that it will always have the corresponding value in any subsequent exchange between them.

Thus, everywhere they strive to establish systematic formal equivalences, which rest on the fact that what is given out will someday come back and therefore remove, where possible, the risk of financial loss and the necessity to protect economic interests by bargaining. Where new relations are established, there lies the greatest risk. Where long-standing relations exist, and particularly within the village, there economic considerations and risk tend to drop out, and the exchanges become systematic, formal, and easily accomplished. Under these circumstances the ritual aspect of the bridewealth exchange particularly stands out.

---

[2] The value of gongs is estimated in the same way, except that attention is given only to the diameter of the gong and not to its depth.

3. SCHEDULE OF PRESTATIONS

The very day of my arrival in Léuwajang (5 October 1969), the village government held a meeting of the village elders in which they introduced alterations in the obligatory schedule of marriage prestations. There are variations from village to village concerning the list of these gifts, but they are generally still very similar everywhere. The alterations introduced in Léuwajang did not make any great change in the over-all value of the exchange. Of principal interest was that the first gift of the wife-takers had now to be paid immediately. Formerly, this would have waited an indefinite period. The reason given for the immediate payment was that now that most of the young people are Christian or Muslim, the wife's parents must sustain the expense of a large feast plus that of household utensils and so on which some now give. Therefore, it was decided to ensure that they receive the first stage immediately to recompense them. In order to avoid misunderstanding, it must be noted, as will be explained later, that the bride's parents have no right to use this prestation to meet the expense of the feast, for it is clan property. On the other hand, they do not bear the expense alone, as these new wedding feasts follow the old pattern in that many people help in providing the food and labour it requires.

As it now stands, the schedule in Léuwajang is as follows:

(1) *ué-mal, bako-oro*, a tusk (or gong) worth five *munaq*, given by the husband's clan to the bride's clan. The name means sirih-pinang, tobacco and the lontar leaf strips used to roll cigarettes; and it refers to the initial gift of these items when the man first tells the woman's parents of his intentions. Formerly, the value of this tusk depended on that received for the girl's mother, and it varied between three and five *munaq*. As it was, the village chose, on democratic principles, to standardize the value at the higher level. There is no return for this gift.

(2) *nolin-wélin*. This consists of two tusks (or gongs), the *nolin-bala*—now reduced in value from forty to twenty-five *munaq* —and the *wélin*—worth fifteen *munaq*. The woman's clan formerly gave in return for this a tusk (or gong), *méhi-mawar*, of eight *munaq*, plus a sarong, five ivory bracelets, one *lipaq* and one *nodéng* (short pants). The tusk has been eliminated to balance the reduction in the *nolin-bala*. The present return is two sarongs, ten

bracelets, two *lipaq*, and two *nodéng*. This final series of prestations may take many decades to be paid and is often redeemed by the children or grandchildren.

The three tusks given the wife-givers in this list are worth about Rp 90,000 or $240. The return is worth around $40, so one might say that a woman costs $200. Actually, they rarely have to pay in a literal sense.

In addition to this standard list are a number of contingent payments. Where a marriage initiates a relation between clans which had never before had any ties, a gift called the *bunga karé* must be given. The amount involved is not standard but is determined in negotiations between the parties involved. A typical exchange would be a goat and silver ear-ring given the bride's clan, and a return of a *lipaq*. Where the man does not marry into his mother's brother's clan, a payment called *hudé-hén* is required. The name means 'to notify and to receive'. In some villages this must be given before the marriage can take place, but in Léuwa-jang it may not be given until all the other bridewealth obligations have been acquitted; thus, it is the last on the list. It consists of a *nobol puén*, 'trunk *nobol*', given to the mother's brother's clan, and a *nobol utuq*, 'tip *nobol*', given to the new wife-giving clan. The first of these is a tusk, or some other valuable, worth two *munaq*; the second is a silver ear-ring.

Further, there is a payment of a tusk of three *munaq*, given to the woman's parents when a man marries an unwed mother with full-grown children. This is intended to compensate the parents for the expense of raising the children. Adultery requires a fine of five *munaq*; molesting an unmarried girl brings a fine of two *munaq*. In the case of elopement, a payment of five *munaq* is added to the normal bridewealth. The *otéq-noloq*, the tusk which the mother's brother of a male deceased or the brother of the female deceased could demand at a funeral, has been dropped within the village.

The custom of acquitting the bridewealth obligations by a period of service for the bride's parents does not exist in Kédang.

4. BRIDEWEALTH TRANSACTIONS

Primary responsibility for all bridewealth transactions lies with the elder, or *aqé-amé*, of each clan. The individual is not allowed to pay his obligations by himself. The pattern which is invariably followed when a man receives a request that he pay his bridewealth obligations is that he first notifies the *aqé-amé* of his clan and the head of the village. Then he and the *aqé-amé* and other members of the clan consult to see what bridewealth is in the possession of the clan and what debts are outstanding to it. Generally a distinction must be made between privately owned objects of wealth and those which are in the clan possession. Under some circumstances, the former may be used to meet a bridewealth obligation. Where nothing else is available, a man might give a personally owned tusk to discharge his own obligation or that of a brother; but he may very well refuse it to a very distantly related member of his own clan. However, bridewealth received is clan property and may not be sold or used for private purposes. Were someone to attempt it, he could be called to trial by the village government. This means on the one hand, the marriage exchanges have a tendency to convert personal wealth into clan-owned wealth. On the other, it means that the individual is usually not forced to rely on his own resources because ultimately any obligation he incurs must be backed by the clan.

It can be seen, then, that the clan as a group, and not the individual, is the bridewealth-giving and bridewealth-receiving unit. Once the available bridewealth has been surveyed, and the outstanding obligations have been reviewed, the clan will hold a meeting, usually with the attendance of the village head, to consider what steps it wishes to take. If, at the time, inadequate bridewealth is held within the clan, they commonly turn to whichever of their wife-takers have obligations against them and ask for a payment. This often initiates a series of negotiations which requires several meetings before the matter is settled. When the whole transaction is entirely within the village, the affair is much simpler and more easily settled. The final details are ultimately worked out in a meeting including the *aqé-amé* of all the clans and the head of the village. It is obligatory that this final negotiation be a village affair, so that whatever is decided upon will be a matter of public record. This requirement relates in part to the fact that there is no permanent record of these things, and in order to insure that obligations acquitted and those outstanding are remembered and disagreement avoided, the details must be made a matter of public memory. It usually happens on such occasions that more is discussed than the transaction at hand and new demands of payment are often brought forward at this time.

The favourite form of settlement, and the one most often employed within the village, is one in which a chain of obligations is found which leads back upon its starting-point. Then the clan which makes the initial payment receives its own goods back at the end, and no clan has actually lost or gained anything. In other words, where possible, the negotiations are primarily concerned with uncovering a cycle which results in an equality of payments for all parties.

The exchange itself does not occur at the meeting where the conclusion of the negotiations is achieved. Rather the bridewealth is given in conjunction with a feast prepared by the participating clans and to which the village government and the elders of the other clans are invited. Before the feast a small ceremony is held, called a *poan loing nobol-téqa*, or 'a ceremony to inform *nobol-téqa*'. In this the guardian spirit of alliance is informed of exchange of

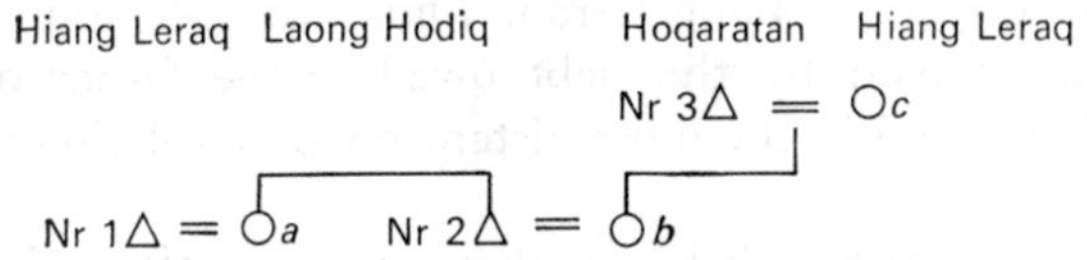

Hiang Leraq   Laong Hodiq   Hoqaratan   Hiang Leraq

$$\text{Nr } 3\triangle \;=\; \bigcirc c$$

$$\text{Nr } 1\triangle = \bigcirc a \qquad \text{Nr } 2\triangle = \bigcirc b$$

FIG. 11. Genealogical ties in an exchange of bridewealth.

the goods. I never had the opportunity to witness this; but the fragments of the chant used which I collected and which are anyhow cited during the accompanying feast, dwell on the fact that the woman has been freed and her bridewealth paid. This ceremony only occurs when it is the final stage which has been paid.

I will describe here one such exchange which demonstrates several characteristic points. It concerned the three clans Hoqaratan, Laong Hodiq, and Hiang Leraq.

Formally, the exchange went as follows. First the man No. 1 of Hiang Leraq gave a tusk to No. 2 of Laong Hodiq in payment of his wife *a*. No. 2 then gave this tusk to No. 3 of Hoqaratan in payment of his wife *b*. No. 3 then returned this tusk to Hiang Leraq in payment of his wife *c*. This transaction shows several characteristic features of an asymmetric alliance system. (1) The importance of the *anaq maqing* (in this case the daughter's husband) for meeting bridewealth obligations. The whole affair began when No. 3 was asked to give bridewealth for his wife. He then

turned to his daughter's husband to find the necessary tusk. (2)
The importance of the *maqing* of *maqing*, or the wife-takers to the
second degree, in providing bridewealth. In order to get the bridewealth from No. 2, they had to go farther to his *maqing*, No. 1.
(3) Their predilection for finding closed cycles in which exchange
results in equilibrium and what goes out comes back. What Hiang
Leraq initially gave, it got back at the end. (4) A practical correspondence to formal structure (at least for Kédang): the *maqing*
of *maqing* are *epu*. Hoqaratan found that the wife-takers of its
wife-takers were in the same clan as its wife-givers. This case
simultaneously demonstrates an instance in which a series of
alliances results in a cycle. (5) The case shows the extent to which
the clans, as bridewealth exchanging groups, are corporately
involved in marriage alliance. Although No. 1 and the father of *c*
are in the same clan, they belong to lines which are only distantly
related, and whose last common ancestor was the eponymous
founder of the clan, Hiang Leraq. Thus, the obligations of No. 1
were actually paid by the debt owed to the father of *c*, even
though they stood in the most distant possible relation within the
clan.

Additionally, although I have shown the genealogical ties which
were directly concerned, the exchange did not take place among
the men shown. Instead, at the formal exchange, the goods were
given and received by the *aqé-amé* of each of the three clans (as it
happened, No. 3 held this position for his clan). Furthermore, not
only did they hold the feast and ceremony, rather than simply
cancelling each debt against the other, but they actually went
through the process of exchanging the prestations. For this purpose they used a huge tusk which belonged to Hiang Leraq, and
the worth of which was out of all proportion to the debts involved.
This was then carried from person to person, as was the counter-
prestation. What this shows is that the process of exchange and
reciprocity is valued in and of itself and that in certain cases—the
most favoured in fact—circumstances allow the separation of this
value from any consideration of economic loss or gain.

An incidental feature of this exchange demonstrates an additional point of interest. No. 3 was completing the bridewealth
payments for his second wife. His mother was from the clan Apé
Labi, as was his first wife. Nevertheless, Apé Labi took this occasion to request that he pay the *hudé-hén* which is given when one

marries outside the mother's brother's clan. Even though his first
marriage satisfied this contingent rule, he was still obliged to pay
hudé-hén by a second marriage which did not.

Figure 11 shows a cycle of exchange of a strictly asymmetric
form. I was told by the village head that they do not allow two
clans to acquit mutual obligations by a direct exchange, as would
often be possible because of the reciprocal marriages between many
of the clans. As a matter of fact, I knew of one case in which a man
of Apé Labi was married to a woman of Laong Hodiq, whose
brother was married to a woman of Apé Labi. A stage of the
obligations of both men were taken care of in a direct exchange
between the two clans. When I called this to the Kepala's attention, he remarked that the man and woman of Apé Labi had
different fathers—they were in fact very distantly related—and
this allowed the transaction to take place. In fact this case shows
how instances of direct exchange can occur without completely
violating the principle of asymmetry. This is a predictable and in
fact necessary feature of segmentary systems. The case was obviously to a great extent irregular, and since it did not lead to an
alteration of the corporate structure, it had no positive systematic
consequences; but it showed how even here, where bridewealth
matters are strictly kept to the structural level of the clan, there is
a tendency for them on occasion to work themselves out on a lower
level.

If these exchanges are easiest to arrange and tend to equilibrium
within the village, they are correspondingly difficult in cases of
marriage outside the village. Here everything is thrown open to
negotiation and bargaining. Even the stages of the schedule of
prestations and the value of each may not be exactly equivalent in
each village, and this will require the arrangement of a special
agreement involving each village as a whole, and binding each of
its clans in any subsequent transactions. Then there is the matter
of agreeing over the actual value of the pieces which are offered.
A gong which has circulated within the village for years at a value
of seven *munaq* may actually not even have that value, either
because at first it was agreed to assign it a more or less fictional
value or because its state has deteriorated. So one village will offer
what it has and claim a certain, perhaps somewhat inflated value
for it, and the other village will assess its value as being much lower.
This then becomes a real matter of competition and concern with

economic advantage; and the bartering is correspondingly long and exhausting.

It must be remarked that in a case like this, it is the two villages themselves which are the alliance groups. If a man is asked to pay bridewealth to his wife-givers in another village, then his clan must often hunt within the village, sometimes even borrowing from another clan when it can find no object of its own or an outstanding equivalent debt owed to it. Then, when the matter has been arranged within the village, this clan calls a meeting of the village elders and government for whom it provides a meal, during which the village discusses the strategy which will be taken with the other village in the bargaining. Once agreement is reached, the *aqé-amé* of the clan involved is told what he should do, and everyone is exhorted to stand behind him and to say nothing which would hinder his role as the chief negotiator. Then on an agreed day a village delegation, including members of the clan involved, elders of all the other clans, the village government and other prominent people in the village, travels in a group to the second village, where they are received. After initial enjoyment of sirih-pinang and cigarettes, the discussions (which have been previously prepared by a series of meetings between the village heads) begin. Only after agreement has been reached, possibly many hours later, are the guests provided with a meal. In an affair of this sort, it is the village having the role of wife-taker which travels, bringing its goods to the village of the wife-giver. They bring no food with them, as would be done on other occasions, for this is all provided by the wife-givers. In the negotiations, they are in the weaker position, and must usually be satisfied with a somewhat unfavourable result.

I accompanied a party from Léuwajang on one such mission and was able to observe how thoroughly it is really the villages and not the clans which are the alliance groups. Most of the people in our party, including some of the principal negotiators, were not even clear about the names of the clans (there was more than one case) with which they were dealing in the other village. Furthermore, the two village heads took care to point out during the proceedings that it was forbidden for two clans of the villages to deal directly with each other in a matter of this sort. And even though the novelty of the relation allowed the introduction of competition and economic interests, all agreements were subsequently binding on both villages, and there was concern to ensure that in a subsequent case of a reversed relationship, equal value would be returned.

5. OBSERVATIONS ON THE SIGNIFICANCE OF BRIDEWEALTH

Fischer (1935: 368) observes that bridewealth is commonly less in Indonesia in the case of marriages which accord with the marriage rules. This is true in Kédang only in the sense that a marriage outside the clan of the mother's brother brings the additional payment of the *hudé-hén* and, if it opens ties between two groups which had never had any relations, of the *bunga karé*. These two payments do not bring a very large increase in the expense of the gifts. However, it is true that marriages which initiate new ties, particularly outside the village, lead to substantial expense for the wife-takers. There is an opposition between safe marriages which lead to no loss or gain and marriages in which there is economic risk; and this opposition poses the question of what the purpose of bridewealth really is.

First to be considered is that it is only in the novel situations that a group may hope to acquire more wealth. The more ties that are established, the more a system begins to appear which tends to prevent permanent imbalances and restricts the possibilities of hoarding. Competition for bridewealth appears then only in the absence of the system. Even in these instances, the appearance of purchase is avoided, and a two-sided exchange is established of which the woman herself is a part. Where the ties become, or rather can be made to be, systematic, the system takes the form of two reciprocal cycles, of which one includes the unilateral circulation of women (Needham 1958: 96).

We have seen that the actual cost of the prestations from the wife-takers is much higher than those from the wife-givers. This suggests that the difference roughly represents the place of the woman in the series of gifts. Since the woman does not take the place of a slave, and since the cost usually disappears, her place in the exchanges is probably not correctly considered in economic terms.

The question arises, then, how the value represented by the woman is to be assessed. Lévi-Strauss (1969: 260) says that 'the bride-price has less to do with sexual rights . . . than with the permanent loss of the wife and her offspring'; and Leach (1961: 101, n. 1) says, 'In most societies, the outcome of marriage exchanges is

concerned with validating the status of the woman's offspring.'
This leads to the by now commonplace observation that what is
given with the woman is the continued life of the clan itself. Van
Ossenbruggen, following Mauss, interprets this as a form of magi-
cal power. According to Mauss's interpretation of the gift, a prestation always carries with it a part of the owner's spirit, and not
to return this with a reciprocal gift is dangerous (1966: 10). Van
Ossenbruggen (1930: 221; 1935: 13, 15) takes this idea over into
his own interpretation of bridewealth. It must be said that this idea
of the danger of a gift and Mauss's view that there is a confusion
between the personality of the giver and the thing given, do not
correspond to Kédangese conceptions. Still Mauss's notion that
gift exchange expresses an opposition between substance and
spiritual essence is probably very much to the point. In my
opinion the most direct view of the marriage system and the system of prestations of which it is a part lies in the opposition
between the giving of substantial values in the form of expensive
but non-consumable tusks and gongs in return for the gift of the
spiritual value life.

XIX

THE SOCIAL ORDER:
A STATISTICAL SUMMARY

THE Indonesian census of 1970 was conducted while I was in the field, and the village government of Léuwajang kindly let me see their records. On the basis of the village census, I was able to collect complete genealogies of all the members of the clans of Léuwajang going back in almost all cases to the founding ancestors. The final lists included many lines which have no living representatives and provide an extensive record of marriages in the village extending nine to ten generations from current adults.

Within the last four or five generations, this record may be taken as nearly complete. Beyond that, marriages in some clans could only be partially remembered, and numerous uncertainties concerning which woman was married to which man and the original clan and village of the spouse began to appear. Nevertheless, in some clans the record is very nearly complete, back to the original ancestor, and is reasonably accurate, as is demonstrated by correspondences among different clans. In the earlier stages of the genealogies, there is a tendency to forget the names of clan sisters, which introduces a distortion not found in recent levels. Nevertheless, the information concerning marriages including even the apical ancestors gives the firm impression of being historical in character, however much it may suffer from the uncertainties of memory.

One of the benefits of this long record is that inspection reveals with a good deal of certainty that there has been no significant change in the extent to which the marriage rule is followed during this period. Since the record goes back well beyond the time (beginning in the early decades of this century) when there was any appreciable external influence from the Dutch colonial government or from Islam or the Catholic mission, we can be certain that we do not need to reckon with these influences in explaining the current state of things. This condition represents a, so to speak, natural possibility for societies with ideologies of asymmetric alliance.

I. THE EVIDENCE

The population of Léuwajang in 1970 was 1,060; the break-down of this figure by clan and sex is given in Appendix III. The genealogical record reveals a total of 419 marriages between men and women of Léuwajang, and an additional 324 marriages outside the village by men of Léuwajang and 195 marriages outside by women. The inequality in the last two figures is explained in part by the fact that women who marry outside the village are charac-teristically forgotten after a few generations. There is a total, then, of 938 marriages recorded, or, if those within the village are counted twice, 1,357.

Of 594 marriages in which it seems possible to trace the relevant relations with a reliable degree of completeness and accuracy, 365, or 62 per cent, were with women in the proper category (*mahan*), 42, or 7 per cent, with women who could only be considered *iné utun* and 187 with women with whom there was no apparent pre-vious relation. When 22 instances in which the closest traceable relation places the woman in the category *iné utun* are removed from the positive side and added to the negative, there are 343, or 58 per cent of marriages with women who are unequivocally *mahan* and 64, or 11 per cent of marriages with women who should probably be regarded as *iné utun*. In either case, 31 per cent are with apparently unrelated women.

This means that there are 407 marriages with women with whom there is a previous traceable relationship, and of these marriages 87 to 90 per cent are in the proper category, while 10 to 13 per cent are with women who may be regarded *iné utun*.

Of the original 594 marriages, 530 to 552, or from 89 per cent to 93 per cent, are into the prescribed category *or* initiate new relations, while 7 to 11 per cent are with women in the prohibited category.

Thus, there is a high degree of correspondence between the actual pattern of marriages and the formal marriage ideology.

Table 14 indicates the number of marriages among the clans of the village. Marriages which end in divorce are not counted, unless the children remain in the father's clan. Each marriage is counted in cases of polygynous marriages. In the table, the number of mar-riages of each type is given in parentheses. For example, for the clan Apé Utung, the entry Apé Labi (3/5) means Apé Utung received three women from Apé Labi and gave five.

This table reveals that there is direct exchange between a high proportion of the clans. This is not an unusual feature, and it occurs in societies where the system of asymmetric affinal alliance is intact (Needham 1957: 178). Still it stands in marked contrast to the fact that it is the clan, and not a smaller segment, which acts as the alliance group in the exchange of bridewealth.

Of the 743 marriages involving men of Léuwajang it is possible in 687 cases to tell with certainty whether the man married into the clan of his mother's brother. This represents a test of the marriage preference as defined by the payment of the form of bridewealth called *hudé-hén*. Of these marriages only 16 or 17 per cent satisfy the preference.

In some societies with a principle of prescribed affinal alliance, the rule is satisfied when one of a set of brothers marries according to the prescribed pattern, the rest being free to choose as they wish. Usually it is the eldest brother who is obligated, but often a younger brother may take his place (Drabbe 1923: 551, 556; Dumont 1957a: 189–90). This contingent arrangement is not recognized in Kédang when considering the rule governing the payment of *hudé-hén*; every marriage of each brother is subject to the rule. Nevertheless, it may prove of use for comparison with a society which allows such freedom to re-examine the evidence from Léuwajang under the assumption that these conditions *do* apply. If each set of brothers numbering one or more is counted as one instance and if at least one marriage, including secondary marriages, is into the clan of the mother's brother (and therefore constitutes a positive instance), then of 383 instances 103, or 27 per cent follow the reinterpreted marriage preference. This means that in an extreme instance, if of several brothers the third wife of one is the only correct partner, this is considered a positive case.

There are some cases, where the wife comes from outside Léuwajang, which are treated as undeterminable because, although the village of origin of mother and wife are identical, the clan in one or other instance or both is unknown. If these are interpreted as all being positive cases (25 in number) then the percentage of marriages into the mother's brother's clan is raised to 20. If the same adjustments are made to the figure for sets of brothers, the positive instances are increased by 22 (to 125) and the negative by 9 (to 271), thus giving 32 per cent of positive instances.

The 17 to 20 per cent of accordance to the marriage preference

TABLE 14

Marriage ties among the clans of Léuwajang

Clan	No relation to	Wife-taking only from	Wife-giving only to	Both
Apé Utung	Ape Worén Boli Leraq	Apé Liling (1) Apé Tatu (2) Laong Hodiq (1)	Apé Nobé (2)	Apé Labi (3/5) Amun Toda (2/5) Hiang Leraq (1/2) Buang Leraq (1/3) Hoqaratan (4/2) Toul Wala (3/2)
Apé Labi		Apé Liling (1)	Boli Leraq (3) Hoqaratan (3)	Apé Utung (5/3) Apé Worén (9/12) Apé Nobé (9/11) Apé Tatu (1/1) Amun Toda (8/16) Hiang Leraq (2/11) Buang Leraq (8/3) Laong Hodiq (11/1) Toul Wala (4/4)
Apé Worén	Apé Utung Apé Liling	Hiang Leraq (4)	Apé Nobé (1) Buang Leraq (8)	Apé Labi (12/9) Apé Tatu (1/2) Amun Toda (11/8) Boli Leraq (2/3) Laong Hodiq (1/2) Hoqaratan (3/1) Toul Wala (6/3)
Apé Liling	Apé Worén Apé Tatu Amun Toda Hiang Leraq Buang Leraq Hoqaratan	Apé Nobé (1) Toul Wala (1) Boli Leraq (1)	Apé Utung (1) Apé Labi (1) Laong Hodiq (1)	
Apé Nobé	Boli Leraq	Apé Utung (2) Apé Worén (1) Apé Tatu (1) Toul Wala (4)	Apé Liling (1) Buang Leraq (8) Laong Hodiq (1) Hoqaratan (4)	Apé Labi (11/9) Amun Toda (3/6) Hiang Leraq (9/2)
Apé Tatu	Apé Liling	Boli Leraq (1) Hoqaratan (3)	Apé Utung (2) Apé Nobé (1) Toul Wala (3)	Apé Labi (1/1) Apé Worén (2/1) Amun Toda (1/1) Hiang Leraq (4/3) Buang Leraq (6/4) Laong Hodiq (1/1)
Amun Toda	Apé Liling	Buang Leraq (4)	Hiang Leraq (3) Boli Leraq (2)	Apé Utung (5/2) Apé Labi (16/8) Apé Worén (8/11) Apé Nobé (6/3) Apé Tatu (1/1) Amun Toda (1/1) Laong Hodiq (1/7) Hoqaratan (5/1) Toul Wala (4/10)

Clan	No relation to	Wife-taking only from	Wife-giving only to	Both
Hiang Leraq	Apé Liling	Amun Toda (3)	Apé Worén(4)	Apé Utung (2/1) Apé Labi (11/2) Apé Nobé (2/9) Apé Tatu (3/4) Buang Leraq (8/7) Boli Leraq (4/3) Laong Hodiq (4/7) Hoqaratan (9/4) Toul Wala (1/1)
Buang Leraq	Apé Liling	Apé Worén (8) Apé Nobé (8)	Amun Toda (4) Toul Wala (5)	Apé Utung (3/1) Apé Labi (3/8) Apé Tatu (4/6) Hiang Leraq (7/8) Boli Leraq (4/4) Laong Hodiq (8/2) Hoqaratan (5/5)
Boli Leraq	Apé Utung Apé Nobé	Apé Labi (3) Amun Toda (2) Laong Hodiq (1) Apé Liling (1)	Apé Tatu (1)	Apé Worén (3/2) Hiang Leraq (3/4) Buang Leraq (4/4) Hoqaratan (1/2) Toul Wala (2/4)
Laong Hodiq		Apé Liling (1) Apé Nobé (1) Hoqaratan (3) Toul Wala (1)	Apé Utung (1) Boli Leraq (1)	Apé Labi (1/11) Apé Worén (2/1) Apé Tatu (1/1) Amun Toda (7/1) Hiang Leraq (7/4) Buang Leraq (2/8) Laong Hodiq (1/1)
Hoqaratan	Apé Liling	Apé Labi (3) Apé Nobé (4)	Apé Tatu (3) Laong Hodiq (3)	Apé Utung (2/4) Apé Worén (1/3) Amun Toda (1/5) Hiang Leraq (4/9) Buang Leraq (5/5) Boli Leraq (5/1) Toul Wala (1/1)
Toul Wala		Apé Tatu (3) Buang Leraq (5)	Apé Liling (1) Apé Nobé (4) Laong Hodiq (1)	Apé Utung (2/3) Apé Labi (4/4) Apé Worén (3/6) Amun Toda (10/4) Hiang Leraq (1/1) Boli Leraq (4/2) Hoqaratan (1/1)

gives little reason to think that there is a systematic pattern of affinal alliances in Léuwajang. Even 27 to 32 per cent accordance with the reinterpreted preference is not very impressive, and this reinterpretation does not, of course, even represent the ethnographic fact. Of the (95) positive instances in which it is possible to determine the exact genealogical relation of the spouse, only 25 or 26 per cent married the genealogical MBD (or in one case the MBSD). There was one case of marriage with the MFFBSD, three with the MFFBSSD, which seemed to be the genealogically closest available member of the category, and 6 with the MFBSD. If these 10 cases are considered as equivalent to MBD, then there were 35 or 37 per cent of the positive instances in which there was simultaneously marriage with the genealogical MBD or equivalent. Where there is no marriage into the clan of the MB, a marriage into the clan of the FMB (if there is a difference of clan) still requires payment of substitute bridewealth; but there were actually 27 instances of this type of marriage. This figure is probably statistically of little significance, but it does show a certain liking for picking up old ties, particularly as it sometimes seems that one line develops a special predilection for it.

Studies of prescriptive alliance systems frequently reveal that the alliance system exists not at the level of the clan but at the level of its segments. For the Kallar, for instance, the system 'is focused on as many centres as there are lines of two or three generations' (Dumont 1957b: 22). The observation that the alliance groups are characteristically smaller than the exogamous group was made by Fischer (1935: 369), and the distinction has since then continually proved to be of essential analytic importance. In Léuwajang, one can find model instances in which marriages are with the same lineage for as many as four generations; but these lineages set themselves apart in this way from the great majority. In practice, repeated marriages with the same lineage seems to be a special preference developed by individual segments, but it is not characteristic for the whole. Furthermore, the inspections of genealogies reveals no system of affinal alliance.

There actually seems to have been no instance of FZD marriage, but more distant marriages, such as to a FZHBD, FZSD, FBDD, and of course instances more distant yet, did occur. Figure 12 demonstrates a genealogically rather close instance of direct exchange.

The genealogies show, in addition to this, three cases of marriage with the ZHFBD and one with the ZHBD. There are even two cases of direct exchange between sets of siblings. As it happened, two closely related lines of one clan were involved in both cases. Its partners were also in a clan together but were not closely related. The exchanges in question are shown in Figure 13.

The two men No. 1 and 2 who were responsible for the reversal in both cases were subject to the fine *poroq-tobuq*, consisting of five ivory bracelets and a sarong, and symbolizing the removal of the objects which represented their position as bride-givers. In these and the other cases of genealogically close reciprocal marriages, it would be necessary to perform the ceremony used in cases of incest. I did not witness such a ceremony in the case of marriage with a woman in the same category as FZD or ZHZ, so I do not know quite how it is arranged; but I was once told that if the relationship

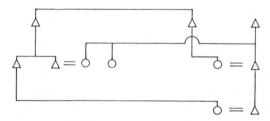

F I G. 12. An example of direct marriage exchange.

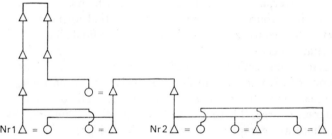

F I G. 13. Direct marriage exchange between sets of siblings.

is permanent, they would wait until the couple had ceased having children before performing the ceremony. I never heard that the woman could be removed from the prohibited category and adopted into the permitted one as sometimes occurs elsewhere (Needham 1961: 107).

I found as well two cases of marriage within the same clan. In one case a man married his FFBD. They were expelled from the clan and now live on another part of the island. In the other, quite ancient case, a man took for his second wife his FBSSD. Far from being expelled, this woman became the mother of what is now a substantial segment of the clan.

2.   A SYNOPTIC VIEW OF MARRIAGE AND ALLIANCE IN
     KÉDANG

Needham (1970: 257; 1964b: 305) gives a list of features which, while not diagnostic of prescriptive alliance, are significantly coherent when found in connection with a prescriptive termin- ology (see also Korn 1971: 119). 'These are: the arranged marriages, corporate involvement of descent groups in marriage payments, widow-inheritance, sororal polygyny, and absence of divorce.' He adds to this the existence of masculine and feminine goods exchanged between descent groups in connection with the con- traction of marriage. It is useful then to consider how far these features are also found in Kédang.

First, arranged marriages are exceptional if they occur at all. This is a fact of considerable importance for the actual pattern of marriages. The second feature, corporate involvement of descent groups in marriage payments, is present and represents the one point where social action comes closest to system. That it is the clan, however, and not the lineage or line, which is the bridewealth exchanging group may be seen as closely tied to the absence of a practically operating system of asymmetric affinal alliance. Widow- inheritance occurs, but only as an optional procedure and not as an obligatory institution. Sororal polygyny occurs. There is no absence of divorce; it is in fact relatively easy, even though there are fines connected with it which are intended to restrict it to a moderate degree. There are no 'masculine' and 'feminine' goods, but there are complementary and oriented prestations, which is the essential aspect of this institution, and we can say then that Kédang exhibits this feature to the required degree.

This review gives rather mixed results, indicating a large degree of latitude in the whole. Furthermore, they do not exploit certain structural possibilities of the principle of descent. Needham (1958: 98) says of matrilateral connubium that it 'can be regarded as one way—and a simple and very effective one—of creating and maintaining counter-fissive relationships in a segmentary society'. It is clear that the successful operation of matrilateral alliance is closely connected to the segmentary character of the principle of descent, and Needham even lists (1961: 107) 'the fission of alliance groups and the subsequent contraction of differential alliances' as one of the forms of the manipulation of alliances which may be resorted to in such a system—and which obviously contribute to its maintainance.

In some societies where the system of affinal alliance is actually in operation, clans may in fact exchange women reciprocally, while the asymmetric pattern is preserved by their segments. This seems often associated with the existence of named lineages, as in eastern Sumba (Needham 1957) and probably in the Ili Mandiri region of East Flores (Arndt 1940: 5; Kennedy n.d.: 161–2, 407–8). Named lineages may not be necessary, but they probably are very helpful to the preservation of such a system. It is characteristic that they do not occur in Kédang. It is also often found that alliance groups maintain a multiplicity of alliances to increase their room for finding marriage partners (Fischer 1935: 369); the lines in Léuwajang commonly show a multiplicity of ties, but these ties have no systematic consequences in the absence of features insuring that they are kept up and renewed. In some societies alliances are kept up by having one of a set of brothers marry a woman from the mother's lineage; but this seems not to be a procedure regularly followed here. It sometimes occurs that it is even prohibited for two brothers to marry two sisters, but in Kédang this is not only possible, it is also a likely consequence of obedience to the rules governing the payment of substitute bridewealth.

Under these conditions there is no point in attempting to find cycles of marriage alliance. They would have no more meaning here than in a society which has no prescribed rule. We have, unfortunately, no information on an operating system of asymmetric affinal alliance comparable to that for Kédang; so we do not know the point where the percentage of irregular marriages becomes so high that the system no longer exists. In fact, there probably is no clear line between functioning and non-functioning systems; but we can be sure that a positive or negative judgement concerning a society near this line could only be made after detailed consideration of its institutions and of the ties among its descent groups. The means of acquiring an understanding of how systems of this type may operate is the collecting and examining of extensive genealogies in society after society.

It may be observed that the analytic tools which have been developed concerning the topic of prescriptive alliance are only useful if they are capable of rendering both negative and positive results. When applied to facts from Kédang, they have shown that there is here an exemplary ideological system of asymmetric prescriptive alliance and a high degree of correspondence to the formal marriage prescription, but that there are several divergences from this ideal system in social action, and that finally there are no set and patent alliances among corporate descent groups.

XX

CONCLUSION

IN this book I have examined the collective representations of Kédang in a series of areas of their life, and I have shown that there is a general concordance throughout all phases of their conceptual order.

This conceptual order is based on a form of dualism consisting of pairs of ranked and complementary opposites. Complementary opposition is the germ of a number of systems of oriented relations which show the features of segmentation, irreversibility, and self-closure.

Structurally equivalent ideas of the golden germ, or pot, and of the initial unity of heaven and earth, and ideas of life fluids in various forms, lie at the heart of all such systems. The separating, splitting or pouring forth of these images leads to being and development. This being and development continue to be governed by those primal forms. The conceptual relation of a source (*matan*) and a trunk (*puén*) is reflected in the relation between a node (*woq*) and a segment (*laru*). The hierarchic character of such complementary relationships leads to orientation of the developed representation. The superiority of right to left—seemingly a universal feature of thought—becomes a law of motion to the right. This law governs the construction of buildings and, as I have argued, the representation of the cycle of human life.

The social order is also represented as consisting of a unilateral and irreversible series of relations between segmentary groups. This series of relations consists of two self-closing cycles of prestations moving in opposite directions. The major prestation in one of these cycles is life in the form of women and their ability to give birth. In return for life, given by a superior to an inferior, is a cycle of counter-prestations of primarily non-consumable valuables given by the inferior to the superior. That there is an exact correspondence in the orientation of the series of social relations, and of the cycles mentioned previously, is suggested by the fact that their Lamaholot neighbours in East Flores, who have an identical social order, designate the prescribed marriage partner *mure wana*, meaning 'take from the right'.

Motion through these cycles in the proper direction insures well-being; reversal of this motion brings disaster. Typical is the custom of laying markers (*bulung éqa*)—consisting of the spines of coconut branches or strips from the trunk of a banana tree— around the edges of fields when the ears of the maize crop begin to develop. These markers must all lie so that they point to the right around the field. Should any be laid out incorrectly, then wild pigs may enter at that point.

In contrast to the irreversibility of such cycles is the procedure of inversion. Certain delicts may only be set right by an intentional inversion of orderly relations. The ceremony for erasing the effects of incest is the prime example. Sexual relations with a prohibited category of person is considered in Kédang a form of inversion comparable to placing a house post in upside-down (*hunéq-koloq*) or, even worse, walking with one's feet to the sky (*ula-lojo*). Such disorder can be set right only by the extreme measure of bringing the sky down and rejoining it to the earth, which is as much as returning to the beginning of time and existence to make an entirely new start. Well-being depends on the irreversibility of relations; but when things are seriously wrong, one must resort to the opposite principle: inversion. An example of the use of this logical technique for putting disorder back in order is the resort which they said one must take when one is hopelessly lost on an unfamiliar trail. The only way one can get out of such a situation is to put one's clothes on upside-down.

On other occasions, disaster may be assumed to be due to the impurity or defilement of a source of life, in particular the village or spring. They then return to this source and subject it to a thorough cleaning.

All things which have being in Kédang are punctuated or articulated by points where life-giving or life-taking spirit may enter and leave. All living things contain life fluids. It would seem then, that the world for the people of Kédang is permeated by the continuous flow of life. Just as water emerging from a spring or sap from a plant, humanity itself may be regarded in Kédangese terms as a form of life flowing through the segmented series of worlds which together form the cycle of the universe.

Categories such as that uniting solids like gold and other metals with life-giving fluids (*werén-lalan*), suggest that it is not the opposition of the material to the immaterial or of body to spirit or even of space to time which is fundamental to the collective thought of Kédang. Perhaps the most irreducible conceptual distinction to be found here is one—more abstract yet than the body/essence pair which Endicott (1970: 96) has argued to be fundamental to Malay magic—in which the form or structure of being, whether material or not, is contrasted to this spiritual essence which moves through it.

APPENDIX I
PULAU LAMA LÉQANG

This is the story of the culture hero of Kédang, whose name has already been translated in the Introduction.

I was given the story by Mamaq Gatang of the village Léuhoéq. He originally heard it from a member of the village Léuwajang living in the hamlet Édang. For this reason I have taken the liberty of changing the name of the heroine from Aréq Muko Paréq to Peni Muko Lolong, the form favoured in Léuwajang. Aréq and Peni are typical names for women; *aréq* in fact means 'woman'. Peni is a favoured name for a mythical heroine in Kédang and Lamaholot. *Muko lolong* is Lamaholot for 'banana leaf' and the reader will soon learn why it appears in her name. *Muko paréq* is also Lamaholot and is, perhaps, a variety of banana. This figure is also known in Kédang as Peni Muko Tapo, Lamaholot for Peni Banana Tree-Coconut Palm.

Ina wai is Lamaholot for 'woman', and *tuan* is a term of honour; so Ina Wai Tuan seems to be archetypical old woman.

In the text she points out that she and Pulau Lama Léqang have entered into a wife-giving/wife-taking relationship as a result of Pulau Lama Léqang's theft of Peni Muko Lolong. As the story develops, it becomes clear that Pulau Lama Léqang is also wife-taker from God.

This is a story about fundamental human concerns, told in Kédangese terms. It may give pleasure to see what depths of meaning lie in it. I think it should not be too difficult for the European reader to interpret if he has read the foregoing attentively. Some comment has been given on pages 110–111. The most obscure point is perhaps the meaning of the fresh egg which Ina Wai Tuan asks in return for Peni Muko Lolong. In my opinion, since it is given her on a plate and cotton, just like that in which Peni Muko Lolong sits, the egg must in some ways be equivalent to the maiden. The story-teller and a friend were once at my house and brought up this passage in conversation among themselves. Not satisfied with the clarity of the passage, they speculated, as I overheard, that she intended to use this egg in a guardian spirit ceremony (*poan tuéng nimon-narin*), in which she would request that Peni be taken back up to the heavens as revenge on Pula Lama Léqang. Sure enough this happens.

A final point to note is that Peni Muko Lolong is herself a golden maiden. This associates her with all those values which the Kédangese regard as being in one way or another golden. She is of course the image of God's creative powers and she stands for all that women mean to the people of Kédang.

Once the Moon and the Sun were vilifying each other.
The Sun said to the Moon, 'Moon, you're a witch.'
The Moon replied, 'Sun, you're a witch.'
'If that's so,' returned the Sun, 'let's check each other's granary.'
'You check mine first', said the Moon.
'Eh! You check mine first', returned the Sun.
Then the Moon went up and inspected the Sun's granary. The Sun's barn contained all the valuables and food to be found in the world (*ihin-werén, matan-méan, utan-watar*). But when the Sun inspected the Moon's barn, he found nothing but skeletons (*matén lurin*) stacked up like ears of maize.
Then the Sun said, 'Moon, you're half blossom [i.e. human], half witch. Now you're full, now you're new. I rise above the mountain and set in the sea [i.e. always in the same place]. For a while you are old, then you are young; but I am always old and always young.'
The Moon responded, 'Ah! If you say I'm a witch, then let's drop a maiden.'
So the two of them prepared to drop a maiden.
The Moon said, 'If I don't eat by the light of the hearth fire, drink by the light of the torch, then my maiden will fall to the centre of the sky and shatter into mosquitoes, gnats, maggots, ants, geckos, iguanas, snakes, and lizards. If I eat by the light of the hearth fire, drink by the light of the torch, my maiden will land in the top of the banana tree.'
Then the Sun said, 'If I eat the ripe, drink the green [i.e. eat stolen crops], then my maiden will just fall to the centre of the sky where she will shatter into mosquitoes, gnats, maggots, ants, snakes, geckos, and iguanas. But if my maiden is golden (*ihin-werén, matan-méan*), then she will land in the top of the banana tree.'
Then each dropped his maiden. The Moon's girl fell to the centre of the sky where she shattered into all the kinds of vermin in the world. The Sun's maiden landed in the banana tree; therefore, she was named Peni Muko Lolon (Peni Banana Leaves).
Ina Wai Tuan went to work in her fields. When she got there she said, 'Ah! The rains are almost here. I have to clean my fields

and plant to be ready for the rains, and those little children, they just cut down the banana leaves and scatter them everywhere, so that I have to clear the fields again!'

The next morning, she came back and found banana leaves again scattered everywhere.

'These little children,' she said, 'everyday they come and strew my banana leaves all over everywhere!' She returned home and was very angry. 'Tomorrow, I'm going to come back and beat you children.'

The next day she came back and the leaves were scattered around as usual. Then she said, 'Child are you up there dropping down those leaves? I'm going to come up too.' Then more leaves fell down. Ina Wai Tuan called, 'Who's up there?'

'I'm up here. My name is Peni Muko Lolong.'

'Eh? Where do you come from?'

'I come from Ula-Lojo [the heavens].'

'Come down, come down, come down! Come down and I will cradle you in my arms.'

'No. If you cradle me, your hair and nails will stick me.'

Ina Wai Tuan asked, 'What do you want then?'

'You go home and wash a plate until it is gleaming white; then get raw cotton and put it in the plate so that I can come down and sit in it.'

Ina Wai Tuan went home and got the plate.

Peni Muko Lolon came down and sat in it. Then her colours (*iréq*) shown like those of a bumble-bee (*woqo-toqo*), a rainbow, gold (*nado-tado, lair-kéu, werén-lalan, matan-méan*).

Ina Wai Tuan carried her home, and they were followed by a light shower containing a rainbow. Ina Wai Tuan took Peni Muko Lolong up to a platform high near the roof of her house. Her big basket had seven levels, and she put Peni Muko Lolong in the very bottom of these levels.

The next morning, the shower and rainbow were over Ina Wai Tuan's house.

Pulau Lama Léqang said, 'Ina Wai Tuan is just a widow, but there is a rainbow over her house. What kind of precious valuables (*werén-lalan, matan-méan*) can she have? I know, I'll trick her.'

The next day he went over to her house and said, 'Eh. Ina Wai Tuan, the market is very crowded.'

'Is that so. Shall we go together tomorrow?'

'All right, tomorrow we'll go to market as soon as I am through tapping palm wine.'

The next morning when Ina Wai Tuan was through with breakfast, she tied up the door to her house and went to get Pulau Lama Léqang.

Pulau Lama Léqang said, 'Eeee . . . Ina Wai Tuan, my stomach is sick, sick, sick. Will you go by yourself?'

She replied, 'Yes, in that case, I'll go by myself.'

Then she went off to market, but before she got as far as the village Léuwehéq, Pulau Lama Léqang's stomach was already well. He said to himself, 'She is already far away. How is it that a widow like her can have a rainbow over her house? She must have some precious valuables (*ihin-werén, matan-méan*). I'll go down there and steal them.'

So he went down to her house. By the time she had gotten to Meru, he began to climb the ladder. When he stepped on the ladder, Peni Muko Lolong began to cry.

'Eeee . . . Ina Wai Tuan eee . . . Pulau Lama Léqang is going to cradle Peni Muko Lolong and carry her away . . .'

But Ina Wai Tuan kept walking. When she got to Balaurin, the market was not yet even half over. And Pulau Lama Léqang climbed another rung of the ladder. Peni Muko Lolong called.

'Eeee . . . Ina Wai Tuan eee . . . Pulau Lama Léqang's going to cradle Peni Muko Lolong and carry her away . . .'

When Pulau Lama Léqang had thus climbed as far as the fifth rung, he entered the house. Once inside he began to open the basket.

But Peni Muko Lolong said, 'Eh, you can't touch me! Go get my mother's plate and clean it and put cotton in it and then I will go with you.'

Then Palau Lama Léqang cleaned the plate and put the cotton in it like Ina Wai Tuan had done. She sat in it, and he took her home.

When Ina Wai Tuan came back, she saw the door to her house ajar and her basket empty.

'Eh! Pulau Lama Léqang cheated me. He said his stomach was sick, but then he stole my maiden.'

So she went up to Pulau Lama Léqang's house and said, 'Pulau Lama Léqang, you tricked me, you stole my golden maiden who came down from Ula-Lojo. How can you do that!'

Pulau Lama Léqang answered, 'I took her because I want to marry her.'

She replied, 'Ah! If you marry her, then let's discuss bridewealth at once.'

'That's right, let's talk bridewealth. Will you take a whole platform full of gongs?'

Ina Wai Tuan replied, 'What use are gongs to me?' I already have gongs.'

'Then, will you take a platform full of elephant tusks?' What use are tusks to me? I already have tusks.'

'Then, a platform of golden chains (*aba*)?'

'What use are golden chains to me? I have them.'

'Then, a platform of golden ear-rings?'

'What use are they, I have them.'

'In that case, what do you want?'

She replied, 'You get a clean plate and cotton as well as a fresh egg.' So Pulau Lama Léqang gave her these things.

After a time, Peni Muko Lolong became pregnant. Then the people in the village asked themselves:

'Pulau Lama Léqang married this maiden, but who is her mother? Who is her father? What is the name of her village? We don't know where she comes from, we don't know who she is. This is what we will do. Tomorrow, we will gather together and then all go hunting.'

So the next morning they shouted the announcement in the village that they should gather for a hunt. The whole village, all the men and all the women, went on the hunt. They hunted until sundown, but there were no pigs or deer. Then they asked Pulau Lama Léqang, 'Pulau Lama Léqang, will you play dead? When we get back to the village, we will tell your wife that the deer pierced you (*ruha tubaq*), the boars gored you (*wawi namang*); so we can find out who her mother is and who her father is and what the name of her village is.'

So they wrapped him in coconut leaves and gathered together his bow and arrows, while he played dead, so that they could carry him back to the village. Those who carried him told the rest to go ahead.

When these reached the village, Peni Muko Lolong was just finishing a basket. She asked, 'Why, you others are already here! Where is my husband?'

They replied, 'Eh, your husband Pulau Lama Léqang, the deer pierced him, the boars gored him. They are carrying him home behind us.'

'Is that true or are you trying to trick me?' she said.

In a short while another three or four people came back to the village.

She asked, 'You others have come back, but where is my husband?'

'Eh, Pulau Lama Léqang, the deer pierced him, the boars gored him. He is being carried behind us.'

Soon, as the group carrying Pulau Lama Léqang neared the village, they began to shout, 'Oha', the way they do when they carry corpses. When they were closer, the villagers showed Peni Muko Lolong that her husband was being carried home. When she saw that she cried:

'My husband, the deer pierced him, the goars gored him, he is dead. They are carrying him home.' Then she went into the house and got two golden bowls. One she set down on the right, the other on the left. Then she began to lament.

The cry 'Oha!' was heard, and she said, 'My husband is really dead.' Then she began to cry:

> 'Mother Bota eee, oh Father Taé.[1]
> Pati Kong eee, oh Ulu Amaq.[2]
> Father White Sun, oh Great Sun eee.
> Pulau Lama Léqang, the deer pierced him,
> Pulau Lama Léqang, the boars gored him.
> Uh, huh, huh, huuh . . .'

The mucus from her nose fell into the right bowl and became a golden chain (*aba*). Her tears fell into the left bowl and became golden ear-rings.

> 'Mother Bota eee, oh Father Taé.
> Pati Kong eee, oh Ulu Amaq.
> Father White Sun, oh Great Sun eee.
> The Evening Star [Uno] precedes at dusk,
> The Morning Star [Lia] follows at dawn.

---

[1] Presumably Bota Ili, the mountain, and in a contracted form 'Tahiq eee', the sea; both taken together being aspects of God.

[2] Perhaps 'Prince Gong' and 'Skin of the Golden Germ', honorific terms for God.

Pulau Lama Léqang, the deer pierced him,
Pulau Lama Léqang, the boars gored him.
Uh, huh, huh, huuh . . .'

The mucus fell into the right bowl again and turned to a golden chain. Her tears fell into the left and became golden ear-rings. When the people carrying Pulau Lama Léqang reached the village, they dropped him on the ground. Jarred by the fall, he moved.

Peni Muko Lolong said, 'Eh! Pulau Lama Léqang tricked me. He made me expose my gold. They said he was dead, but there he is, alive.' Then she cried and wailed so long that the right pot was filled with golden chains and the left was filled with golden ear-rings.

The next morning she decided to trick Pulau Lama Léqang and told him, 'You climb up and get me a white coconut. Then you set the coconut so that its base (*matan*) points up and shave off the covering until you can almost see the water, as they sometimes do in a guardian spirit ceremony. Then you give it to me.'

Pulau Lama Léqang got the coconut and prepared it. Then Peni Muko Lolong took the pin from her hair and pierced the coconut. The water squirted up to the sky taking her with it, where she met her father the Sun again.

The Sun said, 'Eh! Are you here? I thought you had shattered into mosquitoes, gnats, maggots, and ants.'

She replied, 'I fell until I landed on the top of a banana tree. Then my mother found me and took care of me. She is named Ina Wai Tuan. My husband is named Pulau Lama Léqang.'

The Sun said, 'You go back down!'

She said in return, 'Wait until Pulau Lama Léqang comes up and meets you, then I will go back down. If he doesn't come up, I won't go back down.'

Pulau Lama Léqang climbed up to the compartment under the roof, but the water of the coconut had already gone even higher. Then he rushed around looking here and there, at a loss what to do.

Then he went over and asked the Coconut Palm, 'Coconut, how many days before you go up to the sky?'

The Coconut Palm replied, 'I climb at the most only to the centre of the sky. You go over and ask Banyan.'

So he went over and asked Banyan. 'Banyan, how many days before you go to the sky?'

Banyan said, 'Me, go to the sky? Why they cut my branches and aerial roots, and burn them and dig them all out. How can I go up to the sky?'

Then Pulau Lama Léqang said, 'I'll go over and ask Pinang.'

'Pinang, how soon will you go up to the sky?'

'I don't go up that high.'

'Then whom should I ask?'

'I heard that Rotan is going up to the sky.'

So he climbed up the mountain to ask Rotan.

'Rotan, how many days before you go up to the sky?'

'I'm going up in five days.'

Pulau Lama Léqang said, 'Peni Muko Lolong ran away to see her father in the sky. Shall we go together? Will you help carry my gongs and tusks to pay the bridewealth for my wife?'

'How many times should I twist?'

'You twist five times.'

Then Rotan said, 'I'll take you up to the sky, but you must be careful. The wind up there is really strong.'

'Fine, I'll hold on tight.'

So in five days, Rotan began to arrange the gongs and tusks. He twisted five times, and each twist was full of gongs and tusks. Then he said, 'Up in the sky the wind is really strong, so you have to hold on tight! If not you will fall down and split into pieces.'

'Good.'

Then they climbed up to the sky. Once there, they stayed at Rotan's house. At this time Peni Muko Lolong gave birth to a boy. His features resembled Pulau Lama Léqang.

Pulau Lama Léqang said, 'That is my son [Léqang Pulau]. You call him over here.'

So Rotan called him over, and Pulau Lama Léqang cut off the tip of an elephant tusk to serve as a top and gave him a golden chain to play with.

Then Peni's father saw the child playing with his toys and said to himself, 'A few days ago, this child didn't have any tusks or golden chains to play with; his father must have come up and brought them.'

Then he went and said to Pulau Lama Léqang, 'Pulau Lama

Léqang if you want to take this child, then you go back down to earth and gather together enough gongs and tusks to fill all the houses in the village, then you can take him.'

Pulau Lama Léqang said, 'Done. But don't expect me to come back tomorrow. I'll come back in seven days.'

He went down to earth with Rotan and gathered the gongs and tusks. Then he took them back to the sky and gave them to the Sun. There was enough to fill the houses of all the Sun's brothers, clan mates and mother's sister's children (*ariq lai-utun, kangarin, meker-éhoq*). Then Pulau Lama Léqang took his wife and child back down to earth and lived here on our earth.

APPENDIX II

GENEALOGY OF THE CLANS OF LÉUWAJANG

Ula Lojo
Suri Ula

Bujaq Suri = ○ Omé Suri

△ Lojo Bujaq
△ Lia Lojo
△ Tuno Lia
△ Matan Tuno
△ Matur Matan
△ Retung Matur
△ Abé Retung
△ Beni Abé

△ Bujaq Beni (founded Leudanung)   △ Toan Beni (founded Léu Toan, Kalikur)   △ Auq Beni (founded Léuhoéq)   △ Tokan Beni (founded Tokodjain, Gunung Api)   △ Butu Beni (founded Buton and Makasar)   △ Bako Beni   △ Hama Beni (founded Witihama, Adonara)   ○ Boleng Beni (Ili Boleng, Adonara)

△ Koko Bako (founded Bernusa, Pantar)   △ Leki Bako

△ Telu Beni

△ Au Telu

△ Ramuq Au

△ Lalé Ramuq   △ Dahu Ramuq   △ Rian Au
△ Lemur Lalé   △ Etoq Dahu   △ Hoéq Rian (killed Nibanç Naran)
△ Boté Lemur   △ Kiaq Etoq   △ Wehéq Etoq   △ Beni Hoéq
△ Beni Boté   △ Toda Kiaq   △ Maing Wehéq   △ Utung Beni (Apé Utung)
△ Leraq Beni   △ Amun Toda   △ Labi Maing (Apé Labi)   △ Worén Maing (Apé Worén)   △ Liling Maing (Apé Liling)   △ Nobé Maing (Apé Nobé)   △ Tatu Maing (Apé Tatu)

△ Hiang Leraq   △ Buang Leraq   △ Boli Leraq

APPENDIX III

CLANS OF LÉUWAJANG: CURRENT SIZE

Clan	Males	Females	Total
Apé Utung	24	20	44
Apé Labi	65	78	143
Apé Worén	42	58	100
Apé Liling	—	—	—
Apé Nobé	39	54	93
Apé Tatu	20	17	37
Amun Toda	99	70	169
Hiang Leraq	62	51	113
Buang Leraq	45	56	101
Boli Leraq	34	48	82
Laong Hodiq	36	31	67
Hoqaratan	16	19	35
Toul Wala	26	34	60
No clan	1	1	2
From outside	7	7	14
Total	516	544	1,060

BIBLIOGRAPHY

ADAMS, MARIE JEANNE (1969). *System and Meaning in East Sumba Textile Design: a Study in Traditional Indonesian Art.* (Cultural Report Series, no. 16), Yale University Southeast Asia Studies, New Haven.

ANDREE, RICHARD (1893). Die Pleiaden im Mythus und in ihrer Beziehung zum Jahresbeginn und Landbau. *Globus,* **64,** no. 229, 362–6.

ANONYMOUS (1850a). Vulkanische Uitbarsting op Poeloe Komba of Batoetara. *Natuurkundig Tijdschrift voor Nederlandsch-Indië,* **1,** 87.

—— (1850b). Werkzaamheid van den Vulkaan Lobetolle op het Eiland Lomblen. *Natuurkundig Tijdschrift voor Nederlandsch-Indië,* **1,** 153–4.

—— (1851). Uitbarsting van den Vulkaan op Poeloe Komba. *Natuurkundig Tijdschrift voor Nederlandsch-Indië,* **2,** 523.

—— (1852). Eruptie van den Vulkaan van Poeloe Komba. *Natuurkundig Tijdschrift voor Nederlandsch-Indië,* **3,** 639.

—— (1914). De Eilanden Alor en Pantar, Residentie Timor en Onderhoorigheden. *Tijdschrift van het Koninklijk Nederlandsch Aaardrijkskundig Genootschap,* **31,** 70–102.

ARNDT, PAUL (1933). *Li'onesisch-Deutsches Wörterbuch.* Arnoldus-Druckerei, Ende, Flores.

—— (1937). *Grammatik der Solor-Sprache.* Arnoldus-Drukkerij, Ende, Flores.

—— (1938). Demon und Padzi, die feindlichen Brüder des Solor-Archipels. *Anthropos,* **33,** 1–58.

—— (1940). *Soziale Verhältnisse auf Ost-Flores, Adonara und Solor.* (Anthropos, Internationale Sammlung Ethnologischer Monographien, vol. 4), Aschendorffsche Verlagsbuchhandlung, Münster i.W.

—— (1951). *Religion auf Ostflores, Adonara und Solor.* (Studia Instituti Anthropos, vol. 1), Missionsdruckerei St. Gabriel, Wien-Mödling.

—— (1954). *Gesellschaftliche Verhältnisse der Ngadha.* (Studia Instituti Anthropos, vol. 8), Missionsdruckerei St. Gabriel, Wien-Mödling.

—— (1961). *Wörterbuch der Ngadhasprache.* (Studia Instituti Anthropos, vol. 15), Pertjetakan Arnoldus, Posieux, Fribourg, Suisse.

BARNES, R. H. (1973). Two Terminologies of Symmetric Prescriptive Alliance from Pantar and Alor in Eastern Indonesia. *Sociologus,* **23,** 71–89.

BECKERING, J. D. H. (1911). Beschrijving der Eilanden Adonara en

Lomblem, Behoorende tot de Solor-Groep. *Tijdschrift van het Koninklijk Nederlandsch Aardrijkskundig Genootschap*, 2e Serie, **28**, 167–202.

BELO, JANE (1935). A Study of Customs Pertaining to Twins in Bali. *Tijdschrift voor Indische Taal-, Land- en Volkenkunde*, **75**, 483–549.

BOSCH, F. D. K. (1960). *The Golden Germ: an Introduction to Indian Symbolism*. (Indo-Iranian Monographs, vol. 2), Mouton & Co., 's-Gravenhage.

BOUMAN, M. A. (1943). De Aloreesche Dansplaats. *Bijdragen tot de Taal-, Land- en Volkenkunde van Nederlandsch-Indië*, **102**, 481–500.

BROUWER, H. A. (1917a). Geologisch Overzicht van het Oostelijk Gedeelte van den Oost-Indischen Archipel. *Jaarboek van het Mijnwezen in Nederlandsch Oost-Indië*, **46**, 147–452.

—— (1917b). Over het Ontbreken van Werkende Vulkanen tusschen Panter en Dammer, in Verband met de Tektonische Bewegingen in dit Gebied. *Verslagen der Koninklijke Akademie van Wetenschappen*, **25**, 995–1004.

—— (1940). Geological and Petrological Investigations on Alkali and Calc-alkali Rocks on the Islands Adonara, Lomblem and Batoe Tara. In *Geological Expedition to the Lesser Sunda Islands* (ed. H. A. Brouwer), vol. 2, 1–94. Noord-hollandsche Uitgevers Maatschappij, Amsterdam.

COLFS, ALBERT (1888). *Het Journaal van Albert Colfs, eene Bijdrage tot de Kennis der Kleine Soende-Eilanden* (ed. A. G. Vorderman). Ernst & Co., Batavia.

COOMARASWAMY, ANANDA K. (1942). Spiritual Authority and Temporal Power in the Indian Theory of Government. (*American Oriental Series*, vol. 22), American Oriental Society, New Haven.

COVARRUBIAS, MIGUEL (1937). *Island of Bali*. Alfred A. Knopf, New York.

CUNNINGHAM, CLARK E. (1964). Order in the Atoni House. *Bijdragen tot de Taal-, Land- en Volkenkunde*, **120**, 34–68.

—— (1967a). Atoni Kin Categories and Conventional Behaviour. *Bijdragen tot de Taal-, Land- en Volkenkunde*, **123**, 53–70.

—— (1967b). Recruitment to Atoni Descent Groups. *Anthropological Quarterly*, **40**, 1–12.

DEMPWOLF, OTTO (1938). *Austronesisches Wörterverzeichnis*. (*Vergleichende Lautlehre des Austronesischen Wortschatzes*, vol. 3). (Beihefte zur Zeitschrift für Eingeborenen-Sprachen, no. 19), Dietrich Reimer, Berlin.

DIJK, L. J. VAN (1925, 34). De Zelfbesturende Landschappen in de Residentie Timor en Onderhoorigheden. *De Indische Gids*, **47**, 528–42, 618–23; **56**, 708–12.

DRABBE, P. (1923). Het Heidensch Huwelijk op Tanimbar. *Bijdragen tot de Taal-, Land- en Volkenkunde van Nederlandsch-Indië*, **79**, 546–68.

—— (1940). *Het Leven van den Tanémbarees: Ethnografische Studie over het Tanémbareesche Volk*. (Internationales Archiv für Ethnographie, vol. 38, supplement), E. J. Brill, Leiden.

DUBOIS, CORA (1944). *The People of Alor: a Social-psychological Study of an East Indian Island*. 2 vols, University of Minnesota Press, Minneapolis.

DUHEM, PIERRE (1913–17). *Le Système du monde: histoire des doctrines cosmologiques de Platon à Copernic*. 5 vols, Librairie Scientifique A. Hermann et Fils, Paris.

DUMÉZIL, GEORGES (1948). *Mitra-Varuna: essai sur deux représentations Indo-Européenes de la souveraineté*. 2nd edn, Gallimard, Paris.

DUMONT, LOUIS (1957a). *Une Sous-caste de L'Inde du Sud: organisation sociale et religion des Pramalai Kallar*. Mouton & Co., Paris.

—— (1957b). Hierarchy and Marriage in South Indian Kinship. (*Occasional Papers of the Royal Anthropological Institute of Great Britain and Ireland*, no. 12), London.

—— (1961). Marriage in India: the Present State of the Question. *Contributions to Indian Sociology*, **5**, 75–95.

—— (1966). Descent or Intermarriage? A Relational View of Australian Section Systems. *Southwestern Journal of Anthropology*, **22**, 231–50.

ECHOLS, JOHN M. and SHADILY, HASSAN (1970). *An Indonesian-English Dictionary*. Cornell University Press, Ithaca, New York.

ELIADE, MIRCEA (1949). *Le Mythe de l'éternel retour: archétypes et répétition*. Gallimard, Paris.

ENDICOTT, KIRK MICHAEL (1970). *An Analysis of Malay Magic*. Clarendon Press, Oxford.

FISCHER, H. TH. (1932). Der magische Charakter des Brautpreises. *Der Weltkreis*, **3**, 65–8.

—— (1935). De Aanverwantschap bij enige Volken van de Nederlands-Indische Archipel. *Mensch en Maatschappij*, **11**, 285–97.

—— (1936). Het asymmetrisch cross-cousin huwelijk in Nederlandsch Indië. *Tijdschrift voor Indische Taal-, Land- en Volkenkunde*, **76**, 359–72.

FISCHER, H. TH. and RENSELAAR, H. C. VAN (1959). Over enkele Batakse Verwantschapstermen. *Bijdragen tot de Taal-, Land- en Volkenkunde*, **115**, 40–55.

FOX, JAMES J. (1968). 'The Rotinese: a Study of the Social Organization of an Eastern Indonesian People'. D. Phil. thesis, The University of Oxford (unpublished).

—— (1971a). Semantic Parallelism in Rotinese Ritual Language. *Bijdragen tot de Taal-, Land- en Volkenkunde*, **127**, 215–55.

—— (1971b). Sister's Child as Plant: Metaphors in an Idiom of Consanguinity. In *Rethinking Kinship and Marriage* (ed. Rodney Needham). (A.S.A. Monographs 11), Tavistock, London.

GEERTZ, CLIFFORD (1960). *The Religion of Java*. The Free Press, Glencoe, Illinois.

GENNEP, ARNOLD VAN (1960). *The Rites of Passage* (trans. M. B. Vizedom and G. L. Caffee). The University of Chicago Press, Chicago.

GONDA, J. (1952). *Sanskrit in Indonesia*. International Academy of Indian Culture, Nagpur, India.

GORIS, R. (1960). The Religious Character of the Village Community. In *Bali: Studies in Life, Thought, and Ritual* (trans. J. S. Holmes), pp. 77–100. W. van Hoeve, The Hague and Bandung.

GORIS, R. and DRONKERS, P. L. (n.d.). *Bali: Atlas Kebudajaan*. Ministry of Education and Culture of the Republic of Indonesia.

GRANDSAIGNES D'HAUTERIVE, R. (1948). *Dictionaire des racines des langues européennes*. Larousse, Paris.

HARTMANN, M. A. (1935). De Werkende Vulkanen van het Eiland Lomblèn (Solor Archipel). *Tijdschrift van het Aardrijkskundig Genootschap*, **52**, 817–36.

HERTZ, ROBERT (1960). *Death & the Right Hand* (trans. Rodney and Claudia Needham). The Free Press, Glencoe, Illinois.

HOCART, A. M. (1933). *The Progress of Man, a Short Survey of his Evolution, his Customs and his Works*. Methuen & Co., London.

—— (1952). *The Life-giving Myth and Other Essays*. Methuen & Co., London.

HOOYKAAS, JACOBA (1956a). The Balinese Realm of Death. *Bijdragen tot de Taal-, Land- en Volkenkunde*, **112**, 74–93.

—— (1956b). The Rainbow in Ancient Indonesian Religion. *Bijdragen tot de Taal-, Land- en Volkenkunde*, **112**, 291–322.

HUBERT, H. and MAUSS, M. (1909). Étude sommaire de la représentation du temps dans la religion et la magie. *Mélanges d'histoire des religions*. Alcan, Paris.

KATE, H. F. C. TEN (1894). Verslag eener Reis in de Timorgroep en Polynesië. *Tijdschrift van het Koninklijk Nederlandsch Aardrijkskundig Genootschap*, 2e Serie, **11**, 195–246, 333–90, 541–638, 659–700, 765–823.

KENNEDY, RAYMOND (n.d.). 'Field Notes on Indonesia: Flores 1949–1950' (ed. Harold C. Conklin). Human Relations Area Files, New Haven.

KLUPPEL, J. M. (1873). De Solor-Eilanden. *Tijdschrift voor Indische Taal-, Land- en Volkenkunde*, **20**, 378–98.

KORN, FRANCIS (1971). A Question of Preferences: the Iatmul Case, pp. 99–132. In *Rethinking Kinship and Marriage* (ed. Rodney Needham). (A.S.A. Monographs 11) Tavistock, London.

KROL, JAN (n.d.). 'Woordenlijst: Solorees-Nederlands'. (Unpublished manuscript, available on microfilm from The Oriental Manuscript Department, Bibliotheek der Rijksuniversiteit te Leiden, The Netherlands.)

KRUYT, ALB. C. (1941). Rechts en Links bij de Bewoners van Midden-Celebes. *Bijdragen tot de Taal-, Land- en Volkenkunde van Nederlandsch-Indië*, 100, 339–55.

LEACH, E. R. (1954). *Political Systems of Highland Burma: a Study of Kachin Social Structure.* Bell, London.

—— (1961). *Rethinking Anthropology.* (London School of Economics Monographs on Social Anthropology, no. 22), The Athlone Press, London.

—— (1967). The Language of Kachin Kinship: Reflections on a Tikopia Model. In *Social Organization: Essays Presented to Raymond Firth* (ed. M. Freedman), pp. 125–152. Cass, London.

—— (1969). 'Kachin' and 'Haka Chin': A Rejoinder to Lévi-Strauss. *Man*, 4, 277–85.

LEEMKER, H. H. O. (1893). Woordenlijstje van de Soloreesche Taal. *Tijdschrift voor Indische Taal-, Land- en Volkenkunde*, 36, 421–61.

LE ROUX, C. C. F. M. (1929). De Elcano's tocht door den Timorarchipel met Magalhães' ship 'Victoria'. In *Feestbundel Uitgegeven door het Koninklijk Bataviaasch Genootschap van zijn 150 Jarig Bestaan 1778–1928*, vol. 2. Kolff, Weltevreden.

LÉVI-STRAUSS, CLAUDE (1963). *Structural Anthropology* (trans. C. Jacobson and B. G. Schoepf). Basic Books, New York.

—— (1964). *Mythologiques: le cru et le cuit.* Plon, Paris.

—— (1966). *The Savage Mind.* Weidenfeld and Nicholson, London.

—— (1969). *The Elementary Structures of Kinship* (trans. Bell, Sturmer and Needham). Eyre & Spottiswoode, London.

LIE GOAN LIONG (A. ADI SUKADANA) (1962a). Serba Serbi Makanan dan Perabotan dari Pulau Lomblen. ('Flores' 9), *Djaja*, 39.

—— (1926b). Beberapa Tindjauan serta Kebiasaan dari Daerah Kedang. *Madjallah Fakultas Kedoktoran Gigi*, Universities Airlangga, Surabaja.

—— (1963a). Doroawer dan Nahaq dari Daerah Kedang, P. Lomblen. ('Flores' 11), *Djaja*, 50.

—— (1969b). Gigi Bersolak. *Djaja*, 54.

—— (1964a). Mutilasi dan Penghitaman Gigi Ditindjau dari Sudut Anthropologi dan Ethnologi. *Fakultas Kedoktoran Gigi*, Universitas Airlangga Surabaja.

—— (1964b). Beberapa Hasil Palaeoanthropologis dari Penemuan 2 Dipantai Lewoleba, P. Lomblen. *Madjallah Research Kedoktoran*, **3**, 120–37.

—— (1965). Palaeoanthropological Results of the Excavation at the Coast of Lewoleba (Isle of Lomblen). *Anthropos*, **60**, 609–24.

LYNDEN, D. W. C. BARON VAN (1851). Bijdrage tot de Kennis van Solor, Allor, Rotti, Savoe en Omliggende Eilanden, Getrokken uit een Verslag van de Residentie Timor. *Natuurkundig Tijdschrift voor Nederlandsch-Indië*, **2**, 317–36, 388–414.

MAASS, ALFRED (1920/21). Sterne und Sternbilder im malaiischen Archipel. *Zeitschrift für Ethnologie*, **52/53**, 38–63.

—— (1924, 26). Sternkunde und Sterndeuterei im malaiischen Archipel. *Tijdschrift voor Indische Taal-, Land- en Volkenkunde*, **64**, 1–172, 347–445; **66**, 618–70.

—— (1933). Die Sterne im Glauben der Indonesier. *Zeitschrift für Ethnologie*, **65**, 264–303.

MALLINCKRODT, J. (1924). Ethnografische Mededeelingen over de Dajaks in de Afdeeling Koealakapoeas. *Bijdragen tot de Taal-, Land- en Volkenkunde*, **80**, 397–446, 521–600.

MAUSS, MARCEL (1966). *The Gift: Forms and Functions of Exchange in Archaic Societies* (trans. Ian Cunnison). Cohen & West, London.

MUNRO, W. G. (1915). 'Nota over Lomblen (Afdeling Flores)'. (Unpublished).

NEEDHAM, RODNEY (1956). A note on kinship and marriage on Pantara. *Bijdragen tot de Taal-, Land- en Volkenkunde*, **112**, 285–90.

—— (1957). Circulating Connubium in Eastern Sumba: a Literary Analysis. *Bijdragen tot de Taal-, Land- en Volkenkunde*, **113**, 168–78.

—— (1958). A Structural Analysis of Purum Society. *American Anthropologist*, **60**, 75–101.

—— (1960). The Left Hand of the Mugwe: an Analytical Note on the Structure of Meru Symbolism. *Africa*, **30**, 20–33.

—— (1961). Notes on the Analysis of Asymmetric Alliance. *Bijdragen tot de Taal-, Land- en Volkenkunde*, **117**, 93–117.

—— (1962). *Structure and Sentiment: a Test Case in Social Anthropology*. The University of Chicago Press, Chicago and London.

—— (1964a). Descent, Category, and Alliance in Sirionó Society. *Southwestern Journal of Anthropology*, **20**, 229–40.

—— (1964b). A Synoptic Examination of Anāl Society. *Ethnos*, **29**, 219–36.

—— (1966). Age, Category, and Descent. *Bijdragen tot de Taal-, Land- en Volkenkunde*, **122**, 1–35.

—— (1966, 67). Terminology and Alliance: I. Garo, Manggarai; II. Mapuche; Conclusions. *Sociologus*, **16**, 141–57; **17**, 39–54.

—— (1967a). Percussion and Transition. *Man*, **2**, 606–14.

—— (1967b). Right and Left in Nyoro Symbolic Classification. *Africa*, **37**, 425–52.

—— (1968). Translator's note. In *Types of Social Structure in Eastern Indonesia* (by F. A. E. van Wouden), pp. xi–xiv. Nijhoff, The Hague.

—— (1970). Endeh, II: Test and Confirmation. *Bijdragen tot de Taal-, Land- en Volkenkunde*, **126**, 246–58.

NILSSON, MARTIN P. (1920). *Primitive Time-reckoning: a Study in the Origins and First Development of the Art of Counting Time among the Primitive and Early Culture Peoples*. (Skrifter Utgivna av Humanistiska Vetenskapssamfundet I.), Gleerup, Lund.

ONVLEE, L. (1949). Naar Aanleiding van de Stuwdam in Mangili: Opmerkingen over de Sociale Structuur van Oost-Sumba. *Bijdragen tot de Taal-, Land- en Volkenkunde*, **105**, 445–59.

OSSENBRUGGEN, F. D. E. VAN (1930). Verwantschaps- en Huwelijksvormen in den Indischen Archipel. *Tijdschrift van het Aardrijkskundig Genootschap*, **47**, 212–29.

—— (1935). Het Oeconomisch-magisch Element in Tobasche Verwantschapsverhoudingen. (*Mededelingen der Koninklijke Akademie van Wetenschappen*, Afdeeling Letterkunde Deel 80, Serie B, No. 3) Noord-Hollandsche Uitgevers-Maatschappij, Amsterdam.

OUWEHAND, C. (1950). Aantekeningen over Volksordening en Grondenrecht op Oost-Flores. *Indonesië*, **4**, 54–71.

PIET PITU (SARENG ORINBAO) (1969). *Nusa Nipa: Nama Pribumi Nusa Flores (Warisan Purba)*. Penerbitan Nusa Indah, Ende-Flores.

PLEYTE, C. M. (1894). Die Schlange im Volksglauben der Indonesier. *Globus*, **65**, no. 6, 95–100, no. 11, 169–76.

RIENZI, G. L. Domeny de (1836–7). *Oceanie ou cinquième partie du monde*. 5 vol., Firmin Didot Frères, Paris.

SALZNER, RICHARD (1960). *Sprachenatlas des Indopazifischen Raumes*. 2 vols, Wiesbaden.

SCHÄRER, HANS (1963). *Ngaju Religion: the Conception of God among a South Borneo People* (trans. Rodney Needham). Nijhoff, The Hague.

—— (1966). *Der Totenkult der Ngadju Dajak in Süd-Borneo: Mythen zum Totenkult und die Texte zum Tantolak Matei*. 2 vols, Nijhoff, 's-Gravenhage.

SCHOLZ, FRIEDHELM (1962). *Der Herr des Bodens in Ostindonesien*. (Doctoral dissertation, Universität Köln, no publisher given.)

SCHOUTEN, WOUTER (1676). *Wouter Schoutens Oostindische Voyagie* ... Meurs and van Someren, Amsterdam.

SCHULTE NORDHOLT, H. G. (1971). *The Political System of the*

Atoni of Timor. (Verhandelingen van het Koninklijk Instituut voor Taal-, Land- en Volkenkunde, no. 60), Nijhoff, The Hague.

SCHUSTER, CARL (1951). Joint-marks: a Possible Index of Cultural Contact between America, Oceania and the Far East. (*Mededeling* No. XCIV, Afdeling Culturele en Physische Anthropologie no. 39), Koninklijk Instituut voor de Tropen, Amsterdam.

SEEGELER, C. J. (1931). Nota van Toelichting betreffende het Zelfbesturende Landschap Larantoeka . . . (ddo. 29 Augustus 1931, unpublished).

SELL, HANS JOACHIM (1955). *Der Schlimme Tod bei den Völkern Indonesiens.* Mouton, 's-Gravenhage.

SKEAT, WALTER WILLIAM (1900). *Malay Magic: an Introduction to the Folklore and Popular Religions of the Malay Peninsula.* Macmillan, London.

SNOUCK HURGRONJE, C. (1893). *De Atjèhers*, vol. 1. Landsdrukkerij, Batavia.

STEINEN, KARL VON DEN (1894). 'Plejaden' und 'Jahr' bei Indianern des nordöstlichen Südamerika. *Globus*, **65**, no. 15, 243–6.

SWELLENGREBEL, J. L. (1960). Introduction. In *Bali: Studies in Life, Thought, and Ritual* (trans. James S. Holmes), pp. 1–76. W. van Hoeve, The Hague and Bandung.

TOBING, PH. L. (1956). *The Structure of the Toba-Batak Belief in the High God.* Jacob van Campen, Amsterdam.

U.S. NAVY HYDROGRAPHIC OFFICE (1962). *Sailing Directions for Java; Lesser Sundas; South, Southeast and East Coasts of Borneo; and Celebes.* (H.O. Pub. no. 72), 5th edn., United States Government Printing Office.

VATTER, ERNST (1932). *Ata Kiwan, unbekannte Bergvölker im Tropischen Holland.* Bibliographisches Institut A.G., Leipzig.

—— (1934). Der Schlangendrache auf Alor und verwandte Darstellungen in Indonesien, Asien und Europa. *Jahrbuch für Prähistorische und Ethnographische Kunst*, **9**, 119–48.

VERBEEK, R. D. M. (1908). Molukken-verslag: Geologische Verkenningstochten in het Oostelijke Gedeelte van den Nederlandsch Oost-Indischen Archipel. *Jaarboek van het Mijnwezen in Nederlandsch Oost-Indië (Wetenschappelijk Gedeelte)*, **137**, 836 pp.

VERGOUWEN, J. C. (1964). *The Social Organisation and Customary Law of the Toba-Batak of Northern Sumatra.* Nijhoff, The Hague.

VERHEIJEN, J. (1950). De Stem der Dieren in de Manggaraise Folklore. *Bijdragen tot de Taal-, Land- en Volkenkunde*, **106**, 55–8.

VOLKSTELLING 1930 (1936). Vol. V: *Inheemsche Bevolking van Borneo, Celebes, de Kleine Soenda Eilanden en de Molukken.* Landsdrukkerij, Batavia.

VROKLAGE, B. A. G. (1952). *Ethnographie der Belu in Zentral-Timor.* 3 vols, Brill, Leiden.

WICHMAN, ARTHUR (1891). Bericht über eine im Jahre 1888–89 ausgeführte Reise nach dem Indischen Archipel. *Tijdschrift van het Koninklijk Nederlandsch Aardrijkskundig Genootschap*, **8**, 188–293.

WINKLER, JOHS. (1913). Der Kalender der Toba-Bataks auf Sumatra. *Zeitschrift für Ethnologie*, **45**, 436–47.

WOUDEN, F. A. E. VAN (1956). Locale Groepen en Dubbele Afstamming in Kodi, West Sumba. *Bijdragen tot de Taal-, Land- en Volkenkunde*, **112**, 204–46.

—— (1968). *Types of Social Structure in Eastern Indonesia* (*trans.* Rodney Needham). Nijhoff, The Hague.

INDEX OF WORDS AND PHRASES IN
THE KÉDANG LANGUAGE

INDEX OF PERSONS

SUBJECT INDEX